THE PLAYS OF
Richard Steele

S.r Richard Steele K.nt

G. Kneller Eques Baron.t pinx.   G. Vertue Sculp.

RICHARD STEELE

From George Vertue's engraving after the Kit-Cat portrait by Sir Godfrey
Kneller. The engraving was used as a frontispiece for the edition of the
plays published in 1717, the *Dramatick Works* of 1723, and later editions.

THE PLAYS OF
Richard Steele

EDITED BY

SHIRLEY STRUM KENNY

OXFORD

AT THE CLARENDON PRESS

1971

Oxford University Press, Ely House, London W. 1

GLASGOW NEW YORK TORONTO MELBOURNE WELLINGTON
CAPE TOWN SALISBURY IBADAN NAIROBI DAR ES SALAAM LUSAKA ADDIS ABABA
BOMBAY CALCUTTA MADRAS KARACHI LAHORE DACCA
KUALA LUMPUR SINGAPORE HONG KONG TOKYO

FOR

FLORENCE AND MARCUS STRUM

ACKNOWLEDGEMENTS

I OWE a great debt of gratitude to many scholars and librarians who have graciously provided information and assistance as I worked on this edition. I wish particularly to thank Fredson Bowers and Arthur Friedman, whose guidance, suggestions, and criticism have been invaluable. I am also grateful for the advice of Leo Hughes, John Loftis, Giles E. Dawson, and Robert W. Kenny, who read and criticized parts of the introductions.

Of the librarians who contributed their time and knowledge to the project, I am especially indebted to D. G. Neill of the Bodleian Library, Richard A. Christophers of the British Museum, the staff of the Folger Shakespeare Library, and the rare-books staff of the University of Texas Library.

Philip Highfill allowed me access to his files on eighteenth-century performers; Calhoun Winton provided biographical information on Steele; Professor and Mrs. Richmond P. Bond supplied a bibliographical description of their copy of *The Conscious Lovers*; and Albert Wertheim examined a rare Dublin edition at Princeton; to all of them I give my thanks.

A grant from the National Endowment for the Humanities greatly aided me in the completion of my work.

Finally, I wish to thank Florence Strum for her alert and accurate typing and copyreading of the texts of the plays, and Edna Johnson Wills for her very special assistance.

CONTENTS

ABBREVIATIONS FOR REFERENCE WORKS

Aitken   Aitken, George A. *The Life of Richard Steele.* 2 vols. London, 1889.

Avery   Avery, Emmett L. *The London Stage 1660–1800, Part 2: 1700–1729.* 2 vols. Carbondale, Ill., 1960.

Churchill   Churchill, Winston S. *Marlborough: His Life and Times.* 4 vols. London, 1933–8.

Correspondence   *The Correspondence of Richard Steele,* ed. Rae Blanchard. 2nd edn. Oxford, 1968.

Cunnington, *Eighteenth*   Cunnington, C. Willett and Phillis. *Handbook of English Costume in the Eighteenth Century.* London, 1957.

Dennis   *The Critical Works of John Dennis,* ed. Edward Niles Hooker. 2 vols. Baltimore, 1939–43.

DNB   *Dictionary of National Biography.*

Loftis   Loftis, John. *Steele at Drury Lane.* Berkeley, 1952.

Mermaid   *Richard Steele,* ed. G. A. Aitken. Mermaid Series. London, 1894.

Military Dictionary   *A Military Dictionary Explaining All Difficult Terms in Martial Discipline, Fortification, and Gunnery.* 3rd edn. London, 1708.

NQ   *Notes and Queries.*

OED   *Oxford English Dictionary.*

Rolli   *Gli Amanti Interni,* trans. P. Rolli. London, 1724.

SB   *Studies in Bibliography.*

Scouten   Scouten, Arthur H. *The London Stage 1660–1800, Part 3: 1729–47.* 2 vols. Carbondale, Ill., 1961.

Smith   Smith, John Harrington. *The Gay Couple in Restoration Comedy.* Cambridge, Mass., 1948.

Stone   Stone, George Winchester, Jr. *The London Stage 1660–1800, Part 4: 1747–1776.* 3 vols. Carbondale, Ill., 1962.

Van Lennep   Van Lennep, William. *The London Stage 1660–1800, Part 1: 1660–1700.* Carbondale, Ill., 1965.

Verse   *The Occasional Verse of Richard Steele,* ed. Rae Blanchard. Oxford, 1952.

Wheatley	Wheatley, Henry B. *London, Past and Present: Its History, Associations, and Traditions.* 3 vols. London, 1891.
Winton	Winton, Calhoun. *Captain Steele: The Early Career of Richard Steele.* Baltimore, 1964.

In quoting from primary sources I have followed these modern texts:

Andria	Terence, trans. John Sargeaunt. The Loeb Classical Library. 2 vols., London, 1931.
Burnaby	*The Dramatic Works of William Burnaby,* ed. F. E. Budd. London, 1931.
Dryden	*The Poems of John Dryden,* ed. James Kinsley. 4 vols. Oxford, 1958.
Le Menteur	*Œuvres de P. Corneille,* ed. Ch. Marty-Laveaux. 13 vols. 2nd printing. Paris, 1862–68.
Molière	*The Plays of Molière in French, with an English Translation and Notes,* trans. A. R. Waller. 8 vols. Edinburgh, 1926.
She Stoops to Conquer	*Collected Works of Oliver Goldsmith,* ed. Arthur Friedman. 5 vols. Oxford, 1966.
Spectator	*The Spectator,* ed. Donald F. Bond. 5 vols. Oxford, 1965.
Theatre	*Richard Steele's 'The Theatre', 1720,* ed. John Loftis. Oxford, 1962.
Tracts and Pamphlets	*Tracts and Pamphlets by Richard Steele,* ed. Rae Blanchard. Oxford, 1944.

INTRODUCTION

RICHARD STEELE's comedies, like his periodical essays, greatly affected the sensibility of the eighteenth century. All but one of his plays were favourites on stage for decades. With *The Funeral* in 1701 and *The Lying Lover* in 1703 he made his first steps toward the sentimental comedy he was to advocate in essays and epitomize in *The Conscious Lovers* twenty years later. Although he retreated from sentimentalism in *The Tender Husband* in 1705, *The Conscious Lovers*, first staged in 1722, embodied his dramatic theories and reached what he considered his theatrical peak. The comedy not only packed houses and sold copies for many years but also provided a model for younger playwrights.

Steele, who demonstrated great interest in the theatrical productions, showed little concern for the printed versions of his comedies. The first editions of *The Funeral* and *The Tender Husband* contain many errors attributable to hasty and careless printing from poor manuscripts. The second edition of *The Funeral* is the only evidence we have for his ever revising a play after its initial publication. The Tonsons and later booksellers, recognizing profit in the plays, issued unrevised editions repeatedly in the eighteenth and early nineteenth centuries. With few exceptions they are mere reprints of no editorial interest; some are 'adapted for theatrical representation' or 'marked with the variations of the manager's book', that is, stage cuts are either made or marked by inverted commas; most introduce new errors and retain old ones; almost all depart further in successive printings from Steele's intentions. G. A. Aitken edited the last text of the complete dramatic works, published in 1894 and reissued in 1903 in the Mermaid Series. Although his modern-spelling edition long served as a standard one, his bibliographical method was unscientific, and consequently the text is not accurate. In more recent times publishers have confined their interest almost entirely to the influential *Conscious Lovers*, but usually without stress on textual precision. Arthur E. Case undertook a serious bibliographical examination of the play in *British Dramatists from Dryden to Sheridan* (Boston, 1939), but he arrived at some incorrect conclusions. Calhoun Winton's modern-spelling edition of *The Tender Husband* (1967) and mine of *The*

Conscious Lovers (1968), both in the Regents Restoration Drama Series, are the most recent attempts to provide sound texts of Steele's plays.

The present edition tries to make all Steele's plays readily and reliably available to modern readers in an old-spelling text. After collating multiple copies of the first editions and at least one copy of all others that Steele might conceivably have revised, I have selected the first edition of each play, with press corrections when they exist, as copy-text. The text includes a few revisions which are demonstrably Steele's and corrections of obvious errors, some caught by eighteenth-century printing-house employees, some by me. Although routine emendations in early editions have no authorial basis, I have accepted them if they satisfactorily correct errors; if they do not, I have followed copy-text or substituted more appropriate emendations. All editions, with the exception of the Regents, have reprinted gross errors, such as wrong names within speeches and incorrect speech prefixes; many of these are here corrected for the first time. For simplicity in reading, I have regularly standardized characters' names when more than one name or spelling occurs in the speech prefixes and stage directions, following Steele's intentions when they could be determined and arbitrarily choosing a single form when they could not. I have also added necessary stage directions, recording those from early editions in the footnotes and identifying those new to this edition by square brackets. With these few exceptions, the edition adheres as closely as possible to the copy-text, although Steele's unwieldy, sometimes almost incomprehensible sentences tempt one to emend.

Accidentals as well as substantives follow the copy-text very closely. My criterion is spelling and punctuation which is neither confusing nor misleading to readers familiar with eighteenth-century texts. Therefore pointing acceptable in Steele's time but not now (for example, a question mark used for a mild exclamation) stands. But since I consider compositorial foibles far from sacrosanct, I have freely changed obvious errors, such as a lower-case initial beginning a speech or the omission of punctuation at the end of one.

Typography and some accidentals are silently regularized. The edition neither reproduces nor notes initials, factotums, display capitals, swash letters, long ∫'s, *v*'s used for *u*'s, wrong-fount letters and italics used in shortages, turned letters except *u* and *n*, lost letters or words jammed together in tight lines. Regardless of the copy-text, rhymed poetry, quotations, and letters are indented and italicized. Also italicized are characters' names, including genitive *s*'s, in roman passages but not accompanying titles such as 'Sir' or 'Mr.' Characters' names in italic passages and stage directions appear in roman type. Speech prefixes and stage directions, consistently italicized begin with capitals, end with periods or dashes, and contain corrections of obvious misspellings. Entrances are centred, exits set flush right, stage directions between speeches centred, those within speeches enclosed in parentheses, and those incorrectly placed in the text positioned properly. The changes of typography and accidentals in speech prefixes and stage directions do not affect the lines Steele wrote for the stage, but simplify the mechanical elements of the texts for which compositors were responsible.

The introduction to each play briefly treats the composition, sources, first production, theatrical history, critical reception, influence on later drama, textual problems, and history of publication. In tracing sources I do not link plays with earlier ones when the relationships are dubious; seemingly similar passages do not necessarily indicate borrowings, for some merely reflect conventions of the period. Although Steele was obviously familiar with contemporary English comedy, few direct debts can be proved. I am also hesitant to claim Steele's influence over later works, unless there is strong evidence of a specific relationship. The bibliographical section of each introduction describes the printing of the first edition and other significant ones to explain textual cruxes, then briefly surveys later ones printed within Steele's lifetime and shortly after his death.

Footnotes record all substantive emendations of the copy-text and any debatable refusals to emend. Explanations provide information on textual decisions about which questions can reasonably arise. The commentary provides the reader with the necessary background of topical and literary allusions, sources, and occasionally relations to works by Steele or others. Emendations of accidentals list all changes from copy-text in punctuation and spelling, except silent alterations; to prevent misunderstanding of the original accidentals, I include hyphenations of compound words at the ends of lines in both the copy-text and the present edition unless the second part of the compound is capitalized. Press-variants include corrections in the first editions only. The historical collation contains all substantive and semi-substantive changes in editions published by 1732. The abbreviation 'ed.' stands for 'editor', and 'om.' for 'omitted'.

THE PLAYS

THE FUNERAL: OR, GRIEF A-LA-MODE

COMPOSITION AND SOURCES

STATIONED near London at the turn of the century, Richard Steele followed a number of the pursuits of vigorous young men: he attained his captaincy, sired at least one illegitimate child, reluctantly fought a duel in which he almost killed his man, and lost his money in an alchemical venture.[1] Then he made his way into literary London with a moralistic tract, *The Christian Hero*, which made some of his friends cry hypocrite and others avoid or deride him.[2] It was incumbent after this tract, he felt, to write a comedy in order to 'enliven his Character'.[3] He retired in the summer of 1701 to Wandsworth in Surrey to complete a play, hoping thereby not only to regain his reputation as a pleasant companion, but also to free himself from debt. There, with his man Will, perhaps the model for Will Trim, he read 'two or three excellent authors'[4] and he wrote.

Except for Nathaniel Lee, whom he quoted both in a letter from Wandsworth and in *The Funeral*, the excellent authors probably did not influence his pen, for *The Funeral* is the only comedy by Steele which is not even loosely based on a French or classical model; the plot is entirely original. That is not to say, of course, that it is not tied to English tradition. Further, one scene, the ladies' visit in III. ii, seems modelled on a play Steele undoubtedly knew, William Burnaby's *Ladies Visiting-Day*,[5] first acted in January 1701, and published 27 February, nine months before *The Funeral* opened. The two visiting scenes reveal the women's passion for liquor, gossip, and young men. The authors raise similar objections to the behaviour of widows, but

---

[1] Winton, pp. 45–55.

[2] Mary Delariviere Manley, *Secret Memoirs and Manners of Several Persons of Quality, of Both Sexes. From the New Atalantis, an Island in the Mediterranean*, 2nd edn. (London, 1709), p. 188. Richard Steele, *Mr. Steele's Apology for Himself and his Writings; Occasioned by his Expulsion From the House of Commons* (London, 1714), in *Tracts and Pamphlets*, p. 339.   [3] *Tracts and Pamphlets*, p. 339.

[4] Letter to Colonel Edmund Revett, 2 September 1701, in *Correspondence*, p. 10.

[5] He and Burnaby must have known each other fairly well. Both entered Merton College, Oxford, in 1691, and they were perhaps partners in the alchemical venture (*Correspondence*, pp. 429–30, n. 1). They tried to make their literary mark in London at the same time. Both knew the wits of Will's Coffee-house; both contributed to *Commendatory Verses on the Author of the Two Arthurs, and the Satyr against Wit* in 1700, and defended *The Way of the World*. Each sooner or later dedicated a play to the Duke of Ormonde.

the hypocritical mourning is more central to Steele's plot. Burnaby was not the first to ridicule the failings of the ladies; however, Steele's dialogue in III. ii and his commentary on French affectations are so similar to Burnaby's in detail that one suspects at least unwitting echoes.

Beyond the touches from Burnaby, however, it is difficult to show any sizable debt to an antecedent play. John Genest says Steele borrowed the idea of Lady Sharlot's escape in a coffin from Beaumont and Fletcher's *Knight of the Burning Pestle*, in which Jasper comes to Luce in a coffin and slips her out under the pall;[1] indeed, the action in the two scenes is strikingly parallel. John Harrington Smith finds Steele 'owing something to Shadwell's *The Volunteers* as a model',[2] a claim more difficult to sustain. Steele's plot more nearly resembles that of Aphra Behn's *Sir Patient Fancy*, although the comedy had not been performed in London or published since 1678. In Mrs. Behn's play—in which there is a young spark named Fainlove, a name Steele used in *The Tender Husband*—Sir Patient is persuaded by his nephew Leander to play dead in order to discover Lady Fancy's infidelity. They stage a death scene at which Lady Fancy mourns extravagantly, meanwhile asking her lover in an aside if she dissembles well. Later Leander directs his uncle, as Trusty does his master, to eavesdrop on a conversation in which Lady Fancy reveals her true character. The incident is based on one in Molière's *Le Malade imaginaire*, but Steele is closer to Mrs. Behn's version.

STAGE HISTORY

Steele reached an agreement with Christopher Rich of the Drury Lane Theatre on 9 October 1701 for the production of *The Funeral*.[3] It was first acted some time between this date and 11 December when copies of the incidental music composed by William Croft were advertised.[4] The comedy probably opened in the first days of December; however, no theatrical records of the date or length of the first run exist, nor are there newspaper accounts or advertisements, since the *Daily Courant* was not begun until the following year. The cast were players who were to continue famous during Steele's lifetime. Colley Cibber originated the role of the exemplary Lord Hardy and

---

[1] John Genest, *Some Account of the English Stage from the Restoration in 1660 to 1830*, 10 vols. (Bath, 1832), ii. 254.

[2] Smith, p. 202.

[3] Aitken, i, 72, 116.

[4] The music was published 18 December at 1*s*. 6*d*. a set.

Robert Wilks the debonair lover Campley; later, of course, Wilks had comparable major parts in Steele's three other comedies as Young Bookwit, Captain Clerimont, and Myrtle, but Cibber turned to comedy roles such as Latine and the valet Tom. Anne Oldfield played Lady Sharlot, and Jane Rogers Lady Harriot. Daniel Purcell, brother of the composer Henry Purcell and Oxford acquaintance of Steele, who had written music for a number of Drury Lane performances, set four of the songs. William Croft, organist at St. Anne's, Westminster, provided eight act-tunes, scored in four parts, and perhaps wrote the music for Trim's jocular 'Cynderaxa, kind and good', sung to the accompaniment of the kitchen tongs.[1]

How much money Steele received from Rich and the publisher Jacob Tonson is not on record, but he clearly gained fame. The war on theatrical immorality incited by Collier and others was under way, and pamphlets on the subject were multiplying. In November players had been prosecuted for using indecent expressions on stage.[2] But in Steele's play '(tho' full of incidents that move Laughter) Virtue and Vice appear just as they ought to do'.[3] Further, the comedy overflows with patriotic and military fervour in an era of chauvinistic enthusiasm, at least on the part of the Whigs. Steele packed the house with fellow redcoats,[4] but the defensive action proved unnecessary, for *The Funeral* met with 'more than expected Success'.[5] ''Tis a dangerous Matter to talk of this Play,' one critic lamented; 'the Town has given it such applause, 'twill be an ungrateful undertaking to call their Judgments in question.'[6]

The play even gained the attention of the King. Steele reported its success in *Mr. Steele's Apology for Himself and His Writings* (1714): 'Nothing can make the Town so fond of a Man as a successful Play, and this, with some Particulars enlarged upon to his Advantage, (for Princes never hear Good or Evil in the manner others do) obtained him the Notice of the King: And his Name, to be provided for, was in the last Table-Book ever worn by the Glorious and Immortal *William* the Third.'[7] Unfortunately for Steele, William, wasted by illness, died on 8 March 1702, about three months after the opening, never having provided any gift, annuity, or place for the young playwright,

[1] *Verse*, pp. 80–2.   [2] Avery, i. 15.
[3] *Apology*, in *Tracts and Pamphlets*, p. 339.
[4] See Prologue, ll. 23–8, Preface, ll. 13–16.
[5] Colley Cibber, *An Apology for the Life of Mr. Colley Cibber, Comedian, and Late Patentee of the Theatre-Royal* (London, 1740), p. 153.
[6] *A Comparison between the Two Stages*, ed. Staring B. Wells (Oxford, 1942), p. 78.
[7] *Tracts and Pamphlets*, p. 339.

who was forced to continue seeking preferment at other hands.[1] But Steele's reputation, if not his fortune, was made.

The Funeral became a staple of the repertory. Richard Blackmore indicated the acceptance of Steele's work in 1713 when he declined to transcribe an entire speech by Trusty because 'it is so well known on the Stage that there is no need of it'.[2] Between 1703, the date at which the *Daily Courant* advertisements of *The Funeral* began, and 1776 there was a total of 171 performances; 52 of these were benefits, a particularly informative index of popularity. The comedy was acted by royal command of two kings (22 February 1715 and 31 December 1735), of Princess Caroline (29 January 1736), and 'At the Desire of the Two Princes, Brothers to the King of Delago in Africa' (26 May 1721). A census by decades of seventy seasons, beginning with its second season, shows the rises and falls of its popularity on stage:

1702–12	14 performances
1712–22	17 performances
1722–32	30 performances
1732–42	48 performances
1742–52	19 performances
1752–62	29 performances
1762–72	10 performances[3]

Of Steele's three early plays, *The Funeral* was most frequently performed over a seventy-five-year span.

REPUTATION AND INFLUENCE

A Comparison between the Two Stages, anonymously issued soon after *The Funeral*, provided the most detailed critical evaluation. Although the author wrote before the vogue for the sentimental developed, he praised Steele's noble intentions and high-minded characters. He also admired the satirical strokes on widows, knavish lawyers, and undertakers, and the humorous portrayal of the recruits. He admitted, in sum, '. . . that it is a diverting Play, and that it is writ with Care and Understanding; that the Author's Intentions are noble, and that it is in many places a just and lively Satyr . . . that he seems a good judge

---

[1] However, Winton attributes Steele's assignment as captain of the Thirty-fourth Foot to King William's notice. See Winton, pp. 63–4.

[2] *Lay-Monastery*, no. 9.

[3] Avery, Scouten, Stone, *passim*.

of Comedy; that he has touch'd some things very justly, that his Vices are new, and his Characters not ill drawn.'[1] But the bad, according to the author, outweighs the good. Steele is, to generalize, guilty of improbability, poor taste, and faulty style.

Blackmore, writing twelve years after the first performance and doubtless influenced towards the sentimental by such essays as Steele's own periodical pieces, found pleasure in the 'many lively Strokes of Wit and Humour', but he was 'more pleas'd with the fine Touches of Humanity in it, than with any other Part of the Entertainment'.[2]

Several references in the *Spectator* again suggest that the play remained widely known. Eustace Budgell used Mademoiselle D'Epingle's remarks on undressing in front of men as a point of departure for a lecture on proper feminine behaviour.[3] Another essayist talked casually of the mourners in Act I, expecting his readers to recognize the reference.[4] Steele himself discussed the play in the *Spectator* no. 51 and quoted from Act V in the *Theatre* in 1720.[5] Further, poems were written about it. Some years after the opening, for example, Laurence Eusden, poet laureate from 1718 to 1730, lauded Sharlot in a poem 'To the Author of the *Tatler*' as an exemplary heroine to be emulated by genteel young ladies.[6]

The influence of *The Funeral* on later drama is difficult to assess. Smith believes Steele's pattern of two couples, both sincere and honourable, although one is serious and the other 'inclined to be lively', founded a tradition followed in many later plays, including Farquhar's *The Twin-Rivals* (1702), Centlivre's *The Man's Bewitch'd* (1709), Taverner's *The Female Advocates* (1713), and Sturmy's *The Compromise* (1722). Volatil and Arabella in Johnson's *The Wife's Relief* (1711), he says, are obviously modelled on Campley and Harriot, and *The Apparition* (anonymous, 1713) is 'greatly indebted' to *The Funeral*.[7] Smith's estimate is perhaps generous: the frequent revivals and reprints (at least twenty-eight editions in the eighteenth century, including several published in Dublin and Edinburgh, and translations in French (1749) and Italian (1742) made it a familiar play which could have influenced later dramatists, but one cannot draw convincing proof of specific debts. Nevertheless, it should be recognized as a popular and innovative comedy.

---

[1] *Comparison*, p. 78.   [2] *Lay-Monastery*, no. 9.
[3] *Spectator*, no. 506.   [4] *Spectator*, no. 599.   [5] *Theatre*, no. 13.
[6] John Nichols, *A Select Collection of Poems With Notes, Biographical and Historical*, 8 vols. (London, 1780–2), iv. 154.   [7] Smith, p. 202; p. 220, n. 38.

THE TEXT

Four editions of *The Funeral* were published by Jacob Tonson during Steele's lifetime (1672–1729), and one more was issued shortly after his death. Steele revised the second edition, dated 1712, but those of 1717, 1723, and 1730 show no further evidence of his hand. Three other editions were published before his death, two printed for T. Johnson, probably at The Hague, in 1710 and 1721, and a third by Stephen Powell for George Risk in Dublin in 1725.

The first edition was published 20 December 1701 with the date 1702. A quarto with the collational formula π^2 A–L^4, it was printed hurriedly, perhaps to capitalize on unexpected public interest. At least three compositors worked on the book, one setting sheets B, D, F, and H; a second C, E, and G; and a third I, K, L, and probably A.[1] At least seven skeletons were used on at least three presses.[2] An erratum on A4^v corrects an error on I1 (p. 57). The only press corrections appear on D2^v (p. 20). The lack of others, despite a number of mis-spelt words, incorrect marks of punctuation, and botched

---

[1] The first two had very similar compositorial characteristics. Only by tracing individual pieces of broken type could I reach a conclusion about which compositor set which pages, and, of course, the results of such a survey are not complete—none of the traceable pieces appeared on some pages. In general, however, the same broken letters can be found in gatherings B, D, F, and H, and another group in C, E, and G. The third compositor, who set I–L, had more easily distinguishable characteristics. In I, he began setting commas rather than periods after speech prefixes that were not abbreviated, although there is no evidence of a shortage of periods in his case; but he used periods after all speech prefixes later in the gathering. Also, in speech prefixes he chose abbreviations different from those common in B–H: *Trus.* rather than *Tru.* for Trusty and usually *Wi.* rather than *Wid.* for Widow. He set 'The End of the IV. ACT.' instead of spelling out the cardinal, and he set the act heading differently. Further, his composing stick was very slightly shorter than the other compositors'. Since the lines of gathering A are of the same measure, it seems likely that the third compositor also set A.

[2] The distribution between presses was:

Press I:
   Skeleton 1: the outer formes of B, D, F, and H.
   Skeleton 2: the inner formes of B, D, F, and H.

Press II:
   Skeleton 3: outer C and E, inner G.
   Skeleton 4: inner C and E, outer G.

Press III:
   Skeleton 5: outer I, inner K and L.
   Skeleton 6: inner I, outer K.
   Skeleton 7: outer L.

The fact that a new set of running-titles appears in outer L suggests that either a Press IV was introduced to print outer L and A or that the running-titles of Skeleton 6 were prematurely distributed in anticipation of printing A, which did not require them, and then new running-titles had to be set for outer L.

passages, suggests that the play was issued in some haste. The uncorrected errors give evidence of the underlying manuscript as well, for certain slips deny the possibility of promptbook derivation. For example, in a love scene in II. iii, Campley, who is wooing Harriot, calls her 'Sharlot', an error that would not survive in a promptbook. Also, incomprehensible passages occur in more than one gathering, set by more than one compositor. Complicated and remote from usual syntax, they seem to be compositors' guesses at illegible passages in a heavily marked and probably interlineated draft. One compositor, for instance, set the nonsense line, '*Campley,* will you gain Ground ev'n of that his Rival', for a passage interpreted in the second edition as '*Campley* will gain Ground ev'n of that Rival of his'. The extremely erratic punctuation indicates printer's copy which was very lightly and casually pointed: the compositor's faulty punctuation of a passage in I. ii, apparently not pointed in the manuscript, has obscured its meaning by causing each of a series of gestures to accompany the wrong phrase. All these details suggest that the manuscript was the author's papers or a very careless transcript.

The second edition, dated 1712, was published on 25 September 1711 in a collection, *The Funeral; and The Tender Husband: Comedies,* printed 'on a new Elziver Letter'.[1] The first edition served as printer's copy. Several issues of the collection, with different title-pages, appeared. Most extant copies read 'Printed for J. T. And Sold by Owen Lloyd near the Church in the Temple' (copies at the Folger Shakespeare Library, Bodleian, University of Texas, British Museum, Cornell, Yale, University of Pennsylvania, Newberry, and University of Michigan).[2] At least one press-variant state of the imprint exists: 'Printed for Jacob Tonson, at Shakespear's Head over-against Catherine Street in the Strand' (British Museum and Yale). A second issue has a cancel title-page with the imprint 'Printed for Henry Scheurleer at Erasmus's Head in the Market-Place at the Hague' (Bodleian). In still another form, the collection 'Printed for J. T. And Sold by Owen Lloyd. . . .', was combined with the second edition of *The Lying Lover* under the additional title-page *The Lying Lovers; The Funeral; and The Tender Husband: Comedies* (University of Texas) and

---

[1] Advertisement, *Spectator,* no. 187, 4 October 1711. According to Alvin I. Dust, Steele was in Tonson's debt at the time of publication ('An Aspect of the Addison–Steele Literary Relationship', *English Language Notes,* i (1964), 199).

[2] One copy, probably made up, in the University of Texas library, lacks the Dedication to the Duchess of Hamilton (*A3–6), and the title-page to the collection (*A2) replaces the title-page to *The Funeral* (A1).

published on 6 November 1711.[1] Except for the cancel title-page in the Scheurleer issue and the addition of a new general title-page to cover the three plays, all the type is from one setting, but a re-impression from standing type was made of gathering A of *The Funeral* (British Museum and Yale). There is, however, one obvious instance of reset type in the reimpression, a Q replacing a swash Q in the motto on the title-page of *The Funeral* (A1).

Three significant revisions and one substantial addition occur, all incontrovertibly authorial. Two are deletions of passages that Steele considered immoral. One of these had been the subject of a letter to the *Spectator*, no. 51, published 28 April 1711:

Mr. SPECTATOR,

My Fortune, Quality, and Person, are such as render me as Conspicuous as any Young Woman in Town. It is in my Power to enjoy it in all its Vanities, but I have, from a very careful Education, contracted a great Aversion to the forward Air and Fashion which is practised in all Publick Places and Assemblies. I attribute this very much to the Stile and Manners of our Plays: I was last Night at the *Funeral*, where a Confident Lover in the Play, speaking of his Mistress, Cries out—*Oh that* Harriot! *to fold these Arms about the Waste of that Beauteous strugling, and at last yielding Fair!* Such an image as this ought, by no means, to be presented to a Chaste and Regular Audience. . . .

Steele commented of his own play, 'The Complaint of this Young Lady is so just, that the Offence is gross enough to have displeased Persons who cannot pretend to that Delicacy and Modesty, of which she is Mistress.' Donald F. Bond believes that Steele may have composed the young lady's letter himself.[2] At any rate, he felt so strongly about the matter that when the second edition of *The Funeral* was published in September of the same year, he revised the passage and omitted some soldiers' impertinences about the pox. That both deletions were made on cancelled pages indicates that he insisted on the changes after the sheets had been through the press.

The third authorial revision, the substitution in a complimentary passage in the Preface of 'the Duke of Devonshire' for 'a very great Man', is not the result of a cancel. Further, a new Dedication of the collection to the Duchess of Hamilton appears. Steele, then, definitely showed some concern for the second edition and dealt personally with the publisher. To ascertain whether he made minor revisions as well

[1] Advertisement, *Spectator*, no. 215, 6 November 1711.
[2] Donald F. Bond, ed., *The Spectator*, 5 vols. (Oxford, 1965), i. 216, n. 1.

as major, it is necessary to determine the order of printing and revision.

The Funeral; and The Tender Husband: Comedies has the collational formula 12^0: *A^6 A^{12} B^{12} ($\pm B4$) C^{12} ($\pm C12$) D–G^{12} H^4. Gathering *A contains the title-page and Dedication of the collection. The title-page of *The Funeral* is A1; the revision in the Preface occurs on A4^v; the text begins on A7. E1 is the title-page of *The Tender Husband*; H4 is blank and in many copies missing. Two skeletons were used for sheets A and C and two others for B and D. Similarly, in *The Tender Husband*, two were used for E and G, two more for F and H. It seems probable, although it cannot be proved, that one pair of skeletons and one press printed two sheets of *The Funeral* and two of *The Tender Husband*, and that a second pair of skeletons and a second press printed the other four sheets.

The division of labour is suggested by the use of the same recognizable pieces of display type in gatherings A and E and other pieces in D and H. Some were also used in the second edition of *The Lying Lover* published a week later. If, as was frequently the case, compositorial duties were divided at the same points as printing operations, the reused display type would combine with the running-title evidence to indicate that one compositor and one press worked on A, C, E, and G, while a second team set and printed B, D, F, and the sheet containing H, *A, and probably the two cancels, all of which would have fitted on one sheet.

Before or during the printing of *The Funeral* Steele must have consulted Tonson or a printing-house employee about the substitution of 'the Duke of Devonshire' and the new Dedication. The *Spectator* was being published daily except Sunday, and Steele was responsible for the issue of 11 September, no. 167, published by Tonson,[1] which preceded the publication of the plays by two weeks. Possibly the two new compliments to patrons were added or other arrangements were made at this time.

However, Steele did not carefully prepare copy or supervise the printing; in gatherings A, B, and C the inaccuracies of the first edition are either reprinted or changed by compositors or editors unfamiliar with the play. Punctuation and capital letters are regularized; obvious errors, such as the repetition of a word or a blatant instance of misused punctuation, are corrected. There is no evidence

[1] Donald F. Bond, 'The First Printing of the *Spectator*', *Modern Philology*, xlvii (1950), 164–77.

of authorial revision except in the two cancels and in gathering D. During the printing Steele apparently recollected the letter to the *Spectator* and insisted on the deletions on B4^v and C12^v.

The nature of the revisions in the type of sheet D, remarkably different from the casual handling of obvious misprints by the compositors of A–C, suggests that Steele prepared the copy or corrected proofs for it. There are noticeably more corrections, and the kinds of revisions bespeak the work of the author. For example, stage directions for Trusty to enter are added at two points, neither of which immediately precedes a speech by him, but at both of which his presence is necessary to stage action which shortly follows. In a lengthy speech in Act v Lord Brumpton first gives fatherly advice to Campley and then to his own son. In the first edition no attention is drawn to the point at which he turns to Lord Hardy, but in the second the stage direction '*To Lord* Hardy.' marks it; a printing-house employee would not have made such a correction. Also the line 'has Mr. *Cabinet* Visited your Lordship since this calamity—How stands that affair now?' in v. iv would hardly have looked incorrect to a compositor or editor. However, the author knew that 'Lordship' is a misprint for 'Ladyship' and that the line impugns the widow's virtue. The editing is certainly not the work of a compositor, nor does it seem probable that it is attributable to a printing-house editor, for he would have had to be unusually alert and familiar with the play. And he would not have edited the whole volume, but only gathering D. One can only assume that Steele provided the substantive revisions. Possibly he revised accidentals, but there is no conclusive evidence. Certainly he was never a perfectionist in regard to punctuation, and he probably would not have marked many changes on proof. Therefore it seems likely that a compositor was responsible for at least most of the accidentals.

The printing schedule supports the theory that Steele himself corrected copy or proofs of sheet D before the press run. According to running-title evidence, one press printed sheet B and then D.[1] A second press, meanwhile, printed C and A. By the time Steele ordered the cancels on B4^v and C12^v, at least the outer formes of B and C had been printed, or cancellation would not have been necessary. The cancellans B4 reuses the running-title from D10; the cancellans C12, the running-title from D8; and C12^v, the running-title from D5^v. The

[1] The order is established by the press-variant running-title on B5, only the corrected form appearing on D5.

reuse of the running-titles of the inner forme of D indicates that the skeleton of inner D was still standing when the cancels were ordered. Steele, then, must have ordered the cancels at least before D was long off the press. He could well have come into the print shop before D was printing, perhaps when inner B and inner C or one forme of A were on the presses. At this time he presumably corrected D. Meticulous, knowledgeable revisions in both formes show that his changes must have preceded the press run of either.

The second impression of A may also contain Steele's revisions, but there is no conclusive proof. Presumably printed to fill out a shortage, the reimpression was made from standing type in a single skeleton containing running-titles from D7, D8^v, and D11. Five revisions in accidentals were introduced into the type:

	Printer's Copy (First edition)	First Impression	Second Impression
A6	Shakespear's	Skakespear's	Shakespear's
A7	Laughters,	Laughers,	Laughters,
A7^v	Undertaker!	Undertaker	Undertaker!
	Insignificant.	Insignificant.	Insignificant?
	China-ware—	China-ware—	China-ware.

Although the return to 'Laughters' seems an odd change for a proof-reader to make, there is little reason to believe Steele proof-read and asked for the revisions.

He did not, certainly, revise any later editions. In 1717 Tonson published a second edition of the collection called *The Funeral; and The Tender Husband: Comedies*. It is a page-for-page reprint of the edition dated 1712, although p. 35 lacks the catchword 'Enter'. The corrections in punctuation in the second impression of sheet A of the second edition are reproduced, but the more likely word 'Laughers' is substituted for 'Laughters'. The only changes in substantives are compositorial.

The 1723 edition, the first play in *The Dramatick Works of Sir Richard Steele*, derives from the 1717 text and introduces a few new errors. A fifth edition of *The Funeral*, published in 1730, the year after Steele's death, bears on its title-page the words 'The Sixth Edition'. There is, however, no evidence of an intervening edition except those published in Dublin and at The Hague. The copy-text is the second edition with the second impression of A. Introducing relatively few new errors, the fifth is a less corrupt text than that of 1723.

The octavo editions published by T. Johnson at The Hague in 1710 and 1721 are interesting and informative. For the 1710 edition Johnson or a printer's reader painstakingly sought comprehensible readings for obviously confused passages and corrected misleading and inaccurate punctuation. The resulting text, while lacking authority, is helpful to the modern editor; at a number of points it offers more significant information than the Tonson editions. With the 1710 as copy-text, the 1721 reprint contains a few additional enlightening if unauthorized revisions. The Dublin edition of 1725, a careful imitation of Tonson's of 1723, attracts little editorial interest since both errors and attempts to correct the copy-text are sparse.

In all the early editions printers never corrected a few quite obvious errors, for example, the use of *Sharlot* for *Harriot* in II. iii. 123. On the other hand, they consistently regularized accidentals, attempted to make sense of incomprehensible passages, and added or removed stage directions. Only the second edition contains authorial revisions. Therefore, I adopt the following editorial procedures:

1. The first edition serves as copy-text.

2. I accept the revision 'the Duke of Devonshire' in gathering A of the second edition and the substantive revisions in gathering D but not changes in accidentals.

3. I reprint the passages expurgated by Steele, since they were omitted purely on moral rather than literary grounds. Footnotes indicate Steele's expurgations.

4. Since Steele made no other revisions in gatherings A, B, and C of the second edition or any gatherings of other editions, I accept no other changes as authoritative. If the first edition readings are obviously compositorial errors and the revisions are as nearly correct as any I might offer, I incorporate them into the text.

5. I freely correct the position of stage directions.

I have collated the following copies: first edition, Folger, British Museum, University of Chicago, Huntington, University of Texas (two copies); second edition, Folger, Bodleian, British Museum, Yale, University of Texas (two copies); third edition, University of Chicago, Folger; fourth edition, Folger, University of Texas; fifth edition, Folger (four copies), University of Pennsylvania; T. Johnson, 1710, Folger; T. Johnson, 1721, Folger; Dublin, 1725, Newberry.

THE

FUNERAL:

OR,

GRIEF A-LA-MODE.

A COMEDY.

Ut Qui conducti plorant in Funere, dicunt
Et Faciunt prope plura dolentibus ex animo, sic
Derisor Vero plus Laudatore movetur. Horace

ABBREVIATIONS USED IN THE NOTES

The following abbreviations are used in reference to early editions of *The Funeral*:

Q   First edition. London: Tonson, 1702.

D1 Second edition. In *The Funeral; and The Tender Husband: Comedies.* London: Tonson, 1712.

D2 Third edition. In *The Funeral; and The Tender Husband: Comedies.* London: Tonson, 1717.

D3 Fourth edition. In *The Dramatick Works of Sir Richard Steele.* London: Tonson, 1723.

D4 Fifth edition. London: Tonson, 1730.

TJ1 First Johnson edition. [The Hague]: T. Johnson, 1710.

TJ2 Second Johnson edition. [The Hague]: T. Johnson, 1721.

Du First Dublin edition. Dublin: Risk, 1725.

TO THE

Right Honourable

THE

COUNTESS

OF

ALBEMARLE.

MADAM,

Among the many Novelties with which Your Ladyship, a stranger in our Nation, is daily entertain'd, You have not yet been made acquainted with the Poetical *English* Liberty, the Right of Dedication; which Entitles us to a Previlege of Celebrating whatever for 5 it's Native Excellence is the just Object of Praise; and is an Antient Charter, by which the Muses have always a Free Access to the Habitation of the Graces.

Hence it is that this Comedy waits on Your Ladyship, and presumes to Welcome You amongst Us; tho' indeed, Madam, We are 10 surpriz'd to see You bring with You, what we thought was of our own Growth only, an agreeable Beauty; Nay, We must assure You, that We cannot give up so Dear an Article of our Glory, but assert it by our Right in You: For if 'tis a Maxim founded on the Noblest Humane Law, that of Hospitality, that every Soil is a Brave Man's 15 Country, *England* has a very just Pretence of Claiming as a Native, a Daughter of Mr. *Scravenmore.*

But Your Ladyship is not only endear'd to Us by the great Services of your Father, but also by the kind Offices of your Husband, whose Frank Carriage falls in with our Genius, which is 20 Free, Open, and Unreserv'd; In this the Generosity of your Tempers makes You both Excel in so peculiar a Manner, that your Good Actions are their own Reward; nor can they be return'd with Ingratitude, for none can forget the Benefits you Confer so soon as You do Your Selves. 25

But Ye have a more indisputable Title to a Dramatick Performance, than all these Advantages; for You are Your selves in a
Degenerate low Age, the Noblest Characters which that fine
Passion that supports the Stage, has inspir'd; and as You have
30 practis'd as Generous a Fidelity as the Fancies of Poets have ever
drawn in their Expecting Lovers; so may You Enjoy as high a
Prosperity as ever they have bestow'd on their Rewarded: This
You may possess in an happy Security, for Your Fortunes cannot
move so much Envy, as Your Persons Love. I am,

35   *Madam,*

Your LADYSHIP's
Most Devoted Humble Servant,
Richard Steele.

PREFACE.

THE Rehearsal of this Comedy was honour'd with the Presence of the Duke of *Devonshire*, who is as distinguish'd by His Fine Understanding, as High Quality; The Innocence of it Mov'd Him to the Humanity of Expressing Himself in it's favour. 'Tis his Manner to be pleas'd where He is not offended; a Condescension 5 which Delicate Spirits are oblig'd to for their Own Ease, for they would have but a very ill time of it, if they suffer'd themselves to be diverted with nothing, but what could bear their Judgment.

That Elegant, and Illustrious Person, will, I hope, pardon My 10 Gratitude to the Town, which obliges Me to report so Substantial a reason for their Approbation of this Play, as that He permitted it: But I know not in what words to thank my Fellow-Soldiers for their Warmth and Zeal in my behalf, nor to what to attribute their Undeserv'd favour, except it be that 'tis Habitual to 'em to run to 15 the Succour of those they see in Danger.—

The Subject of the *Drama* 'tis hop'd will be acceptable to all Lovers of Mankind, since Ridicule is partly Levell'd at a Sett of People who live in Impatient hopes to see Us out of the World, a Flock of Ravens that attend this Numerous City for their Carkases; 20 but indeed 'tis not in the power of any Pen to speak 'em better than they do themselves; As for Example, On a Door I just now past by, a Great Artist thus informs Us of his Cures upon the Dead;

W. W. *Known and approved for his Art of Embalming, having preserved the Corps of a Gentlewoman Sweet and Entire Thirteen Years, without* 25 *Embowelling, and has reduced the Bodies of several Persons of Quality to Sweetness in* Flanders, *and* Ireland, *after Nine Months Putrefaction in the Ground, and they were known by their Friends in* England. *No Man performeth the like.*

He must needs be strangely in Love with this Life, who is not 30 touch'd with this Kind Invitation to be Pickled; and the Noble

2 the Duke of *Devonshire*] D1; a very Great Man.

Operator must be allow'd a very Useful Person for bringing old
Friends together: nor would it be unworthy his Labour to Give Us
an Account at large of the sweet Conversation, that arose upon
35 Meeting such an Entire Friend as He mentions.

But to be Serious; Is there any thing, but it's being downright
Fact, could make a Rational Creature believe 'twere possible to
arrive at this Phantastick Posthumous folly? Not at the same time
but that 'twere Buffoonery rather than Satyr to Explode all Funeral
40 Honours; but then it is Certainly Necessary to make 'em such that
the Mourners should be in Earnest, and the Lamented worthy of
our Sorrow: but this Purpose is so far from being serv'd, that it is
Utterly destroy'd by the Manner of Proceeding among Us, where
the Obsequies which are due only to the Best and Highest of
45 Humane Race (to admonish their short Survivors that neither Wit,
nor Valour, nor Wisdom nor Glory can suspend our Fate) are
prostituted, and bestow'd upon such as have nothing in Common
with Men, but their Mortality.

But the Dead Man is not to pass off so easily, for his Last Thoughts
50 are also to suffer Dissection, and it seems there is an Art to be learn't
to Speak our own Sense in other Mens words, and a Man in a Gown
that never saw his Face shall tell you immediately the Design of the
deceas'd, better than all his Old Acquaintance; Which is so perfect
an *Hocus Pocus*, that without you can repeat such and such words,
55 you cannot convey what is in your hands into another's; but far
be it from any Man's Thought to say there are not Men of Strict
Integrity of the Long Robe, tho' it is not every body's good fortune
to meet with 'em.

However the Daily legal Villanies we see committed, will also be
60 esteem'd things proper to be prosecuted by Satyr, nor could our
Ensuing Legislative do their Country a more seasonable office than
to Look into the Distresses of an Unhappy People, who groan
perhaps in as much Misery under intangled, as they could do under
Broken Laws; Nor could there be a Reward High enough assign'd
65 for a Great Genius, if such may be found, who has Capacity sufficient to glance through the false colours that are put upon Us, and
propose to the *English* World, a Method of making Justice flow in
an uninterrupted Stream; There is so Clear a Mind in being, whom

we will name in Words that of all Men breathing can be only said
of Him; 'Tis He that is Excellent   70

> *Seu linguam causis acuit, seu Civica Jura*
> *Responsare parat, seu condit amabile carmen.*

Other Enemies that may arise against this Poor Play are indeed
less terrible, but much more powerful than these, and they are the
Ladies; but if there is any thing that argues a Sower'd Man, who 75
lashes all for Lady *Brumpton*; we may hope there will be seen also a
Devoted Heart, that esteems all for Lady *Sharlot*—

PROLOGUE,

Spoken by Mr. *Wilks*.

Nature's Deserted, and Dramatick Art,
To Dazle now the Eye, has left the Heart;
Gay Lights, and Dresses, long extended Scenes,
Dæmons and Angels moving in Machines,
All that can now or please or fright the Fair   5
May be perform'd without a writer's Care,
And is the Skill of Carpenter, not Player;
Old Shakespear's *Days could not thus far Advance,*
But what's his Buskin to our Ladder Dance?
In the mid Region a silk Youth to stand,   10
With that unweildy Engine at Command!
Gorg'd with intemp'rate Meals while here you sit,
Well may you take Activity for W it:
Fie, Let confusion on such Dulness seize.
Blush you're so Pleas'd, as we that so we Please;   15
But we still kind to your inverted Sence,
Do most unnatural Things once more dispense;
For since You're still prepost'rous in Delight,
Our Author made, a full House to invite
A Funeral a Comedy to night.   20
Nor does he fear that you will take the Hint,
And let the Funeral his own be meant;
No, in Old England *nothing can be won*
Without a Faction Good or Ill be done;
To own this our Frank Author does not fear,   25
But Hopes for a prevailing Party here,
He knows h' has num'rous Friends, nay knows they'll show it,
And for the Fellow-Soldier save the Poet.

DRAMATIS PERSONAE.

[MEN.]

Lord *Brumpton*.	Mr. *Thomas*.
Lord *Hardy* Son to Lord *Brumpton*.	Mr. *Cibber*.
Mr. *Campley*.	Mr. *Wilks*.
Mr. *Trusty* Steward to Lord *Brumpton*.	Mr. *Mills*.
5 *Cabinet*.	Mr. *Toms*.
Mr. *Sable* an Undertaker.	Mr. *Johnson*.
Puzzle a Lawyer.	Mr. *Bowen*.
Trim, Servant to Lord *Hardy*.	Mr. *Pinkethman*.
Tom, the Lawyer's Clerk.	Mr. *Fairbanck*.

WOMEN.

10 *Widow* [Lady *Brumpton*].	Mrs. *Verbruggen*.
Lady *Sharlot*.　⎰ Orphan-Sisters left in ⎱	Mrs. *Oldfeild*.
Lady *Harriot*.　⎱ ward to Lord *Brumpton*. ⎰	Mrs. *Rogers*.
Mademoiselle *D'Epingle*.	Mrs. *Lucas*.
Tattleaid.	Mrs. *Kent*.
15 Mrs. *Fardingale*.	Mr. *Norris*.
Kate Matchlock.	Mr. *Bullock*.

Visitant-Ladies, Sable's *Servants*, [*Grave-digger, Boys, Servants,*]
Recruits, &c.

SCENE *Covent-Garden*.

THE FUNERAL:

OR,

Grief A-la-Mode.

Act I. Scene i.

Enter Cabinet, Sable, Campley.

Cabinet. I Burst into Laughter, I can't bear to see Writ over an Undertaker's Door, Dresses for the Dead, and Necessaries for Funerals! Ha! ha! ha!

Sable. Well Gentlemen, 'tis very well, I know you are of the Laughers, the Wits that take the Liberty to deride all things that 5 are Magnificent and Solemn.

Campley. Nay, but after all, I can't but admire *Sable's* nice discerning on the superfluous cares of Mankind, that could lead him to the thought of raising an Estate by providing Horses, Equipage, and Furniture, for those that no longer need 'em.   10

Cabinet. But is it not strangely contradictory, that Men can come to so open, so apparent an Hypocrisy, as in the Face of all the World, to hire profess'd Mourners to Grieve, Lament, and Follow in their stead, their nearest Relations, and suborn others to do by Art, what they themselves should be prompted to by Nature?   15

Sable. That's reasonably enough said, but they regard themselves only in all they Act for the Deceas'd, and the poor Dead are deliver'd to my Custody, to be Embalm'd, Slash'd, Cut, and Drag'd about, not to do them Honour, but to satisfy the Vanity or Interest of their Survivors.   20

5 Laughers] D1; Laughters   'Laughters' in Q was changed to 'Laughers' in D1; in the second impression of outer A of D1 the only correction was the return to the copy-text spelling 'Laughters'. Although this perhaps seems an odd change for a printing-house editor to make, there is no reason to believe Steele was responsible. Since the word 'Laughters' for 'those who laugh' is suspect, unlisted for example in the *OED*, I have chosen the more likely form.

Campley. (*Aside to* Cabinet.) This Fellow's every way an Undertaker! How well and luckily he talks! His prating so aptly, has methinks something more Ridiculous in it, than if he were Absurd!

Cabinet. But as Mr. *Campley* says, how could you Dream of making
25 a Fortune from so Chimerical a Foundation, as the Provision of things wholy Needless and Insignificant.

Sable. Alas Gentlemen, the Value of all things under the Sun is merely Fantastick: We run, we strive, and Purchase things with our Blood and Money, quite foreign to our Intrinsick real Happi-
30 ness, and which have a being in Imagination only, as you may see by the pudder that is made about Precedence, Titles, Court Favour, Maidenheads, and China-ware—

Campley. Ay, Mr. *Sable*, but all those are Objects that promote our Joy, are bright to the Eye, or stamp upon our Minds, Pleasure, and
35 Self-satisfaction.

Sable. You are extremely mistaken Sir, for one would wonder to consider that after all our Outcrys against Self-interested Men, There are few, very few in the whole World that Live to themselves, but Sacrifice their Bosom-Bliss to Enjoy a Vain Show, and
40 appearance of Prosperity in the Eyes of others, and there is often nothing more inwardly distress'd, than a Young Bride in her Glittering Retinue, or deeply Joyful, than a Young Widow in her Weeds and Black Train; of both which, the Lady of this House may be an Instance, for she has been the one, and is, I'll be sworn the other.
45 *Cabinet*. You talk Mr. *Sable*, most Learnedly!

Sable. I have the deepest Learning, Sir, Experience, remember your Widow Cousin that Married last Month.

Cabinet. Ay! But how cou'd You Imagine she was in all that Grief an Hypocrite?—could all those Shreiks, those Swoonings, that
50 Rising falling Bosome be constrain'd? You'r Uncharitable, *Sable* to believe it—what Colour, what Reason had you for it.

Sable. First, Sir, her Carriage in her concerns with Me, for I never yet could meet with Sorrowful relict but was her self enough to make an hard bargain with Me—Yet I must confess they have
55 frequent Interruptions of Greif and sorrow when they read my Bill— but as for her, nothing she resolv'd that look'd Bright or Joyous, should after her Love's Death approach Her. All her Servants that

were not Cole black must turn out; A fair Complection made her
Eyes and Heart Ake, she'd none but downright Jet, and to exceed all
example she hir'd my Mourning Furniture by the Year, and in case 60
of my Mortality Ty'd my Son to the same Article; so in six weeks
time ran away with a Young Fellow—Prethee Push on Briskly, Mr.
Cabinet, now is your time to have this Widow for *Tattleaid* tells me
she always said she'd never Marry—

 Cabinet. As You say that's Generally the most hopeful sign.   65

 Sable. I tell you Sir, 'tis an Infalliable one, You know those professions
are only to introduce Discourse of Matrimony and Young Fellows.

 Cabinet. But I swear I could not have Confidence ev'n after all our
Long Acquaintance, and the Mutual Love which his Lordship (who
indeed has now been so Kind as to leave us) has so long interrupted 70
to mention a thing of such a Nature so unseasonably—

 Sable. Unseasonably! Why I tell you 'tis the only Season (granting
her Sorrow unfaign'd) when would You speak of Passion? but in the
midst of Passions? There's a what de' call a Crisis—the Lucky
minute that's so talk'd of, is a moment between Joy and Grief, 75
which You must take hold of, and push your Fortune—But get you
in, and you'll best read your Fate in the Reception Mrs. *Tattleaid*
gives you: All she says and all she does, nay her very Love, and
Hatred are mere repetition of her Ladyship's Passions: I'll say that
for her, she's a True Lady's Woman and is her self as much a second 80
hand thing as her Cloaths. But I must beg your pardon Gentlemen,
my People are come I see—

       Exeunt Cabinet *and* Campley.

     Enter Sable's *Men*.

Where in the name of Goodness have you all been! have you brought
the Saw-dust and Tarr for Embalming? have you the Hangings and
the Six-penny Nails, and my Lord's Coat of Arms?   85

     Enter Servant.

 Servant. Yes Sir, and had come sooner, but I went to the Heralds
for a Coat for Alderman *Gathergrease* that Dy'd last night—he has
promis'd to invent one against to morrow.

Sable. Ah! Pox take some of our Cits, the first thing after their
90 Death is to take care of their Birth—Pox let Him bear a Pair of
Stockings, he's the first of his Family that ever wore one: Well come
you that are to be Mourners in this House put on your sad Looks,
and walk by Me that I may sort you: Ha you! a little more upon
the Dismal; (*Forming their Countenances—*) this Fellow has a good
95 Mortal look—place him near the Corps: That Wanscoat Face must
be o'top of the Stairs, that Fellow's almost in a Fright (that looks as
if he were full of some strange misery) at the Entrance of the Hall—
So—but I'll fix you all my self—Lets have no Laughing now on any
provocation: (*Makes faces.*) Look Yonder that Hale Well-looking
100 Puppy! You ungrateful Scoundrel; Did not I pity you, take you out
of a Great Man's Service, and show you the Pleasure of receiving
Wages? Did not I give you Ten, then Fifteen, now Twenty shillings
a Week, to be Sorrowful and the more I give you, I think, the Glader
you are?

Enter a Boy.

105 *Boy.* Sir the *Grave-digger* of St. *Timothie's* in the Fields would speak
with you.
Sable. Let Him come in.

Enter Grave-digger.

Grave-digger. I carry'd home to your House the Shrowd the
Gentleman was buried in last Night; I could not get his Ring of very
110 easily; therefore I brought the Finger and all; and Sir the Sexton
gives his Service to you, and desires to know whether you'd have
any Bodies remov'd or not: if not He'll let 'em lie in their Graves a
week longer.
Sable. Give him my Service, I can't tell readily, but our Friend,
115 tell Him Dr. *Passeport* with the Powder has promised me Six or
Seven Funeralls this Week. I'll send to our Country-Farm at
Kensington Gravel-Pits; and our City-house in *Warwick-lane* for
News, you shall know time enough; Hark'e be sure there's care
taken to give my Lady *Languishe's* Woman a Fee, to keep out that
120 Young Fellow came last from *Oxford*; He'll ruine us all:

Enter Goody Trash.

I wonder Goody *Trash* you could not be more punctual; when I told
you I wanted you, and your two Daughters to be three Virgins to
Night to stand in White about my Lady *Katherine Grissel's* Body,
and you know you were privately to bring her home from the Man-
Mid-wifes, where she Dy'd in Child-birth to be Buried like a Maid; 125
But there is nothing minded: Well I have put of that till to morrow;
go and get your Bagg of Brick-dust and your Whiting. Go and sell
to the Cook-maids; know who has Surfeited about Town: bring me
no bad news none of your Recoverys again; And you Mr. Blockhead
I warrant you have not call'd at Mr. *Pestles* the Apothecary: Will 130
that fellow never pay me? I stand Bound for all the Poison in that
starving Murderers shop: He serves me Just as Dr. *Quibus* did, who
promis'd to write a Treatise against Water-gruel, a Damn'd
Healthy slop, that has done Me more Injury than all the Faculty:
Look you now you're all upon the Sneer, let me have none 135
but downright stupid Countenances—I've a good mind to turn
you all off and take people out of the Play-house; but hang 'em
they are as Ignorant of their Parts as you are of yours, they never
Act but when they speak; when the Cheif indication of the Mind is
in the Gesture, or indeed in case of Sorrow in no Gesture, except 140
you were to Act a Widow, or so—But yours you Dolts, is all in
Dumb show; Dumb show? I mean expressive Eloquent show: as
who can see such an horrid Ugly Phiz as that Fellow's, and not be
shock'd, offended, and kill'd of all Joy while he beholds it? But we
must not Loiter—ye stupid Rogues whom I have pick'd out of all 145
the rubbish of Mankind, and fed for your Eminent worthlessness
attend and know, that I speake you this Moment stiff and Immutable to all sense of Noise, Mirth, or Laughter: (*Makes mouths at 'em*
as they pass by him to bring 'em to a constant Countenance.) So they are
pretty well—pretty well—   150

[Act I. Scene ii.]

Enter Trusty, *Lord* Brumpton.

Trusty. 'Twas fondness Sir, and tender duty to you who have been so Worthy, and so Just a Master to me, made me stay near you; they left me so, and There I found you wake from your Lethargick-slumber; on which I will assume an Authority to beseech you, Sir
5 to make Just use of your reviv'd Life, in seeing who are your True Friends, and knowing Her who has so wrought upon your noble nature, as to make it Act against it self in Dis-inheriting your Brave Son.

Lord Brumpton. Sure 'tis impossible she should be such a Creature
10 as you tell me—My mind reflects upon Ten Thousand endearments that plead unanswerably for Her: Her chast reluctant Love, her easy Observance of all my wayward Humours to which she would accommodate her self with so much ease, I could scarce observe it was a Virtue in her; she hid her very Patience.

15 *Trusty.* It was all Art Sir or indifference to you, for what I say is downright matter of Fact.

Lord Brumpton. Why did'st thou ever tell me it, or why not in my life-time, for I must call it so, nor can I date a minute mine, after her being False, all past that Moment is Death, and Darkness: Why
20 did'st thou not tell me then I say?

Trusty. Because you were too much in Love with Her to be inform'd, nor did I ever know a man that touch'd on Conjugal affairs could ever reconcile the Jarring humours, but in a common Hatred of the intermedler: But on this most extraordinary Occasion,
25 which seems pointed out by Heav'n it self to disengage you from your Cruelty and Banishment of an Innocent Child, I must, I will Conjure you to be conceal'd, and but contain your self, in hearing one Discourse with that Curs'd Instrument of all her Secrets that *Tattleaid*, and you'll see what I tell you, you'll call me then your
30 Guardian and good Genius.

Lord Brumpton. Well you shall Govern me, but would I had Dy'd
in Earnest, e're I'd known it; my Head swims as it did when I fell
into my Fit at the thoughts of it—How dizzy a place is this World
You Live in! All Human Life's a mere Vertigo!

Trusty. Ay, Ay, My Lord, fine Reflections, fine Reflections but 35
that does no Business, Thus Sir, we'll stand conceal'd and hear I
doubt not a much sincerer Dialogue than Usual between Vitious
Persons, for a late Accident has giv'n a little Jealousy which makes
'em over-act their Love and confidence in each other. (*They Retire.*)

Enter Widow *and* Tattleaid *meeting*
and running to each other.

Widow. Oh *Tattleaid*! His and our hour is come!   40
Tattleaid. I always said by his Church-yard-Cough, you'd Bury
him, but still you were impatient—
Widow. Nay, thou hast ever been my Comfort, my Confident, my
Friend, and my Servant; and now I'll reward thy Pains; for tho' I
scorn the whole Sex of Fellows, I'll give 'em hopes for thy sake; 45
every Smile, every Frown, every Gesture, Humor, Caprice and
Whimsey of mine, shall be Gold to thee Girl; thou shalt feel all the
Sweet and Wealth of being a Fine Rich Widow's Woman: Oh! how
my Head runs my first Year out, and jumps to all the Joys of Widowhood! If Thirteen Months hence a Friend should haul one to a Play 50
one has a mind to see: What Pleasure 'twill be when my Lady
Brumpton's Footman's call'd (who kept a place for that very purpose)
to make a suddain Insurrection of Fine Wigs in the Pit, and Side-
Boxes. Then with a pretty sorrow in one's Face, and a willing Blush
for being Star'd at, one ventures to look round and Bow, to one of 55
one's own Quality, Thus: (*Very Derectly.*) To a Smug Pretending
Fellow of no Fortune, Thus: (*As scarce seeing him.*) To one that Writes
Lampoons, Thus: (*Fearfully.*) To one one really Loves, Thus: (*Looking
down.*) To one's Woman Acquaintance, from Box to Box, Thus:
(*With looks differently Familiar.*) And when one has done one's part, 60

55–60 one . . . *Familiar.*)] ed.; one of one's own Quality. Thus [*very Derectly*] to
a Smug Pretending Fellow of no Fortune: Thus [*as scarce seeing him*] to one that
Writes Lampoons: Thus [*Fearfully*] to one one really Loves: Thus [*looking down*] to
one's Woman, Acquaintance, from Box to Box: Thus [*with looks differently Familiar*]
    The punctuation in all the Tonson editions, reproduced by Aitken in the Mer-
maid edition, assigns the wrong gesture to each phrase. Oddly enough, T. Johnson

observe the Actors do theirs, but with my mind fixt not on those I
look at, but those that look at me—Then the Serenades! The Lovers!

Tattleaid. Oh Madam, you make my Heart bound within me; I'll
warrant you Madam, I'll manage 'em all, and indeed Madam, the
65 Men are really very silly Creatures, 'tis no such hard matter—They
Rulers! They Governours I warrant you indeed!

Widow. Ay *Tattleaid*, they imagine themselves mighty things,
but Government founded on Force only, is a Brutal Power—We
rule them by their Affections, which blinds them into a belief that
70 they rule us, or at least are in the Government with us—But in this
Nation our Power is Absolute; Thus, thus, we sway—(*Playing her
Fan.*) A Fan is both the Standard, and the Flag of *England*: I Laugh
to see the Men go our Errands, Strut in Great Offices, Live in
Cares, Hazards and Scandals, to come home and be Fools to Us in
75 Brags of their Dispatches, Negotiations, and their Wisdoms—as my
good Dear Deceas'd us'd to Entertain me; which I to releive my
self from—would lisp some silly Request, pat him on the Face—He
shakes his Head at my pretty Folly, Calls me Simpleton; Gives Me
a Jewel, then goes to Bed so Wise, so Satisfyed and so Deceiv'd!

80 *Tattleaid.* But I protest Madam, I've always wonder'd how you
could accomplish my Young Lord's being disinherited.

Widow. Why *Tatty*, you must know my Late Lord, how prettily
that sounds, my Late Lord! But I say my Late Lord's Foible was
generosity—I press'd Him there, and whenever you, by my order,
85 had told him Stories to my Son in Law's Disadvantage, in his Rage,
and Resentment, I (whose interest lay otherwise) always fell on my
knees to implore his Pardon, and with Tears, Sighs, and Importunities for Him prevail'd against Him: Besides this You Know I had
90 when I pleas'd Fits; Fits are a mighty help in the Government of a
Good natur'd Man; but to an Ill Natur'd Fellow have a Care of 'em
—He'll hate you for Natural Infirmities: will remember your Face
in it's Distortion, and not value your return of Beauty.

corrected the error. The present reading remains as close as possible to the accidentals of Q but corrects the misleading punctuation.

83 Lord's Foible] ed.; Lord *Frible*   The original 'Lord *Frible*' is suspect, since
Frible, meaning a frivolous fellow, would be a peculiarly inappropriate name for the
widow to call Lord Brumpton. The present emendation, suggested by a correction
in the Leeds copy in an eighteenth-century hand, is both logical and easily ex-
plicable as a compositor's misreading of the manuscript.

Tattleaid. Oh rare Madam! Your Ladiship's a Great Head-peice
but now Dear Madam, is the hard Task, if I may take the Liberty 95
to say it—to Enjoy all Freedoms, and seem to Abstain, to manage
the number of Pretenders and keep the disoblig'd from prating—

Widow. Never fear *Tattleaid*, while you have Riches if you affront
one to Abuse, you can give hopes to another to defend you: these
Maxims I have been laying up all my Husbands Life-time, for we 100
must provide against Calamities—

Tattleaid. But now Madam, a Fine Young Gentleman with a Red
Coat that Dances—

Widow. You may be sure the happy man (if it be in Fate that
there is an Happy man to make me an Unhappy Woman) shall not 105
be an Old one again: Age and Youth Married, is the Cruelty in
Dryden's Virgil, where *Mezentius* Tyes the Dead and living together:
I'm sure I was ty'd to a Dead Man many a long Day before I durst
Bury Him—But the Day is now my own—Yet now I think on't
Tattleaid, be sure to keep an Obstinate Shyness to all our old 110
Acquaintance: Let 'em talk of Favours if they please, if we grant
'em still they'll grow Tyrants to us, if we Discard 'em the Chast
and Innocent will not believe we could have Confidence to do
it, were it so, and the Wise if they believe it, will applaud our
Prudence.   115

Tattleaid. Ay Madam—I believe Madam—I speak Madam, but
my Humble Sence—Mr. *Cabinet* would Marry you.

Widow. Marry me! No *Tattleaid*. He that is so mean as to Marry
a Woman after an affair with her, will be so base as to Upbraid that
very Weakness: He that Marries his Wench will Use her like his 120
Wench—Such a pair must sure live in a Secret Mutual Scorn of each
other—and Wedlock is Hell, if at least one side does not Love, as it
would be Heav'n if both did; and I believe it so much Heav'n as to
think it was never Enjoy'd in this World.

Enter a Woman.

Woman. A Gentleman to Mrs. *Tattleaid*—   125
Widow. Go to him—

Exit Tattleaid.

99 give] D1; gives

Bless me how careless and open have I been to this Subtle Creature
in the case of *Cabinet*, she's Certainly in his Interests—We People of
condition are never Guarded enough against those about us: They
130 watch when our Minds boil over with Joy, or Greif to come in upon
us: How Miserable 'tis to have One one hates always about one,
and when One can't endure ones own Reflection upon some Actions,
who can bear the thoughts of another upon 'em: But she has me by
Deep Deep Secrets—The *Italians* they say can readily Remove the
135 too much intrusted—Oh their pretty scented Gloves! This Wench
I know has play'd me False, and Horn'd me in my Gallants: Oh
Italy I could resign all my Female *English* Liberty, to thee for thy
much Dearer Female Pleasure Revenge!

Enter Tattleaid.

well what's the matter, Dear *Tatty*—
140   *Tattleaid.* The matter Madam, why Madam, Councellor *Puzzle* is
come to wait on your Ladiship about the Will, and the Conveyance
of the Estate—there must it seems be no time lost for fear of things;
Fie, Fie, Madam you a Widow these Three hours, and not look'd
on a Parchment Yet—Oh Impious to neglect the Will of the Dead!
145   *Widow.* As you say indeed there is no Will of an Husbands so
willingly Obey'd as his Last. But I must Go in, and receive Him in
my Formalities leaning on a Couch, as necessary a Posture as his
going behind his Desk when he speaks to a Client—But do you
bring him in hither till I'm ready—

Exit.

150   *Tattleaid. (Calling.)* Mr. Councelour, Mr. Councelour—

Enter Puzzle *and* Clerk.

Puzzle. Servant Good Madam *Tattleaid*, my Ancient Friend is
gone, but Business must be minded—
Tattleaid. I told my Lady twice or thrice, as she lies in Dumb Grief
on the Couch within, that you were here, but she regarded me not,
155 However since you say 'tis of such Moment, I'll venture to introduce you, please but to repose here a little while I step in; For methinks I would a little prepare her.

149.1 *Exit.*] D1; [om.]

Puzzle. Alas! Alas! Poor Lady!

              Exit Tattleaid.

Damn'd Hypocrites! Well this Noble's Death is a little sudden:
Therefore pray let me recollect: Open the Bagg good *Tom*; now 160
Tom thou art my Nephew, my Dear Sister *Kate's* only Son, and my
Heir, therefore I will conceal from Thee on no occasion, any thing;
For I would enter Thee into Business as soon as possible: Know then
Child that the Lord of this House was one of your Men of Honour,
and Sense, who lose the latter in the former, and are apt to take all 165
men to be like themselves; Now this Gentleman intirely trusted
me, and I made the only use a man of Business can of a Trust, I
cheated Him; for I, imperceptibly, before his Face made his whole
Estate liable to an Hundred *per Annum* for my self, for good Services
&c. As for Legacies they are good or not, as I please, for let me tell 170
you, a man must take Pen, Ink and Paper, sit down by an Old
Fellow, and pretend to take directions, but a True Lawyer never
makes any man's Will but his own, and as the Priest of Old among
us Got near the Dying Man, and gave all to the Church, so now the
Lawyer gives all to the Law. 175

 Clerk. Ay Sir, but Priests then Cheated the Nation by doing their
Offices in an unknown Language.

 Puzzle. True, but Ours is a way much surer, for we Cheat in no
Language at all, but Loll in our own Coaches, Eloquent in Gibbrish,
and Learned in Juggle—Pull out the Parchment there's the Deed, I 180
made it as long as I could—Well I hope to see the Day, when the
Indenture shall be the exact measure of the Land that passes by it—
For 'tis a Discouragement to the Gown—that every Ignorant Rogue
of an Heir should in a word or two understand his Father's meaning,
and hold Ten Acres of Land, by half an Acre of Parchment—Nay I 185
hope to see the time when what there is indeed some Progress made
in shall be wholly affected, and by the improvement of the noble
Art of Tautology every Inn in *Holborn* an Inn of Court—Let others

---

186 what] ed.; that The misprint 'that' made nonsense of Steele's rather bulky
sentence. Compositors and editors of later editions made some attempts to bring
meaning to the passage (see Historical Collation). None, however, chose the sim-
plest explanation, the misprinting of 'that' for 'what', as a basis for emendation.
The phrase 'what there is indeed some Progress made in' refers to the lawyers' improvement in the art of tautology.

188 an Inn] D1; or Inn's This revision appears in the portion of D1 that Steele
did not correct, but it doubtless reflects his original intentions.

Think of logick Rhetorick and I Know not what impertinence but
190 mind thou Tautology—What's the first Excellence in a Lawyer—
Tautology? What the second? Tautology? What the third Tautology, as an old Pleader said of Action: But Turn to the Deed; (*Pulls
out an imeasurable Parchment.*) For the Will is of no force if I please,
for he was not capable of making one after the former—as I manag'd
195 it—upon which account I now wait on my Lady; By the way do you
Know the True meaning of the word a Deed?

Clerk. Ay, Sir, a Deed is as if a man should say the Deed.

Puzzle. Right: 'Tis emphatically so call'd, because after it—all
Deeds and Actions are of no effect, and you have nothing to do but
200 hang your self—the only Obliging thing you can then do—But I
was telling you the Use of Tautology—Read toward the Middle of
that Instrument.

Clerk. (*Reads.*) I the said Earl of *Brumpton*, Do give, Bestow, Grant
and Bequeath over and above the said Premises, all the site and
205 Capital Messuage call'd by the name of *Oatham*, and all Outhouses,
Barns, Stables and other Ædifices, and Buildings, Yards, Orchards,
Gardens, Feilds, Arbors, Trees, Lands, Earths, Medows, Greens,
Pastors, Feedings, Woods, Underwoods, Ways, Waters, Water-
courses, Fishings, Ponds, Pools, Commons, Common of Pasture,
210 Paths, Heath-Thickets, Profits, Commodities, and Emoluments
with their, and every of their Appurtenances whatsoever, (Puzzle
nods and snears as the Synonimous words are repeating, whom Lord
Brumpton *scornfully mimicks.*) to the said Capital Messuage, and
site belonging or in any wise appertaining, or with the same hereto-
215 fore used, occupied, or enjoy'd, accepted, executed, known, or taken
as part, parcel, or member of the same containing in the whole, by
Estimation four Hundred Acres of the large Measure, or thereabouts,
be the same more or less, all and singular, which the said site
Capital Messuage, and other the Premises with their, and every
220 of their Appurtenances are situate, lying and being—

Puzzle. Hold hold good *Tom*; you do come on indeed in Business,
but don't use your Nose enough in Reading—Why you're quite
out—you Read to be Understood—let me see it—I the said Earl
(*Reads in a Ridiculous Law-Tone, till out of breath.*)—Now again suppose
225 this were to be in Latin—Making Latin, is only making it no

English—(*Runs into Latin Terminations.*) *Ego Predict—Comes de Brumpton—Totas meas Barnos—Outhousas, & Stabulas—Yardos*—But there needs no further perusal—I now Recollect the whole—My Lord, by this Instrument, Disinherits his Son utterly—Gives all to my Lady—and moreover, Grants the Wards of two Fortune-Wards 230 to her—*Id est*, to be Sold by her; which is the Subject of my Business to her Ladyship, who methinks a little overdoes the affair of Grief, in letting me wait thus long on such Welcome Articles—But here—

Enter Tattleaid *Wiping her Eyes.*

Tattleaid. I have in vain done all I can to make her regard me—Pray Mr. *Puzzle*, you're a Man of Sense, come in your self, and 235 speak Reason to bring her to some Consideration of her self, if possible.

Puzzle. Tom, I'll come down to the Hall to you; Dear Madam, lead on?

Exeunt Clerk *one way*, Puzzle, Tattleaid *another.*

Lord Brumpton *and* Trusty *Advance from their
concealment after a long Pause and
staring at each other.*

Lord Brumpton. Trusty on thy sincerity, on thy Fidelity to me thy 240 Friend, thy Patron, and thy Master, answer me directly to One Question: Am I really Alive? Am I that Identical, that Numerical, that very same Lord *Brumpton* that—

Trusty. That very Lord—that very Lord *Brumpton*, the very Generous Honest, and Good Lord *Brumpton*, who spent his strong 245 and riper Years, with Honor and Reputation, but in his Age of Decay declin'd from Virtue also—that very Lord *Brumpton* who Buried a Fine Lady, who brought him a Fine Son, who is a Fine Gentleman, but in his Age that very Man unseasonably Captivated with Youth and Beauty, Married a very Fine Young Lady, who has 250 dishonour'd his Bed, Disinherited his Brave Son, and Dances o're his Grave.

Lord Brumpton. Oh! that Damn'd Tautologist too—That *Puzzle* and his Irrevocable Deed! (*Pausing.*) Well I know I do not really

240 thy sincerity] D1; the ~

255 Live, but wander o're the place, where once I had a Treasure—I'll
haunt her *Trusty*, Gaze in that False Beauteous Face: 'till she
Trembles, 'till she looks Pale, nay till she Blushes—

Trusty. Ay Ay My Lord, you speak a Ghost very much,
There's Flesh, and Blood in that Expression, that False Beauteous
260 Face!

Lord Brumpton. Then since you see my Weakness, be a Friend,
and Arm me with all your Care, and all your Reason—.

Trusty. If you'll condescend to let me direct you—you shall cut
off this rotten Limb your False Disloyal Wife, and save your Noble
265 Parts, your Son, your Family, your Honour.

Short is the Date in which Ill Acts prevail,
But Honesty's a Rock can never fail.

The End of the First Act.

Act II. [Scene i.]

Enter Lord Hardy Solus.

Lord Hardy. Now indeed, I am Utterly Undone, but to expect an
Evil softens the weight of it when it happens, and pain no more than
pleasure is in reality so great as in expectation: But what will become of me? How shall I keep my Self ev'n above Worldly want?
5 Shall I live at Home a stiff, Melancholy, Poor man of Quality, grow
uneasy to my Acquaintance as well as my self, by Fancying I'm
slighted where I am not; with all the Thousand particularities,
which attend those whom low Fortune, and high Spirit make Malecontents? No! we've a Brave Prince on the Throne, whose Commis-
10 sion I bare, and a Glorious War in an Honest Cause, Approaching
(*Clapping his Hand on his Sword.*) in which this shall Cut Bread for me,
and may perhaps Equal that Estate to which my Birth Entitled me
—But what to do in present Pressures—(*Calling.*) ha! *Trim*.

Enter Trim.

Trim. My Lord.

Lord Hardy. How do the Poor Rogues, that are to recruit my 15 Company?

Trim. Do Sir? they've Eat you to your last Guinea.

Lord Hardy. Were you at the Agent's?

Trim. Yes?

Lord Hardy. Well? and how?   20

Trim. Why Sir for your Arrears, You may have Eleven Shillings in the Pound; but he'll not Touch your Growing Subsistence under Three Shillings in the Pound Interest—besides which You must let his Clerk *Jonathan Item*, Swear the Peace against you to keep you from Duelling—or insure your life, which you may do for Eight 25 *percent*. On these terms He'll Oblige you; which he would not do for any Body else in the Regiment, but he has a Friendship for You.

Lord Hardy. Oh I'm his Humble Servant; But he must have his own terms, we can't Starve, nor must my Fellows want. But me-thinks this is a Calm Mid-night I've heard no Duns to-Day—   30

Trim. Duns My Lord? Why now Your Father's dead and they can't Arrest you; I shall grow a little less upon the Smooth with 'em then I have been: Why Friend, says I, how often must I tell you my Lord is not stirring: His Lordship has not Slept well, you must come some other time, Your Lordship will send for Him when you 35 are at Leisure to look upon Money-affairs or if they are so Sawcy, so Impertinent as to press to a man of your Quality for their own— there are Canes, there's *Bridewel*, there's the Stocks for your Ordin-ary Tradesmen. But to an Haughty Thriving, *Covent-Garden* Mercer, Silk or Lace-man, Your Lordship gives your most Humble Service 40 to Him, hopes his Wife's well; you have Letters to Write, or you'd see him your self, but you desire he would be with you Punctually such a Day, that's to say, the Day after you are gone out of Town.

Lord Hardy. Go, Sirrah you're Scurrilous I won't believe there are such Men of Quality—d'ye hear give my Service this Afternoon to 45 Mr. *Cutpurse* the Agent, and tell him I am oblig'd to him for his readiness to Serve me, for I'me resolv'd to pay my Debts forth-with—

A Voice. (Without.) I don't know whether he's within or not, Mr.
50 *Trim* is my Lord Within?

 Lord Hardy. Trim see who it is, I an't within you know—

               [*Exit* Trim.]

 Trim. (Without.) Yes Sir, my Lord's above, Pray Walk up—

 Lord Hardy. Who can it be he owns me to?

      Enter Campley *and* Trim.

Dear *Tom Campley* this is kind—You are an Extraordinary Man
55 indeed, who in the sudden accession of a Noble Fortune can be still
Your self, and Visit your less happy Friends.

 Campley. No You are, my Lord, the Extraordinary Man, who on
the loss of an almost Princely Fortune, can be Master of a Temper,
that makes you the envy rather than Pity of your more Fortunate,
60 not more happy Friends.

 Lord Hardy. Oh Sir, your Servant—But let me Gaze on thee a
little—I han't seen thee since I came home into *England*—most
Exactly, Negligently, Gentielly Dress'd! I know there's more than
Ordinary in this—(*Beating* Campley's *Breast.*) Come,—Confess,
65 who shares with me here—I must have her Real and Poetical Name
—Come—She's in Sonnet *Cynthia*—In Prose Mistress.

 Campley. One you little Dream of, tho' she is in a manner of your
placing there?

 Lord Hardy. My placing there?

70 *Campley.* Why, my Lord, all the fine things you've said to me
in the Camp of my Lady *Sharlot* your Father's Ward, ran in my Head
so very much, that I made it my Business to become Acquainted in
that Family, which I did by Mr. *Cabinet's* means, and am now in
Love in the same place with your Lordship.

75 *Lord Hardy.* How! in Love in the same place with me Mr.
Campley?

 Campley. Ay, my Lord, with t'other Sister, with t'other Sister.

 Lord Hardy. What a Dunce was I, not to know which without

53 Who can it be he owns me to?] ed.; Who can it be, he owns me too? The
punctuation and the rather unusual spelling 'too' for the preposition in Q led subsequent compositors to 'improve' the line by distorting its original meaning to 'Who
can it be? he owns me too.' Aitken followed this interpretation. The correct reading
is, however, obvious from the context. The accidentals are here changed for clarity.
 58 loss] D1; lose

your Naming her? Why thou art the only Man breathing fit to deal
with her—But my Lady *Sharlot*, there's a Woman—So easily 80
Vertuous!—So agreeably severe! Her Motion so Unaffected, yet so
Compos'd! Her Lips breath nothing but Truth, Good Sense, and
Flowing Wit.

Campley. Lady *Harriot*! there's the Woman, such Life, such Spirit,
such warmth in her Eyes—Such a Lively Commanding Air in her 85
Glances; so Spritely a Mein, that carries in it the Triumph of
Conscious Beauty; her Lips are made up of Gum, and Balm—
There's something in that Dear Girl that fires my Blood Above—
Above—Above—

Lord Hardy. Above what?   90

Campley. A Granadier's March.

Lord Hardy. A soft Simile I must confess—but oh that *Sharlot*! to
recline this Aching Head, full of Care on that Tender Snowy—
Faithful Bosom!

Campley. Oh that *Harriot*! to fold these Arms about the Wast of 95
that Beauteous Strugling—and at last Yeilding Fair!

Lord Hardy. Ay *Tom*; but methinks your Head runs too much on
the Wedding-Night only, to make your Happiness lasting, mine is
fixt on the Married State; I expect my Felicity from Lady *Sharlot*, in
her Friendship, her Constancy, her Piety, her Houshold Cares, her 100
Maternal Tenderness—You think not of any Excellence of your
Mistress, that is more than Skin-deep—

Campley. When I know her further than Skin-deep, I'll tell you
more of my mind.

Lord Hardy. Oh fie *Tom*, how can you talk so lightly of a Woman 105
you Love with Honour—But tell me, I wonder how you make your
Approaches in Beseiging such a sort of Creature; she that Loves
Addresses, Gallantry, Fiddles? That Reigns and Delights in a
Crowd of Admirers—If I know her, she's one of those you may
easily have a general Acquaintance with, but hard to make 110
Particular—

95–96 to fold . . . Fair!] This line brought a prim complaint to the *Spectator*,
allegedly from a young lady who had seen *The Funeral* performed on 26 April 1711.
The letter was the occasion of Steele's revision in D1 to 'to Embrace that Beauteous—'.
Since the revision, which required the cancellation of B4, was made purely on moral
rather than literary grounds, the original reading is retained in the present edition.

Campley. You understand her very well—you must know I put her out of all her Play, by carrying it in an Humorous manner; I took care in all my Actions, before I discover'd the Lover, that she
115 should in general have a good Opinion of me; and have ever since behav'd my self with all the good Humour, and ease I was able; so that she is now extremely at a loss, how to throw me from the Familiarity of an Acquaintance, into the distance of a Lover; But I Laugh her out of it, when she begins to Frown, and look Grave at
120 my Mirth, I Mimick her till she bursts out a Laughing—

Lord Hardy. That's Ridiculous enough.

Campley. By *Cabinet's* Interest over my Lady *Brumpton*, and with Gold and Flattery to Mrs. *Fardingale*, an Old Maid her Ladyship has plac'd about the Young Ladies, I have easy access at all times,
125 and am this very day to be admitted by her into their Apartment— I have found you must know that she is my Relation—

Lord Hardy. Her Ladyship has chose an odd Companion for young Ladies—

Campley. Oh my Lady's a Politician; she told *Tattleaid* one day,
130 that an Old Maid was the best Guard for Young ones, for they, like Eunuchs in a *Saraglio*, are Vigilent, out of Envy of Enjoyments they cannot themselves arrive at—But as I was saying, I've sent my Cousin *Fardingale* a Song, which she and I are to practise to the Spinet—The Young Ladies will be by—and I am to be left alone
135 with Lady *Harriot*, then I design to make my grand Attack, and to day, Win or Lose her: I know Sir, this is an opportunity you want —If you'll meet me at *Tom's*, have a Letter ready, I'll my self deliver it to your Mistress, conduct you into the House, and tell her you are there—and find means to place you together—You must March
140 under my Command to day, as I have many a one under yours—

Lord Hardy. But Faith *Tom* I shall not behave my self with half the Resolution you have under mine, for to confess my Weakness, tho' I know she Loves me, tho' I know she is as Stedfastly mine, as her Heart can make her—I know not how I have so sublime an Idea
145 of her high Value, and such a melting Tenderness dissolves my

---

122 *Brumpton,* and] This is the reading intended in the first edition. D1 was printed from one of the relatively few copies of Q which read '*Brumpton* , ' because of type lost during the run. The error was retained in later editions, including Aitken's.

whole Frame, when I am near her, that my Tongue Faulters, my
Nerves Shake, and my Heart so alternately Sinks and Rises that my
premeditated Resolves vanish into Confusion, Down-cast Eyes,
and Broken utterance—

Campley. Ha! ha! ha! this in a Campagner too! Why, my Lord, 150
that's the condition *Harriot* would have me in, and then she thinks
she could have me, but I that know her better than she does her
self, know she'd insult me, and lead me a Two years Dance longer,
and perhaps in the end turn me into the Herd of the many Neglected
Men of better Sense, who have been Ridiculous for her sake—But 155
I shall make her no such Sacrifice—'Tis well my Lady *Sharlot*'s a
Woman of so Solid an Understanding, I don't know another that
would not Use you ill for your High Value—

Lord Hardy. But *Tom* I must see your Song, you've sent your
Cousin *Fardingale*, as you call her.   160

Campley. (*Aside*.) This is Lucky enough. [*To Lord* Hardy.] No hang
it, my Lord, a Man makes so Silly a Figure when his Verses are
reading—*Trim*—Thou hast not left of thy Loving and thy Rhiming,
Trim's a Critick, I remember him a Serviture at *Oxon*, (*Gives a Paper
to Trim*—) I give my self into his hands, because you shan't see 'em 165
till I'm gone.

My Lord your Servant you shan't stirr.

Lord Hardy. Nor you neither then. (*Strugling*.)

Campley. You will be Obey'd.

                              Exeunt. Lord Hardy *waits on him down.*

Trim. What's in this Song—Ha—don't my Eyes deceive me,— a 170
Bill of Three Hundred pounds—

  Mr. Cash,
  Pray Pay to Mr. William Trim, *or Bearer, the Summ of Three
  Hundred Pounds, and place it to the Accoumpt of,*

                                        SIR,   175
                              Your Humble Servant,
                              Thomas Campley.

(*Pulling off his Hat and Bowing*.) Your very Humble Servant Good
Mr. *Campley*, Ay, this is Poetry, this is a Song indeed? Faith I'll Set
it, and Sing it my self—Pray Pay to Mr. *William Trim*—so far in 180

recitativo—Three Hunddred (*Singing ridiculously*—) Hun— dred—
Hundred—Hundred thrice repeated, because 'tis Three Hundred
Pounds, I Love repetitions in Musick, when there's a good reason
for it, Po—unds after the *Italian* Manner—If they'd bring me such
185 Sensible words as these, I'd Out-strip all your Composers, for the
Musick Prize—This was honestly done of Mr. *Campley*—Tho' I
have carry'd Him many a Purse from my Master when He was
Ensign to Our Company in *Flanders*—

Enter Lord Hardy.

My Lord I am your Lordships Humble Servant.
190   *Lord Hardy.* Sir your Humble Servant. But pray my Good
Familiar Friend, How come You to be so very much my Humble
Servant all of a Sudden.

Trim. I beg pardon, Dear Sir, My Lord, I am not your Humble
Servant.
195   *Lord Hardy.* No.

Trim. Yes my Lord I am, but not as you mean—but I am—I am
My Lord—in short I'm overjoy'd.

Lord Hardy. Overjoy'd! Thou'rt Distracted—what Ails the
Fellow—Where's *Campley's* Song?
200   *Trim.* Oh! my Lord one would not think 'twas in him Mr.
Campley's really a very Great Poet—as for the Song, 'tis only as they
all end in Rhime—Ow—Woe—Isses—Kisses—Boy—Joy—But my
Lord The other in Long Heroick Blank Verse. (*Reading it with a
great Tone*—) *Pray Pay to Mr.* William Trim, *or Order, the Summ of*—
205 How sweetly it runs?—Pactolian Guineas Chink every Line—

Lord Hardy. How very handsomely this was done in *Campley*? I
wonder'd indeed he was so willing to shew his Verses—in how
careless a manner that Fellow does the Greatest Actions?—

Trim. My Lord, Pray my Lord, shan't I go Immediately to
210 *Cutpurse's.*

Lord Hardy. No Sirrah—now we've no occasion for it—

Trim. No my Lord, only to Stare at him full in the Face after I've
receiv'd this Money, not say a word, but keep my Hat on, and walk
out—Or perhaps not hear, If any I meet with speak to me—But
215 grow Stiff, Deaf, and Shortsighted to all my old Acquaintance, like

a Sudden Rich Man as I am—Or perhaps, My Lord, desire
Cutpurse's Clerk to let me leave Fifty Pounds at their House Payable
to Mr. *William Trim,* or Order—till I come that way—or a Month
or two hence, may have occasion for it—I don't know what Bills
may be drawn upon me—Then when the Clerk begins to Stare at   220
me, 'Till he puls the Great Goose-quill from behind His Ear—(*Pulls
a Handful of Farthings out*—) I fall a reckoning the Peices as I do
these Farthings.

    Lord Hardy. Well Sirrah, you may have your Humour, but besure
you take Fourscore pounds, and pay My Debts immediatly—if you   225
Meet any Officer you ever see Me in Company with, that looks
Grave at *Cutpurse's* house, tell him I'd speak with him—We must
help our Friends—But learn moderation, You Rogue, in your
Good-Fortune, Be at home all the Evening after, while I wait at
Tom's to meet *Campley* in order to see Lady *Sharlot*—   230
       My Good or Ill in her Alone is Found,
       And in that thought all other cares are Drown'd.
                                        Exeunt.

[Act II. Scene ii.]

    Enter Sable, *Lord* Brumpton, Trusty.

    Sable. Why my Lord, you can't in Conscience put me of so; I must
do according to my Orders, Cut you up, and Embalm you, except
you'll come down a little deeper than you Talk of, you don't consider the Charges I have been at already.

    Lord Brumpton. Charges? for what?   5

    Sable. First Twenty Guineas to my Lady's Woman for notice of
your Death (a Fee I've, before now, known the Widow her self go
halfs in but no matter for that)—in the next place Ten Pounds for
watching you all your Long fit of Sickness last Winter—

10   *Lord Brumpton.* Watching me? Why I had none but my own
Servants by Turns—

   Sable. I mean attending to give notice of your Death, I had all
your long fit of Sickness last Winter, at Half a Crown a day, a Fellow
waiting at your Gate, to bring me Intelligence, but you Unfortun-
15 ately recover'd and I Lost all my Obliging pains for your Service.

   Lord Brumpton. Ha! ha! ha! *Sable* Thou art a very Impudent
Fellow, Half a Crown a Day to attend my Decease, and dost thou
reckon it to Me—

   Sable. Look you Gentlemen, don't stand Staring at me—I have a
20 Book at home which I call my Dooms-day-Book, Where I have every
man of Quality's, Age and Distemper in Town, and know when you
should Drop—Nay my Lord if you had Reflected upon your
Mortality half so much as Poor I have for you, you would not desire
to return to Life Thus—in short I cannot keep this a Secret, under
25 the whole Money I am to have for Burying You.

   Lord Brumpton. *Trusty* if you think it safe in you to Obey my
Orders after the Deed *Puzzle* told his Clerk of, Pay it Him—

   Trusty. I should be glad to give it out of my own Pocket, rather
than be without the Satisfaction of seeing you Witness to it.

30   *Lord Brumpton.* I heartily Believe thee Dear *Trusty*—

   Sable. Then my Lord the Secret of your being Alive, is now safe
with me.

   Trusty. (*Aside.*) I'll Warrant I'll be reveng'd of this Unconscionable Dogg—[*To Lord* Brumpton.] My Lord you must to your
35 Closet—I fear some Bodies coming—

        Exit Sable *one way*, **Lord** Brumpton *and* Trusty *another*.

[Act II. Scene iii.]

Scene *Draws and Discovers Lady* Sharlot,
Reading at a Table—Lady Harriot *playing
at a Glass to and fro, and Veiwing her self.*

Lady Harriot. Nay, good Sage Sister, you may as well talk to
(*Looking at her self as she speaks.*) me, as sit Staring at a Book which I
know you can't attend—Good Dr. *Lucas* may have writ there what
he pleases, but there's no putting *Francis* Lord *Hardy*, now Earl of
Brumpton out of your Head, or making him absent from your Eyes, 5
do but look at me now, and Deny it if you can—

Lady Sharlot. You are the Maddest Girle—(*Smiling.*)

Lady Harriot. Look'e you, I knew you could not say it and forbear
Laughing—(*Looking over Lady* Sharlot.) Oh I see his Name as plain
as you do—F—r—a—n Fran—c—i—s, cis Francis 'Tis in Every line 10
of the Book.

Lady Sharlot. (*Rising.*) 'Tis in Vain I see to mind any thing in such
Impertinent Company—but Granting 'twere as you say, as to my
Lord *Hardy*—'Tis more excuseable to admire another than One's
self—   15

Lady Harriot. No I think not—Yes I Grant you than really to be
vain at One's person, But I don't admire my self—Pish! I don't
believe my Eyes have that Softness—(*Looking in the Glass.*) They
A'n't so peircing: No 'tis only a Stuff the Men will be talking—
Some People are such admirers of Teeth—Lord what signifies 20
Teeth? (*Showing her Teeth.*) A very Blackamore has as White Teeth
as I—No Sister, I Don't admire my self, but I've a Spirit of Contradiction in me: I don't know I'm in Love with my self, only to Rival
the Men—

Lady Sharlot. Ay, but Mr. *Campley* will gain Ground ev'n of that 25
Rival of his, your Dear self—

25–6 *Campley* will gain Ground ev'n of that Rival of his] ed.; *Campley*, will you
gain Ground ev'n of that his Rival The precise wording Steele intended for this

Lady Harriot. Oh! what have I done to you, that you should name that Insolent intruder—A Confident Opinionative Fop—No indeed If I am as a Poetical Lover of mine Sigh'd and Sung, of both Sexes;

30   *The Publick Envy, and the Publick Care.*

I shan't be so easily Catch'd—I thank him—I want but to be sure, I shou'd Heartily Torment Him, by Banishing him, and then consider whether he should Depart this Life, or not.

Lady Sharlot. Indeed Sister to be Serious with you, this Vanity in 35 your Humour does not at all become you!

Lady Harriot. Vanity! all the Matter is we Gay People are more Sincere than you wise Folks: All your Life's an Art—Speak your Soul—Look you there—(*Halling her to the Glass.*) Are you not Struck with a Secret Pleasure, when you view that Bloom in your Looks, 40 that Hormony in your Shape, that Promptitude of your Mein!

Lady Sharlot. Well Simpleton, if I am, at First so Silly, as to be a little taken with my self, I know it a Fault, and take Pains to Correct it.

Lady Harriot. Psaw! Psaw! talk this Musty Tale to Old Mrs. 45 *Fardingale,* 'tis too soon for me to think at that Rate—

Lady Sharlot. They that think it too soon to Understand themselves, will very soon find it too Late—But tell me honestly don't you like *Campley*?

Lady Harriot. The Fellow is not to be Abhorr'd, if the Forward 50 thing did not think of Getting me so easily—Oh—I hate a Heart I can't break when I please—What makes the Value of Dear China, but that 'tis so Brittle—were it not for that, you might as well have Stone-Muggs in your Closet—

Lady Sharlot. Hist, Hist, Here's *Fardingale*—

Enter Fardingale.

55 *Fardingale.* Lady *Harriot,* Lady *Sharlot*—I'll entertain you now, I've a new Song Just come Hot out of the Poet's Brain: Lady *Sharlot,* My Cousin *Campley* writ it, and 'tis Set to a pretty Air I warrant you.

passage, jumbled by the compositor, remains unclear. None of the early editions contain convincing emendations. The emendation printed here follows as closely as possible the wording in Q.
29 am] D1; [om.]

Lady Harriot. 'Tis like to be Pretty indeed of his writing. (*Flings away.*)

Fardingale. Come, Come—This is not one of your Tringham 60 Trangham Witty things, that your Poor Poets write, no 'tis well known my Cousin *Campley* has Two Thousand pounds a Year—But this is all Dissimulation in you.

Lady Sharlot. 'Tis so indeed, for your Cousins Song's very pretty Mrs *Fardingale*: (*Reads.*) 65

> Let not Love on me bestow
> Soft Distress, and tender Woe;
> I know none but substantial Blisses,
> Eager Glances, solid Kisses;
> I know not what the Lovers feign, 70
> Of finer Pleasure mix'd with Pain,
> Then prethee give me gentle Boy,
> None of thy Grief but all thy Joy.

But *Harriot* thinks that a little unreasonable, to expect one without enduring t'other. 75

Enter Servant.

Servant. There's your Cousin *Campley* to wait on you without—
Fardingale. Let him come in—We shall have the Song now—

[*Exit* Servant.]

Enter Campley.

Campley. Ladies your most Obedient Servant—Your Servant Lady *Sharlot*—Servant Lady *Harriot*—(*Lady* Harriot *looks Grave upon him*—) what's the Matter Dear Lady *Harriot*—Not well? I protest to you, 80 I'm mightily concern'd—(*Pulls out a Bottle.*) This is a most Excellent Spirit—Snuff it up Madam—

Lady Harriot. [*Aside.*] Pish—The Familiar Coxcomb Frets me Heartily—

Campley. 'Twill over I hope immediately. 85

Lady Sharlot. Your Cousin *Fardingale* has shown us some of your Poetry, there's the Spinet Mr. *Campley*, I know you're Musical.

Campley. She should not have call'd it my Poetry.

Fardingale. No: Who waits there—Pray bring my Lute out of the next Room— 90

Enter Servant *with a Lute.*

You must know, I con'd this Song before I came in, and find 'twill go to an excellent Air of Old Mr. *Laws's*, who was my Mother's intimate Acquaintance; my Mother's, what do I talk of? I mean my Grand-Mother's—Oh here's the Lute—(*Aside to him.*) Cousin
95 *Campley,* hold the Song upon your Hat. 'Tis a pretty Gallantry to a Relation. (*Sings and Squales.*) *Let not Love,* &c. Oh! I have left of these things many a day.

Campley. No; I profess Madam you do it Admirably—But are not assur'd enough—Take it higher Thus (*In her own Squale.*)—I know
100 your Voice will bear it.

Lady Harriot. [*Aside.*] Oh hideous! Oh the gross Flatterer—I shall burst——[*To* Fardingale.] Mrs. *Fardingale* pray go on, the Musick Fits the words most aptly—Take it higher as your Cousin advises—

105 *Fardingale.* Oh dear Madam, do you really like it—I do it purely to please you—for I can't Sing alas!

Lady Sharlot. We know it good Madam, we know it—But pray—

Fardingale. Let not Love, and substantial Blisses, is Lively enough, and ran accordingly in the Tune (*Curtsies to the Company.*) Now I took
110 it higher—

Lady Harriot. Incomparably done! Nothing can equal it, except your Cousin Sang his own Poetry—

Campley. (*Delivers a Letter to Lady* Sharlot.) [*Aside to Lady* Sharlot.] Madam from my Lord *Hardy*—[*To Lady* Harriot.] How do you say
115 my Lady *Harriot,* except I Sing it my self; then I assure you I will—

Lady Sharlot. [*Aside.*] I han't patience, I must go Read my Letter.

Exit.

Campley. (*Sings.*) *Let not Love,* &c.

Fardingale. Bless me, what's become of Lady *Sharlot.*

Exit.

Lady Harriot. Mrs. *Fardingale,* Mrs. *Fardingale,* what must we
120 lose you—(*Going after her.*)

Campley *runs to the Door, takes the Key out, and locks her in.*

118.1 *Exit.*] D1; [om.]

What means this Insolence, a Plot upon me—Do you know who I am—

Campley. Yes Madam, you're my Lady _Harriot Lovely_, with Ten Thousand Pounds in your Pocket: and I am Mr. _Campley_, with Two Thousand a Year—Of Quality enough to pretend to you—And I 125 do design before I leave this Room, to hear you talk like a reasonable Woman, as Nature has made you—Nay 'tis in vain to Flounce —and Discompose your self and your Dress—

Lady Harriot. If there are Swords, if there are men of Honour, and not all Dastards, Cowards that pretend to this Injur'd Person— 130 (_Running round the room._)

Campley. Ay Ay, Madam, let 'em come—That's putting me in my way, Fighting's my Trade—But you've us'd all mankind too ill to expect so much service—In short Madam, were you a Fool I should not desire to expostulate with You—(_Seizing her hand._) But— 135

Lady Harriot. Unhand me Ravisher—(_Pulls her hand from him, Chafes round the Room_, Campley _after her_—)

Campley. But Madam, Madam, Madam, why Madam! (_Sings._)

> _Prethee_ Cynthia _look behind you,_
> _Age and Wrinkles will o'retake You._ 140

Lady Harriot. Age, Wrinkles, Small-Pox, nay, any thing that's most Abhorrent to Youth and Bloom, were welcome in the place of so detested a Creature!

Campley. No such matter Lady _Harriot_; I would not be a Vain Coxcomb, but I know I am not detestable, nay know where you've 145 said as much, before you Understood me for your Servant. Was I immediately transform'd because I became Your Lover?

Lady Harriot. My Lover, Sir, Did I ever give you reason to think I admitted you as such?

Campley. Yes you did in your using me ill—for if you did not 150 assume upon the Score of my pretending to you; How do you

123 _Harriot_] ed.; _Sharlot_ By some curious slip the first edition contained the name '_Sharlot_' rather than '_Harriot_', and every subsequent edition repeated the error. Possibly the mistake originated in the manuscript, or, equally likely, a printer may have carelessly glanced at the abbreviation '_Har._' and mistaken it for '_Shar._' The present edition is the first to carry the correct name for the lady being wooed in this scene, although the error certainly never once occurred on stage.

137 _Chafes_] All eight early editions contain 'Chafes'. Steele probably intended the rather unusual metaphorical use of the verb; the dialectical 'Chases' is of course a likely emendation.

answer to your self some parts of your behaviour to me as a Gentleman—'Tis trivial all this in you, and derogates from the Good
Sense I know you Mistress of; Do but consider, Madam; I have long
155 Lov'd you—Bore with your Phantastick humour through all its
Mazes—Nay do not Frown—for 'tis no better—I say I have bore
with this Humour, but would you have me with an Unmanly Servi-
tude Feed it—No I Love You with too sincere, too honest a
Devotion—and would have your Mind as faultless as your Person,
160 which 'twould be, if you'd lay aside this Vanity of being pursued
with Sighs, with Flatteries, with Nonsense—(*She walks about less
violently but more confus'd.*) (*Aside.*) Oh my Heart akes at the disturbance which I give her but she must not see it—[*To Lady* Harriot.]
Had I not better tell you of it Now, then when you're in my Power,
165 I should be then too Generous to thwart your Inclination.

 Lady Harriot. (*Aside.*) That is indeed very handsomely said. Why
should I not obey Reason as soon as I see it? [*To* Campley.] Since so,
Mr. *Campley*, I can as ingenuously as I should then acknowledge
that I have been in an errour. (*Looking down on her Fan.*)
170 *Campley.* Nay that's too Great a Condescension: Oh! Excellence!
I repent! I see 'twas but Justice in you to demand my Knees,
(*Kneeling.*) my Sighs, my constant Tenderest regard, and Service—
And you shall have 'em, since you are Above 'em—

 Lady Harriot. Nay Mr. *Campley*, you won't recall me to a Fault you
175 have so lately shown me—I will not suffer this—No more Extasies!
But pray, Sir, what was't you did to get my Sister out of the room?

 Campley. You may know it, and I must desire you to assist my
Lord *Hardy* there, who Writ to her by me—For he is no Ravisher,
as you call'd me just now—He is now in the House—And would
180 fain gain an Interview—

 Lady Harriot. That they may have—but they'le make little use
of it; for the Tongue is the Instrument of Speech to us of a lower
Form; They are of that high Order of Lovers, who know none but
Eloquent Silence, and can utter themselves only by a Gesture that
185 speaks their Passion Inexpressible—and what not Fine things?

 Campley. But pray let's go into your Sister's Closet, while they
are together.

179 And] ed.; And I

Lady Harriot. I swear I don't know how to see my Sister—she'll
Laugh me to Death to see me out of my Pantofles, and you and I
thus Familiar—However, I know she'll approve it—   190

Campley. You may boast your self an Heroine to her, and the first
Woman that was ever Vanquish'd by hearing Truth, and had
sincerity enough to receive so rough an Obligation, as being made
acquainted with her Faults—Come Madam, stand your Ground
bravely, we'll March in to her thus. (*She leaning on* Campley.)   195

Lady Harriot. Who'll believe a Woman's Anger more, I've betray'd the whole Sex to you Mr. *Campley.*

Exeunt.

Re-enter Lord Hardy, Campley.

Campley. My Lord, her Sister who now is mine, will immediately
send her hither—But be your self—Charge her Bravely—I wish she
were a Cannon—an Eighteen Pounder for your sake—Then I know   200
were there occasion, you'd be in the mouth of Her—

Lord Hardy. I long yet fear to see her—I know I am unable to
utter my self—

Campley. Come retire here till she appears. (*Go back to the door.*)

Enter Lady Sharlot.

Lady Sharlot. (*Aside.*) Now is the tender Moment now approach-   205
ing. There he is. (*They approach and salute each other Trembling.*) Your
Lordship will please to sit; (*After a very long pause, stoln Glances, and
irresolute Gesture.*) Your Lordship I think has travell'd those parts of
Italy where the Armies Are—

Lord Hardy. Yes Madam—   210

Lady Sharlot. I think I have Letters from You Dated *Mantua.*

Lord Hardy. I hope you have, Madam, and that their purpose—

Lady Sharlot. My Lord?—(*Looking serious and confus'd.*)

Lord Hardy. Was not your Ladiship going to say something?

Lady Sharlot. I only attended to what your Lordship was going to   215
say—that is my Lord—But you were I believe going to say something of that Garden of the World *Italy*—I am very sorry your
Misfortunes in *England* are such as may make you Justly regret your
leaving that place.

220 *Lord Hardy.* There is a Person in *England* may make those losses insensible to me—

Lady Sharlot. Indeed my Lord there have so very few of Quality attended his Majesty in the War, that your Birth and Merit may well hope for his favour.

225 *Lord Hardy.* I have, indeed, all the Zeal in the World for His Majesties Service and most Grateful affection for His Person, but Did not then mean Him—

Lady Sharlot. But can you indeed impartially say that our Island is really preferable to the rest of the World, or is it an Arrogance 230 only in us to think so?

Lord Hardy. I profess Madam, that little I have seen has but more endear'd *England* to me; for that Medley of Humours which perhaps distracts our Publick Affairs, does, methinks, improve our Private Lives, and makes Conversation more Various, and consequently 235 more pleasing—Every where else both Men and Things have the same Countenance—in *France* you meet much Civility and little Friendship, in *Holland* deep Attention, but little Reflexion, in *Italy* all Pleasure but no Mirth—but here with us, where you have every where Pretenders, or Masters in every Thing, you can't fall into 240 Company wherein you shall not be Instructed or Diverted.

Lady Sharlot. I never had an Account of any thing from you my Lord, but I mourn'd the loss of my Brother, you would have been so happy a Companion for Him—with that right Sense of yours—My Lord you need not bow so Obsequiously, for I do you but Justice— 245 But you sent me Word of your seeing a Lady in *Italy* very Like me —Did you Visit her often?

Lord Hardy. Once or twice but I observ'd her so loose a Creature that I could have Kill'd her for having your Person—

Lady Sharlot. I thank You Sir, But Heav'n that preserves me 250 Unlike her, will I hope make her more like me—But your Fellow-Traveller—His Relations Themselves know not a Just account of Him—

Lord Hardy. The Original cause of his Feavour was a Violent Passion for a fine Young Woman, he had not power to speak to— 255 but I told her his regard for her, as passionately as possible—

242 would have] D1; would [followed by catchword 'have']

Lady Sharlot. You were to him, what Mr. _Campley_ has been to You
—Whither am I running?—Poor your Friend—Poor Gentleman—
Lord Hardy. I hope then as _Campley's_ Eloquence is greater, so has
been his Success—
Lady Sharlot. My Lord?   260
Lord Hardy. Your Ladyship's.

Enter Lady Harriot.

Lady Harriot. Undone! Undone! _Tattleaid_ has found by some
means or other, that _Campley_ brought my Lord _Hardy_ hither, we are
Utterly ruin'd, my Ladies coming—
Lord Hardy. I'll stay and confront her—   265
Lady Sharlot. It must not be—we are too much in her Power.

Enter Campley.

Campley. Come, Come my Lord, we're routed Horse and Foot—
down the Back-stairs, and so out.
Ladies. Ay, Ay—
                              Exeunt [Campley _and Lord_ Hardy].
Lady Harriot. I Tremble every Joint of me—   270
Lady Sharlot. I'm at a stand a little, but rage will Recover me
she's coming in—

Enter Widow.

Widow. Ladies your Servant—I fear I Interrupt you, have you
Company? Lady _Harriot_ your Servant, Lady _Sharlot_ your Servant,
What not a word—Oh I beg your Ladyship's Pardon—Lady _Sharlot_ 275
did I say? My young Lady _Brumpton_, I wish you Joy.
Lady Sharlot. Oh your Servant Lady Dowager _Brumpton_—That's
an Appellation of much more Joy to you—
Widow. So smart Madam! But you should methinks have made
one acquainted—Yet Madam your Conduct is seen Through—   280
Lady Sharlot. My Conduct Lady _Brumpton_!
Widow. Your Conduct Lady _Sharlot_! (_Coming up to each other._)
Lady Sharlot. Madam, 'Tis you are seen through all your Thin
Disguises—

285 *Widow.* I seen? by Whom?

Lady Sharlot. By an all peircing Eye, nay by what you much more fear, The Eye of the World—The World sees you, or shall see you; It shall know your Secret Intemperance, your Publick Fasting— Loose Poems in your Closet, an Homily on your Toilet—Your Easy
290 skilfull practis'd Hypocrisy, by which you wrought upon your Husband, basely to Transfer the Trust, and Ward of Us two helpless Virgins into the hands, and Care of—I cannot name it—you'r a Wicked Woman—

Lady Harriot. (*Aside.*) Oh Rare Sister! 'tis a fine thing to keep
295 ones Anger in stock by one, we that are Angry and Pleas'd every half hour, have nothing at all, of all this High-Flown-Fury! Why she Rages like a Princess in a Tragedy! Blessings on her Tongue—

Widow. Is this the effect of your Morning Lectures, your self-
300 examination all this Fury?

Lady Sharlot. Yes it is Madam, if I take Pains to Govern my Passions, it shall not give License to others to Govern 'em for me—

Widow. Well Lady *Sharlot* however you ill deserve it of me, I shall
305 take care while there are Locks and Bars to keep you from Lord *Hardy*—From being a Leiger Lady, From carrying a Knapsack.

Lady Sharlot. Knapsack! Do you upbraid the Poverty your own Wicked Arts have brought him to—Knapsack! Oh grant me Patience, can I hear this of the Man I Love? Knapsack! I have not
310 words—(*Stamps about the Room.*)

Widow. I leave you to Cool upon it, Love and Anger are very warm Passions—

Exit.

Lady Harriot. She has Lock'd us in—

Lady Sharlot. Knapsack? Well I will break Walls to go to Him—I
315 could sit down and Cry my Eyes out! Dear Sister what a Rage have I been in? Knapsack! I'll give vent to my Just resentment—Oh how shall I avoid this Base Woman, how meet that Excellent Man!— What an helpless Condition are you and I in now? If We run into the World, that youth and Innocence which should demand assist-

319 and Innocence] D1; Innocence and

ance, does but attract Invaders: Will Providence Guard us: How do 320
I see that our Sex is Naturally Indigent of Protection?—I hope 'tis
in Fate to Crown our Loves; For 'tis only in the Protection of Men
of Honour, that we are, Naturally, Truly safe;

> *And Woman's happiness, for all her Scorn,*
> *Is only by that Side whence she was Born.*   325

[*The End of the Second Act.*]

Act III. [Scene i.]

Enter Lord Hardy, Campley, Trim.

Lord Hardy. That Jade *Tattleaid* saw me upon the Stairs, for I had
not Patience to keep my Concealment, but must Peep out to see
what was become of you.

Campley. But we have advice however it seems from the Garrison
already—this Mistress of *Trim's* is a mighty Lucky Accident—   5

Trim. Ay Gentlemen, she has free Egress, and Regress, and you
know the French are the best Bred People in the World—She'll be
Assistant—But Faith I have one Scruple that hangs about me—
and that is—Look you my Lord, we Servants have no Masters in
their Absence—In a word when I am with Mademoiselle, a talk of 10
your Lordship as only a Particular Acquaintance, that I do Business

320–1 How . . . Protection?] TJ1 emends convincingly to 'Now do I see that our
sex is naturally indigent of protection.' However, the reading of Q is satisfactory
when the question mark is recognized as a mild exclamation point.

1–3 That . . . you.] The opening line of Act III is not a satisfactory explanation of
the Widow's unexpected arrival, which interrupts the love scene in Act II. If Lord
Hardy has indeed been spotted by Tattleaid, surely he would mention the fact when
he goes with Campley to find Sharlot, but his fears are confined to his inability to
converse with her. In his meeting with her, he gives no indication of the danger of
detection. Since the line is not at all necessary to begin Act III, it seems likely that
it is a vestige of an earlier form of the play. Possibly the shy lovers' meeting was not
included or had a different form which gave credence to this line. It is also possible,
of course, that Steele merely neglected to unify the details of his plot. The line is
printed in the present edition since Steele never deleted it.

indeed for you sometimes—I must needs say, Crys I, that indeed
my Lord *Hardy* is really a Person I have a great Honour for—

Lord Hardy. Pish! is that all? I understand you—your Mistress
15 does not know that you do me the Honour to Clean my Shooes or
so upon occasion—Prethee *Will* make your self as considerable as
you please.

Trim. Well then, your Lesson is this—She out of her Respect to
me, and understanding Mr. *Campley* was an Intimate, of my
20 Friend my Lord *Hardy*, and condescending (tho she is of a Great
House in *France*) to make Manto'es for the Improvement of the
English—which gives her Easy admittance—she I say mov'd by
these Promises has vouchsaf'd to bring a Letter from Lady *Harriot*
to Mr. *Campley*, and came to me to bring her to him. You are to
25 understand also that she is Dress'd in the latest French Cut; Her
Dress is the Model of their Habit, and her self of their Manners—for
she is—But you shall see Her—

Exit.

Lord Hardy. This gives me some life—Chear up *Tom*—but behold
the Solemnity—Do you see *Trim's* Gallentry? I shall Laugh out.

Enter Trim *Leading in Mademoiselle*
D'Epingle.

30   *Trim.* My Dear Lord *Hardy* this is Mademoiselle *D'Epingle*, whose
name you've often heard me Sigh—(*Lord* Hardy *salutes her.*) Mr.
Campley—Mademoiselle *D'Epingle*—(Campley *salutes her.*)

Mademoiselle D'Epingle. Votre Servante Gentlemen, Votre
Servante—

35   *Campley.* I protest to you, I never saw any thing so Becoming as
your Dress—shall I beg the Favour you'd condescend to let Mr.
Trim lead you once round the Room, that I may admire the Elegance
of your Habit—(Trim *leads her round.*—)

Lord Hardy. [*Aside to* Campley.] How could you ask such a thing?
40   *Campley.* [*Aside to Lord* Hardy.] Pshaw my Lord, you are a Bashful
English Fellow—You see she is not surpriz'd at it, but thinks me
Gallant in desiring it—[*To Mademoiselle* D'Epingle.] Oh! Madam!

---

23 Promises] *A Comparison between the Two Stages* suggested the emendation
'Premises'.   31 heard] D1; hear   40 you] D1; your

your Air—! The Negligence, the Disengagement of your Manner!
Oh how Delicate is your Noble Nation—I Swear there's none but
the Clumsy Dutch and English would oppose such Polite Con- 45
querors—When shall you see an English Woman so Dress'd?

Mademoiselle D'Epingle. De Englise! Poor Barbarians, poor Savages,
Dey Know no more of De Dress, but to Cover Dere Nakedness
(*Glides along the Roome.*) Dey be cloded, but no Dress'd—But
Monsieur *Terim* which Monsieur *Campley*?   50

Trim. That's Honest *Tom Campley*.

Campley. At your Service Mademoiselle—

Mademoiselle D'Epingle. (*Pulling out the Letter, and Recollecting as
loath to deliver it—*) I fear I incur de Censure, but Mr. *Terim*, being
your Intimate Friend, and I designing to Honour Him, in De way 55
of an Husband—So—So—how I do run away in Discourse—I never
make promise to Mr. *Terim* before, and now to do it par accident—

Campley. Dear *Will Trim* is extreamly obliging in having prevail'd
upon you, to do a thing, that the Severity of your Virtue, and the
Greatness of your Quality (tho' a Stranger in the Country, you now 60
honour by your Dwelling in it) would not let you, otherwise,
condescend to—

Mademoiselle D'Epingle. Oh Monsieur, Oh Monsieur! You speak
my very Toughts—Oh! I don't know how! Pardon me to give a
Billet—it so look—Oh Fie! I can no stay (*Drops it.*) after it—(*Runs* 65
affectedly to the other end of the Room. Then quite out. Re-enters.) I begg
ten tousand pardons for go away so mal-propos—(*Curtsies as going.*)

Lord Hardy. Your Servant Good Madam—Mr. *Trim* you know
you Command here—pray if Madam *D'Epingle* will Honour our
Cottage with longer stay, wait on her in, and Entertain Her—Pray 70
Sir, be Free—

Trim. My Lord you know your Power over me I'm all Complaisance—(*Leads her out.*)

Campley. Now to my Dear Epistle—

SIR,   75
*There is One thing which you were too Generous to touch upon in our
last Conversation—We have reason to fear the Widow's practices in*

relation to our Fortunes, if you are not too quick for her—I ask Lady
Sharlot *whether this is not her Sense to Lord* Hardy—*She says*
80 *nothing, but lets me Write on—These People always have, and will*
have admittance every where, therefore we may hear from you.

I am,

SIR,

Your most Obedient Servant,

85   Harriot Lovely.

My Obedient Servant! thy Obedience shall ever be as voluntary as
now—Ten Thousand, Thousand Kisses on Thee—Thou Dear
Paper—Look you my Lord—what a pretty hand it is?
   Lord Hardy. Why *Tom,* thou dost not give me leave to see it—
90 you Snatch it to your Mouth so—you'll stifle the Poor Lady—
   Campley. Look you my Lord, all along the Lines here went the
Pen. And through the White-Intervals her Snowy Fingers. Do you
see this is her Name—
   Lord Hardy. Nay there's Lady *Sharlots* Name too in the mid'st of
95 the Letter—Why you'll not be so unconscionable—you're so
gready, you'll give me one Kiss sure—
   Campley. Well you shall, but you're so Eager—Don't Bite me—for
you shan't have it in your Own hands—there, there, there—Let
go my hand—
100   *Lord Hardy.* What an Exquisite pleasure there is in this Foolery—
But what shall we do?
   Campley. I have a Thought, Prethee my Lord call *Trim.*
   Lord Hardy. Ha *Trim*—
   Campley. Hold Mr. *Trim*—You forget his Mistress is there.
105 *Lord Hardy.* Gra'mercy—Dear *Will Trim,* step in hither.
   Campley. Ay that's something—

Enter Trim.

Trim have Not I seen a Young Woman sometimes carry Madam
D'Epingles Trinkets for her coming from my Lady *Brumpton's*—
   Trim. Yes, you might have seen such a one, she waits for her now—

---

92 the White-Intervals] ed.; them~ The compositorial error in Q, 'them' for
'the', was retained in all later editions. There can be no doubt, however, about
Steele's intentions.

Campley. Do you think you could not prevail for me to be dress'd 110
in that Wenches Cloaths, and attend your Mistress in her stead
thither? They'll not Dream we should so soon attempt again—

Trim. Yes I'll Engage it—

Campley. Then we'll trust the rest to our good Genius I'll about
it instantly—*Harriot Lovely*—   115

Exit kissing the Letter.

[Act III. Scene ii.]

Enter Widow, Tattleaid.

Widow. This was well done of you; be sure you take care of their
Young Ladyships; You shall I promise you have a Snip in the Sale
of 'em.

Tattleaid. I thank your Good Ladyship.

Widow. Is that the Porter's Paper of How Dee's?   5

Tattleaid. Yes Madam he just sent it up—His General Answer is,
that your're as well as can be expected in your condition, but that
you see no Body—

Widow. That's right—(*Reading names.*) Lady *Riggle*, Lady *Formal*
—oh that *Riggle*, a pert Ogler—an indiscreet silly thing, who is 10
really Known by no man, yet for her carriage Justly thought
common to all, and as *Formal* has only the appearance of Virtue so
she has only the appearance of Vice—what chance, I wonder, put
these contradictions to each other into the same Coach, as you say
they call'd—Mrs. *Francis*, and Mrs. *Winifred Glebe*—who are they? 15

Tattleaid. They are the Country Great Fortunes, have been out
of Town this whole Year; they are those whom your Ladyship said
upon being very well born, took upon 'em to be very ill bred—

Widow. Did I say so? really I think 'twas apt enough now I
remember 'em; Lady *Wrinkle* oh that Smugg old Woman, there's 20
no enduring her affectation of Youth, but I plague her; I always ask

whether her Daughter in *Wiltshire*, has a Grandchild yet or not—
Lady *Worthy*—(*Aside.*) I can't bear her Company she has so much
of that Virtue in her heart, which I have in my mouth only. [*To*
25 Tattleaid.] Mrs. *After-Day*—Oh that's she that was the Great
Beauty—the mighty Toast about Town, that's Just come out of
the Small-Pox, she's horridly pitted they say; I long to see her and
plague her with my Condolance—'Tis a pure ill-natur'd satisfaction
to see one that was a Beauty unfortunately move with the same
30 languor, and softness of behaviour, that once was Charming in
her—To see, I say, her Mortify that us'd to Kill—ha ha ha! The
rest are a Catalogue of mere Names, or Titles they were Born
to, an insipid croud of the neither Good, nor Bad—But you are
sure these other Ladies suspect not in the least that I Know of their
35 Coming—

Tattleaid. No, Dear Madam, they are to ask for me—

Widow. I hear a Coach—

Exit Tattleaid.

I've now an Exquisite pleasure in the Thought of surpassing my
Lady *Sly*, who pretends to have Outgriev'd the whole Town for her
40 Husband—They are certainly coming—Oh no! here let me—Thus
let me sit and Think—(*Widow on her Couch while she is raving as to her
self*, Tattleaid *softly brings in the Ladies.*) wretched disconsolate as I
am! oh wellcome—wellcome, dear killing Anguish—oh that I could
lie down, and die in my present heaviness—But what—how? Nay
45 my Dear Dear Lord—Why do you look so Pale so Gastly at me,
Wottoo, Wottoo Fright thy own Trembling shivering Wife—

Tattleaid. Nay good Madam be Comforted.

Widow. Thou shalt not have me—(*Pushes* Tattleaid.)

Tattleaid. Nay, Good Madam, 'Tis I, 'Tis I your Ladiships own
50 Woman—'Tis I, Madam, that Dress you, and talk to You, and tell
you all that's done in the House every day 'tis I—

Widow. Is it then possible? is it then possible that I am left—
speak to me not—hold me not—I'll Break the Listning Walls with
my Complaints. (*Looks surpriz'd at seeing Company, then severely at*
55 Tattleaid.) Ah! *Tattleaid*—

First Lady. Nay, Madam, be not Angry at her we would come in
in spite of her—We are your Friends, and are as concern'd as you—

Widow. Ah! Madam, Madam, Madam, Madam I am an undone
Woman—oh me! Alas! Alas! Oh! Oh! (*All join in her Notes.*) I swoon,
I expire. (*Faints.*)   60

Second Lady. Pray Mrs. *Tattleaid* Bring something that is Cordial
to her.

Exit Tattleaid.

Third Lady. Indeed, Madam, you should have Patience, his Lordship was Old. To Die is but going before in a Journey we must all
take.   65

Enter Tattleaid *loaded with Bottles.* Third Lady
takes a Bottle from her and Drinks.

Fourth Lady. Lord! How my Lady *Fleer* Drinks; I've heard indeed
but never could believe it of her. (*Drinks also.*)

First Lady. But Madam, Don't you hear what the Town says of
the Jilt *Flirt* the men lik'd so much in the *Park*—Harkee (*Whispers
by interruptions.*)—was seen with Him in an Hackney-Coach—and 70
Silk-Stockins—Key-hole—his Wigg—on the Chair—

Second Lady. Impudent *Flirt* to be found out!

Third Lady. But I speak it only to you—

Fourth Lady. Nor I but to one more—(*Whispers next Woman.*)

Fifth Lady. I can't believe it, Nay I always thought it Madam— 75
(*Whispers the Widow.*)

Widow. Sure 'tis impossible! The Demure Prim thing—sure all
the World's Hypocrisy—Well I thank my Stars whatsoever sufferings I have, I've none in Reputation. I wonder at the Men, I could
never think her handsome. She has really a good Shape and Com- 80
plexion, but no Mein. And no Woman has the use of her Beauty
without Mein. Her Charms are Dumb they want utterance. But
whither does distraction lead me to talk of Charms?

First Lady. Charms? a Chit's, a Girl's Charms—Come let us
Widows be true to our selves, keep our Countenances, and our 85
Characters, and a Fig for the Maids, I mean for the Unmarried.

Second Lady. Ay since they will set up for our Knowledge, why
should not we for their Ignorance?

Third Lady. But Madam o' *Sunday* Morning at Church I curtsied
to You; and look'd at a Greate Fusse in a Glaring light Dress next 90

Pew. That strong Masculine thing is a Knight's Wife, pretends to all the Tenderness in the World! and would Fain put the Unweildy upon us for the Soft the Languid! She has of a sudden left her Dayry, and sets up for a fine Town Lady, calls her Maid *Sisly* her Woman,

95 speaks to her by her Sirname Mrs. *Cherryfist*, and her great Foot-Boy of Nineteen big enough for a Trooper, is strip'd into a Lace-Coat, now Mr. Page forsooth.

Fourth Lady. Oh! I have seen her—Well I heartily Pity some People for their Wealth, they might have been unknown else!

100 You'd Die, Madam to see her and her Equipage—I thought the honest Fat Tits, her Horses were asham'd of their Finery; they Drag'd on, as if they were still at the Plough, and a great Bashful-look'd Booby behind, grasp'd the Coach as if he held one.

Fifth Lady. Alas some People think there's nothing but being Fine

105 to be Gentile but the high Prance of the Horses, and the Brisk Insolence of the Servants in an Equipage of Quality, are Inimitable, but to our own Beasts and Servants.

First Lady. Now you talk of Equipage, I Envy this Lady, the Beauty she'll appear in, in a Mourning Coach, 'twill so become her

110 Complexion; I confess I my self mourn'd Two Years for no other reason. Take up that Hood there, oh! that Fair Face with a Vail. (*They take up her hoods.*)

Widow. Fie Fie Ladies—But I've been told indeed Black does become—

115 *Second Lady.* Well I'll take the Liberty to speak it, There's young *Nutbrain* has long had (I'll be Sworn) a Passion for this Lady; But I'll tell you one thing I fear she'll dislike, that is, he's younger than she is.

Third Lady. No that's no exception: But I'll tell you one, He's

120 younger than his Brother.

Widow. Ladies, talk not of such Affairs: Who cou'd Love such an unhappy relict as I am? But Dear Madam, what Grounds have you for that Idle story?

Fourth Lady. Why he toasts you and trembles when you're spoke

125 of, it must be a Match.

Widow. Nay, Nay; you rally, you rally: But I Know you mean it Kindly.

First Lady. I swear we do.

Tattleaid *whispers the* Widow

Widow. But I must beseech You Ladies, since you have been so compassionate, as to visit, and accompany my sorrow, to give me the 130 only comfort I can now Know, to see my Friends Chearful, and to honour an Entertainment *Tattleaid* has prepar'd within for You: If I can find strength enough, I'll attend you: But I wish you'd excuse me, for I've no relish of Food or Joy, but will try to get a Bit down in my own Chamber. 135

All. No no, you must go with us.

First Lady. There's no pleasure without You.

Widow. But, Madam, I must beg of your Ladiship not to be so importune to my fresh Calamity, as to mention *Nutbrain* any more: I'm sure there's nothing in it; In Love with me quoth a'. (*Is* 140 *help'd of*.)

Exeunt.

[Act III. Scene iii.]

Enter Mademoiselle D'Epingle, *and* Campley
in Woman's Cloaths carrying her things.

Mademoiselle D'Epingle. I ver'y glad us be in de Ladies Antichamber; I was sham'd of you. You you such an impudent look: Besides me wonder you were not seiz'd by the Constable, when you push'd de man into de Kennell.

Campley. Why, should I have let him Kiss'd me? 5

Mademoiselle D'Epingle. No: But if you 'had hit him wit Fan, and say why sure sawcy-box, it been enough; beside what you hitted de Gentleman for offer Kisse me.

Campley. I beg pardon, I did not know you were pleas'd with it.

Mademoiselle D'Epingle. Please no, but me rader be Kisse, den you, 10 Mr. *Terim*'s Freind, be found out. Could not you say when he Kisse me, sure sawcy-box dat's meat for your Master. Besides you take such strides when you Walk—Walk—oh Fie; dese littill pette Tiny bits a Woman steps. (*Shewing her step*.)

15 *Campley.* But Preethee *Madamoiselle* why have you lost your English Tongue all of a sudden; methought when the Fellow call'd us French Whores, as we came along, and said we came to Starve their own People, Ye gave him pretty plain English; he was a Dog, a Rascall, you'd send him to the Stocks—

20 *Mademoiselle D'Epingle.* Ha! ha! ha! I was in a Passion and betray'd my self, but you're my Lover's Friend, and a man of Honour, therefore know you'll do nothing to injure us: Why, Mr. *Campley,* you must know I can speak as good English as you, but I don't for fear of Losing my Customers; The English will never give a Price
25 for any thing they Understand. Nay I've known some of your Fools pretend to buy with good breeding, and give any rate rather than not be thought to have French enough to know what they were doing; strange and farfetch'd things they only like: Don't you see how they swallow Gallons of the Juice of Tea; while their own
30 Dock-leaves are trod under Foot. But Mum. My Lady *Harriot.*

Enter Lady Harriot.

Madam, vostre Servante servante—
    Lady Harriot. Well *Madamoiselle,* did you Deliver my Letter?
    Mademoiselle D'Epingle. Oui—
    Lady Harriot. Well and How—is that it in your Hand?
35 *Mademoiselle D'Epingle.* Oui—
    Lady Harriot. Well then, why don't you give it me?
    Mademoiselle D'Epingle. Oh Fie! Lady, dat be so right Englise, de Englise mind only de Words of de Lovers, but de Words of de Lovers are often Lye, but de Action no Lye.—
40 *Lady Harriot.* What does the thing mean? Give me my Letter—
    Mademoiselle D'Epingle. Me did not deliver your Letter—
    Lady Harriot. No?
    Mademoiselle D'Epingle. No. Me tell you, me did drop it, to see Mr. *Campley* how Cavalier to take it up. As dese me Drop it so Monsieur
45 Run take it up—([*Drops it.*] *They both run to take it up. Mademoiselle* D'Epingle *takes it.*)
    Lady Harriot. Will you give me my Letter or not?
    Mademoiselle D'Epingle. Oui—But dus he do—Dere de Letter—
(*They both run,* Harriot *gets it.*) ver'y well, very well. O L'amour!

You Act de manner Mr. *Campley*—take it up better den I, do' you 50
no see it.

    Lady Harriot. (*Reads.*)

    Madam,
    I *Am glad you mention'd what indeed I did not at that time think of,*
    nor if I had shou'd I have known how to have spoken of. But bless me 55
    more than Fortune can by turning those Fair Eyes upon, Madam
                           Your most Faithfull,
                   Most Obedient humble Servant,
                           Tho. Campley.

What does he mean? But bless me more—by turning—(*Looking* 60
about observes Campley *smile.*) Oh 'tis He Himself—Oh the Hoiden—
The Romp—I did not think any thing could add to your Native
confidence, but you look so very Bold in that Dress—and your
Arms will fall of—And your Petticoats how they hang?

    Campley. Madamoiselle Voulez vous De *Salville Leau D'Hongrie,* 65
Chez Monsieur Marchand de *Montpelier*—Dis for your Teet, (*Show-*
ing his Trinkets.) De Essence, a little Book French for teach De elder
Broders make Compliments. Will you I say have any thing that
I have, Will you have all I have?—Madam.

    Lady Harriot. Yes, and for the Humour's sake, will never part 70
with this Box, while I Live, ha, ha, ha!

    Campley. But Lady *Harriot* we must not stand Laughing, as you
observe in your letter, delays are dangerous in this Wicked Woman's
Custody of you—Therefore I must, Madam beseech you, and pray
stay not on Niceties but be advis'd.   75

    Lady Harriot. Mr. *Campley* I have no Will but yours.

    Campley. Thou Dear Creature—but (*Kisses her hand.*) Harkee then
you must Change Dresses with *Madamoiselle,* and go with me
instantly.

    Lady Harriot. What you please—   80

    Campley. Madam *D'Epingle* I must desire you to comply with a
Humour of Gallentry of ours, you may be sure I'll have an Eye over
the Treatment you have upon my account, only to Change Habits
with Lady *Harriot,* and let her go, while you stay.

85 *Mademoiselle D'Epingle.* Wit all my Heart. (*Offers to undress her self.*)
Lady Harriot. What before Mr. *Campley?*
Mademoiselle D'Epingle. (*Apart to* Harriot.) Oh Oh very *Anglaise*!
Dat is so Englise, all Women of Quality en *France* are Dress and
Undress, by a Valet de-Chambre, De man Chambermaid Help
90 Complexion, better Den de Woman.
Lady Harriot. Nay, that's a Secret in Dress *Madamoiselle*, I never
knew before, and am so unpolish'd an English Woman as to resolve
never to learn ev'n to Dress before my Husband, Oh! indecency!
Mr. *Campley* do you hear what *Madamoiselle* says—
95 *Mademoiselle D'Epingle.* Oh! Hist—Bagatelle.
Lady Harriot. Well We'll run in and be ready in an instant.

            Exeunt Lady Harriot *and Mademoiselle* D'Epingle.
Campley. Well I like her every Minute better and better. What a
delicate Chastity she has! There's something so gross in the Carriage
of some Wives (tho' they're Honest too) that they lose their Hus-
100 bands Hearts for Faults, which if they have either Good Nature, or
Good Breeding, they know not how to tell 'em of. But how Happy
am I in such a Friend as *Hardy*, such a Mistress as *Harriot*!

       Continue Heav'n, a Grateful Heart to bless
       With Faith in Friendship, and in Love Success.

       The End of the Third Act.

Act IV. [Scene i.]

Enter Widow *and* Trusty.

Widow. Mr. *Trusty*, You have I do assure you, the same Place and
Power, in the Management of my Lord *Brumpton's* Estate, as in his
Life-time. (*Aside.*) (I am reduc'd to a necessity of Trusting him.)
[*To* Trusty.] However *Tattleaid* Dissembles the matter she must be
Privy to Lady *Harriot's* Escape, and *Fardingale's* as deep with 'em
5 both, and I fear will be their Ruin, which 'tis my Care and Duty to

       96.1 *Exeunt*] D1 (*Exe.*); *Exit*

prevent. Be Vigilant and you shall be Rewarded. I shall Employ you wholly in Lady *Sharlot's* Affairs, she is able to pay Services done for her. You've Sense, and Understand me.

Exit Widow.

Trusty. Yes, I do indeed Understand you, and could wish, 10 another could with as much Detestation as I do, but my Poor Old Lord is so strangely, so Bewitchedly Enamour'd of her; that ev'n after this Discovery of her Wickedness, I see he could be Reconcil'd to her, and tho he is Asham'd to confess to me, I know he longs to Speak with her. If I tell Lord *Hardy* all to make his Fortune, He 15 would not let his Father be Dishonour'd by a Publick way of Separation. If things are acted Privately, I know she'll throw us all; there's no Middle way, I must Expose her to make a Re-union Impracticable: Alas how is Honest Truth Banish'd the World, then we must Watch the Seasons and soft Avenues to Mens Hearts, to 20 Gain it Entrance ev'n for their own Good and Interest!

Exit.

[Act IV. Scene ii.]

Enter Lord Hardy, Campley, Trim.

Lord Hardy. I forget my own Misfortunes, Dear *Campley*, when I reflect on your Success.

Campley. I assure you, it Moderates the Swell of Joy that I am in, to think of your Difficulties. I hope my Felicity is Previous to yours; my Lady *Harriot* gives her Service to you, and we both think it but 5 decent to Suspend our Marriage till your, and Lady *Sharlot's* Affairs are in the same Posture.

Lord Hardy. Where is my Lady?

Campley. She's at my Ant's my Lord. But my Lord, if you don't interpose, I don't know how I shall adjust matters with Mr. *Trim*, for 10 Leaving his Mistress behind me, I fear he'll demand Satisfaction of me.

Trim. No Sir, alas I can know no Satisfaction, while she is in Jeopardy. Therefore would rather be put in a way to recover her, by Storming the Castle, or other feat of Arms, like a true enamour'd
15 Swain as I am.

Campley. Since we are all Three then expecting Lovers my Lord, Prethee let's have that Song of yours which Suits our common purpose.

Lord Hardy. Call in the Boy.
20 *Boy.* (*Sings.*)

[I.]

Ye Minutes bring the happy Hour,
And Chloe *Blushing to the Bower:*
Then shall all Idle Flames be o're,
Nor Eyes or Heart e're wander more:
25 *Both,* Chloe, *fix'd for e're on Thee,*
For Thou art all thy Sex to Me.

II.

A Guilty is a false Embrace,
Corinna's *Love's a Fairy-Chace:*
Begone, thou Meteor, Fleeting Fire,
30 *And all, that can't survive Desire.*
Chloe *my Reason moves and Awe,*
And Cupid *shot Me, when he Saw.*

Trim. Look you, Gentlemen, since as you are pleas'd to say we're all Lovers, and consequently Poets, pray do me the honour to hear
35 a little Air of mine: You must know then, I once had the misfortune to fall in Love below my self, but things went hard with us at that time, so that my Passion, or as I may Poetically speak, my Fire was in the Kitchin: 'Twas towards a Cook-Maid; but before I ever saw Mrs. *Deborah.*
40 *Lord Hardy.* Come on then, *Trim,* let's have it.
Trim. I must run into next Room for a Lute.

Exit.

Campley. This must be diverting! can the Rogue Play?

Re-enter Trim, *with a pair of Tongs.*

Trim. Dear *Cynderaxa* her self very well understood this Instrument, I therefore always sung this Song to it, as thus.

I.

Cynderaxa *Kind and Good,*   45
Has all my Heart and Stomach too;
She makes me love, not hate, my Food,
As other peevish Wenches do.

II.

When Venus *leaves her* Vulcan's *Cell,*
Which all but I a Cole-hole call;   50
Fly, fly yee that above Stairs dwell,
Her Face is wash'd, yee vanish all.

III.

And as she's Fair, she can impart
That Beauty, to make all things Fine;
Brighten's the Floor with wondrous Art,   55
And at her touch the Dishes shine.

Lord Hardy. I protest, *Will,* thou art a Poet indeed. And at her touch the Dishes shine—And you touch your Lute as finely.

Enter Boy.

Boy. There's one Mr. *Trusty* below wou'd speak with my Lord.
Lord Hardy. Mr. *Trusty*? My Father's Steward? What can he 60 have to say to me?
Campley. He's very honest to my knowledge.
Lord Hardy. I remember indeed when I was turn'd out of the House, he follow'd me to the Gate, and wept over me, for which I've heard he'd like to have lost his Place. But however I must Advise 65 with you a little, about my Behaviour to him; Let's in, *Boy* bring him up hither, tell him I'll waite on him presently.

Exit Boy.

I shall want you I believe here *Trim.*

Exeunt.

Re-enter Boy, *and* Trusty.

Boy. My Lord will waite on you here immediately.

Exit Boy.

70 *Trusty.* 'Tis very well—These Lodgings are but homely for the Earl of *Brumpton*—Oh that damn'd Strumpet—that I shou'd ever know my Master's Wife for such—How many Thousand things does my Head run back to? After my poor Father's Death the good Lord took me, because he was a Captain in his Regiment, and gave 75 me Education. I was I think Three and Twenty when this Young Lord within was Christned; what a do there was about calling him *Francis*? (*Wipes his Eyes.*) These are but poor Lodgings for him. I cannot bear the Joy to think that I shall save the Family, from which I've had my Bread.

Enter Trim.

80 *Trim.* Sir my Lord will wait you immediately.

Trusty. Sir 'tis my duty to waite him—(*As* Trim *is going.*) but Sir, are not you the Young Man that attended him at *Christ-Church* in *Oxford*, and have follow'd him ever since.

Trim. Yes Sir, I am.

85 *Trusty.* Nay Sir, No harm, but you'll thrive the better for it.

Trim. (*Aside.*) I like this Old Fellow, I smell more Money.

Exit.

Trusty. I think 'tis now Eight Years since I saw him, he was not then Nineteen, when I follow'd him to the Gate, and gave him Fifty Guineas, which I pretended his Father sent after him.

Enter Lord Hardy.

90 *Lord Hardy.* Mr. *Trusty* I'm very glad to see you look very hale and Jolly; you wear well—I'm glad to see it—but your Commands to me Mr. *Trusty*.

Trusty. Why my Lord I presume to waite on Your Lordship; my Lord you're strangely grown; you're your Father's very Picture; 95 you're he my Lord: You are the very Man that look'd so pleas'd, to see me look so fine in my Lac'd Livery, to go to Court. I was his Page when he was just such another as you. He Kiss'd me afore a great many Lords, and said I was a brave Man's Son that taught

him to Exercise his Arms. I remember he carry'd me to the great
Window, and bid me be sure to keep in your Mother's Sight in all 100
my Finery. She was the Finest Young Creature, the Maids of
Honour hated to see her at Court. My Lord then Courted my good
Lady: She was as kind to me on her Death Bed, she said to me, Mr.
Trusty take care of my Lord's Second Marriage for that Child's sake:
She pointed as well as she could to you; You fell a Crying and said 105
she should not Die; but she did my Lord; she left the World, and
no one like her in't. (*Weeps, runs to my Lord, and hugs him.*)
Forgive me my honour'd Master, I've often carry'd you in these
Arms that Grasp you, they were stronger then, but if I Die to
morrow, you're worth 5000 *l.* by my Gift, 'tis what I've got in the 110
Family, and I return it to you with thanks—But alas, do I Live to
see you want it?

    Lord Hardy. You confound me with all this Tenderness and
Generosity.

    Trusty. I'll trouble you no longer my Lord—But—   115

    Lord Hardy. Call it not a trouble, for—

    Trusty. My good Lord, I will not, I say, Indulge my self in talking
fond Tales that Melt me, and Interrupt my Story: My business to
your Lordship in one word is this; I am in good Confidence at
present with my Lady *Dowager,* and I know she has some Fears upon 120
her, which depend upon the Nature of the Settlement to your Dis-
favour, and under the Rose. Be your self: I fear your Father has not
had fair play for his Life; be compos'd my Lord, what is to be done
is this, we'll not apply to Publick Justice in this case, till we see
farther; 'Twill make it Noisy, which we must not do, if I might 125
Advise. You shall with a Detachment of your Company, Seize the
Corps as it goes out of the House this Evening to be Interr'd in the
Country, 'twill only look like taking the Administration upon your
self, and Commencing a Suit for the Estate, she has put of the Lying
in State, and Lady *Harriot's* escape with Mr. *Campley,* makes her fear 130
he will prove a Powerful Friend, both to the Young Ladies and your
Lordship. She cannot with Decency be so busie, as when the Corps
is out of the House, therefore hastens it. I know your whole Affair,
leave the care of Lady *Sharlot* to me, I'll Pre-acquaint her, that she
mayn't be Frightned, and dispose of her safely, to Observe the Issue. 135

Lord Hardy. I wholly understand you, it shall be done.

Trusty. I'm sure I am wanted this Moment for your Interest at home. This Ring shall be the Pass-port of Intelligence, for whom you send to Assault us, and the remittance of it Seal'd with this, shall
140 be Authentick from within the House.

Lord Hardy. 'Tis very well.

Trusty. Hope all you can wish my Lord, from a certain Secret relating to the Estate, which I'll acquaint you with next time I see you.

Lord Hardy. Your Servant—

Exit Trusty.

145 This Fellow's strangely honest—Ha! *Will.*

Enter Campley *and* Trim.

Will, don't the recruits waite for me to see 'em at their Parade before this House.

Trim. Yes, and have waited these three Hours.

Lord Hardy. Go to 'em, I'll be there my Self Immediately, we must
150 Attack with 'em if the Rogues are Sturdy this very Evening.

Trim. I guess where—I'm overjoy'd at it. I'll warrant you they do it, if I Command in Chief.

Lord Hardy. I design you shall.

Trim *runs out jumping.*

Campley. You seem my Lord to be in deep Meditation.

155 *Lord Hardy.* I am so, but not on any thing that you may not be acquainted with.

[Act IV. Scene iii.]

Enter Trim, *with a Company of Ragged Fellows,
with a Cane.*

First Soldier. Why then I find Mr. *Trim* we shall come to Blows before we see the French—

Trim. Harkee, Friend, 'tis not your Affair to Guess or Enquire what you are going to do, 'tis only for us Commanders—

Swagger. The French, Pox, they are but a Company of Scratching 5
Civet-Cats—They Fight!

Trim. Harkee don't bluster—were not you a little mistaken in
your Facings at *Steinkirk?*—

Swagger. I grant it; you know I have an Antipathy to the *French*—
I hate to see the Dogs—look you here, Gentlemen, I was shot quite 10
through the Body—look you.

Trim. Prethee look where it enter'd at your back.

Swagger. Look you Mr. *Trim*, you will have your Joke, we know
you are a Wit—but what's that to a Fighting Man.

Enter Kate.

Kate. Mr. *Trim*—Mr. *Trim*—.   15

Trim. Things are not as they have been Mrs. *Kate*, I now pay the
Company—and we that pay Money expect a little more Ceremony—.

Kate. Will your Honour please to taste some right *French* Brandy?

Trim. Art thou sure, Good Woman, 'tis right (*Drinks.*) How— 20
French—pray—nay if I find you deceive me, who pay the Men—.
(*Drinks.*)

Kate. Pray, good Master, have you spoke to my Lord about Me?

Trim. I have, but you shall speak to him your self—thou hast
been a true Campayneer *Kate*, and we must not neglect thee—do 25
you sell Grey-pease yet of an Evening—Mrs. *Matchlock*—. (*Drinks
again.*)

Kate. Any thing to turn the Penny, but I got more by crying
Pamphlets this Year then by any thing I have done a great while—
now I am Married into the Company again, I design to cross the 30
Seas next Year. But Master, my Husband, a Temple Porter, and
a Parliament Man's Footman Last Night by their talk made me
think there was Danger of a Peace, why they said all the prime
People were against a War.

<hr/>

5, 9, 13 *Swagger*] ed.; *Sw.* Swagger, the traditional boastful soldier, has three
speeches in this scene, but he is never called by name. It is not until Act V that he is addressed by Trim as Swagger; but in Act V he has no speeches, and therefore the speech
prefix '*Sw.*' does not appear. Nor is he listed in the Dramatis Personae. In the first
edition the abbreviation '*Sw.*' was used as a speech prefix in IV. iii. The compositor
or printing-house editor of D1, presumably considering '*Sw.*' a misprint for '*So.*',
changed the speech prefix to '2 *Sol.*', T. Johnson similarly used '2d. *So.*' The error
was consistently retained in later editions.

8 Facings] Q erratum on A4v; Sayings.

35   *Trim.* No, no, *Kate*, never fear, you know I keep great Company, all Men are for a War, but some would have it abroad, and some would have it at home in their own Country.

  Kate. Ay, say you so, Drink about Gentlemen, not a Farthing to pay, a War is a War, be it where it will;—but pray Mr. *Trim*, speak
40 to my Lord, that when these Gentlemen have Shirts I may Wash for 'em.

  Trim. I tell you, if you behave well to Night, you shall have a Fortnights Pay, each Man as a Reward; but there's none of you Industrious, there's a thousand things you might do to help out
45 about this Town—as to cry—Puff—Puff Pyes. Have you any Knives or Syzzars to Grind—or late in an Evening, whip from *Grub-Street* strange and bloody News from *Flanders*—Votes from the House of Commons—Buns, rare Buns—Old Silver-Lace, Cloaks, Sutes or Coats—Old Shoes, Boots or Hats—but here, here, here's My Lord a
50 coming—here's the Captain, fall back into the Rank—there move up in the Center.

Enter Lord Hardy *and* Campley.

  Lord Hardy. Let me see whether my ragged Friends are ready and about me.

  Kate. Ensign *Campley*, Ensign *Campley*, I am over-joy'd to see your
55 Honour, ha' the Worlds surely alter'd ha'.

  Campley. 'Tis so Faith *Kate*, why thou art true to the Cause, with the Company still Honest *Amazon*.

  Kate. Dear Soul, not a bit of Pride in him, but won't your Honour help in my Business with my Lord, speak for me, noble Ensign,
60 do.

  Campley. Speak to him your self I'll second you.

  Kate. Noble Captain, my Lord, I suppose Mr. *Trim* has told your Honour about my Petition, I have been a great Sufferer in the Service; 'tis hard for a poor Woman to lose nine Husbands in a War,
65 and no Notice taken; nay three of 'em alas in the same Campaigne, here the Woman stands that say's it, I never stript a Man till I first try'd if he could stand on his Legs, and if not, I think 'twas fair Plunder, except our Adjutant, and he was a Puppy that made my eighth Husband run the Gantlet for not turning his Toes out.

Lord Hardy. Well, we'll consider thee *Kate*, but fall back into the 70
Rear. A Role of what? Gentleman Soldiers.

Trim. (*To* Bumpkin.) Do you hear that, my Lord himself can't
deny but we are all Gentlemen as much as his Honour.—

Lord Hardy. (*Reading.*) Gentleman Soldiers Quarter'd in and about
Guy-Court in *Vinegar-Yard*, in *Russel-Court* in *Drury-Lane*, belonging 75
to the Honourable Captain *Hardy's* Company of Foot—So Answer
to your Names and March off from the left—*John Horseem* Corporal
March easie, that I may view you as you pass by me: Drums. *Simon
Ruffle*, ha! *Ruffle*, what's the meaning you Stride and Founder at
that rate. 80

Ruffle. I'm Pox't like your Honour.

Lord Hardy. *Trim* let him be carry'd to our Surgeon's Mate,
Poxt you Brute Beast! have you no Shame? The next time you shall
Rot: *Darby Tattoo*—there's a Shilling for you—*Tattoo* be always so
tight, how does he keep himself so clean. 85

Trim. Sir, he is a Tragedy-Drum to one of the Play-
Houses.

Lord Hardy. Private Gentlemen—*Alexander Cowitch, Humphrey
Mundungus, William Faggot, Nicholas Scab, Timothy Megrim, Philip
Scratch, Nehemiah Dust, Humphrey Garbage, Nathaniel Matchlock.* 90

Campley. What is *Matchlock* come back to the Company? That's
the Fellow that brought me off at *Steinkirk*.

Lord Hardy. No: Sir, 'tis I am oblig'd to him for that; (*Offering to
give him Money.*) there Friend; you shall want for nothing, I'll give
thee a Halbert too. 95

Kate. O brave me! Shall I be a Sergants Lady—I faith I'll make the
Drums, and the Corporal's Wives, and Company-keepers know
their Distance.

Campley. How far out of the Country did you come to List, don't
you come from *Cornwall*, how did you bear your Charges? 100

Matchlock. I was Whipt from Constable to Constable.—

Trim. Ay, my Lord, that's due by the Courtesie of *England* to all

72 Bumpkin.] TJ2 (*Bumkin.*); *Pumkin*
74 Quarter'd] D1; are Quarter'd
79–84 ha! *Ruffle. . . Rot:*] Here Steele made his second revision on moral
grounds. On the cancel in D1 he merely excised the lines he considered to be
in bad taste, and later editions, including the Mermaid, followed D1. The entire
passage is printed in this edition.

that want in red Coats; besides there's an Act that makes us Free of all Corporations, and that's the Ceremony of it.

105 *Campley.* But what pretence had they for using you so ill, you did not Pilfer?

Matchlock. I was found guilty of being Poor.

Campley. Poor Devil!

Lord Hardy. Timothy Ragg—Oh *Ragg*! I thought when I gave you 110 your Discharge, just afore the Peace, we should never have had you again, how came you to List now?

Ragg. To pull down the *French* King.

Lord Hardy. Bravely resolv'd—but pull your Shirt into your Breeches, in the mean time. *Jeoffrey Tatter*—what's become of the 115 Skirts and Buttons of your Coat?

Tatter. In our last Cloathing in the Regiment I serv'd in afore, the Collonel had one Skirt before, the Ajent one behind, and every Captain of the Regiment a Button.

Lord Hardy. Hush, you Rogue you talk Mutiny. (*Smiling.*)

120 *Trim.* Ay Sirrah, what have you to do with more knowledge than that of your Right-hand, from your Left. (*Hits him a blow on the Head.*)

Lord Hardy. Hugh Clump—Clump thou growest a little too heavy for Marching.

Trim. Ay, my Lord, but if we don't allow him the Pay he'll 125 Starve, for he's too Lame to get into the Hospital.

Lord Hardy. Richard Bumpkin! Ha! a perfect Country Hick,—how came you Friend to be a Soldier.

Bumpkin. An't please your Honour, I have been cross'd in Love, and am willing to seek my Fortune.

130 *Lord Hardy.* Well I've seen enough of 'em, if you mind your Affair, and Act like a wise General, these Fellows may do—come take your Orders. (Trim *puts his Hat on his Stick, while my Lord is giving him the Ring and whispers Orders.*)

Well Gentlemen do your Business Manfully and nothing shall 135 be too good for you.

All. Bless your Honour.

Exeunt Lord Hardy *and* Campley.

114 in] D1; [om.] This is the first of the readings taken from gathering D of D1. The other substantive revisions in gathering D follow but are not individually discussed.

Trim. Now, my brave Friends and Fellow Soldiers—(*Aside.*) I must Fellow Souldier 'em just afore a Battle, like a true Officer tho' I cane 'em all the Year round beside—(*Struting about.*) Major General *Trim*, no, Pox *Trim* sounds so very short and Priggish—that 140 my Name should be a Monosyllable! but the Foreign News will write me, I suppose, Mounsieur, or Chevalier *Trimont*, Seigneur *Trimoni*, or Count *Trimuntz*, in the *German* Army I shall perhaps be call'd; ay, that's all the Plague and Comfort of us great Men they do so toss our Names about—but Gentlemen you are now under my 145 Command—Hussa! thrice—Faith, this is very pleasing this Grandeur! why after all 'tis upon the Neck of such Scoundrells as these Gentlemen, that we great Captains, build our Renown—a Million or two of these Fellows make an *Alexander*, and as that my Predecessor said in the Tragedy of him on the very same occasion 150 going to storm for his *Statira*, so do I for my Dear Sempstress, Madam *D'Epingle.*

> *When I rush on, sure none will dare to stay;*
> *'Tis Beauty calls, and Glory leads the way.*

The End of the Fourth Act.

Act V. Scene i.

Enter Trusty *and Lord* Brumpton.

Trusty. She knows no Moderation in her good Fortune, she has out of Impatience to see her self in her Weeds, order'd her Manto-Woman to stich up any thing immediately—you may hear her and *Tattleaid* Laugh aloud—she is so wantonly Merry.

Lord Brumpton. But this of Lady *Sharlot* is the very utmost of all 5 ill—pray read—but I must sit—my late Fit of the Gout makes me act with Pain and Constraint—let me see.—

Trusty. She writ it by the Page who brought it me, as I had Wheedled him to do all their Passages.

10 *Lord Brumpton.* (*Reads.*)

> *You must watch the Occasion of the Servants being gone out of the House, with the Corps,* Tattleaid *shall Conduct you to my Lady* Sharlots *Appartment—away with her—and be sure you bed Her.—*
> *Your Affectionate Sister,*
15 Mary Brumpton.

Brumpton? The Creature—she call'd as *Franks* Mother was? *Brumpton*! The Succaba! What a Devil Incarnate have I had in my Bosome? Why the common abandon'd Town-women would scruple such an Action as this—tho' they have lost all regard to their own
20 Chastity they would be Tender of another's—why sure she had no Infancy—she never had Virginity to have no Compassion through Memory of her own former Innocence—this is to forget her very Humanity—her very Sex—where is my poor Boy? Where's *Frank*? Does not he want! How has he liv'd all this time—not a Servant I
25 Warrant to attend him—what Company can he keep? What can he say of his Father?

Trusty. Tho' you made him not your Heir, he is still your Son— and has all the Duty and Tenderness in the World, for your Memory—

30 *Lord Brumpton.* It is impossible *Trusty*, it is impossible—I will not rack my self with the Thought, that one I have injur'd can be so very Good—keep me in Countenance—tell me he hates my very Name—wou'd not assume my Title, because it descends from me— what's his Company?

35 *Trusty.* Young *Tom Campley* they are never asunder.

Lord Brumpton. I am glad he has my pretty Tattler—the Chearful Innocent—*Harriot*—I hope he'll be good to her—he's good Natur'd and well Bred—

Trusty. But my Lord, she was very punctual in Ordering the
40 Funeral—she bid *Sable* be sure to lay you deep enough—she had heard such Stories of the Wicked Sextons taking up People—but I

wish, my Lord, you would please to hear her, and *Tattleaid* once
more.—

Lord Brumpton. I know to what thy Zeal tends—but I tell you
since you cannot be convinc'd but that I have still a softness for 45
her—I say tho' I had so, it should never make me transgress that
scrupulous Honour that becomes a Peer of *England*—if I could forget
Injuries done my self thus gross—I never will those done my
Friends—you knew *Sharlots* worthy Father—no—there's no need
of my seeing more of this Woman—I behold her now with the same 50
Eyes that you do—there's a meanness in all she says or does—
she has a great Wit, but a little Mind—some thing ever wanting
to make her appear my Lady *Brumpton*—she has nothing natively
Great—you see I Love her not—I talk with Judgment of her.—

Trusty. I see it, my good Lord, with Joy I see it—nor care how 55
few things I see more in this World—my satisfaction is Compleat—
Welcome old Age—Welcome Decay—'Tis not Decay but growth
to a latter Being.

Exit, Leading Lord Brumpton.

Re-enter Trusty *meeting* Cabinet.

Trusty. I have your Letter Mr. *Cabinet.*

Cabinet. I hope Sir, you'll believe it was not in my Nature to be 60
guilty of so much baseness, but being born a Gentleman, and Bred
out of all Roads of Industry in that idle manner too many are; I soon
spent a small Patrimony, and being Debauch'd by Luxury, I fell
into the narrow Mind to dread no Infamy like Poverty—which
made me Guilty as that Paper tells you—and had I not writ to you 65
I am sure I never could have told you of it.

Trusty. It is an Ingenious, Pious Penitence in you—My Lord
Hardy—(to whom this Secret is inestimable) is a noble natur'd Man
—and you shall find him such—I give you my Word.—

Cabinet. I know, Sir your Integrity.— 70

Trusty. But pray be there—all that you have to do is to ask for the
Gentlewoman at the House at my Lord *Hardy's*—she'll take care of
you.—and pray have Patience, where she places you till you see
Me—

Exit Cabinet.

75 My Lord *Hardy's* being an House where they receive Lodgers, has
allow'd me convenience to place every Body I think necessary to be
by at her Discovery—This Prodigious Welcome Secret! I see however impracticable honest Actions may appear, we may go on with
just Hope.

80   *All that is Ours, is to be justly bent,*
          And Heav'n in its own Cause will bless th' Event.

                                                  Exit.

[Act V. Scene ii.]

Enter Trim *and his Party.*

   Trim. March up, march up—Now we are near the Citadel—And
I halt only to give the Necessary Orders for th' Engagement—Ha!
Clump, Clump—When we come to Lord *Brumpton's* Door, and you see
us conveniently dispos'd about the House—You are to wait till you
5 see a Corps brought out of the House—Then to go up to him, you
observe the Director; and ask importunately for an Alms to a poor
Soldier—For which you may be sure you shall have a good Blow or
two—But if you have not, be Sawcy till you have—Then when you
see a File of Men got between the House and the Body—A File of
10 Men, *Bumpkin*, is six Men—I say, when you see the File in such a
Posture, that half the File may Face to the House, half to the Body
—You are to fall down, crying, Murder, that the Half-file fac'd to
the Body, may throw it, and themselves, over you——I then march
to your Rescue—Then, *Swagger*, you, and your Party, fall in to
15 secure my Rear; while I march off with the Body—These are the
Orders—And this, with a little Improvement of my own, is the
same Disposition *Villeroy* and *Catinat* made at *Chiari.*

                                        Marches off with his Party.

81.1 *Exit*] D1; [om.]

[Act V. Scene iii.]

Enter Widow *in deep Mourning, with a*
dead Squirrel on her Arm, and Tattleaid.

Widow. It must be so—It must be your carelessness—What had
the Page to do in my Bedchamber?

Tattleaid. Indeed, Madam, I can't tell—But I came in and catch'd
him wringing round his Neck—   5

Widow. Tell the Rascal from me—He shall Romp with the
Footmen no more—No—I'll send the Rogue in a Frock, to learn
Latine among the dirty Boys that come to good—I will—But 'tis
ever so among these Creatures that live on one's superfluous
Affections, a Ladies Woman, Page, and Squirrel, are always Rivals. 10
Poor Harmless Animal—Pretty ev'n in Death:
Death might have overlook'd thy little Life—
How could'st thou, *Robin*, leave thy Nuts and me?
How was't, import'nat Dearest, thou should'st die?
Thou never did'st Invade thy Neighbour's Soils:
Never madest War with specious Shews of Peace: 15
Thou never hast depopulated Regions,
But chearfully didst bear thy little Chain
Content—So I but fed thee with this Hand.

Tattleaid. Alass, alass! We are all Mortal: Consider, Madam, my
Lord's dead too. (*Weeps.*)   20

Widow. Ay, but our Animal Friends do wholly die; an Husband
or Relation after Death, is rewarded or tormented—That's some
Consolation—(*Aside.*) I know her Tears are false for she hated
Robin always—But she's a well-bred dishonest Servant, that never
speaks a painful Truth—[*To* Tattleaid.] But I'll resolve to conquer 25
my Affliction—Never speak more of *Robin*—Hide him there—But
to my Dress—How Soberly Magnificent is Black—and the Train—
I wonder how Widows came to wear such long Tails!

Tattleaid. Why, Madam, the stateliest of all Creatures has the
30 longest Tayl, the Peacock; nay 't has of all Creatures the finest Mein
too—except your Ladyship, who are a Phenix—

Widow. Ho! Brave *Tattleaid*—But did not you observe what a
Whining my Lady *Sly* made, when she had drank a little? Did you
believe her? Do you think there are really People sorry for their
35 Husbands?

Tattleaid. (*Speaks with Pins in her mouth.*) Really, Madam, some
Men do leave their Fortunes in such Distraction, that I believe it
may be—

Widow. But I swear I wonder how it came up to dress us thus—I
40 protest, when all my Equipage is ready, and I move in full Pageantry,
I shall fansie my self an Embassadress from the Commonwealth of
Women, the distressed State of *Amazonia*—to treat for Men—But
I protest I wonder how two of Us thus clad can meet with a grave
Face—Methinks they should laugh out like two Fortune-tellers,
45 or two opponent Lawyers that know each other for Cheats—

Tattleaid. Ha! ha! ha! I swear to you, Madam, your Ladyship's
Wit will choak me one time or other—I had like to have swallow'd
all the Pins in my mouth—

Widow. But, *Tatty*, to keep house six Weeks, that's another
50 barbarous Custom; but the Reason of it, I suppose, was that the
base People should not see People of Quality may be as afflicted as
themselves—

Tattleaid. No; 'Tis because they should not see 'em as merry as
themselves.

55 *Widow.* Ha! ha! ha! Hussey, you never said that you spoke last—
Why 'tis just—'Tis Satyre—I'm sure you saw it in my Face, that I
was going to say it—'twas too good for you—Come, lay down that
Sentence and the Pin-cushion, and Pin up my shoulder—Harkee,
Hussey, if you should, as I hope you wo'n't, out-live me, take care
60 I an't buried in Flannen, 'twould never become me, I'm sure—That
they can be as Merry? Well, I'll tell my New Acquaintance—What's
her Name?—She that reads so much, and writes Verses—Her
Husband was dead the first Quarter of a Year—I forget her Name

63 dead] ed.; deaf   The reading 'dead' for 'deaf', required by context, has never
previously been printed.

—That Expression she'll like—Well, that Woman does divert me strangely—I'll be very great with her—She talk'd very learnedly of 65 the Ridicule, till she was ridiculous, then she spoke of the Decent— of the Agreeable—of the Insensible—she Designs to Print the Discourse—But of all things I like her Notion of the Insensible.

Tattleaid. Pray, Madam, how was that?

Widow. A most useful Discourse to be inculcated in our Teens 70 —the purpose of it is to disguise our Apprehension in this ill Bred Generation of Men who speak before Women what they ought not to hear—As now suppose you were a Spark in my Company, and you spoke some double entendre—I look thus! But be a Fellow, and you shall see how I'lle Use you—The insensible is useful upon any 75 occasion where we seemingly Neglect, and secretly Approve, which is our ordinary common Case—Now suppose a Coxcomb Dancing, Prating and Playing his Tricks before me to move me—without Pleasure or Distaste in my Countenance I look at him—just thus— but—Ha, ha, ha! I have found out a Supplement to this Notion of 80 the insensible, for my own use which is infallible, and that is to have always in my Head, all that they can say or do to me—so never be surpriz'd with Laughter, the occasion of which is always sudden.—

Tattleaid. Oh my Lady *Brumpton* (Tattleaid *Bows and Cringes.*) My 85 Lady—your most Obedient Servant.—

Widow. Look you, Wench, you see by the Art of Insensibility I put you out of Countenance though you were prepar'd for an ill reception.—

Tattleaid. Oh! Madam—How Justly are you form'd for what is 90 now fall'n to you the *Empire* of Mankind.—

Widow. O Sir, that puts me out of all my insensibility at once— That was so Gallant! Ha! What noise is that—That noise of Fighting—Run I say—Whither are you going—What are you Mad —Will you leave me alone—Can't you stir—What you can't take 95 your Message with you—What ever 'tis I suppose you are not in the *Plot*; not you—Nor that now they're breaking open my house for *Sharlot*—Not you—Go see what's the Matter I say I have no body I can trust—

Exit Tattleaid.

100 One minute I think this wench honest and the next false—Whither
shall I turn me?

Tattleaid. (*Re-entring.*) Madam—Madam.

Widow. Madam, Madam will you swallow me Gapeing.—

Tattleaid. Pray good my Lady be not so out of Humour—But
105 there is a Company of Rogues have set upon our servants and the
Burial Man's while others ran away with the Corps.—

Widow. How! What can this mean? What can they do with it—
Well 'twill save the Charge of interment—but to what end?

Enter Trusty *and a* Servant *Bloody and*
Dirty haling in Clump *and* Bumpkin.

Servant. I'le teach you better manners—I'le poor Souldier you.—
110 You Dog you, I will—Madam, here are two of the Rascals that were
in the Gang of Rogues that Carryed away the Corps—

Widow. We'll examine 'em apart—Well Sirrah what are You?
Whence came You? What's your Name? Sirrah? (Clump *makes Signs*
as a Dumb Man.)

115 *Servant.* O you Dog, you could speake loud enough Just now
Sirrah, when your Brother Rogues mauld Mr. *Sable*—we'll make
you speak Sirrah.—

Widow. Bring the other fellow hither—I suppose you will own
you Knew that man before you saw him at my door?

120 *Clump.* I think I have seen the Gentleman's face. (*Bowing to*
Bumpkin.)

Widow. The Gentleman's! the Villiain Mocks me—but Friend,
you look like an Honest man, what are you, whence come you?
What are you Friend?

125 *Bumpkin.* I'se at present but a Private Gentleman, but I was listed
to be a Sergeant in my Lord *Hardy's* Company—I'se not asham'd
of my name nor of my Koptin.—

Widow. Leave the Room all;

Exeunt all but Trusty, Tattleaid, [Widow].

Mr. *Trusty*—Lord *Hardy*! O that Impious young Man—Thus with
130 the Sacrilegious hands of Ruffians to divert his Father's Ashes from
their urn, and rest—

105 servants] D1; servant's   108.1 Trusty *and a*] D1; [om.]

(*Aside.*) I suspect this fellow. [*To* Trusty.] Mr. *Trusty* I must
desire you to be still near me—I'le know the bottom of this, and to
Lord *Hardy's* Lodgings as I am, instantly—'Tis but the backside of
this Street I think—Let a Coach be call'd—*Tattleaid* as soon as I am 135
gone—Conduct my Brother and his Friends to Lady *Sharlot*, away
with her—Bring *Mademoiselle* away to me—That she may not be a
Witness—Come good Mr. *Trusty*.

Exeunt.

[Act V. Scene iv.]

Enter Lord Hardy *leading Lady* Harriot—
Campley, Trim.—

Lady Harriot. Why then I find this Mr. *Trim* is a perfect General
—but I'le assure you, Sir, I'le never allow you an Heroe, who could
leave your Mistress behind you, you should have broke the house
down, but you should have brought *Mademoiselle* with you.—

Trim. No really Madam, I have seen such strange fears come into 5
the Men's heads, and such strange resolutions into the Women's
upon the Occasion of Ladies following a Camp, that I thought it
more discreet to leave her behind me—my success will naturally
touch her as much as if she were here.—

Lady Harriot. (*Aside.*) A good intelligent Arch fellow this; [*To* 10
Lord Hardy.] But were not you saying, my Lord, you believed Lady
Brumpton would follow hither—if so, pray let me be gone—

Lord Hardy. No Madam; I must beseech your Ladyship to Stay for
there are things alledg'd against her which you who have liv'd in the
Family may, perhaps give light into, and which I can't believe ev'n 15
she could be guilty of.

Lady Harriot. Nay, my Lord, that's Generous to a folly, for e'ven
for her Usage of you, (without regard to my self) I am ready to

138.1 *Exeunt.*] D1; *Exeunt omnes.*

believe she would do any thing that can come into the head of a
20 Close, Malicious Cruel, designing Woman—

Enter Boy.

Boy. My Lady *Brumpton*'s below—
Lady Harriot. Ill run then.—
Campley. No, no, stand your Ground; you a Souldiours Wife?
Come we'll rally her to death.—
25 *Lord Hardy.* Prethee entertain her a little while I go in for a
Moment's thought on this Occasion.

Exit.

Lady Harriot. She has more Wit than us both—
Campley. Psaw, no matter for that—Besure assoon as the Sentence
is out of my mouth to Clap in with something else—and laugh at
30 all I say; I'll be grateful and burst my self at my pretty Witty Wife
—We'll fall in slap upon her,—she shan't have time to say a Word
of the running away.

Enter Lady Brumpton *and* Trusty.

O my Lady *Brumpton,* your Ladyships most obedient Servant:
this is my Lady *Harriot Campley*—Why, Madam, your Ladyship is
35 immediately in your mourning—nay as you have more Wit than
any body, so (what seldome Wits have) you have more prudence
too—Other Widows have nothing in a readiness but a Second
Husband—But you I see had your very weeds and dress lying by
you—
40 *Lady Harriot.* Ay, Madam; I see your Ladyship is of the Order of
Widowhood for you have put on the habit.—
Widow. I see your Ladyship is not of the Profession of Virginity
for you have lost the look on't.—
Campley. You are in the Habit—That was so pretty nay without
45 Flattery Lady *Harriot* you have a great deal of Wit ha! ha! ha!
Lady Harriot. No my Lady *Brumpton* here is the Woman of Wit,
but indeed she has but little enough considering how much her
Ladyship has to defend ha! ha! ha!
Widow. I am sorry, Madam, your Ladyship has not what's

32.1 *and* Trusty] D1; [om.

sufficient for your Occasions, or that this pretty Gentleman can't 50
supply 'em—(Campley *Danceing about and Trolling.*)

Hey day! I find, Sir, your heels are a great help to your head—
They relieve your Wit I see; and I don't Question but 'ere now they
have been as kind to your Valour: ha! ha!

Campley. (*Aside.*) Pox I can say nothing 'tis always thus with your 55
Endeavourers to be Witty [*To* Widow.] I saw Madam your Mouth
go but there could be nothing offer'd in answer to what my Lady
Harriot said—'Twas home—'Twas cutting Satire.—

Lady Harriot. Oh Mr. *Campley*? But Pray, Madam, has Mr. *Cabinet*
Visited your Ladyship since this calamity—How stands that affair 60
now?—

Widow. Nay Madam, if you already want instructions—I'll
acquaint you how the World stands if you are in Distress—but I
fear Mr. *Campley* over-hears us.—

Campley. And all the Tune the Pipers Play'd—was Toll-toll-dorol 65
—I swear Lady *Harriot* were I not already yours I could have a
Tender for this Lady.

Widow. Come good Folks I find we are very free with each other
—What makes you two here, Do you board my Lord, or He you;
come come ten Shillings a head will go a great way in a Family— 70
what do you say Mrs. *Campley* is it so: Does your Ladiship go to
Market your self—Nay you're in the right of it—come—can you
imagine what makes my Lord stay—He is not now with his Land-
steward—not Signing Leases I hope ha, ha, ha!

Campley. (*Aside.*) Hang her to have more Tongue than a Man and 75
his Wife too.—

Enter Lord Hardy.

Lord Hardy. Because your Ladyship is I know in very much Pain
in Company you have injur'd—I'll be short—open those Doors—
There lies your Husbands my Father's Body—And by you stands
the Man Accuses you of Poisoning Him.—   80

Widow. Of Poisoning him!—

Trusty. The Symptoms will appear upon the Corps.—

Lord Hardy. But I am seiz'd by Nature—How shall I View A

53 They] D1; Thus   56 Mouth] D1; Month   60 Ladyship] D1; Lordship

Breathless lump of Clay—Him whose high Veins Convey'd to me
85 this Vital Force, and Motion.
I cannot bear that Sight.—
I am as fix'd and Motionless as he.—

They open the Coffin, out of which
jumps Lady Sharlot.

Art thou the gastly Shape my Mind had form'd,
Art thou the cold Inanimate—Bright Maid!
90 Thou giv'st new higher Life to all around,
Whither does Fancy fir'd with Love convey me;
Whither Transported by my pleasing Fury,
The Season Vanishes at thy approach,
'Tis Morn, 'tis Spring—
95 Daysies and Lillies strow thy Flowr'y Way,
Why is my fair unmov'd—My Heav'nly Fair;
Does she but Smile at my Exalted Rapture?
     Lady Sharlot. Oh! Sence of Praise to me unfelt before,
Speak on, speak on, and Charm my attentive Ear:
100 How sweet Applause is from an Honest Tongue.
Thou lov'st my Mind—Hast well Affection plac'd;
In what, nor Time, nor Age, nor Care, nor Want can alter.—
Oh how I Joy in thee—My Eternal Lover;
Immutable as the Object of thy Flame!
105 I Love, I'm Proud, I Triumph that I Love,
Pure I approach Thee—Nor did I with empty Showes,
Gorgeous Attire, or studied Negligence;
Or Song, or Dance, or Ball, Allure thy Soul,
Nor want, or fear, such Arts to keep, or lose it:
110 Nor now with fond reluctance doubt to enter,
My Spacious, Bright Abode this Gallant Heart. (*Reclines on Lord*
Hardy.)
     Lady Harriot. Ay Marry—These are high doings indeed, the
greatness of the occasion has burst their Passion into Speech—Why
115 Mr. *Campley*, when we are near these fine Folks, you and I are but

mere Sweet Hearts—I protest—I'll never be won so; you shall
begin again with me.

Campley. Prethee, why dost Name us poor Animals! They have
forgot there are any such Creatures as their old Acquaintance *Tom*
and *Harriot.*   120

Lord Hardy. So we did indeed, but you'll pardon us.

Campley. My Lord, I never thought to see the Minute wherein I
should rejoice at your forgetting me, but now I do heartily. (*Embracing.*)

Lady Sharlot. Harriot. ⎤   125
Lady Harriot. Sharlot. ⎦ *Embracing.*

Widow. Sir, You're at the bottom of all this—I see you're skill'd
at close Conveyances—I'll know the meaning instantly of these
Intricacies, 'tis not your seeming Honesty and Gravity shall save
you from your Deserts—My Husband's Death was sudden—You 130
and the Burial Fellow were observ'd very familiar—Produce my
Husband's Body—Or I'll Try you for his Murder; which I find
you'd put on me thou Hellish Engine!

Trusty. Look you Madam, I could answer you, but I scorn to
reproach People in Misery—You're undone—Madam.—   135

Widow. What does the Dotard mean. Produce the Body Villain,
or the Law shall have thine for it—

Trusty *Exit Hastily.*

Do you design to let the Villain escape. How justly did your Father
Judge, that made You a Beggar with that Spirit—You meant just
now you could not bear the Company of those you'd injur'd.   140

Lord Hardy. You are a Woman, Madam, and my Father's Widow
—but sure you think you've highly injur'd me.

Here my Lord Brumpton *and* Trusty
half enter and observe.

Widow. No, Sir, I have not, will not, Injure you—I must Obey
the Will of my Deceas'd Lord to a Tittle—I must justly pay
Legacies. Your Father, in Consideration that you were his Blood, 145

123 do] D1; did
129 your] D1; the   The word 'the' in Q is clearly a misprint, probably for 'thy';
Steele, when he corrected the D gathering of D1, changed 'the' to 'your'. I accept
this reading.
139 that Spirit] D1; hat ∼

would not wholly Alienate you—He left you Sir, this Shilling with which Estate you now are Earl of *Brumpton*.—

Lord Hardy. Insolent Woman—It was not me my good Father Disinherited, 'twas him you represented. The Guilt was thine, he
150 did an Act of Justice.

Lord Brumpton *entering with* Trusty.

Lord Brumpton. Oh unparallel'd Goodness!

Tattleaid *and Mademoiselle* D'Epingle
at the other Door entring.

Trusty. Oh *Tattleaid*—His and our Hour is come.

Widow. What do I see my Lord, my Master, Husband Living!

Lord Brumpton. (*Turning from her, running to his Son.*) Oh my Boy,
155 my Son—Mr. *Campley*—*Sharlot*—*Harriot.*—(*All Kneeling to him.*) O my Children—Oh, oh! These Passions are too strong for my old Frame—Oh the sweet Torture! My Son, my Son! I shall expire in the too mighty Pleasure! my Boy!

Lord Hardy. A Son, an Heir, a Bridegroom in one Hour!
160 Oh! Grant me, Heav'n, Grant me Moderation!

Widow. A Son an Heir! Am I neglected then?
What? can my Lord revive, Yet Dead to me?
Only to me Deceas'd—To me alone,
Deaf to my Sighs, and Senceless to my Moan.
165   *Lord Brumpton.* 'Tis so long since I have seen Plays, good Madam, that I know not whence thou dost repeat, nor can I answer.

Widow. You can remember tho' a certain Settlement in which I am thy Son and Heir—Great Noble, that I suppose not taken from
170 a Play, that's as irrevocable as Law can make it, that if you Scorn me—Youre Death and Life are Equal—Or I'll still wear my Mourning 'cause you're Living.

Trusty. Value her not, my Lord, a Prior Obligation made you incapable of settling on her your Wife.
175   *Lord Brumpton.* Thy Kindness, *Trusty*, does distract thee—I would indeed disengage my self by any Honest Means, but alas I know no Prior Gift that avoids this to her—Oh my Child.

Trusty. Look you, Madam, I'll come again immediately—Be not troubled my dear Lords.—

Exit.

Campley. Trusty looks very Confident, there is some good in that. 180

Re-enter Trusty *with* Cabinet.

Cabinet. What my Lord *Brumpton* Living, nay then?

Trusty. Hold, Sir, you must not stir, nor can you, Sir, retract this for your Hand-writing—my Lord, this Gentleman since your suppos'd Death has lurk'd about the House, to speak with my Lady, or *Tattleaid,* who upon your Decease have shun'd him, in hopes, I 185 suppose, to buy him off for ever—Now as he was prying about, he peep'd into your Closet—where he saw your Lordship Reading—struck with horrour, and believing himself (as well he might) The Disturber of your Ghost for Alienation of your Fortune from your Family—He writ me this Letter, wherein he acknowledges a 190 Private Marriage with this Lady half a Year before you ever saw her.

All. How! (*All turn upon her disdainfully*—)

Widow. (*Recovering from her Confusion*—) No more a Widow then, but still a Wife,

I am thy Wife—Thou Author of my Evil.   195
Thou must partake with me an homely Board,
An homely Board that never shall be Chearful;
But ev'ry Meal embitter'd with Upbraidings.
Thou that could'st tell me, Good and Ill were Words,
When thou coul'st basely let me to another,   200
Yet could'st see Sprights, great Unbeliever!
Coward! Bugg-bear'd Penitent—
Stranger henceforth to all my Joys, my Joys
To thy Dishonour; Dispicable Thing,
Dishonour thee? Thou Voluntary Couckold.   205

Cabinet *sneaks of,* Widow *Flings after*
him, Tattleaid *Following.*

Lord Brumpton. I see you're all confus'd as well as I—Yee are my Children—I hold you all so. And for your own use will speak plainly to you, I cannot hate that Woman: Nor shall she ever want. Tho' I

scorn to bear her injuries—Yet had I ne're been rous'd from that low
210 Passion to a Worthless Creature—But by disdain of her attempt on
my Friend's Child. I am glad that Scorn's confirm'd by her being
that Fellows—whom for my own sake I only will contemn. Thee
Trusty how shall we prosecute with equal Praise and Thanks for
this great Revolution in our House?

215   *Trusty*. Never to speak on't more my Lord.

   Lord Brumpton. You are now, Gentlemen, going into Cares at a
Crisis in your Country.
And on this great Occasion *Tom*—I'll mount
Old *Campley* which thy Father gave me,
220 And attend thee, a chearful gay old Man,
Into the Field to represent our County.
My rough *Plebeian Britains* not yet Slaves
To *France*, shall mount thy Father's Son
Upon their Shoulders. Eccho Loud their Joy—
225 While I and *Trusty* follow Weeping after:
But be thou Honest, Firm, Impartial,
Let neither Love, nor Hate, nor Faction move thee,
Distinguish Words from Things, and Men from Crimes;
Punctual be thou in Payments, nor basely
230 Screen thy Faults 'gainst Law, behind the Laws
Thou makest.—(*To Lord* Hardy.) But thou against my Death,
    must learn
A supererogatory Morality.
As he is to be Just, be Generous thou:
235 Nor let thy reasonable Soul be struck,
With Sounds and Appellations, Title is
No more, if not significant
Of something that's Superiour in thy self
To other Men, of which thou may'st be
240 Conscious yet not Proud—But if you swerve
From higher Virtue than the Crowd Possess,
Know they that call thee Honourable, mock thee.
You are to be a Peer, by Birth a Judge

---

209 had] D1; should   211 am] D1; am's   219 me] D1; thee
231 (*To Lord* Hardy)] D1; [om.]

Upon your Honour of others Lives and Fortunes;
Because that Honour's dearer than your own.   245
Be good my Son, and be a Worthy Lord:
For when our Shineing Virtues bless Mankind,
We Disappoint the lived Malecontents,
Who long to call our Noble Order Useless,
[*To both.*] Our All's in Danger, Sirs, nor shall you dally   250
Your Youth away with your fine Wives.
No in your Countries Cause you shall meet Death,
While feeble we with minds resign'd do wait it.
Not but I intend your Nuptials as soon as possible to draw Intails
and Settlements. How necessary such things are I had like to have 255
been a fatal Instance.

Campley. But my Lord here are a Couple [*Motioning toward* Trim
and Mademoiselle D'Epingle.] that need not wait such Ceremonies.
Please but to sit: You've been extremely mov'd and must be tir'd.
You say we must not spend our time in Daliance, you'll see, my 260
Lord, the Entertainment reminds us also of Nobler things, and what
I design'd for my own Wedding I'll Complement the General with.
The Bride Dances finely—*Trim* will you Dance with her?

Trim. I will, but I cant—There's a Country-man of hers without
by Accident.   265

Campley. Ay but is he a Dancer?

Trim. Is a *French-man* a Dancer, is a *Welshman* a Gentleman? I'll
bring him in.—

Here a Dance and the following Songs.

[Song.]

Set by Mr. *Daniel Purcell.*
Sung by *Jemmie Bowin.*

I.

On Yonder Bed supinely laid,
Behold thy Lov'd Expecting Maid: 270
In Tremor, Blushes, half in Tears,

247 when] D1; which   250 Sirs] TJ1; Sir

Much, much she Wishes, more she fears,
Take, take her to thy Faithful Arms
Hymen bestows thee all her Charms.

II.

275   *Heav'n to thee Bequeaths the Fair*
To raise thy Joy, and lull thy Care,
Heav'n made Grief, if Mutual, cease,
But Joy, divided, to encrease
To Mourn with her exceeds delight,
280   *Darkness with her, the Joys of Light.*

[Song.]

Sung by Mr. *Pate.*

I.

Arise, arise great Dead for Arms renown'd,
Rise from your Urns, and save your Dying story,
Your Deeds will be in Dark Oblivion Drown'd
For Mighty William *Seizes all your Glory.*

II.

285   *Again the* British *Trumpet Sounds,*
Again Britannia *Bleeds;*
To Glorious Death, or comely Wounds,
Her Godlike Monarch Leads.

III.

Pay us, kind Fate, the Debt you Owe,
290   *Cælestial Minds from Clay untye,*
Let Coward Spirits dwell below,
And only give the Brave to Die.

Lord Brumpton. Now Gentlemen let the Miseries which I have but
miraculously Escap'd, admonish you to have always inclinations
295 proper for the Stage of Life you're in. Don't follow Love when
Nature seeks but Ease: Otherwise you'll fall into a Lethargy of your

275 *Bequeaths*] D1; *Bequeath,*

Dishonour, when warm Pursuits of Glory are over with you; For
Fame and Rest are utter Opposites.

> *You who the Path of Honour make your Guide,*
> *Must let your Passion, with your Blood subside;*   300
> *And no untim'd Ambition, Love, or Rage*
> *Employ the Moments of Declining Age:*
> *Else Boys will in your Presence lose their Fear,*
> *And laugh at the Grey-head they should revere.*

[*The End of the Fifth Act.*]

EPILOGUE,

Spoken by Lord *Hardy*.

Love, Hope and Fear, Desire, Aversion, Rage, ⎫
All that can move the Soul, or can asswage, ⎬
Are drawn in Miniature of Life the Stage. ⎭
Here you can View your Selves, and here is shown
5   *To what you're born in Sufferings not your own,*
The Stage to Wisdom's no Fantastick Way,
Athens her self learn't Virtue at a Play
Our Author me to-Night a Souldier drew:
But faintly Writ, what warmly you pursue:
10   *To his great purpose, had he Equal Fire,*
He'd not aim to please only, but inspire;
He'd sing what hovering Fate attends our Isle,
And from base Pleasure rouse to glorious Toil:
Full time the Earth t'a new Decision brings;
15   *While* William *gives the* Roman *Eagle Wings:*
With Arts and Arms shall Brittain *Tamely end,*
Which naked Picts *so bravely could Defend?*
The Painted Heroes on th' Invaders press,
And think their Wounds Addition to their Dress;
20   *In Younger Years we've been with Conquest Blest,*
And Paris *has the* Brittish *Yoke confess'd;*
I'st then in England, *in lost* England *known,*
Her King's are nam'd from a Revolted Throne.
But we offend—You no Examples need,
25   *In Imitation of your selves proceed;*
'Tis you your Countries Honour must secure,
Be all your Actions Worthy of Namure:
With Gentle Fires your Gallantry improve,
Courage is Brutal if untouch'd with Love:

If soon our utmost Bravery's not display'd,
Think that Bright Circle must be Captives made.
Let Thoughts of saving them our Toils beguile,
And they Reward our Labours with a Smile.

31 Bright] D1; Right

FINIS.

DEDICATION OF THE FIRST EDITION OF
THE FUNERAL; AND THE TENDER
HUSBAND: COMEDIES

To Her GRACE the
DUTCHESS
OF
HAMILTON.

MADAM,

It is frequent to make Addresses of this Nature at the Front of
Books to implore future Patronage, but I do not know of any
Acknowledgments expressed this way for Favour towards Writings,
5 after they have appear'd in the World. I am sure there is a juster
Pretence for taking the Liberty of presenting a Dedication in
Gratitude for Protection already granted, than to supplicate such
an Obligation. Your Grace will, therefore, forgive me, that I lay
before You an Edition of a Book, which I believe would never have
10 appeared, had not these Plays been acted at Your Request, long
after the Run of them, as the Phrase is, was over in the Town. If
You will please to continue to them, by Your Influence, the Life to
which You restored 'em, You will, I hope, do an Act not unworthy
that Ingenuous Temper, which makes You so Affectionately
15 promote the more liberal Entertainments of the Stage. I have the
Confidence to say thus much for these Comedies, because they are
certainly Inoffensive, if they do not deserve to be called Instructive.
But I have said the best thing I can to recommend them, when I
have declared they have Your Grace's Approbation.

20   For, in Writing Plays, not to displease such whose Minds are
filled with the worthiest Ideas of what is Laudable in real Life, is
much more than to escape the Censure of such as are more inclined
to observe the Conduct of the Characters, as they are part of a
Dramatick Entertainment.

If this elegant Taste (with relation to Writings) in which your 25 Grace excels, were more frequently the Ambition of Ladies to attain, I do not know but a Conversation built upon the Characters in a well-wrought Play, might be almost as Instructive as the common Practice among them, of pulling to Pieces the Conduct of familiar Friends, or rehearsing defamatory Reports of those to 30 whom they are Strangers.

But such Meanness ought not to be mentioned in an Epistle to the Dutchess of HAMILTON, whose whole Behaviour is the lively Expression of that sort of good Breeding which is founded on the Principles of good Nature and Generosity. 35

Your Favour is ever bestowed on the Unfortunate, and Your Praise on the Absent. The just Condescension with which Your Conversation is always adorned, at once gives Speech to the Humble, and Silence to the Presumptuous. Your Affability to me, when I have the Honour to wait upon You, and the very kind 40 Things You have so frequently said of these Writings in my Absence, put me under a Temptation of falling into the usual Language of Dedications. But I know this would be highly Offensive to You, and for this Reason I forbear to tell You, that Your High Station in the World is as easie to Your Inferiors as Your Self; that 45 were You to appear any where unknown, all that should converse with You, would believe or wish Your Quality what it is; and that all who know You think it as impossible to Envy You, as not to Esteem You. As for this Acknowledgment which I here make You, for Your Partiality to these Comedies, all I can say is, that I shall 50 think my self very happy, if you find, upon reading them again, that it is no Diminution to You, (what is a great Addition to me) that I am,

MADAM,
   Your Grace's 55
     Most Oblig'd and
     Most Obedient,
      Humble Servant,
       Richard Steele.

THE LYING LOVER: OR, THE
LADIES FRIENDSHIP

COMPOSITION AND SOURCES

ACCORDING to local tradition, Steele wrote *The Lying Lover* while stationed at Landguard Fort, Suffolk, retreating to a farmhouse near Walton or the Queen's Arms in Harwich to write.[1] His Dedication to the Duke of Ormonde, scholars agree, was attributable not only to appreciation for past favours but also to his desire to join the Duke's new regiment and thus escape the boredom of Landguard.[2]

His chief source was Corneille's *Le Menteur* (1642), derived in turn from Juan Ruiz de Alarcón's *La Verdad Sospechosa*. Corneille's play had been translated into English, acted at the Theatre Royal at least by 1684 and probably some twenty years earlier,[3] and published as *The Mistaken Beauty, or the Lyar A Comedy* (1685, anonymous). Steele, however, seems to have turned to Corneille rather than to the English translation. It would be unlikely, in fact, that he knew the English version, which had not been performed or republished during his years in and around London; certainly *The Lying Lover* bears no greater resemblance to it than one might expect from two adaptations of one original.

He carefully followed *Le Menteur* in the main outline and some of the dialogue of the first three acts, broke from it in all but one of the five scenes of Act IV, and completely departed from the text in the last act, except for the final disposition of the lovers. His alterations are of two kinds. First, he created a number of new characters and situations more broadly humorous than those found in his model. He chose for comic valet not the expected prating servant but rather the young gentleman Latine, fresh from Oxford and full of witticisms, yet wise also in the ways of footmen and abigails; the comic climax of this invention comes in IV. ii, when Latine dazzles maid and mistress alike with his verbal pyrotechnics. Through Latine and genuine servants he ridiculed life below stairs: Lettice weeps copiously

---

[1] Winton, pp. 68–9. *Gentleman's Magazine*, lx (1790), Part ii, 993.
[2] Winton, pp. 70–1. *Correspondence*, p. 447, n. 1.
[3] Van Lennep, pp. 17, 124, 333. Pepys in his diary of 1667 refers to *The Mistaken Beauty* as an old play.

over the romance of Argalus and Parthenia before coolly conducting
a real-life romance of her own (IV. ii); the bright cookmaid masters
her emotions ('Good Madam, excuse me, I can't touch him.—I have
Bowels for him') to give Latine a sound drubbing. The masters and
mistresses as well as their servants are given new comic scenes. In
one of the funniest passages Steele ever wrote, the two loving cousins
Victoria and Penelope blight each other's beauty by applying excessive
powder and patches with enthusiastic malice (III. i). Old Bookwit
displays absurd delight at finding his abilities at courtship less rusty
than he believed (II. i); Penelope and Victoria gull Young Bookwit;
the girls unwittingly bare their jealousies in hypocritically polite
conversations. Finally, Steele introduced the bumbling watch and
the gaol-birds Charcole and Storm. In these added comic touches
he exceeded Corneille in social commentary, amusement at the
idiosyncrasies of the times, and satire on social foibles.

The second innovation shaped the fifth act, which differed so
radically and so suddenly from the rest of the play that Steele found
cause to defend it on grounds of morality. He claimed to have been
affected by Jeremy Collier's *Short View of the Immorality and Profaneness
of the English Stage* (1698):

> Mr. *Collier* had, about the Time wherein this was published, written
> against the Immorality of the Stage. I was (as far as I durst for fear of witty
> Men, upon whom he had been too severe) a great Admirer of his Work, and
> took it into my Head to write a Comedy in the Severity he required. In this
> Play I made the Spark or Heroe kill a Man in his Drink, and finding himself
> in Prison the next Morning, I give him the Contrition which he ought to
> have on that Occasion.[1]

Act V is a highly emotional condemnation of duelling; there is not
one humorous line or one unworthy sentiment. The tone is highly
serious, even tragic; the lines are largely blank verse, or what
approximates blank verse.

The English comic tradition was strong in Steele, and there are
echoes of earlier plays in *The Lying Lover*, but no startling resemblances. Smith claims that Steele's 'general model' for administering
'a pill to purge the rakishness of a thoughtless young gallant' was
Shadwell's *The Scowrers* (1690),[2] but there is no noticeable similarity
between the two plays, much less any borrowing. There is an echo
from Burnaby's *The Ladies Visiting-Day* (1701), but this and many other

---

[1] *Apology*, in *Tracts and Pamphlets*, pp. 311–12.   [2] Smith, p. 202.

casual similarities to earlier plays point to a general familiarity with the theatre rather than debts to specific authors.

STAGE HISTORY

The *Daily Courant* of 29 November 1703 advertised for Wednesday, 1 December, the *première* of 'a new Comedy never acted before, call'd *The Lying Lover*, or, *The Lady's Friendship*. Written by the Author of *The Funeral; or, Grief all-Amode*'. The advertisement for 1 December, however, announced postponement till the following day, and *The Lying Lover* opened at the Drury Lane Theatre on Thursday, 2 December. William Croft composed a set of eight act-tunes, probably used for special effects.[1] Four new songs, at least three set by Croft, Daniel Purcell, and Richard Leveridge, were introduced. Three were sung in comical circumstances obviously intended to produce hearty laughter: Penelope reads her admirer's lyrics 'To *Celia's* Spinet', interspersing self-adulatory commentary; Young Bookwit with great flourishes directs his band of musicians in '*Venus* has left her Grecian Isles'; and he reels drunkenly as he sings 'Since the Day of poor Man'. A cast of the leading performers of the company, most of whom also played in *The Funeral*, was assembled. Robert Wilks played Young Bookwit; Colley Cibber, Latine; and the sedate John Mills, Lovemore. Anne Oldfield and Jane Rogers acted Victoria and Penelope.

The comedy ran six nights, closing on 8 December with an author's benefit; the satisfactory initial run, however, must be attributed to excitement over a new comedy by the author of the popular *Funeral* rather than to any intrinsic merit. The play then disappeared from the stage for almost forty-three years; in the spring of 1746 a revival ran for four nights, and then again Steele's only stage failure vanished from the repertoire, this time permanently.

REPUTATION AND INFLUENCE

Oddly enough, the comedy even vanished from the minds of those most intimately connected with it or at least became hazy, for, from earliest references, a few years after the run, Steele and others either neglected it or confused its chronology. In the legal tussle between Steele and the manager Christopher Rich over the unfinished *Election of Gotham*, *The Lying Lover* received no notice; in printed

[1] *Verse*, p. 82.

accounts, from 1718 on, it was listed as Steele's third play, produced after *The Tender Husband*.[1] Only the newspaper advertisements provide a reliable first-hand account of its date. The two other early comedies were linked in people's minds and were twice published together in editions which did not include *The Lying Lover*, although the latter was sometimes bound with them. Except for reprints, indeed, the comedy was completely forgotten, edged into obscurity by the apathy of everyone including its author. Steele said it was 'damn'd for its Piety',[2] a view perhaps justified to some extent, but the play was, after all, an inferior work.

Uninteresting as *The Lying Lover* might seem, it was a part of the canon. It was therefore occasionally published for inclusion in the collections of Steele's works that were purchased by Englishmen throughout the century. At least thirteen editions appeared in London, Dublin, and Glasgow by 1776; copies were often bound with his other plays and sold under various title-pages.

One such collection rested in the library of Henry Fielding.[3] There are many touches in his works reminiscent of Steele; for example, the garnish scene in *Amelia*, Book I, Chapter iii, recalls IV. iv of *The Lying Lover*. Smith points out that 'the coquette-taming in *The Lying Lover* is closely imitated by Fielding in *Love in Several Masques*',[4] a comedy first staged in 1728. Indeed v. xii, xiii of Fielding's comedy are strikingly similar to *The Lying Lover*, v. iii. Wisemore comes to Lady Matchless, the widow he loves, disguised, as is Steele's Lovemore, 'in a Serjeant's Gown, his Hat over his Ears'. Enter Malvil, claiming he has slain Wisemore in a duel, and Lady Matchless, who has shied away from a second marriage, reveals her true feelings for her suitor. When he discovers himself, they are reunited in highly emotional speeches. Although Fielding did not specifically paraphrase Steele, the two actions bear such a strong resemblance that, in light of other literary connections, there can be little doubt that *The Lying Lover* influenced the scene.

Samuel Foote in 1762 produced *The Lyar*; but he acknowledged as source Lope de Vega, whom he mistakenly believed to be the author of the Spanish version. Later commentators have doubted his word. John Genest believed he had never seen the original but did know Steele: 'whether he had seen the Lying Lover or not, let any body

[1] Aitken, i. 92.

[2] *Apology*, in *Tracts and Pamphlets*, p. 312.

[3] Austin Dobson, *Eighteenth Century Vignettes*, Third Series (New York, 1896), p. 173.　　　　　　　　　　　　　　　　　　　　　　[4] Smith, p. 220, n. 37.

judge!'[1] A. W. Ward and Aitken continued the tradition that Foote borrowed from Steele. Examination of *The Lyar*, however, shows no incontrovertible debt; Foote may have worked from *Le Menteur* or even *The Mistaken Beauty*, because there are no instances of his having borrowed from Steele's many alterations rather than the translated passages.[2]

<h3 style="text-align:center">THE TEXT</h3>

Four editions of *The Lying Lover: Or, The Ladies Friendship* appeared in London during Steele's lifetime and a fifth three years after his death. A Dublin edition was published in 1725.

Bernard Lintott first published it on 26 January 1704, almost two months after the run opened. According to John Nichols, Lintott paid £21. 10s. for the rights.[3] It was the only play by Steele first issued under Lintott's imprint. Steele wrote some of the preliminary material within nine days before publication, for he mentioned a royal proclamation of 17 January in the Preface.

The text is relatively free from the verbal tangles that marred the first edition of *The Funeral*. The collational formula is $[A]^4$ a^4 $B-I^4$. Printing is regular and apparently unhurried; the work seems to have been distributed evenly between two presses. According to running-title evidence, two skeletons were used for sheets B, C, E, G, and I; the inner formes were imposed in one skeleton, the outer formes in another. Two more skeletons were used with equal regularity for the inner and outer formes of sheets D, F, and H. The preliminary sheets, [A] and a, were probably printed on the second press, but no running-title evidence exists.

The second edition, dated 1712, was advertised in the *Spectator*, no. 187, on 4 October 1711. While most extant copies have the imprint 'Printed for Bernard Lintott at the Cross Keys between the Two Temple-Gates in Fleetstreet. MDCCXII.', a copy at the University of Texas reads 'Printed for Bernard Lintott at the Middle-Temple-Gate in Fleet-Street. MDCCXII.' The most plausible

[1] Genest, iv. 649.

[2] For a different view of the ancestry and influence of *The Lying Lover* see Dorothea Frances Canfield, *Corneille and Racine in England* (New York, 1966), pp. 119-27.

[3] Nichols provides a list of 'copies when purchased' from a notebook of the Lintotts, including '1703-4, June 11, Lying Lovers [sic] £21. 10s. od.' 'June' is undoubtedly a misreading for 'Jan.' (John Nichols, *Literary Anecdotes of the Eighteenth Century*, 9 vols. (London, 1812-16), viii. 301.)

explanation for the two states is that the compositor followed the
copy-text, the first edition, without changing the imprint to match
Lintott's intervening change of address.[1] The error was caught and
the correction made during the run. This duodecimo was often bound
with the 1712 edition of *The Funeral; and The Tender Husband: Comedies*,
and a title-page was printed for the combined volumes.

The second edition was printed with some care. Obvious errors
were corrected; a few words were added or changed to render passages more graceful; necessary stage directions were added. However,
there are no corrections that suggest the hand of Steele. His concern
with the second edition of *The Funeral* had been dictated by his role
as public reformer; there was no need to curb the youthful enthu-
siasms of the characters in his second play, for he had done that as he
had written the play.

Nor do the other editions printed within his lifetime show evidence
that he revised them. The third, copied from the second, bears the
imprint 'Printed for William Mears at the Lamb without Temple
Bar. 1717.' The fourth, for which the third was copy-text, appeared
in the *Dramatick Works* of 1723. Although the title-pages of *The Funeral*
and *The Tender Husband* in this collection read 'Printed for J. Tonson',
the title-page of *The Lying Lover*, bound last in the volume, reads
'Printed for B. Lintot'. In 1725 an edition was printed by Stephen
Powell for George Risk in Dublin. This 16mo printing used the
1723 edition as copy-text. No more were published until the fifth
edition in 1732, 'Printed for Bernard Lintot; and sold by Henry
Lintot.'[2]

I use the first edition as copy-text. Since a few corrections made in
the second, for example an occasional addition of the stage direction
'*Aside*', obviously reflect the intentions of Steele although he did not
make them, I incorporate them in this edition. However, other
'improvements', such as the addition of an article to smooth a phrase

---

[1] Henry R. Plomer gives Lintott's address as the Middle Temple Gate in 1701–4
and the Cross Keys after 1709 (*A Dictionary of the Printers and Booksellers . . . From 1668
to 1725* (Oxford, 1922), pp. 189–90).

[2] D. F. Foxon identified a piracy of the fifth, possibly published by William Feales,
recognizable by the following details: on the title-page l. 3 reads 'OR THE' and the
penultimate line, 'overagainst'; the edition lacks press figures; also, the signatures
vary from those of Tonson ('A Piracy of Steele's *The Lying Lover*', *The Library*, Fifth
Series, x (1955), 127–9). In the British Museum Richard A. Christophers found a
collection of plays published by Feales containing the piracy with a cancel title-page
bearing the imprint 'London: Printed for W. Feales, at Rowe's-Head, over-against
St. Clement's Church in the Strand. M.DCC.XXXVI.' Christophers suggested in a
letter to me that the cancellation 'seems to pass the guilt even more positively on to
Feales than Mr. Foxon first suggested'.

('out of the College' for 'out of College'), have not been included, since Steele's intentions are by no means clear.

I have collated the following copies: first edition, University of Texas (two copies), Folger, Yale, Library of Congress; second edition, Folger; third edition, Folger; fourth edition, Folger; fifth edition, Folger; Dublin, 1725, Yale.

THE

LYING LOVER:

OR, THE

LADIES FRIENDSHIP.

A COMEDY.

Haec nôsse salus est adolescentulis.   Terence

[motto] Terence] ed.; Tertul. The source of the motto was misprinted in the first edition as 'Tertul.', i.e. Tertullian, an error retained as late as the Mermaid edition. Whether the error is Steele's or the compositor's cannot be ascertained. 'Terence' or 'Ter.' in manuscript would, at any rate, lend itself to misinterpretation as 'Tertul.'

ABBREVIATIONS USED IN THE NOTES

The following abbreviations are used in reference to early editions of *The Lying Lover*:

Q   First edition. London: Lintott, 1704.

D1   Second edition. London: Lintott, 1712.

D2   Third edition. London: Mears, 1717.

D3   Fourth edition. In *The Dramatick Works of Sir Richard Steele*. London: Lintott, 1723.

D4   Fifth edition. London: Lintott, 1732.

Du   First Dublin edition. Dublin: Risk, 1725.

TO HIS
GRACE
THE
DUKE of ORMOND.

My Lord,

Out of Gratitude to the Memorable and Illustrious Patron of my
Infancy, Your Grace's Grandfather, I presume to lay this Comedy
at Your Feet: The Design of it is to banish out of Conversation all
Entertainment which does not proceed from Simplicity of Mind, 5
Good-nature, Friendship, and Honour: Such a purpose will not,
I hope, be unacceptable to so great a Lover of Mankind as Your
Grace; and if Your Patronage can recommend it to all who love and
honour the Duke of ORMOND, its Reception will be as extensive
as the World it self.   10

'Twas the irresistible Force of this Humanity in Your Temper
that has carry'd You through the various Successes of War, with
the peculiar, and undisputed Distinction, That You have drawn
Your Sword without other Motive, than a passionate Regard for
the Glory of Your Country; since before You entred into its Ser- 15
vice, You were possess'd of its highest Honours, but could not be
contented with the Illustrious Rank Your Birth gave You, without
repeating the glorious Actions by which it was acquir'd.

But there cannot be less expected from the Son of an OSSORY,
than to contemn Life, to adorn it, and with Munificence, Affability, 20
Scorn of Gain, and Passion for Glory, to be the Honour and Example
to the Profession of Arms: All which engaging Qualities Your Noble
Family has exerted with so stedfast a Loyalty, that in the most
adverse Fortune of our Monarchy, Popularity, which in Others had
been invidious, was a Security to the Crown, when lodg'd in the 25
House of ORMOND.

Thus Your Grace enter'd into the Business of the World with so
great an Expectation; that it seem'd impossible there could be any

thing left, which might still conduce to the Honour of Your Name.
30 But the most memorable Advantage Your Country has gain'd this
Century, was obtain'd under Your Command; and Providence
thought fit to give the Wealth of the *Indies* into His Hands, who
only could despise it; while with a superiour Generosity, He knows
no Reward but in Opportunities of Bestowing. The great Personage
35 whom You succeed in Your Honours, made me feel, before I was
sensible of the Benefit, that this glorious Bent of Mind is Hereditary
to You; I hope, therefore, You will pardon me that I take the Liberty
of expressing my Veneration for his Remains, by assuring Your
Grace that I am,

40   MY LORD,
         Your Grace's most obedient,
            and most devoted,
              humble Servant,
                RICHARD STEELE.

THE
PREFACE,

Tho' it ought to be the Care of all Governments, that publick
Representations should have nothing in 'em but what is agreeable
to the Manners, Laws, Religion and Policy of the Place or Nation
in which they are exhibited; yet is it the general Complaint of
the more Learned and Virtuous amongst Us, that the English 5
Stage has extremely offended in this kind: I thought therefore
it would be an honest Ambition to attempt a Comedy, which
might be no improper Entertainment in a Christian Common-
wealth.

In order to this, the Spark of this Play is introduc'd with as much 10
Agility and Life, as He brought with Him from *France*; and as much
Humour as I could bestow upon Him in *England*. But he uses the
Advantages of a learned Education, a ready Fancy, and a liberal
Fortune, without the Circumspection and good Sense which should
always attend the Pleasures of a Gentleman; that is to say, a reason- 15
able Creature.

Thus he makes false Love, gets drunk, and kills his Man;
but in the fifth Act awakes from his Debauch, with the Compunction and Remorse which is suitable to a Man's finding Himself in a Gaol for the Death of his Friend, without His knowing 20
why.

The Anguish He there expresses, and the mutual Sorrow between
an only Child, and a tender Father in that Distress, are, perhaps, an
Injury to the Rules of Comedy; but I am sure they are a Justice to
those of Morality: And Passages of such a Nature being so frequently 25
applauded on the Stage, it is high time that we should no
longer draw Occasions of Mirth from those Images which the
Religion of our Country tells us we ought to tremble at with
Horrour.

But Her Most Excellent Majesty has taken the Stage into Her 30

20 His knowing] D1; knowing His

Consideration; and we may hope, by Her gracious Influence on the Muses, Wit will recover from its Apostacy; and that by being encourag'd in the Interests of Virtue, 'twill strip Vice of the gay Habit in which it has too long appear'd, and cloath it in its native
35 Dress of Shame, Contempt, and Dishonour.

PROLOGUE.

All the commanding Powers that awe Mankind
Are in a trembling Poet's Audience join'd,
Where such bright Gallaxies of Beauty sit,
And at their Feet assembled Men of Wit:
Our Author therefore owns his deep Despair   5
To entertain the Learned or the Fair:
Yet hopes that both will so much be his Friends,
To pardon what he does, for what h' intends;
He aims to make the coming Action move
On the dread Laws of Friendship, and of Love: 10
Sure then he'll find but very few severe,
Since there's of both so many Objects here;
He offers no gross Vices to your Sight,
Those too much Horrour raise for just Delight,
And to detain th' attentive knowing Ear   15
Pleasure must still have something that's severe;
If then you find our Author treads the Stage
With just Regard to a reforming Age;
He hopes, he humbly hopes, you'll think there's due
Mercy to him, for Justice done to you.   20

DRAMATIS PERSONAE.

MEN.

Old *Bookwit.*
Young *Bookwit.*
Lovemore.
Frederick.
5 *Latine.*
Storm.
Charcole.

Captain *Griffin.*
Mr. *Wilks.*
Mr. *Mills.*
Mr. *Toms.*
Mr. *Cibber.*
Mr. *Pinkethman.*
Mr. *Bullock.*

WOMEN.

Penelope.
Victoria.
10 *Betty.*
Lettice.

Mrs. *Rogers.*
Mrs. *Oldfield.*
Mrs. *Cox.*
Mrs. *Lucas.*

[*Simon, Servants, Chairman,*] Constable, *Watchmen, Turn-key,*
Maid, [*Gaoler*], *and several Gaol-birds.*

SCENE, *LONDON.*

12 *Constable*] ed.; *Constables*   12 *Watchmen*] ed.; *Watch*   13 *Maid*] ed.; *Cookmaid*

THE
LYING LOVER:
OR, THE
LADIES FRIENDSHIP.

Act I.

Scene, *St.* James's *Park.*

Enter Young Bookwit *and* Latine.

Latine. But have you utterly left *Oxford?*

Young Bookwit. For ever, Sir, for ever; my Father has given me
leave to come to Town, and I don't question but will let my return
be in my own Choice.—But *Jack*, you know we were talking in
Maudlin Walks last Week of the necessity, in Intrigues, of a faithful, 5
yet a prating Servant.—We agreed therefore to cast Lots who should
be the other's Footman for the present Expedition.—Fortune, that's
always blind, gave me the Superiority.

Latine. She shall be call'd no more so for that one Action: And I
am, Sir, in a literal Sense, your very humble Servant,— 10

Young Bookwit. Begin then the Duty of an useful Valet, and flatter
me egregiously—Has the Fellow fitted me? How is my Manner?
my Mein? Do I move freely? Have I kick'd off the Trammels of a
Gown? Or does not the Tail on't seem still tuck'd under my Arm?
where my Hat is with a pert Jirk forward, and little Hitch in my 15
Gate like a Scholastick Beau?—This Wigg, I fear, looks like a Cap.

Latine. No, faith, it looks like a Cap and Gown too; tho' at the
same time you look as if you ne'er had worn either—

Young Bookwit. But my Sword,—does it hang careless?—Do I look
bold, negligent, and erect? that is, do I look as if I cou'd kill a Man 20

<hr>

0.2 *Young* Bookwit] D1; Bookwit   In Q speech prefixes and stage directions
read 'Bookwit' when Old Bookwit is not on stage. In the present edition 'Young
Bookwit' is consistently used.

without being out of Humour? I horridly mistrust my self.—Am I
military enough in my Air? I fancy People see I understand Greek.
Don't I pore a little in my Visage?—Han't I a down bookish Lour?
a wise Sadness?—I don't look gay enough and unthinking, I fancy.

25   *Latine.* I protest you wrong your self:—You look very brisk, and
very ignorant.

    Young Bookwit. Oh fie:—I am afraid you flatter me.

    Latine. I don't, indeed.—I'll be hang'd if my Tutor wou'd know
either of us.—But good Master, to what use do you design to put
30 the noble Arts and Sciences he taught us.—The Conduct of our
Lives, the Government of our Passions were his daily talk to us,
good Man!

    Young Bookwit. Good Man! Why I'll obey his Precepts, but abridge
'em.—For as he us'd to advise me, I'll contract my Thoughts,—as
35 I'll tell you, *Jack.*—For the Passions, I'll turn 'em all into that one
dear Passion, Love; and when that's the only Torture of my Heart,
I'll give that tortur'd Heart quite away, deny there's any such
thing as Pain, and turn Stoick a shorter way than e'er thy Tutor
taught thee.—This is the new Philosophy, you Rogue you—

40   *Latine.* But you wou'd not in earnest be thought wholly illiterate?

    Young Bookwit. No; for as when I walk, I'd have you know by my
Motion I can dance; so when I speak I'd have you see I read,—yet
wou'd ordinarily neither cut Capers, nor talk Sentences.—But you
prate as if I came to Town to get an Employment;—No, hang
45 Business,—hang Care, let it live and prosper among the Men;—
I'll ne'er go near the solemn ugly things again,—I'll keep Company
with none but Ladies,—bright Ladies:—Oh *London! London!* Oh
Woman! Woman! I am come where thou livest, where thou shinest.

    Latine. Hey day! why, were there no Women in *Oxford*?

50   *Young Bookwit.* No, no; why, do you think a Bedmaker's a Woman?

    Latine. Yes, and thought you knew it.

    Young Bookwit. No, no, 'tis no such thing.—As he that is not
honest or brave is no Man; so she that is not witty or fair is no
Woman.—No, no, *Jack,*—to come up to that high Name, and
55 object of Desire—She must be gay and chast, she must at once
attract, and banish you.—I don't know how to express my self,—but
a Woman methinks is a Being between us and Angels:—She has

something in her that at the same time gives Awe and Invitation;
and I swear to you I was never out in't yet,—But I always judg'd
of Men, as I observ'd they judg'd of Women: There's nothing shews 60
a Man so much as the Object of his Affections.—But what do you
stare at so considerately?

Latine. Faith, Sir, I am wondring at you,—how 'tis possible you
could be so janty a Town-spark in a Moment, and have so easie a
Behaviour.—I look methinks to you as if I were really your 65
Footman—

Young Bookwit. Why, if you're serious in what you say—I owe it
wholly to the Indulgence of an excellent Father, in whose Company
I was always free, and unconstrain'd.—But what's this to Ladies,
Jack, to Ladies:—I was going to tell you I had study'd 'em, and 70
know how to make my Approaches to 'em by contemplating their
Frame, their inmost Temper:—I don't ground my hopes on the
scandalous Tales and Opinions your wild Fellows have of 'em,—
Fellows that are but mere Bodies,—Machines,—which at best can
but move gracefully,—No, I draw my Pretences from Philosophy, 75
from Nature,—

Latine. You'll give us by and by a Lecture over your Mistress;
you can dissect her.

Young Bookwit. That I can indeed, and have so accurately observ'd
on Woman, that I can know her Mind by her Eye, as well as her 80
Doctor shall her Health by her Pulse.—I can read Approbation
through a Glance of Disdain:—Can see when the Soul is divided by
a sparkling Tear that twinkles and betrays the Heart; a sparkling
Tear's the Dress and Livery of Love—Of Love made up of Hope and
Fear, of Joy and Grief.—   85

Latine. But what have the Wars to do with all this? Why must
you needs commence Soldier all of a sudden?

Young Bookwit. Were't not a taking Complement with my College
Face and Phrase t'accost a Lady—Madam, I bring your Ladyship a
learned Heart, one newly come from the University.—If you want 90
Definitions, Axioms, and Arguments, I am an able Schoolman,—
I've read *Aristotle* twice over, compar'd his jarring Commentators
too, examin'd all the famous Peripateticks, know where the Scotists,
and the Nominals differ: This certainly must needs enchant a Lady.

95   *Latine.* This is too much on th'other side.

Young Bookwit. The Name of Soldier bids you better welcome: 'Tis Valour and Feats done in the Field, a Man shou'd be cry'd up for;—nor is't so hard to atchieve—

Latine. The Fame of it you mean—

100   *Young Bookwit.* Yes; and that will serve.—'Tis but looking big, bragging with an easie Grace, and confidently mustering up an hundred hard Names they understand not: Thunder out *Villeroy*, *Catinat*, and *Bouffleurs*, speak of strange Towns and Castles, whose barbarous Names, the harsher they're to the Ear, the rarer and more
105   taking.—Still running over Lines, Trenches, Outworks, Counterscarps, and Forts, Citadels, Mines, Countermines, Pickeering, Pioneers, Centinels, Patroles, and others, without Sense or Order, that matters not, the Women are amaz'd, they admire to hear you rap 'em out so readily; and many a one that went no farther for't,
110   retailing handsomely some warlike Terms, passes for a brave Fellow. —Don't stand gaping, but live and learn, my Lad,—I can tell thee ten thousand Arts, to make thee known and valued in these Regions of Wit, and Gallantry, the Parks—the Playhouse—

Latine. Now you put me in mind where we are,—What have we
115   to do here thus early—now there's no Company?—

Young Bookwit. Oh! Sir, I have put on so much of the Soldier with my Red-coat, that I came here t'observe the Ground I am to engage upon.—Here must I act I know some Lover's Part, and therefore came to view this pleasant Walk.—I privately rambled to Town last
120   *November.*—Here, ay here,—I stood and gaz'd at high Mall, 'til I forgot 'twas Winter, so many pretty she's marched by me.—Oh! to see the dear things trip, trip along, and breath so short, nipt with the Season.—I saw the very Air not without Force leave their dear Lips.—Oh! they were intollerably handsome.

125   *Latine.* You'll see, perhaps, such to Day;—but how to come at 'em—

Young Bookwit. Ay, there's it, how to come at 'em—

Latine. Are you generous?

Young Bookwit. I think I am no Niggard.

130   *Latine.* You must entertain them high, and bribe all about 'em. They talk of *Ovid*, and his Art of loving, be liberal and you out do

his Precepts,—The Art of Love, Sir, is the Art of giving—Be free
to Women, they'll be free to you. Not ev'ry open handed Fellow
hits it neither. Some give by Lapfulls, and yet ne'er oblige. The
manner, you know, of doing a thing is more than the thing it 135
self—Some drop a Jewel which had been refus'd, if bluntly
offer'd.

Young Bookwit. Some lose at Play what they design a Present.

Latine. Right—the Skill is to be generous, and seem not to know
it of your self, 'tis done with so much ease; but a liberal Blockhead 140
presents his Mistress as he'd give an Alms—

Young Bookwit. Leaving such Blockheads to their deserv'd ill
Fortune—Tell me if thou know'st these Ladies?

Latine. No, not I, Sir; they are above an Academick Converse many
Degrees—I've seen ten thousand Verses writ in the University on 145
Wenches not fit to be either of their Handmaids.—I never spoke to
such a fine thing as either in my whole Life.—I'm downright asleep
o'sudden,—I must fall back, and glad it is my place to do so: Yet I
can get you Intelligence perhaps.—I'll to the Footman.

Young Bookwit. Do you think he'll tell?—   150

Latine. He wou'd not to you perhaps,—but to a Brother Footman
—Do but listen at the Entrance of the Mall at Noon, and you'll
have all the Ladies Characters in Town among their Lacquies.—You
know all Fame begins from our Domesticks—

Young Bookwit. That was a wise Man's Observation,—Follow 155
him, and know what you can.

                                        Exit Latine.

               Enter Penelope, Victoria, Simon, *and*
                            Lettice.

Penelope. A Walk round wou'd be too much for us,—we'll keep
the Mall.—But to our Talk.—I must confess I have Terrors when
I think of marrying *Lovemore*: He is indeed a Man of an honest
Character,—he has my good Opinion, but Love does not always 160
follow that.—He is so wise a Fellow, always so precisely in the
right, so observing and so jealous,—he's blameless indeed, but not
to be commended: What good he has, has no Grace in't; he's one

                   147 asleep] D1; sleep

of those who's never highly mov'd, except to Anger.—Give me a
165 Man that has agreeable Faults rather than offensive Virtues.

Victoria. Offensive Virtues, Madam?

Penelope. Yes,—I don't know how,—there's a sort of Virtue, or
Prudence, or what you'll call it, that we can but just approve.—
That does not win us,—*Lovemore* wants that Fire—that Conversa-
170 tion-spirit I wou'd have—They say he's learned as well as discreet,
but I'm no Judge of that: I'm sure he's no Woman's Scholar; his
Wisdom he should turn into Wit, and his Learning into Poetry or
Humour.

Victoria. Well, I'm not so much of your Mind, I like a sober
175 Passion.

Penelope. A sober Passion! you took me up just now when I said
an offensive Virtue.—Bless me: (*Stumbling almost to a Fall.*)

Young Bookwit. (*Catching her.*) How much am I indebted to an
Accident, that favours me with an Occasion of this small Service! for
180 'tis to me an Happiness beyond Expression thus to kiss your Hand.

Penelope. The occasion, methinks, is not so obliging, nor the
Happiness you mention worth that Name, Sir.

Young Bookwit. 'Tis true, Madam, I owe it all to Fortune, neither
your Kindness nor my Industry had any share in't: Thus am I still
185 as wretched as I was, for this Happiness I so much prize had doubtless been refus'd my want of Merit.

Penelope. 'T has very soon you see lost what you valued in it: But
I find you and I, Sir, have a different Sense; for in my Opinion we
enjoy with most Pleasure, what we attain with least Merit.—Merit
190 is a claim, and may pretend justly to favour, when without it what's
conferr'd is more unexpected, and therefore more pleasing.

Young Bookwit. You talk very well, Madam, of an Happiness you
can't possibly be acquainted with, the enjoying without Desert.
But indeed you have done me a very singular good Office, in letting
195 me know my self very much qualify'd for Felicity.

Victoria. [*Aside.*] I swear he's a very pretty Fellow, and how readily
the thing talks.—I begin to pity *Lovemore*, but I begin to hate
Penelope. How he looks! he looks at her!

179 (*Catching her*)] D1; [om.]

Young Bookwit. But judge, Madam, what the condition of a passionate Man must be, that can approach the Hand only of her 200 he dies for, when her Heart is inaccessible—

Penelope. 'Tis very well the Heart lies not so easily to be seiz'd as the Hand.—I find—Pray, Sir,—[*Aside.*] I don't know what there's in this very odd Fellow, I'm not angry, tho' he's down right rude.— But I must—   205

Young Bookwit. But your Heart, Madam, your Heart—(*Pressingly.*)

Penelope. You seem'd, Sir, I must confess, to have shewn a ready Civility, when I'd like to fall just now, for which I cou'd not but thank you, and permit you to say what you pleas'd on that occasion —But your Heart, Madam! 'tis a sure Sign, Sir, you know not me. 210 —Or if you are what indeed you seem—a Gentleman—Sure you forget your self, or rather you talk by Memory, a Form of Cant which you mistake for something that's gallant.

Young Bookwit. Madam, I very humbly beg your Pardon, If I press'd too far, and too abruptly.—I forgot indeed that I broke 215 through Decencies, and that tho' you have been long a Familiar to me, I am a Stranger to you.

Penelope. Pray, familiar Stranger, what can you mean? I never saw you before this instant, nor you me, I believe.

Young Bookwit. Perhaps not that you know of, Madam,—For your 220 Humility, it seems, makes you so little sensible of your own Perfec- tion, that you o'erlook your Conquest; nor have you e'er observ'd me, tho' I hover Day and Night about your Lodging, haunt you from Place to Place, at Balls, in the Park, at Church.—I gave you all the Serenades you've had, yet never till this Minute cou'd I find, 225 and this Minute an unfortunate one—But this is always my Luck, when I'm out of the Field.

Victoria. You've travail'd then, and seen the Wars, Sir?

Young Bookwit. I—Madam—I—All that I know of the matter is, that *Lewis* the Fourteenth mortally hates me. They talk of French 230 Gold.—What Heaps have I refus'd!—Yet to be generous e'en to an Enemy, I must allow that Prince has Reason for his Rancour to me. —There has not been a Skirmish, Siege, or Battel since I bore Arms, I made not one in: No, nor the least Advantage got o' the Enemy but

212 of] ed.; or   216 tho'] D1; [om.]

235 I had my Share, tho' perhaps not all my Share o'th' Glory.—You've seen my Name, tho' you don't know it, often in the *Gazette*.

Penelope. I never read News.

Enter Latine.

Latine. What Tale's he telling now Tro?

Young Bookwit. You've never heard, I suppose, of such Names as
240 *Ruremonde*, *Keyserwart*, and *Leige*: Nor read of an English Gentleman left dead by his Precipitancy upon a Parapet at *Venlo*.—I was thought so indeed, when the first account came away.—Every Man has his Failings.—Rashness is my Fault.

Latine. Don't you remember a certain Place call'd *Oxford* among
245 your Towns, Sir.

Young Bookwit. Shaw, away—oh!—oh!—I beg your Pardon, Ladies; this Fellow knows I was shot in my left Arm, and cannot bear the least Touch, yet will still be rushing on me.

Latine. (*Aside.*) He has a Lie, I think, in every Joint.

250 *Penelope.* Do you bear any Commission, Sir?

Young Bookwit. There's an Intimate of mine, a General Officer, who has often said, *Tom*, if thou would'st but stick to any one Application, thou might'st be any thing—'Tis my Misfortune, Madam, to have a Mind too extensive. I began last Summer's
255 Campaign with the renowned Prince *Eugene*, but was forc'd to fly into *Holland* for a Duel with that rough Captain of the *Hussars*, *Paul Diack*—They talk of a Regiment for me—But those things—besides it will oblige me to attend it, and then I can't follow Honour where'er she's busiest, but must be confin'd to one Nation—
260 When indeed 'tis rather my way of serving with such of our Allies as most want me.

Penelope. But I see you Soldiers never enjoy such a thing as Rest— You but come home in Winter to turn your Valour on the Ladies, 'tis but just a change of your Warfare.

265 *Young Bookwit.* I had immediately return'd to *Holland*, but your Beauties at my Arrival here disarm'd me, Madam, made me a Man of Peace, or rais'd a Civil War within me rather.—You took me Prisoner at first sight, and to your Charms I yielded up an Heart, till then unconquer'd. Martial Delights (once best and dearest to

me) vanish'd before you in a Moment, and all my Thoughts grew 270
bent to please and serve you.

Lettice. *Lovemore*'s in the Walk, Madam, he'll be in a fit.

Young Bookwit. Rob me o'th' sudden thus of all my Happiness!
Yet e're you quite forsake me, authorize my Passion, licence my
innocent Flames, and give me leave to love such charming Sweetness. 275

Penelope. He that will love, and knows what 'tis to love, will ask
no Leave of any but himself.

Exit Ladies [with Servants].

Young Bookwit. Follow 'em, *Jack.*

Latine. I know as much of 'em already as needs. The Footman was
in his talking Vein—The handsomer of the two, says he, I serve, 280
and she lives in the Garden.

Young Bookwit. What Garden?

Latine. *Covent Garden*: The other lies there too, I did not stay to
ask her Name, but I shall meet him again, I took particular notice
of the Livery.   285

Young Bookwit. Ne'er trouble thy self to know which is which,
my Heart and my good Genius tell me 'tis she, that pretty she I
talk'd to.

Latine. If, with respect to your Worship's Opinion, I might presume to be of a contrary one, I should think the other the handsomer 290
now.

Young Bookwit. What the dumb thing! the Picture—No, Love is
the Union of Minds, and she that engages mine must be very well
able to express her own. But I suppose some scolding Landlady has
made you thus enamour'd with Silence. But here are two o'th' 295
dearest of my old Comrades, they seem amaz'd at something by
their Action.

Enter Lovemore *and* Frederick.

Frederick. How! a Collation on the Water, and Musick too?

Lovemore. Yes, Musick and a Collation.

Frederick. Last Night?   300

Lovemore. Last Night too.

Frederick. An handsome Treat?

Lovemore. A very noble one.

Frederick. Who gave it?

305 *Lovemore.* That I'm yet to learn.

Young Bookwit. How happy am I to meet you here?

Lovemore. When I embrace you thus—no Happiness can equal mine. (*Saluting.*)

Young Bookwit. I thrust my self intrudingly upon you; but you'll

310 pardon a Man o'erjoy'd to see you.

Lovemore. Where you're always welcome you never can intrude.

Young Bookwit. What were you talking of?

Lovemore. Of an Entertainment.

Young Bookwit. Given by some Lover?

315 *Lovemore.* As we suppose.

Young Bookwit. That Circumstance deserves my Curiosity; pray go on, and let me share the Story.

Lovemore. Some Ladies had the Fiddles last Night.

Young Bookwit. Upon the Water too methought you said?

320 *Lovemore.* Yes, 'twas upon the Water.

Young Bookwit. Water often feeds the Flame.

Lovemore. Sometimes.

Young Bookwit. And by Night too?

Lovemore. Yes, last Night.

325 *Young Bookwit.* He chose his time well—The Lady is handsome?

Lovemore. In most Mens eyes she is.

Young Bookwit. And the Musick?

Lovemore. Good as we hear.

Young Bookwit. Some Banquet follow'd?

330 *Lovemore.* A sumptuous one they say.

Young Bookwit. And neither of you all this while know who gave this Treat? ha, ha.

Lovemore. D'ye laugh at it?

Young Bookwit. How can I chuse to see you thus admire a slight

335 Divertisement I gave my self?

Lovemore. You?

Young Bookwit. Ev'n I—

Lovemore. Why have you got a Mistress here already?

Young Bookwit. I should be sorry else: I've been in Town this

340 Month and more, though for some Reasons I appear but little yet

by Day. I'th' dark o'th' Evening I peep out, and *incognito* make some
Visits. Thus had I spent my time but ill, were not—

Latine. [*Aside to Young* Bookwit.] Do you know what you say,
Sir?—Don't lay it on so thick—

Young Bookwit. Nay, you must be sure to take care to be in the 345
way as soon as they land, to shew up Stairs—I beg Pardon, I was
giving my Fellow some Directions about receiving some Women of
Quality that sup with me to Night *incog*—But you're my dearest
Friends, and shall hear all—

Frederick. ([*Aside*] *to* Lovemore.) How luckily your Rival dis- 350
covers himself.

Young Bookwit. I took five Barges, and the fairest kept for my
Company; the other four I fill'd with Musick of all sorts, and of all
sorts the best; in the first were Fiddles, in the next Theorbo, Lutes,
and Voices.   355
Flutes and such Pastoral Instruments i'th' third.
Loud Musick from the fourth did pierce the Air;
Each Consort vy'd by turns,
Which with most Melody shou'd charm our Ears.
The fifth the largest of 'em all was neatly hung,   360
Not with dull Tapistry, but with green Boughs,
Curiously interlac'd to let in Air,
And every Branch with Jessemins, and Orange Posies deckt.
In this the Feast was kept.
Hither with five other Ladies I led her, whose Beauty alone governs 365
my Destiny. Supper was serv'd up straight; I will not trouble you
with our Bill of Fare, what Dishes were best lik'd, what Sauces most
commended; 'tis enough I tell you this delicious Feast was of six
Courses, twelve Dishes to a Course.

Latine. (*Aside.*) That's indeed enough of all Conscience.   370

Lovemore. (*Aside.*) Oh the Torture of Jealousie! [*To Young* Bookwit.] But, Sir, how seem'd the Lady to receive this Entertainment?
We must know that.

Young Bookwit. Oh! that was the height on't.—She, I warrant you,
was quite negligent of all this matter. You know their way. They 375
must not seem to like—No, I warrant it wou'd not so much as smile

to make the Fellow vain, and believe he had Power to move Delight
in her—ha, ha.

    Lovemore. But how then?

380   *Young Bookwit.* Why you must know my Humour grew Poetick.—
I pull'd off my Sword-knot, and with that bound up a Coronet of
Ivy, Laurel, and Flowers, with that round my Temples, and a Plate
of richest Fruits in my Hand; on one Knee I presented her with it
as a *Cornucopia,* an offering from her humble Swain of all his Harvest
385 —To her the *Ceres* of our genial Feast, and rural Mirth.—She
smil'd,—The Ladies clap'd their Hands, and all our Musick struck
sympathetick Rapture at my Happiness;
While gentle Winds, the River, Air, and Shore
Eccho'd the Harmony in Notes more soft
390 Than they receiv'd it. Methought
All Nature seem'd to die for Love like me.
To all my Heart and every Pulse beat time.—
Oh the Pleasures of successful Love!
ha, *Lovemore!* ha! What hast thou got a good Office lately.—
395 You're afraid I shou'd make some Request. Prithee ben't so shy, I
have nothing to ask but of my Mistress; what's the matter?

    Lovemore. I only attend, Sir, I only attend—

    Young Bookwit. Then I'll go on.

As soon as we had supp'd the Fireworks play'd,
400 Squibbs of all sorts were darted through the Skies,
Whose spreading Fires made a new Day.
A flaming Deluge seem'd to fall from Heaven,
And with such Violence attack'd the Waves,
You wou'd have thought the fiery Element
405 Had left his Sphere, to ruine his moist Enemy.
Their Contest done, we landed, danc'd till Day,
Which hasty *Sol* disturb'd us with too soon.
Had he ta'en our Advice, or fear'd my Anger,
He might in *Thetis'* Lap have slept as long
410 As at *Alcmena's* Labour he's reported:
But steering not as we wou'd have prescrib'd,
He put a Period to our envy'd Mirth.

Lovemore. Trust me, you tell us Wonders, and with a Grace as
rare as the Feast it self, which all our Summer's Mirth can't equal.

Young Bookwit. My Mistress took me o'th' sudden—I had not a 415
Day's Warning.

Lovemore. The Treat was costly tho', and finely order'd.

Young Bookwit. I was forc'd to take up with this Trifle. He that
wants time can't do as he wou'd.

Lovemore. Farewel, we shall meet again at more Leisure.   420

Young Bookwit. Number me among your Creatures.

Lovemore. [*Apart to* Frederick.] Oh Jealousie! Thou Rack, Jealousie!

Frederick. What Reason have you to feel it; the Circumstances of
the Feast, nothing agree—

Lovemore. In Time and Place they do; the rest is nothing.   425

                     Exeunt Frederick *and* Lovemore.

Latine. May I speak now, Sir, without Offence.

Young Bookwit. 'Tis in your Choice now to speak or not, but
before Company you'll spoil all.

Latine. Do you walk abroad and talk in your Sleep? or do you use
to tell your Dreams for current Truth?   430

Young Bookwit. Dull Brain!

Latine. Why you beat out mine, with your Battels, your Fireworks, your Musick, and your Feasts. You've found an excellent
way to go to the Wars, and yet keep out of Danger—Then you feast
your Mistresses at the cheapest rate that e'er I knew: Why d'ye 435
make 'em believe you ha' been here these six Weeks?

Young Bookwit. My Passion has the more Growth, and I the better
Ground to make Love.

Latine. You'd make one believe fine things that wou'd but hearken
to you.—But this Lady might soon have found you out—   440

Young Bookwit. Some Acquaintance I have got however; this is
making Love, Scholar, and at the best rate too.

Latine. To speak Truth, I'm hardly come to my self yet, your
great Supper lies on my Stomach still. I defie *Pontack* to have
prepar'd a better o'th' sudden. Your inchanted Castles, where 445
Strangers found strange Tables strangely furnish'd with strange
Cates, were but sixpenny Ordinaries to the fifth Barge; you were

an excellent Man to write Romances, for having Feasts and Battels
at Command, your *Quixot* in a Trice wou'd over-run the World,
450 revelling and skirmishing cost you nothing; then you vary your
Scene with so much ease, and ship from Court to Camp with such
Facility—

Young Bookwit. I love thus to outvie a News-monger; and as soon
as I perceive a Fellow thinks his Story will surprize—I choke him
455 with a Stranger, and stop his Mouth with an *ex tempore* Wonder:
Didst thou but know what Pleasure 'tis to cram their own News
down their Throats again!—

Latine. 'Tis fine, but may prove dangerous Sport, and may
involve us in a Peck of Troubles: Prithee, *Tom*, consider that I am
460 of Quality to be kick'd or cain'd by this L—

Young Bookwit. Hush, hush, call it not Lying, as for my waging
War it is but just I snatch and steal from Fortune that Fame which
she denies me Opportunity to deserve—My Father has cramp'd me
in a College, while all the World has been in Action. Then as to my
465 lying to my Mistress, 'tis but what all the Lovers upon Earth do.—
Call it not then by that course Name a Lie. 'Tis Wit, 'tis Fable,
Allegory, Fiction, Hyperbole, or be it what you call it—The
World's made up almost of nothing else. What are all the grave
Faces you meet in publick?—Mere silent Lies, dark solemn Fronts,
470 by which they wou'd disguise vain empty silly Noddles.—But after
all, to be serious, since I am resolv'd honestly to love, I don't care
how artfully I obtain the Woman I pitch upon.—Besides, did you
ever know any of them acknowledge they lov'd as soon as they
lov'd.—No, they'l let a Man dwell upon his Knees—whom they
475 languish to receive into their Arms.—They're no fair Enemy—
Therefore 'tis but just that—

> *We use all Arts the Fair to undermine,*
> *And learn with Gallantry to hide Design.*

Exeunt.

[*The End of the First Act.*]

Act II. Scene i.

Enter Old Bookwit, Penelope, *and* Lettice.

Old Bookwit. Mistress *Penelope*, I have your Father's Leave to wait upon you, Madam, and talk to you this Morning; nay, to talk to you of Marriage.

Penelope. To talk to me of Marriage, Sir?

Old Bookwit. Yes, Madam, in behalf of my Son *Tom Bookwit*.   5

Penelope. (*Aside.*) Nay, there may perhaps be something said to that.

Old Bookwit. I sent for him from *Oxford* with that Design, he came to Town but Yesterday; and if a Father can judge, he brings from a College the Mein and Air of a Court—I love my Son entirely, and hope, Madam, you take my Thoughts as to you, to be no want of 10 Respect to you.

Penelope. 'Twere want of Sense, Sir, to do that.

Old Bookwit. (*Aside.*) If I can remember my Stile to my Mistress of old, I'll ease *Tom's* way, and raise her Expectation of my Son. [*To* Penelope.] Madam, had I my Hat, my Feather, Pantaloons, and 15 Jerkin on, as when I woo'd your humble Servant's Mother, I wou'd deliver you his Errand. I married her just such a young thing as you; her Complexion was charming, but not indeed with all your Sweetness.

Penelope. Oh! Sir!   20

Old Bookwit. Her Neck and Bosom were the softest Pillows, her Shape was not of that nice sort; some young Women suffer in Shapes of their Mother's making, by spare Diet, straight Lacing, and constant Chiding. But 'twas the Work of Nature, free, unconstrain'd, healthy and—But her Charms had not all that Emanation which 25 yours have.

Penelope. Oh fie! fie!

Old Bookwit. Not those thousand thousand Graces, that soft Army of Loves and Zephirs, Millions of airy Beings that attend around you, and appear only to the second Sight of Lovers.   30

13 (*Aside.*)] D1; [om.]

Penelope. Oh fie! Pray, good Sir, you'll leave nothing for your Son to say.

Old Bookwit. (*Aside.*) I did not think I had such a Memory. I find the Women are now certainly Daughters of the Women before 'em.
35 —Flattery still does it. [*To* Penelope.] *Tom* is my only Son, and I extremely desire to have him settled.—I own I think him of much Merit.

Penelope. He wou'd derogate from his Birth were he not much a Gentleman. But to receive a Man in the Character of a Pretender at first sight—
40 *Old Bookwit.* I'll walk him by and by before your Window, where your own Eyes shall judge.—I think there's nothing above his Pretences but your self; but when one of so many excellent Qualities bestows her self it must be Condescension.—You shall not answer —Farewel, Daughter: We are but too apt to believe what we wish—
Exit Old Bookwit.

45 *Penelope.* 'Tis as you said, *Lettice,* Old *Bookwit* came to propose his Son.

Lettice. I over heard the old Gentleman talk of it last Night.—But, Madam, you han't heard the Song that was made on you.—Oh! 'tis mighty pretty. The Gentleman is dying for you, he says it, pure
50 pure Verses.

Penelope. Whoever writ 'em, he's not the first Poet I have made. They may talk, and say Nature makes a Poet, but I say Love makes a Poet. Don't you see elder Brothers, who are by Nature born above Wit, shall fall in Love, and write Verses—nay, and pretty good ones,
55 considering they can tagg 'em to Settlements: But let's see, (*Reading.*)

To *Celia's* Spinet.

Thou soft Machine that do'st her Hand obey,
Tell her my Grief in thy harmonious Lay.

Poor Man—

60
To shun my Moan to thee she'll fly,
To her Touch be sure reply,
And, if she removes it, die.

The Device is just and truly poetical.
Know thy Bliss—

Ay, ay, there I come in.   65

> *Know thy Bliss, with Rapture shake,*
> *Tremble o'er all thy numerous Make;*
> *Speak in melting Sounds my Tears,*
> *Speak my Joys, my Hopes, my Fears.*

Which all depend upon me.   70

> *Thus force her when from me she'd fly,*
> *By her own hand, like me, to dye.*

Well, certainly nothing touches the Heart of Woman so much as Poetry. I suppose the Master is in the next Room, 'tis his Hour, desire him to walk in. 'Twill make ones Ears tingle, a Song o' one's 75 self! (*Here the Song is perform'd to a Spinet.*)

Well, dost think, *Lettice*, my grave Lover writ this fine thing—say'st thou?

Lettice. No, Madam,—no body writes Songs on those they are sure of.   80

Penelope. Sure of me, the Insolent!

Lettice. Nay, I know no more but that he said he'd turn me away as soon as he had married you.

Penelope. 'Tis like enough.—That's the common Practice of your jealous headed Fellows.—Well, I have a good mind to dress my self 85 anew, put on my best Looks, and send for him to dismiss him.—I know he loves me.

Lettice. I never knew him shew it but by his Jealousie.

Penelope. As you say, a jealous Fellow Love?—'tis all Mistake, 'tis only for himself he has Desires; nor cares what the Object of his 90 Wishes suffers so he himself has Satisfaction.—No, he has a Gluttony, an Hunger for me.

Lettice. An Hunger for you!—I protest, Madam, if you'd let me be his Cook, and make you ready, I'd poison him. But I'm glad *Simon* disobey'd you, and told the Gentleman's Servant who you 95 were, and your Lodging—

Penelope. Did the Rogue do so?—Call him hither.

Lettice. Simon, why *Simon*.

Enter Simon.

Penelope. Sirrah, I find I must at last turn you off, you saucy

100 Fellow; don't stand staring and dodging with your Feet, and wearing out your Livery Hat with squeezing for an Excuse, but answer me, and that presently.

Simon. I will, Madam, as soon as you ask me a Question.

Penelope. Not afore then,—Mr. Pert: Don't you know you told the
105 Gentleman's Footman in the Park who I was, against my constant Order, when I walk early. Come, Sirrah, tell all that pass'd between you.

Simon. Why, Madam, the Gentleman's Gentleman came up to me very civilly, and said his Master was in Discourse with my Lady
110 he suppos'd.—Then he fell into talk about Vails,—about Profits in a Service: At last, after a deal of civil Discourse between us—

Penelope. Come, without this Preamble,—what he ask'd you, Impertinence,—tell that, do—

Simon. He ask'd about you, and Madam *Victoria.*—I said, the
115 handsomest of the two is my Lady.

Penelope. Speak on boldly, *Simon*, I'm never angry at a Servant that speaks truth.

Simon. He told me he shou'd be very proud of my Acquaintance: Indeed, Madam, the Man was very well spoken, and shewed a
120 great deal of Respect for me, on your Ladyship's Account.—He is a mighty well spoken Man, and said, he found I was a smart Gentleman—Said he'd come again.

Penelope. Go, you have done your Business—Go down.

Exit [Simon].

Lettice. Well, after all, Madam, I did not think that Gentleman
125 displeas'd you.

Penelope. Had but young *Bookwit* his Mein and Conversation, how easily would he exclude *Lovemore.*

Enter Servant.

Servant. Mr. *Lovemore* is coming up, Madam.

Penelope. He has not heard sure of this new Proposal.

Lettice. 'Tis possible he may, and come to rant, or upbraid your
130 Ladyship; I wonder you endure him on these Occasions.

Penelope. I'll rack his very Heart-strings. He shall know all that Man e'er suffer'd for his native Mistress, Woman.

128 *Servant.*] D1 (*Ser.*); [om.]

Lettice. His Father, Madam, has been so long coming out of *Suffolk.*—There are strange Tricks in the World, but 'tis not my 135 place to speak—

Penelope. However his Father may come at last, I will not wholly lose him, as bad as he is he's better than no Husband at all.—Stay in the Room, I'll talk to you as if he were not present.—

Enter Lovemore.

Lovemore. Ah! *Penelope!* inconstant! fickle *Penelope!*   140

Penelope. But, *Lettice,* you don't tell me what the Gentleman said; now there's no Body here you may speak—

Lovemore. Now there's no Body here!—Then I am a Thing, an Utensil.—I am no body,—I have no Essence that I am sensible of—I think 'twill be so soon.—This ingrate,—this perjur'd!   145

Penelope. Tell me, I say—How the Match happened to break off?

Lovemore. This is downright Abuse. What! don't you see me, Madam?

Lettice. He had the Folly, upon her being commonly civil to him, to talk of directing her Affairs before his time: In the first place he 150 thought it but necessary her Maid, her faithful Servant Mrs. *Betty* shou'd be remov'd.

Lovemore. Her faithful Servant, Mrs. *Betty,*—Her Betrayer, her Whisperer Mrs. *Lettice.*—Madam, wou'd you but hear me.—I will be heard—   155

Penelope. Prithee step, *Lettice,* and see what Noise is that without.

Lovemore. The Noise is here, Madam; 'tis I that make what you call Noise.—'Tis I that claim aloud my right, and speak to all the World the Wrongs I suffer.

Penelope. Cooling Herbs well steep'd—a good Anodine at Night, 160 made of the Juice of Hellebore, with very thin Diet, may be of use in these Cases. (*Both looking at him as disturb'd.*)

Lovemore. Cases!—What Cases! I shall downright run mad with this damn'd Usage. Am I a Jest?

Lettice. A Jest!—no Faith, this is far from a merry Madness.— 165 Ha! ha! ha!

Lovemore. Hark'e, *Lettice*—I'll downright box you—Hold your Tongue, Gipsy—

Lettice. Dear Madam, save me.—Go you to him—

170 *Penelope.* Let him take you.—Bless me—how he stares,—take her.

Lettice. Take her. ⎫
⎬ (*Running round each other.*)
Penelope. Take her. ⎭

Lovemore. Very fine.—No, Madam, your Gallant, your Spark last Night; your fine Dancer, Entertainer shall take you.—He that was 175 your Swain, and you, I warrant, a fantastick Nymph of the Flood, or Forest; ha! ha! ha! to be out all Night with a young Fellow.— Oh! that makes you change your Countenance, do's it so?—Fine Lady,—You wonder how I came to know,—why chuse a discreeter the next time—he told me all himself.—Swoon,—die for Shame at 180 hearing of these Words—do—

Penelope. I am indeed downright asham'd for him that speaks 'em; whence this Insolence, if not from utter Distraction, under this Roof?

Lovemore. Oh! the Ingrate! Have not I, Madam, two long Years, two Ages, with humblest Resignation depended on your Smile; and 185 shall I suffer one of Yesterday's—to treat you, to dance all Night with you.

Penelope. Speak softly—my Father's coming down.

Lovemore. Thy Father's coming down! faithless!—Thou hast no Father. But to cross me by Night upon the Water!

190 *Penelope.* Well, by Night upon the Water!—What then?—

Lovemore. Yes, all Night.

Penelope. What of that?

Lovemore. Without blushing when you hear of't.

Penelope. Blush for what!—What do you drive at?

195 *Lovemore.* Can you then cooly ask what 'tis I mean, thou Reveller, thou Rambler, a fine young Lady, with your Midnight Frolicks: But what do I pretend to?—I know not how with bended Knees to call you *Ceres*,—make you an Offering of Summers Fruits, and Deifie your Vanity.—Thou art no Goddess, thou'rt a very Woman, 200 with all the Guile.—your Barges! your Treats! your Fireworks!

Penelope. What means the Insolent!—You grow insufferable.

Lovemore. Oh *Penelope*! that Look, that disdainful Look has pierc'd my Soul, and ebb'd my Rage to Penitence and Sorrow.—I own my Fault,—I'm too rash—

205 *Penelope.* Th' imaginary Enemies you raise are but mere Forms of

your sickly Brain;—so I think, and scorn 'em. A diffident, an
humerous, and ungenerous Man, who without Grounds calls me
inconstant, shall surely find me so: She will be very happy that takes
a constant Man with twenty thousand Humours.

Lovemore. Is it a Fault my Life's bound up in thee,   210
That all my Powers change with thy Looks,
That my Eyes glote on thee when thou'rt present,
And ake and roll for Light when thou'rt absent?

Penelope. (*Aside.*) A little ill Usage, I see, improves a Lover
strangely; I never heard him speak so well in my Life before.   215

Lovemore. Of you I am not jealous
'Tis my own Indesert that gives me Fears,
And Tenderness forms Dangers where they're not;
I doubt and envy all things that approach thee:
Not a fond Mother of a long wish'd for only Child beholds with 220
such kind Terrours her Infant Offspring as I do her I love. She
thinks it's Food, if she's not by, unwholsome; and all the ambient
Air made up of Fevers and of Quartan Agues: Except she shrouds
it in her Arms.—Such is my unpitied anxious Care for you, and
can I see another—   225

Penelope. What other?

Lovemore. Nay, if you make a Secret of your meeting,—there's all
that I suspect in't.—Another?—Young *Bookwit* is another.

Penelope. I never saw his Face.—Young *Bookwit*?

Lovemore. What! not tho' he solicited a Glance, with Symphonies 230
of charming Note, with sumptuous Dishes!—Not when the flying
Meteors from the Earth made a new Day!—Not see him!—Oh! that
was hard,—That was unkind, not one Look for all this Gallantry!—
But Love is blind,—You can be all Night with the Son, all Day with
the Father, and never see either.—His Father was here this 235
Morning; seek not to excuse,—I find your Arts, and see their Aim
too—Go, go, take your *Bookwit*,—Forget your Lover as he now
must you. (*Going.*)

Penelope. Hear but three words.

Lovemore. What shall they be?   240

Penelope. Prithee hear me.

Lovemore. No, no, your Father's coming down.

Penelope. He is not coming, nor can he overhear us. There's Time and Privacy enough to disabuse you.

245 *Lovemore.* I'll hear nothing unless you will be married, unless you give me as a present Earnest of your self three Kisses, and your Word for ever.

Penelope. To give way to my Satisfaction then—and be Friends again,—you wou'd, Mr. *Lovemore*, have three Kisses—

250 *Lovemore.* Three Kisses, your Faith, and Hand.

Penelope. Nothing else; will you be so contented?

Lovemore. I'll expect higher Terms, if you accept not these— Quickly then.

Penelope. Well then,—No, my Father's coming? ha, ha, ha.

255 *Lovemore.* Laugh at my Sufferings!—slight my Anger.
Is this your base Requital of my Love;
Revenge, Revenge,—I'll print on thy Favourite in his Heart's Blood my Revenge. Our Swords—our Swords shall dispute our Pretences, rather than he enjoy what my long Services entitle me to,

260 which is to do my self Right for what he intends an Injury; tho' perhaps what we shall dispute for is better lost.

Penelope. Mr. *Lovemore*, you have taken very great Liberties; you say I have injur'd you in my Regard to another.—Is your Opinion then of what you say you will dispute for, such as you just now said

265 —better lost.

Lovemore. Look you, Madam,—so—therefore—as to that—this is such—for that it—You don't consider what you said to me—

Penelope. Ha! ha! ha!

Lovemore. You shall by all that's—You shall repent this.

Flings out.

270 *Penelope.* This is all we have for't, a little Dominion before hand.— These are the Creatures that are born to rule us, who creep, who flatter, and servily beseech our Favour; which obtain'd, they grow sullen, proud, and insolent; pry into the Gift, the manner of bestowing, with all the little Arts th' ungrateful use to hide, or kill their

275 Sense and Conscience of a Benefit—

Lettice. Ay, ay, Madam, 'tis so.—I had a Sweetheart once, a Lady's Butler, to whom I gave a Lock of my Hair; and the Villain when we quarrell'd, told me half of 'em were grey.

Penelope. Ha! ha! ha! the ingrate,—the faithless, as *Lovemore*
says—   280

Lettice. And yet, Madam, the Rogue stole a Letter out of a Book
to ask me for it—as my next Suiterer found out.

Penelope. However, I am sure 'tis in my Fate to be subject to one
of 'em very suddenly.

Lettice. Ah! Madam! the Gentleman this Morning—   285

Penelope. The Fellow's very well, and I am mightily mistaken if
my Cousin *Victoria* did not think so—

Lettice (Aside.) And so do you heartily.

Penelope. Yet I wish I had seen this young *Bookwit* before *Lovemore*
came to Day.—   290

Lettice. I'll tell you how, Madam.—*Victoria* has ne'er a Lover, and
is your entire Friend.—Now, Madam, suppose you got her to write
a Letter to this young Gentleman in her own Name.—You meet
him under that Name *incognito*; then if an Accident should happen,
both you and she may be safe, and puzzle the Truth: You never writ 295
to him, she never met him—

Penelope. A lucky Thought,—step to her immediately.—I'll come
to her, or she to me.

Lettice. I fly, I fly—

                                                                      Exit.

Penelope. This is indeed a lucky hint of the Wench, in which I have 300
another drift too.—Now shall I sift my Friend *Victoria*, and perfectly
understand whether she likes that agreeable young Fellow; for if
her reserv'd Humour easily falls in with this Design on *Bookwit*,
she's certainly smitten with the other, and suspects me to be so
too.—What is this dear, this sudden Intruder Love, that *Victoria's* 305
long and faithful Friendship, *Lovemore's* anxious and constant
Passion, both vanish before it in a Moment?—Why are our Hearts
so accessible at our Eyes! my dear—

                        Enter Victoria.

Victoria. Dear *Penelope* I ran to you,—well, what is't?

Penelope. Set Chairs, and the *Bohee* Tea, and leave us.   310

                                                            Exit Lettice.

Dear *Victoria*,—you have always been my most intimate Bosom-friend.—Your wary Carriage, and Circumspection have often been a Safety against Errors to me,—I must confess it. (*Filling her Tea.*)

315 *Victoria.* But, my dear, why this Preface to me.—To the matter.—

Penelope. You know all that has pass'd between me and Mr. *Lovemore*?

Victoria. I have always approv'd him, and do now more than ever.—For 'tis not a Mein and Air, that makes that worthy Crea-

320 ture, a kind Husband. But—

Penelope. True, but here was old *Bookwit* this Morning, with my Father's Authority to talk to me of the Subject of Love.

Victoria. Nay, Madam, if so, and you can resolve to obey your Father—I contend not for *Lovemore*; for tho' the young Men of this

325 Age are so very vitious, so expensive both of their Health, and Fortune—

Penelope. (*Aside.*) How zealous she is to put me out of her way. False Creature!—[*To* Victoria.] But, my Dear Friend, you don't take me—your Friendship outruns my Explanation.—'Twas for

330 his Son at *Oxford* he came to me,—he is to walk with him before the Door that I may view him,—by and by—

Victoria. Nay, as one must obey their Parents wholly—I think a raw young Man that never saw the Town, is better than an old one that has ran through all its Vices.—I congratulate your good

335 Fortune.—There's a great Estate,—and he knows nothing, just come to Town.—The Furniture, and the Horse-Cloaths will be all your own Device for the Wedding, and the Horses when and where you please.—He knows no better—

Penelope. But one shall be so long teaching a raw Creature a

340 manner—

Victoria. Never let him have one,—'twill make him like himself, and think of making Advances elsewhere: You'd better have him a Booby.—How cou'd I think of the old Fellow for you.—Look you, *Penelope* old Age has its Infirmities, and 'tis a sad Prospect for an

345 honest young Woman to be sure of being a Nurse, and never being a Mother—

Penelope. Oh! that I had but your Prudence! But, my dear, I have a Request to make to you, and that is, that you wou'd write him

an Assignation this Evening in the Park.—I'll obey the Appointment, and converse with him under that Disguise; for the old 350
People will clap up a Match before I know any thing of the real
Man.—And if one don't know one's Husband, how can one manage
him? that is to say, obey him?

Victoria. Oh! pray, my dear, do you think I don't understand
you?—Oh! and there's another thing,—A Scholar makes the best 355
Husband in the World.

Penelope. Because they're the most knowing—

Victoria. No, because they are least knowing.—But I'll go
immediately and obey your Commands.—I wish you heartily well,
my dear, in this matter. (*Kissing her.*)   360

Penelope. I thank you, dearest.—I don't doubt it indeed.

Victoria. Where are you going now, my dear?—Oh fie! this is not
like a Friend.—Do I use you so, dear Madam?

Penelope. Nay, indeed, Madam, I must wait on you—

Victoria. Indeed you shan't,—indeed you shan't. (Penelope *follows.*) 365

Penelope. Well, Madam, will you promise then to be as free with
me?

[*Exit* Victoria.]

Thus does she hope to work me out of my Lover, by being made
my Confident.—But that Baseness has been too fashionable to pass
any more.—I have not trusted her.—The cunning Creature.—I 370
begin to hate her so—I'll never be a Minute from her.

Exit.

[Act II. Scene ii.]

Enter Old Bookwit, *Young* Bookwit, *and* Latine.

Old Bookwit. Well, *Tom,* where have you saunter'd about since I
saw you? Is not the Town mightily increas'd since you were in it?—

Young Bookwit. Ay, indeed, I need not have been so impatient to
have left *Oxford;* had I staid a Year longer they had builded to me—

5 *Old Bookwit*. But I don't observe you affected much with the Alterations.—Where have you been?

Young Bookwit. No Faith, the New Exchange has taken up all my Curiosity.

Old Bookwit. Oh! but, Son, you must not go to Places to stare at 10 Women. Did you buy any thing?

Young Bookwit. Some Bawbles.—But my Choice was so distracted among the pretty Merchants and their Dealers, I knew not where to run first.—One little lisping Rogue, Ribbandths, Gloveths, Tippeths.—Sir, cries another, will you buy a fine Sword-knot; then 15 a third, pretty Voice and Curtsie,—Does not your Lady want Hoods, Scarfs, fine green Silk Stockins.—I went by as if I had been in a Seraglio, a living Gallery of Beauties,—staring from side to side, I bowing, they laughing,—so made my Escape, and brought your Son and Heir safe to you, through all these Darts and Glances.— 20 To which indeed my Breast is not impregnable.—But I wonder whence I had this amorous Inclination—

Old Bookwit. Whoever you had it from, Sirrah, 'tis your Business to correct it—by fixing it upon a proper Object.—But, *Tom*, you know I am always glad to hear you talk with the Gaiety before me, 25 that you do elsewhere.—But I have now something of Consequence (*Aside*.) (that sudden serious look was so like me.) [*To Young* Bookwit.] What I am going to say now, I tell you is extraordinary—

Young Bookwit. I cou'd not indeed help some seeming Extravagancies I have been forc'd to.—But—

30 *Old Bookwit*. I do not grudge you your Expences, I was not going to speak on't,—for I decay, and so do my Desires, while yours grow still upon you.—Therefore what may be spar'd from mine, I heartily give you to supply yours.—'Tis but the just Order of things.—I scorn to hoard what I only now can gaze at, while your 35 Youth and Person want those Entertainments you may become and tast.—All your just Pleasures are mine also.—In you my Youth and gayer Years methinks I feel repeated.

Young Bookwit. Then what can give you, Sir, Uneasiness?

Old Bookwit. Your Affectation of a Soldier's Dress makes me think 40 you bent upon a dangerous, tho' noble Course.—That you'll expose a Life that's dearer to your Father than your self, to daily Hazards;

I therefore have resolv'd to settle thee, and chosen a young Lady, witty, prudent, rich and fair—

Young Bookwit. (*Aside.*) Oh, *Victoria*! [*To Old* Bookwit.] You cannot move too slowly in such a Business.   45

Old Bookwit. Nay, 'tis no sudden thing.—Her Father and I have been old Acquaintance, and I was so confident of her Worth, and your Compliance, that I can't with Honour disengage my self.

Young Bookwit. How, Sir! when Honour calls me to the Field, where I may perpetuate your Name by some brave Exploit!—   50

Old Bookwit. You may do it much better, *Tom*, at home by a brave Boy.—Come, come, it must be so—

Young Bookwit. (*Aside.*) What shall I do for some Invention?

Old Bookwit. Let it be so, dear *Tom*, it must be so.

Young Bookwit. What if it be impossible?   55

Old Bookwit. Impossible! as how?

Young Bookwit. Upon my Knees I beg your Pardon, Sir. I am—

Old Bookwit. What!—

Young Bookwit. At *Oxford*—

Old Bookwit. What art thou at *Oxford*? Rise and tell me.   60

Young Bookwit. Why I am married there, since you needs must know.

Old Bookwit. Married without my Consent!

Young Bookwit. There was a Force upon me; you'll easily get all annull'd if you desire it:—It was the crossest, most unhappy Accident.—Yet indeed she is an excellent Creature!   65

Latine. (*Aside.*) How cou'd he conceal this all this while from me. —But I remember he us'd to be out of College whole Nights,—we knew not where—

Penelope *and* Victoria *at the Window.*

Penelope. [*Aside.*] The very Man we met this Morning; and I employ my Rival to write to him! how confidently she stares at the 70 Fellow, and observes his Action!

Victoria. [*Aside to* Betty.] *Betty*, do you see with what Intent, and with what Fire in her Eyes, *Penelope* gazes yonder?—But take you that Letter and give it when the old Gentleman's gone.—Goodness! how concern'd she seems!—Well, some Women!—   75

Exeunt Ladies from above.

66 (*Aside.*)] D1; [om.]

Old Bookwit. Let that pass, since the Business is irrevocable.—
What is her Name?

Young Bookwit. Matilda, and her Father's *Newtown*.

Old Bookwit. They're Names I never heard before, but go on.

80 *Young Bookwit.* This Lady, Sir, I saw in a Publick Assembly, at the
first sight she made me hers for ever: From that instant I languish'd.
—Nor had Vital Heat out of her Presence.—The Sun to me shed
Influence in vain.—He rose and set both unobserv'd, nor was to any
living this human Life, so much a Dream as me: All this she
85 observ'd, but not untouch'd observ'd. She shew'd a noble Gratitude t'a noble Passion; Favours I soon receiv'd, but severely modest
ones.

Latine. (*Aside.*) Oh! that's presuppos'd, you to be sure wou'd
ne'er desire any other.

90 *Young Bookwit.* We had contriv'd to meet o' Nights,
The sweetest Hours of Love, and there was I
One Evening in her Lodging,—'Twas as I remember,
Yes 'twas on the second of *December*;
That's the very Night I was caught—

95 *Latine.* (*Aside.*) 'Tis strange a Fellow of his Wit to be trapan'd
into a Marriage—

Young Bookwit. Her Father supp'd abroad that Night, which made
us think our selves secure.—But coming home by Accident sooner
than we expected, we heard him at the Door.—How did that Noise
100 surprize us! She hid me behind the Bed, then lets him in.

Old Bookwit. I tremble for the poor young Lady.—Pray go on.—
How did she recover her self?

Young Bookwit. She fell into the prettiest artful little Tales to
divert him, and hide her Discomposure,—which he interrupted by
105 telling her she must be married suddenly to one propos'd to him
that Evening.—This was to me Daggers.

Old Bookwit. But she!—

Young Bookwit. She by general Answers in that case manag'd it so
well, that he was going down, when instantly my Watch in my
110 Pocket struck ten.—He turns him short on his amazed Daughter,
asked where she had it.—She cried, her Cousin *Martha* sent it out

of the Country to be mended for her.—He said he would take care on't; she comes to me, but as I was giving it her, the String was so entangled in the Cock of a Pistol I always had about me on those Occasions, that my haste to disengage it fir'd it off.—My Mistress 115 swoons away.—The Father ran out crying out Murder.—I thought her dead, fear'd his Return, which he soon did, with two boistrous Rogues his Sons, and his whole Family of Servants.—I wou'd have made my Escape, but they oppos'd me with drawn Swords, I wounded both; but a lusty Wench with a Fireshovel at one blow 120 struck down my Sword, and broke it all to pieces—

Old Bookwit. But still the poor young Lady!—

Young Bookwit. Here was I seiz'd.—Mean time *Matilda* wakes from her Trance,—beholding me held like a Ruffian, both her Brothers bleeding—She was returning to it.—What shou'd I do? 125 I saw the hoary Father in the divided Sorrow for his Sons' Lives, and Daughter's Honour, of both which he thought me th' Invader. —She with pitying, dying and reproaching Looks beseech'd me,— and taught me what I ow'd her constant Love.—I yielded, Sir, I own I yielded to the just Terrour of their Family Resentment, and my 130 Mistresses more dreadful upbraiding. Thus am I, Sir, the Martyr of an honest Passion—

Old Bookwit. That I most blame is that you conceal'd it from me, your best Friend.—I'll instantly to *Penelope's* Father, and make my Apology.—He is my Friend—   135

Exit.

Latine. This Marriage strangely surpriz'd me—

Young Bookwit. Why did you believe it too, as well as the old Gentleman? Why then I did it excellently.—Ha! ha! ha!

Latine. What! the Watch!—The Pistol!—Lady swooning, her pitying, upbraiding Looks! all Chimæra?   140

Young Bookwit. Nothing but downright Wit to keep my self safe for *Victoria*.

Latine. May I desire one Favour.

Young Bookwit. What can I deny thee, my Privado?

Latine. Only that you'd give me some little secret hint—when 145 next you L—are going to be witty.—But to jumble Particulars so

<hr>

126 Sons'] ed.; Son's

readily! 'tis impossible you cou'd, I believe, at the beginning of your Tale know the ending.—Yet—

Young Bookwit. These are Gifts, Child, mere Gifts; 'tis not to be
150 learnt—the Skill of Lying,—Except Humour, Wit, Invention, Presence of Mind, Retention, Memory, Circumspection, &c.— were to be attain'd by Industry.—You must not hum, nor haw, nor blush for't—

Latine. Who have we got here?

Betty *entring.*

155 *Betty.* May I be so bold as to crave the Liberty to ask your Name.
Young Bookwit. My bright Handmaid, my little she *Ganimede.*— Thou charming *Hæbe*,—You may ask me my Name,—for I won't tell it you,—till you do—because I'd have the more words with you—
Betty. Are not you Mr. *Bookwit*?
160 *Young Bookwit.* The very same, my dear.
Betty. There then. [*Gives him the Letter.*]—[*Aside.*] He's a mighty pretty Man.

Exit Betty.

Young Bookwit. (*Reading.*)

You may wonder.—Your Person, and Character—this Evening near
165 *Rosomond's Pond, on the other side the Park.*

Victoria.

Oh the Happiness! What is become of the Girl?—Oh! *Latine*! *Latine*! ask me fifty Questions all at once! What ails me? Why this Joy!—who is this from?—Oh I cou'd die methinks this moment, lest
170 there shou'd be in Fate some future Ill to dash my present Joy.— Why, *Jack*, why dost not ask me what's the matter?
Latine. If you'd but give me Leave—
Young Bookwit. No, do not speak.—Let me talk all, I fain wou'd celebrate my fair one's Praise, her every Beauty! But the Mind's too
175 full to utter any thing that is articulate, and will give way to nothing but mere Names and Interjections.—Oh!—*Victoria*!— *Victoria*!—*Victoria*!—Oh my *Victoria*!—Read there.
Latine. Well, I own this subscrib'd *Victoria.*—But still I am afraid of Mistakes.
180 *Young Bookwit.* No.—Kneel down and ask Forgiveness.—You

don't believe that she that wou'd not speak to me wou'd write.—
But after all Raptures and Extasies—Prithee step after the Maid,
learn what you can of her Fortune, and so forth.—Get Interest to be
admitted another time.

Exit Latine.

Enter Frederick.

Frederick. Sir, your Servant.   185
Young Bookwit. Yours, Sir, have you Business with me?
Frederick. This Paper speaks it.
Young Bookwit. (Reading.)

> *Of a Friend you've made me your mortal Enemy.—With your Sword*
> *I expect Satisfaction to morrow Morning at six in* Hide-Park.   190
> Lovemore.

Do you know the Contents of this Letter?
Frederick. Yes, Sir, it is a Challenge from *Lovemore.*
Young Bookwit. Are you to be his Second?
Frederick. I offer'd it, but he will meet you single.   195
Young Bookwit. The fewer the better Cheer.
Frederick. You're very pleasant, Sir.
Young Bookwit. My good Humour was ever Challenge Proof.—I
will be very punctual.

Exit Frederick.

I fall into Business very fast.—There, thou dear Letter of Love.—Be 200
there, thou of Hatred.—There—Men of Business must sort their
Papers.—I fear he saw me put up two Letters.

Enter Latine.

Oh, *Jack*, more Adventures, another Lady has Writ.
Latine. Let's see it.
Young Bookwit. No, always tender of Rep.—she is of Quality.—A 205
Gentleman Usher came with it.—I can't believe there's any thing
in that old whim of being wrap'd in ones Mother's Smock to be thus
lucky.—I suppose I was used like other Children.—They clap'd me
on a Skul-cap,—swath'd me hard, play'd me in Arms, and shew'd
me *London.*—But however it comes about, I have strange luck with 210
the Women.

Latine. But, let us see this Letter.

Young Bookwit. (*Reading.*) *No, No,—a Woman of Condition to go so far.—But indeed your Passion—your Wit.—My Page, at the back-stairs.*
215 *—Secrecy, and your Veracity.—*

Latine. There her Ladyship nicked it.—Pox, i'll be as humerous and as frolick as you—you pert Fellows are the only successful.—

Young Bookwit. Well said Lad—and as Mr. *Bays* says, now the Plot thickens upon us, we'll spend our time as gaily as the best of
220 'em—and all of it in Love.—

> For since through all the Race of Man we find, ⎫
> Each to some darling Passion is Inclin'd, ⎬
> Let Love be still the Biass of my Mind. ⎭

Exeunt.

The End of the Second Act.

Act. III. Scene i.

Enter Victoria *and* Betty.

Victoria. This was indeed, *Betty*, a very diverting accident that I should be employ'd to write to her Lover—now I can't but think how angry my Cousin *Penelope* is—she frets, I warrant, at her very Looking-glass, which us'd to be her comforter upon all occasions.
5 Ha, ha, ha!

Betty. I would not be in poor Mrs. *Lettices* place for all the World.—Nothing to be sure can please to Day, did you mind how she nestled and fum'd inwardly to see your Ladyship look so well.— Nay indeed, Madam, you were in high Beauty.—

10 *Victoria.* Yet I must confess I was my self a little discompos'd—I was asham'd for my Friend—and then to see her shew such regard for a Fellow—

Betty. But I swear, were I to have my will, you should be always angry at me.—It gives your Ladyship such a pretty fierceness, and quick-spirit to your Features—not that you want it.—Yet it adds— 15

Victoria. There are some People very unhappily pretend to Fire, and Life; there's poor stupid insipid Lady *Fad*, has heard of the word Spleen, and Distast, and sets up for being out of Humour, with that unmeaning Face of hers.

Betty. You're in a fine Humour, Madam— 20

Victoria. Her Ladyship's Physician prescrib'd Anger to her—upon which she comes in publick with her Eyes staringly open—this she designs for Vivacity, and gapes about like a wandering Country Lady.—She pretends to be a Remarker, and looks at every body— but alas she wants it here—and knows not that to see, is no more 25 to look, than to go, is to walk.—For you must know, *Betty*, every Child can see—but 'tis an observing Creature that can look—as every pretty Girl can go, but 'tis a fine Woman that walks.

Both. Ha! Ha! Ha!

Victoria. But, by the way, there's Mrs. *Penelope*, methinks, does 30 neither; I have a kindness for her, but she has no Gesture in the least—

Enter Penelope.

My Dear.—

Penelope. Well, my dear—

Betty. (*Aside.*) How civilly People of Quality hate one another. 35

Penelope. Well, my dear, were not you strangely surpriz'd to see that this young *Bookwit* should be the Soldier we met this Morning?

Victoria. The confident lying Creature! Indeed I wonder'd you'd suffer him to entertain you so long.

Penelope. You must know, Madam, he's married too at *Oxford*. 40

Victoria. The ugly Wretch! I think him downright disagreeable. —(*Aside.*) But perhaps this is a fetch of hers; he had no married Look.

Penelope. Yet I am resolv'd to go to your Assignation, if it be but to confront the Coxcomb, and laugh at his Lies.—Such Fellows 45 shou'd be made to know themselves, and that they're under-stood.

Victoria. I'll wait upon you, my dear.—(*Aside.*) She's very prettily dress'd. [*To* Penelope.] But indeed, my dear, you shan't go with

35 (*Aside.*)] D1; [om.]

50 your Hoods so.—It makes you look abominably, with your Head
so forward.—There—(*Displacing her Head.*) That's something.—
You had before a fearful, silly, blushing Look.—Now you command
all Hearts—

Penelope. Thank you, my dear—

55 *Victoria.* Your Servant, dearest—

Penelope. But alas, Madam, who patch'd you to Day?—Let me
see.—It is the hardest thing in Dress.—I may say without Vanity—
I know a little of it.—That so low on the Cheeks pulps the Flesh
too much.—Hold still, my dear, I'll place it just by your Eye.—
60 (*Aside.*) Now she downright squints.

Victoria. There's nothing like a sincere Friend,—for one is not a
Judge of one's self.—I have a Patch-box about me. Hold, my dear,
that gives you a sedate Air, that large one near your Temples—

Penelope. People, perhaps, don't mind these things:—But if it be
65 true, as the Poet finely sings, That all the Passions in the Features
are, We may shew, or hide 'em, as we know how to affix these pretty
artificial Moles—

Victoria. And so catch Lovers, and puzzle Physiognomy.

Penelope. 'Tis true; then pray, my dear, let me put a little Disdain
70 in your Face.—For we'll plague this Fopp.—There—that on your
Forehead does it.

Victoria. Hold, my dear, I'll give Indifference for him, a Patch just
at the Pout of your Lip exactly shews it.—And that you're dumb to
all Applications.

75 *Penelope.* (*Aside.*) You wish I wou'd be.

Victoria. There, my dear.

Penelope. But, dear Madam, your Hair is not half powder'd.—
Betty, bring the Powder Box to your Lady.—It gives one a clean
Look (tho' your Complexion does not want it) to enliven it.

80 *Victoria.* Oh! fie, this from you! but I know you won't flatter me,
you're too much my Friend.

Penelope. Now, Madam, you shall see. (*Powders her.*)—(*Aside.*)
Now she looks like a Spright.

Victoria. Thank you, my dear, we'll take an Hack—Our Maids
85 shall go with us.—Come, dear Friend.

Exeunt [Penelope *and* Victoria] *Arm in Arm.*

Betty. Pray, Madam *Lettice* be pleas'd to go on.
Lettice. Indeed, Madam *Betty*, I must beg your Pardon.
Betty. I am at home, dear Madam *Lettice*—
Lettice. Well, Madam, this is unkind.—I don't use you with this
Ceremony—   90

Exeunt.

[Act III. Scene ii.]

Enter Young Bookwit *and* Latine *after a Flourish.*

Young Bookwit. Victoria! Victoria! Victoria!
Latine. Make way, make way.—By your Leave.—Stand by.—
Victoria!

Formosam resonare doces Amaryllida Sylvas.

Young Bookwit. Well said, *Jack.*—Let me see any of your Sparks 5
besides my self, keep such an Equipage! I don't question but in a
little time I shall be a finer Fop than the Town has yet seen.—All
my Lacquies shall be Linguists as thou art—While thus I ride
immortal Steeds.—How my Horses stare at me!—They see I am
a very new sort of Beau—   10
Latine. This is rare.—The having this Noise of Musick.—But
won't it be reckon'd a Disturbance?—
Young Bookwit. No, no, it is an usual Gallantry here.—But the
Vocal is an Elegance hardly known before me here,—who am the
Founder of accomplish'd Fools.—Of which I'll institute an Order.— 15
All Coxcombs of Learning and Parts shall after me be call'd *Book-*
wits.—A Sect will soon be more numerous, and in more Credit than
your Aristotelians, Platonists, and Academicks—
Latine. Sir, 'twill be extraordinary, and you are really a wise
Person.—You put your Theory of Philosophy into Practice.— 'Tis 20
not with you a dead Letter—

Young Bookwit. Oh! Sir, no: The Design of Learning is for the Use of Life.—Therefore I'll settle a Family very suddenly, and shew my Literature in Oeconomy—

25 *Latine.* As how, pray?

Young Bookwit. I'll have four Peripatetick Footmen, two Followers of *Aristippus* for *Valets de Chambre*, and an Epicurean Cook—with an Hermetical Chymist (who are good only at making Fires) for my Skullion, and then I think all is disposed.—But, methinks, this Fair
30 One takes state upon her.—But I am none of your Languishers,—I am not known in Town, and if I misbehave, 'tis but being sent back again to my small Beer, and three half-penny Commons.—And I, like many another Beau, only blaz'd and vanish'd—

Latine. But you know I love Musick immoderately.—How do
35 you dispose your Entertainment, let 'em begin—

Young Bookwit. Well, give me but leave.—The Fiddles will certainly attract the Ladies, I mean the Nymphs who have Grotto's round this enchanted Forest.—In the first place, you Intelligences that move this Vehicle.—How the Fellows stare!—

40 *Chairman.* Good your Honour, speak to us in English.—

Young Bookwit. Why then you Chairmen,—whereever I move you are to follow me.—For I mean to strut, shine through the Dusk of the Evening, and look as like a lazy Town Fool as I can to charm 'em—

Latine. Well, but the Musick—

45 *Young Bookwit.* But remember, ye Sons of *Phœbus*, Brethren of the String, and Lyre; that is to say, ye Fidlers.—Let me have a Flourish as I now direct.—When I lift up my Cane, let it be Martial.—If I but throw my self just forward on it, or but raise it smoothly—Sigh all for Love to shew, as I think fit,—That I wou'd die, or fight for her
50 you see me bow to—Well then strike up—

SONG,

by Mr. *Leveridge.*

I.

Venus has left her Grecian Isles,
With all her gaudy Train
Of little Loves, soft Cares and Smiles
In my larger Breast to reign.

II.

Ye tender Herds, and list'ning Deer,   55
Forget your Food, forget your Fear,
The bright Victoria *will be here.*

III.

The Savages about me throng,
Mov'd with the Passion of my Song,
And think Victoria *stays too long.*   60

Young Bookwit. There's for you, *Jack*; is not that like a fine Gentleman that writes for his own Diversion?

Latine. And no bodies else.

Young Bookwit. Now I warrant one of your common Sparks woul'd have stamp'd, fretted, and cry'd, what the Devil! fool'd! 65 jilted! abus'd! while I in metre, to shew you how well nothing at all may be made to run—

The Savages about me throng,
Mov'd with the Passion of my Song,
And think Victoria *stays too long.*   70

Latine. I begin to be one of those Savages.

Enter Victoria, Penelope, Lettice *and* Betty.

Victoria. We had better have stayed where we were, and listned to that charming Ecchoe, than have come in Search of that Liar.

Latine. Do you see yonder?

Young Bookwit. (Gives the Sign and sings himself.) Thus, Madam, 75 have I spent my Time almost ever since I saw you; repeated your Name to the Woods, the Dales and ecchoing Groves—

Penelope. [*Aside to* Victoria.] Prithee observe him.—Now he begins—

Young Bookwit. I had not time to carve your Name on every Tree, 80 but that's a melancholly Employment, not for those Lovers that are favour'd with Assignation—

Victoria. [*Aside to* Penelope.] Prithee, Cousin, do you talk to him in my Name.—I'll be silent till I see farther—

85 *Penelope.* The Spring is now so forward, that it must indeed be attributed to your Passion that you are not in the Field—

Young Bookwit. You do me Justice, Madam, in that Thought, for I am strangely pester'd to be there.—Well, the French are the most industrious People in the World.—I had a Letter from one of their
90 Generals, that shall be nameless, (it came over by the way of *Holland*) with an Offer of very great Terms, if I wou'd but barely send my Opinion in the Use of Pikes,—about which he tells me their Prince and Generals have lately held a grand Court Marshal—

Both. Ha! ha! ha!

95 *Latine.* [*Aside.*] These cunning things keep still together to puzzle us.—I'll allarm him.—[*To Young* Bookwit.] Sir, one word—

Victoria. Come, come, we'll have no Whispering, no Messages at present.—Some other Ladies have sent, but they shan't have you from us—

100 *Both.* Ha! ha! ha!

Young Bookwit. I hold my self oblig'd to be of the same Humour Ladies are in.—Ha! ha! ha!—Now pray do me the Favour to tell me what I laugh'd at.

Penelope. Why you must know.—Your talking of the French and
105 War, put us in mind of a young Coxcomb that came last Night from *Oxford*, calls himself Soldier, treats Ladies, fights Battels, raises Jealousies with downright Lies of his own inventing, ha, ha, ha.

Young Bookwit. That must be an impudent young Rascal certainly;
110 ha, ha, ha.

Victoria. [*Aside to* Penelope.] Nay, this is beyond Comparison—

Young Bookwit. I can't conceive how one of those sneaking Academicks cou'd personate such a Character; for we bred in Camps, have a Behaviour that shews we are us'd to act before Crouds—

115 *Penelope.* 'Tis certainly so.— Nay, he has been confronted with it, as plainly as I speak to you, and yet not blush'd for it, but carryed it as if he knew not the Man—

Young Bookwit. That may be,—'tis want of knowing themselves, makes those Coxcombs so confident.

120 *Penelope.* [*Aside to* Victoria.] The Faithless! Shameless! [*To Young* Bookwit.] Well, then to see if possible, such a one may be brought

to that Sense, I tell you, this worthy Heroe, two days agoe, was in hanging-sleves at *Oxford*, and is call'd Mr. *Bookwit*. Ha! Ha!

Young Bookwit. Well, was it not well enough carried.—Poo, I knew you well enough, and you knew me, before you writ to me for Mr. *Bookwit's* Son.—But I fell into that way of talking purely to divert you.—I knew you a Woman of Wit and Spirit—and that acting that Part, woud at least shew I had Fire in me, and wish'd my self what I woud be half an Age to serve and please you.—Suffer in Camps, all the Vicissitudes of burning heats, and sharp afflicting colds—

Victoria. Look you, Sir, I shall tell Mrs. *Matilda Newtown* your Spouse at *Oxford*, what you are saying to another Lady.—

Penelope. Prethee Cousin, never give your self the trouble, to meddle in such a Work—one hardly knows how to speak it to a Gentleman, but don't touch the Affairs of so impudent a Lyar.—

Young Bookwit. Ha, ha, ha,—Why, Madam, have they told you of the Marriage too?—Well, I was hard put to it there.—I had like to have been gravell'd, Faith,—you were more beholden to me for that, than any thing.—Had it not been for that, they had Marryed me to Mrs. *Penelope*, old *Getwel's* Grandaughter. The great Fortune. —(*Aside.*) But I refus'd her for you, who are a greater.—

Latine. Sir, Sir, pray Sir, one Word—

Penelope and Victoria. Stand off, Sirrah.

Victoria. You shan't come near him, none of your Dumb Signs.

Penelope. Then you have refus'd *Penelope*, tho' a great Fortune— what cou'd you dislike in her?

Young Bookwit. The whole Woman.—Her Person, nor Carriage please me.—She is one of those Women of Condition, who do and say what they please with an assur'd Air, and think that's enough, only to be call'd fine Mrs. such a ones manner—

Penelope. [*Aside.*] This is not to be endur'd—[*To Young* Bookwit.] I do assure you, Sir, Mrs. *Penelope* has refus'd your Betters.

Young Bookwit. I don't much value my Betters in her Judgment.— But am sorry to see you concern'd for her, when I have been at Church where I first saw you—I've seen the gay giddy thing in a Gallery, watching Eyes to make Courtesies.—She is indeed a very Ceremonious Church-woman, and never is guilty of a Sin of

125

130

135

140

145

150

155

134 such a] D1; a such

Omission to any Lady of Quality, within Eye-shot.—In short, I
don't like the Woman, and wou'd go to *Tunis* or *Aleppo* for a Wife,
160 before I'de take her.—

Victoria. I cannot bear this of my Friend, if you go on Sir, at
this rate, *Tunis* or *Aleppo* are the properest places for you to shew
your Gallantry in—'twil never be receiv'd by any here—(*Aside.*) I
hope she believes me.

165 *Penelope.* The Lady's in the right on't,—who can confide in a
known common Impostor?

Young Bookwit. Ah Madam! how can you use a Man that loves
you so unjustly?—But call me what you will, Lyar, Cheat, Impostor.—Do but add your Servant, and I am satisfied.—I have
170 indeed, Madam, ran through many Shifts, in hopes to gain you—
and cou'd be contented to run through all the Shapes in *Ovid's*
Metamorphosis, cou'd I but return to this on my bended Knees, of my
fair ones humblest Servant.

Victoria. [*Aside to* Penelope.] Prethee let us leave him,—as you told
175 me, I wonder you can suffer him to entertain you so long.—Leave
him, let him kneel to the Trees, and call to the Woods—if he will—
(*Aside.*) Oh, I could brain him—how ugly he looks kneeling to her.

Penelope. [*Aside to* Victoria.] No, I'll stay to plague him more.—[*To*
Young Bookwit.] But what Opinion can I have of this sudden
180 Passion.—You hardly know me, I believe, or my Circumstances?—

Young Bookwit. No, no, not I.—I don't know you.—Your Mother
was not Alderman *Sterling's* Daughter.—Your Father Mr. *Philips* of
Greys-Inn, who had an Estate and never practis'd? You had not a
Brother kill'd at *Landen*? Your Sister *Diana* is not dead; nor you are
185 not Co-heiress with Miss *Molly.*—No, Madam, I don't know you,
no, nor love you?

Penelope. [*Aside.*] I wish I had taken her Advice in going.—He
means her all this while.—[*To* Victoria.] Pshaw, this is downright
fooling. Let's go, my dear, leave him to the Woods, as you say.
190 (*Aside.*) I wish 'twas full of Bears.

Victoria. [*Aside to* Penelope.] No.—Now I'll stay to plague him.

Penelope. [*Aside to* Victoria.] No, you shan't stay.—[*To Young*
Bookwit.] Sir, we have given our selves the Diversion to see you,
and confront you in your Falshoods; in which you have intangled

your self to that degree, you know not even the Woman you pretend 195
to; and therefore, Sir, I so far despise you, that if you shou'd come
after me with your Fiddles—I'll have a Porter—(*Aside.*) Ready to
let you in.

Victoria. I don't know how to threaten a Gentleman in that
manner; but I'm sure I shall never entertain any Man that has 200
disoblig'd my Friend while my Name's *Victoria*—

                         Exeunt [Penelope *and* Victoria] *Arm in Arm*,
                                 [*followed by* Betty *and* Lettice.]

Latine. Master,—methinks, these Ladies don't understand Wit.—
They were very rough with you.

Young Bookwit. Ay, they were somewhat dull.—But really *Victoria*
discover'd her self at her going, methinks, agreeably enough—   205

Latine. I believe they are irrecoverably lost.—Pox on't, when I
gave you so many Signs too—

Young Bookwit. Well, hang thinking.—Let's to the Tavern, and in
every Glass name a new Beauty, till I either forget, or am inspir'd
with some new Project to attain her.   210

        While in a lovely Bowl I drown my Care,
        She'll cease to be, or I to think her Fair.

                                     Exeunt.

        [*The End of the Third Act.*]

Act IV. [Scene i.]

                  Scene, *Covent-Garden.*

              Enter Young Bookwit *and* Latine.

Young Bookwit. This Roebuck has almost done my Business.—
Rigby's an honest Fellow, and wou'd not poison us. The Wine had
good Humour, Mirth, and Joy in't.—My Blood beats high and
frolick; what says my dear Lacquie? ha!

5   *Latine.* Why, Sir, I say, Sir, that I am in so noble, so exalted a Condition, that I almost forget I am your Honour's Footman—

Young Bookwit. Do but your Business well to Night—

Latine. Who says the Tongue stutters, Legs falter, and Eyes fail with Drink.—'Tis false, my dear Master, my Tongue runs faster

10 than ever.—My Legs so brisk and nimble, that I can't stand still, and my Eyes are better than ever they were; for I see every thing double.—But the Letter, the Letter, I warrant I give it her.

Young Bookwit. Here, here, *Jack*, take it.

Latine. Let's come nearer the Lamp.—This is the foul Copy of it

15 that 'tis wrap'd in.—Let me judge.—Now I'll be sedate.—Let me read it again.

Young Bookwit. But you look cursedly fluster'd.—They'll say you're drunk.—Let's see, I must comb your Wig a little.

Latine. I shall be kick'd for this Letter here about the middle.—

20 You shou'd not talk of Joys so soon.—You shou'd write miserable a Fortnight, or three Weeks longer.—I shall be kick'd.

Young Bookwit. What then, what then? A Man of your Philosophy must needs remember—The Body's but the mere Organ of the Mind.—Kicks come under the Topick of things without.—What shall

25 I do for Powder for this smart Bob. (*Combs out his own Wig into* Latine.)

Latine. 'Tis no matter, Sir; Powder comes under the notion of things without.

Young Bookwit. Oh! but Ladies are no Philosophers; but as to being drub'd (these Stockins too) you must fix your Imagination

30 upon some other Object, and you may by force of Thought suspend your feeling.—The Body is but the Instrument of the Mind.—And you may command an Instrument—

Latine. No, Sir, I'll have you to know, I'll save my Carcass by mere dint of Eloquence. You have no other Orders?—

35 *Young Bookwit.* No; but may Persuasion, Grace, and Elocution hang on thy Lips.—But if you can come into *Victoria*, she and the Wine you've drank will inspire you. Farewel.

              Exit.

Latine. This is the inchanted Castle which the Lady fair inhabits. Ha! Mr. *Simon*, Sir, I am your most humble Servant.—My dear

40 Friend—

Enter Simon.

Simon. Your Servant, good Sir, my Lady is with Madam *Victoria* at Cards.—She'll lie here to Night.—But all's ruin'd.—They are both huge angry with your Master. But *Lettice* having taken a Fancy to you, Mr. *John*, spoke up rarely, that she did indeed.

Latine. Can't one come to the Speech of her? 45

Simon. I was order'd to have a strict Eye to the Door, and let no body in whatever.—I don't care for going up, because she'll see I have made a Cap of one of the finest Napkins, for which she'll make a plaguy Noise.

Latine. Nay, nay, you are exactly of my Mind, I love to avoid 50 Anger.

Simon. You are a little disguis'd in Drink tho', Mr. *John*.—But I han't seen you not I.—Go strait up.—Mrs. *Lettice* is in the Anti-chamber.

Latine. I thank you, dear Friend. My Master bids me upon these 55 Occasions—(*Gives him Money.*)

Simon. I beg your Pardon, good Mr. *John*.

Latine. Look you, I am a Servant as well as you, what do you mean, Mr. *Simon*? Come, come, Time's precious.—When your Lady's marry'd all these Vales will end— 60

Simon. Nay, I said behind your Back, Mr. *John*, that you were very well spoken.—Well—Put up briskly, I'll stand your Friend as much as one Servant can to another, against all Masters and Mistresses whatever.

Latine. Thanks, good Mr. *Simon*. 65

Exeunt.

[Act IV. Scene ii.]

Scene opens and discovers Lettice *reading by a
small Candle. Two large ones by her unlighted.*

Lettice. 'Tis a most sad thing, one dare not light a large Candle,
except Company's coming in,—and I scarce can see to read this
pitious Story.—*Well, in all these Distresses, and Misfortunes, the faithful*
Argalus, *was renown'd all over the Plains of* Arca—Arca—Arcadia—*for*
5 *his loyal and true Affection to his charming Paramour,* Parthenia.—
Blessings on his Heart for it,—there are no such Suiterers now a
Days.—(*Weeping.*) But I hope they'll come together again at the
end of the Book.—And marry, and have several Children—Oh!
Bless me! A Man here! (*Turns over the Leafs.*) (*Aside.*) The Gentle-
10 man's pretty Man—

Enter Latine.

I wonder by what means, with that Impudence, you
could offer to come up Stairs, at this time o'th Night—and
my Lady in the next Room—I protest I'll cry out. (*In a low
Voice all.*)
15 *Latine.* (*Aloud.*) Dear Mrs. *Lettice,* my Love to you.—
Lettice. Hist—hist! I am methinks, however, loath to discover
you, because Servants must do as they're bid—for I know it was
not to see me—but some Message from your Master you came
about.
20 *Latine.* I offer'd to bring a Letter from him, in hopes to see you,
my dearest. I'll not give it at all, I don't care, my dearest. (*Kisses her
hand.*)
Lettice. Pho! pho! now you are rude, because you know one dare
not discover you.—You do what you will. [*Aside.*] How he kisses
25 one's Hand.—I warrant he has kiss'd his Betters.—[*To* Latine.]
Pray, did you never live in a Lady's Service?
Latine. No, nor do I value any of the Sex but your dear self, Mrs.

Lettice.—(*Aside.*) I wou'd be discover'd. [*To* Lettice.] I'm in a Rapture! in a Flame!

Penelope. (*Within.*) Who's there? (*Voice Within.*)   30

Lettice. [*Softly.*] Hist! hist! cou'd you not have forc'd a Kiss quietly.—[*Calling.*] Madam—Madam.—[*Softly.*] Hold me fast.— Shew the Letter, my Lady's coming.—[*Aloud.*] I tell you, Sir, she will receive no Messages at all.—Get you down Stairs, you impudent! (*Softly aside to* Latine.) Hold me faster yet, she loves your 35 Master.

Enter Penelope, Victoria.

Penelope. What can this mean?—What Fellow's that has seiz'd the Wench?

Lettice. Madam, Madam, here's Mr. *Bookwit's* Footman drunk, and has directly stole up Stairs with some ill Design, I fear, on me.— 40 But has a Letter from his Master to your Ladyship.

Penelope. Call up the Servants; *Simon, William, Kate, Alse*; I'll have the Rascal well basted for his Insolence.—Serv'd just as his Master deserves.

Latine. (*Kneeling.*) Let not those Lips more sweet than Labour of 45 Hyblæan Bees, utter a Sentence as if a Lybian Lioness on a Mountain gave thee suck, and thou wert the obdurate Offspring of a Rock.

Victoria. Hyblæan! Lybian! Obdurate! Ridiculous.—The Fellow has got his Master's cant; ha, ha, ha.

Penelope. I'll put him out of it I'll warrant you.—What will no one 50 come up there?

Enter Servants with Brooms, &c.

Latine. Oh! for the force of Eloquence to allay and reconcile the Passions of this angry Mansion.—[*Aside.*] I had like to have said plain House, which had been against the Laws of Buskin, in which I wou'd at present talk.   55

Penelope. Did you ever hear any thing like this. Ha! ha!

Maid. Madam, shall I beat him?

Latine. Ah! culinary Fair, compose thy Rage; thou whose more skilful Hand is still employ'd in Offices for the Support of Nature, descend not from thy self, thou bright Cook-maid.—[*Aside.*] There 60

I sunk again! [*To* Maid.] With heightned Gusts, and quickning
'Ta s, by you, what wou'd be Labour else is made Delight. Thou
g eat Robust, let not thy Hand all red assault a Life it rather should
preserve.

65   *Maid.* Good Madam, excuse me, I can't touch him.—I have
Bowels for him. (*Weeping.*)

   Simon. I wish I had his Learning, I'll warrant he buys in every
thing where ever he lives—

   Latine. This, Madam, this faithful Paper tells you the Passions of
70 the tenderest Heart that ever bled for cruel Maid.—Oh *Victoria*!
Did you but hear his Sighs, his restless Hours!—how often he
repeats *Victoria*!

   Lettice. (*Aside.*) *Victoria*! Then I find this is none on't meant to
my Lady.—Nor to me neither.—The Master and Man are both
75 Rogues.

   Penelope. [*Aside to* Victoria.] Receive your seasonable Epistle now
at Midnight.

   Victoria. [*Aside to* Penelope.] He can't mean me.—To you
he all along address'd.—(*Aside.*) Wou'd I cou'd read it with-
80 out her.

   Penelope. To shew you I value neither Author nor Bearer of it—
Kick the Fellow down.

   Latine. Nay, Madam, since matters must come to Extremities,
I'd rather have the Honour of your Ladyship's Command, to be
85 cudgel'd by your good Family, than have it from my Master.—A
disappointed Lover in his Rage will strike Stone-walls, and things
inanimate, much more a poor live Footman. Therefore I must
deliver my Message.—I'll read it to you Ladies, for I see you are
Friends.

90   *Penelope.* Away with him.

   Latine. If the Sincerity of my Intentions were not—

   Lettice. Get out, false Wretch.

   Latine. Demonstrable in spite of—

   Maid. Take that—

95   *Latine. These Accidents in which I have been involv'd, I should not dare
to tell you how alternately Joys, Raptures, Extasies, Miseries, Doubts, and
Anxieties do attack a Breast devoted to you.*

Whither shall injur'd Virtue fly for shelter,
When Love and Honour suffer thus in me!
Oh! I cou'd rage, call Elements about me, spout Cataracts.—   100
Must I be drub'd with Broom-staves?

Exeunt Latine, &c.

Penelope. Come in, my dear, again.—The Night is cold.

Exeunt.

[Act IV. Scene iii.]

Enter Lovemore, Frederick.

Lovemore. It is so pleasant a Night, that I will see you over the Garden to your Lodgings—

Frederick. That Complement won't pass upon me.—Your Reason for sauntring this way is that 'tis near *Penelope's.*

Lovemore. I come for her sake! No, shou'd she write, beseech, 5 kneel to me, I think I ne'er shou'd value her more. No I'll be no longer her Tool, her Jest; she shall not dally with a Passion she deserves not—

Frederick. 'Twere very well were this Resolution in your Power; but believe me, Friend, one Smile, one Glance that were but 10 doubtful, whether favourable, wou'd conquer all your Indignation.

Lovemore. Faith, I'm afraid what you say is true.

Frederick. Then strive not to be rationally mad, which you attempt, if you think you can at once be at your own Command, and at another's.—Wou'd you be Master of your self, and have a 15 Mistress?

Lovemore. But I can rebel against that Mistress.

Frederick. Do if you can.—Nay, I'm sure 'tis in your Power, because to Morrow Morning you are to fight a Rival for her;— because tho' you know she lies backwards, and you can't so much as 20 see her Chamber-window, you must needs walk hither.—Well, I

protest I'm of your Mind; there is, methinks, now a particular
amiable Gloom about that House.—Tho' perhaps to ordinary
Beholders it is exactly like the others.

25   *Lovemore.* You are very witty, I must confess, at your Friend's
Follies, Mr. *Frederick.*

Frederick. I won't then any longer disturb your Meditation, but
e'en go home like a dull Rogue as I am, and without Love enough to
any Woman, or Hatred enough to any Man to keep me awake—
30 Fall fast asleep.—I was going to wish you Rest, but you are above
all that.—If it shou'd rain, I'd advise you not to forget it does,—but
go into the *Piazza.*

Exit.

Lovemore. 'Tis very well, I am deservedly laugh'd at.—But the
Door opens.—*Bookwit's* Footman!

Latine crosses the Stage.

35 The Master I suppose is there too: I'll watch for his coming out.—
The Morning approaches too slowly.—He shall not sleep to Night,
except it be for ever.—Oh Revenge! Oh Jealousie!—

Enter Young Bookwit *with Bottle and
Glass singing.*

*Young Bookwit. Since the Day of poor Man,
        That little little Span,*
40   *Tho' long it can't last,*
        For the future, and past
    Is spent with Remorse and Despair.
        With such a full Glass
        Let that of Life pass,
45   *'Tis made up of Trouble,*
        A Storm tho' a Bubble,
    There's no Bliss but forgetting your Care.

I wonder what's become of poor *Latine.* I wish he had a Bumper of
this—(*Drinks.*)

50   *Lovemore.* I have no Patience to observe his insolent Jollity; How
immoderately joyful my Misery has made him! *Bookwit!*

Young Bookwit. Lovemore?

Lovemore. What! Sir, are you diverting the Thought of to Morrow
Morning's Business, with Midnight Riot? Or is it an Assignation
keeps you out of Bed thus late.   55

Young Bookwit. An Hour or two till Morning is not much in either
of our Lives.—Therefore I must tell you now, Sir, I am ready for
your Message.

Lovemore. That conscious Light, and Stars are Witnesses of—

Young Bookwit. I want no Witnesses.—I have a Sword as you bid 60
me meet you.

They draw and fight.

Lovemore. You've done my Business. (*Falls.*)

Young Bookwit. Then I've done what you desir'd me. But this is
no Place for me.

Exit.

Enter Constable *and* Watchmen.

Constable. Where, where was this clashing of Swords! so ho! so ho! 65
you Sir, what are you dead, speak, Friend, what are you afraid of?
If you are dead the Law can't take hold of you.

Watchman. I beg your Pardon, Mr. *Constable*, he ought by the Law
to be carried to the Round House for being dead at this time of
Night.   70

Constable. Then away with him you three.—And you, Gentlemen,
follow me, to find out who kill'd him.

Exeunt.

Enter Simon.

Simon. What's the matter, good Gentlemen, what's the matter?
Oh me!—Mr. *Lovemore* kill'd!—Oh me! my Mind gives me that it
must be about our young Lady.   75

Watchman. Does it so, Sir, then you must stay with us.

Some hold Simon, *whilst others carry* Lovemore *off*.

Simon. I stay with you! Oh gemini! Indeed I can't.—They can't
be without me at our House.

68, 76, 79 *Watchman.*] ed.; *Watch.*

Watchman. But they must, Friend.—Hark'e, Friend,—I hope
80 you'll be hang'd. (*Whispers him.*)

Simon. I hang'd! pray, Sir, take care of your words. Madam
Penelope's, our young Lady's Servant hang'd! take care what you
say.

Enter Latine.

Latine. Whither can this *Bookwit* be gone?
85 *Simon.* Oh! Mr. *John,* Mr. *Lovemore* is kill'd just now, since you
went out of our House; and you and your Master must have an
hand in't.

Latine. How! *Lovemore* kill'd!—(*They seize* Latine.)

Enter others with Young Bookwit.

Young Bookwit. Hands off, you dirty Midnight Rascals.—Let me
90 go, or—

Constable. Sir, what were you running so fast for.—There's a Man
kill'd in the Garden, and you're a fine Gentleman, and it must be
you—for good honest People only beat one another—

Latine. Nay, nay, we are all in a fair way to be fine Gentlemen,
95 Mr. *Simon* and all—

Constable. Hands off Rascals, you said just now—do you know
what a Constable is?

Young Bookwit. The greatest Man in the Parish, when all the rest
are asleep.

100 *Constable.* Come, come—I find they are desperate Fellows, we'll
to the Justice, and commit 'em immediately. I'll teach Rascals to
speak High-Treason against a Petty-Constable—

Exeunt.

[Act IV. Scene iv.]

Enter Frederick *and* Old Bookwit.

Old Bookwit. You well may be surpriz'd at my waiting here for your coming home.—But you'll pardon me, since it is to ease me of an Anxiety that keeps me waking.

Frederick. I shall be very glad if I am capable of doing that.

Old Bookwit. You knew my *Tom* at *Oxford*,—and I believe were 5 not so hard a Student, but you made some Acquaintance in the Town.—Therefore, pray tell me—do you know Mr. *Newtown* there?—his Family, Descent, and Fortune?

Frederick. What *Newtown*?

Old Bookwit. I'll tell you, Sir, what you young Fellows take most 10 notice of old ones for—a Token that you needs must know him by. —He is the Father of the fair *Matilda*, your celebrated Beauty of that Town.

Frederick. I assure you, Sir, I never heard of the Father or Daughter, 'til this instant,—therefore I'm confident there's no such Beauty— 15

Old Bookwit. Oh Sir, I know your drift—you're tender of inform-ing me for my Son's sake!—He told me all himself—I know all the Progress of his Love with the young Lady—How he was taken in the Night in her Bed-chamber by his Pistol going of—the Family disturbance, that was rais'd upon't, which he compos'd by marry- 20 ing—I know it all—

Frederick. Is *Tom Bookwit* then marryed at *Oxford*?

Old Bookwit. He is indeed, Sir, therefore our affairs are now so link'd that 'twill be an ill Office both to the *Newtowns*, and to us, to conceal any thing from me, that relates to them. 25

Frederick. A Man can't be said to conceal what he does not know —But it seems, it was Mr. *Bookwit* gave you this Account himself—

Old Bookwit. Yes, Sir, I told you, Sir, I had it from himself—

Frederick. Then I'm sure there was nothing left out, he never tells a Story by halves— 30

Old Bookwit. Why then you think my Son's a Lyar.

Frederick. Oh fie, Sir, but he enlivens a mere Narration with variety of Accidents,—to be plain, his Discourse gains him more applause than credit.—You cou'd not, I believe, have Marryed your 35 Son to a less expensive Lady in *England*, than this Mrs. *Matilda*— I'll be sworn you'l avoid all the charge of gay Dress, high Play, and stately Child-birth—you understand me Sir?—

Old Bookwit. I never cou'd see any thing in my Son, that's disengenuous, to put his aged Father to this Shame.

40 *Frederick.* Never fret or grieve for't.—He told *Lovemore* this Morning, such a Relation of his feasting Ladies, and I know not what—That he has brought a tilt upon his Hands, to morrow Morning—therefore keep him at home—I'll to his Adversary, so we'll convince him of a Fault which has so ill (tho' not intended) 45 Consequences.

Old Bookwit. You'll highly oblige me, Sir, I'll trouble you no longer.

Exeunt.

[Act IV. Scene v.]

Scene *Newgate*, *Young* Bookwit, Latine, Simon, Storm, *with the Crowd of Jayl-birds.*

Storm. I apprehend, Sir, by Mr. *Turn-key*, the Gentleman there with a broken Nose, that you're brought in for Murther,—I honour you Sir.—I don't question but 'twas done like a Gentleman—

Young Bookwit. I hope it will appear so.

5 *Storm.* I come, I fear Sir, to your Acquaintance with some prejudice, because you see me thus in Irons,—but Affliction is the Portion of the Virtuous, and the Gallant—

Young Bookwit. It does not depress, Sir, but manifest the Brave.

Storm. Right, Sir,—I find you'r Noble—you may perhaps have

heard of me—my Name is *Storm*.—This Person my Friend who is 10
call'd *Faggot*, and my self being expos'd by an ungrateful World, to
feel its Cruelty, and Contempt of ragged Virtue—made War upon
it—and in open Day, infested their High-road.

Young Bookwit. Your humble Servant, Gentlemen—I do conceive
you—your Spirits cou'd not stoop to Barter on the Change, to sneer 15
in Courts, to Lye, to Flatter, or to creep for Bread.—You therefore
chose rather to prey like Lyons, than betray like Crocodiles, or fawn
like Dogs—you took upon you to interrupt the commerce of a
cheating World.—To unload the Userer of his Anxious Pelf—and
save the thoughtless landed Boy, he travel'd to undoe—with 20
thousand such good Actions, by which means you two are infamous,
for what two millions of you had been Glorious.

Storm. Right, Sir,—I see you're knowing, Sir, and learned in
Man.—This Gentleman, Mr. *Charcole* the Chymist was our secret
Correspondent, and as we never robb'd a poor Man—so he never 25
cheated a Fool,—But still impos'd on your most sprightly Wits and
Genius—Fellows of Fire, and Metal, whose quick Fancies, and eager
Wishes, form'd Reasons for their undoing—He is a follower of the
great *Raimundus Lullius*; the publick think to frighten him into their
own purposes.—But he'll leave the ungrateful World without the 30
secret—

Charcole. You know, Sir, he that first asserted the Antipodes, dyed
for that Knowledge; and I, Sir, having found out the melioration of
Metals, the ignorant will needs call it Coining,—and I am to be
hang'd for't, wou'd you think it? 35

Young Bookwit. When pray, Sir, are you to be immortal?

Charcole. On Friday next.—I'm very unhappy our Acquaintance
is to be short.—I'm very sorry your Business is not over, Sir, that
if it must be, we might go together.

Young Bookwit. I'm highly obliged to you, Sir. 40

Charcole. Yet let me tell you, Sir, because by secret Sympathy I'm
yours—I must acquaint you, if you can obtain the favour of an
opportunity and a crucible—I can shew projection—directly *Sol*,
Sir, *Sol*, Sir, more bright than that high Luminary the Latines call'd
so—Wealth shall be yours.—We'll turn each Bar about us into 45
golden Ingots.—Sir, can you lend me half a Crown?—

Young Bookwit. Oh, Sir, a trifle between such old Acquaintance.

Storm. You'll be Indited, Sir, to morrow—I wou'd advise you, when your Indictment's read—to one thing.—That is,—don't cavil
50 at false Latine; but if by chance, there should be a word of good, except to that, and puzzle the whole Court.

Young Bookwit. Sir, I'm oblig'd—

Storm. I defie the World to say, I ever did an ill thing. I love my Friend,—but there is always some little trifle given to Prisoners, they
55 call Garnish; we of the Road are above it, but o't'other side of the House, silly Rascals that came voluntarily hither.—Such as are in for Fools, sign'd their own *Mittimus*, in being bound for others, may perhaps want it: I'll be your faithful Almoner.

Young Bookwit. O, by all means, Sir.—(*Gives him Money.*)
60 *Storm.* Pray, Sir, is that your Footman?

Young Bookwit. He is my Friend, Sir.

Storm. Look you, Sir, the only time to make use of a Friend is in Extremity; do you think you cou'd not hang him, and save your self? Sir, my Service to you, your own Health. [*Drinks and passes the*
65 *bottle.*]

First Prisoner. Captain, your Health. (*Gives it to the next Prisoner.*)

Second Prisoner. Captain, your Health.

Storm. But perhaps the Captain likes Brandy better.—So ho!
70 Brandy there.—(*Drinks.*) But you don't perhaps like these strong Liquors.—Sider Ho!—Drink to him in it.—Gentlemen all.—But Captain, I see you don't love Sider neither.—You and I will be for Claret then.—Ay marry! I knew this wou'd please (*Drinks.*) you. (*Drinks again.*) Faith we'll make an end on't, I'm glad you like it.
75 *Turn-key.* I'm sorry, Captain *Storm*, to see you impose upon a Gentleman, and put him to Charge in his Misfortune.—If a petty Larceny Fellow had done this—But one of the Road!

Storm. I beg your Pardon, Sir, I don't question but the Captain understands there is a Fee to you for going to the Keeper's side.
80 (*Young* Bookwit *and* Latine *give him Money.*)

Exeunt Turn-key, Simon *following.*

Nay, nay, you must stay here.

80 *give*] D1; *gives*

Simon. Why I am *Simon,* Madam *Penelope's* Man.

Storm. Then Madam *Penelope's* Man must strip for Garnish; indeed, Master *Simon,* you must.

Simon. Thieves! Thieves! Thieves!			85

Storm. Thieves! Thieves! Why you senseless Dog, do you think there's Thieves in *Newgate?* Away with him to the Tap-house. (*Pushes him off.*) We'll drink his Coat off. Come, my little Chymist, thou shalt transmute this Jacket into Liquor, Liquor that will make us forget the evil Day.—And while Day is ours, let us be 90 merry.

> For *little Villains must submit to Fate,*
> *That great ones may enjoy the World in State.*
>
> 						*Exeunt omnes.*

The End of the Fourth Act.

Act V. [Scene i.]

Scene, *Newgate.*

Scene *opens, and discovers Young* Bookwit
on a Couch asleep, Latine *looking on him.*

Latine. How quietly he rests! Oh that I could by watching him, hanging thus over him, and feeling all his Care, protract his Sleep! Oh sleep! thou sweetest Gift of Heav'n to Man, Still in thy downy Arms embrace my Friend, Nor loose him from his inexistent Trance			5 To sense of Yesterday, and pain of Being; In thee Oppressors sooth their angry Brow, In thee th' oppress'd forget tyrannick Pow'r, In thee— The Wretch condemn'd is equal to his Judge,			10

And the sad Lover to his cruel Fair;
Nay, all the shining Glories Men pursue,
When thou art wanted, are but empty Noise;
Who then wou'd court the Pomp of guilty Power,
15 When the Mind sickens at the weary Shew,
And flies to temporary Death for Ease;
When half our Life's Cessation of our Being—
He wakes—
How do I pity that returning Life,
20 Which I cou'd hazard thousand Lives to save!

   Young Bookwit. How heavily do I awake this Morning! Oh this senseless drinking! To suffer a whole Weeks Pain for an Hour's Jollity.—Methinks my Senses are burning round me.—I have—But interrupted Hints of the last Night.—Ha! in a Gaol;—Oh! I
25 remember, I remember: Oh *Lovemore*! *Lovemore*! I remember—

   Latine. You must have Patience, and bear it like a Man.

   Young Bookwit. Oh! whither shall I run, t'avoid my self?
Why all these Bars? These bolted Iron Gates?
They're needless to secure me.—Here, here's my Rack,
30 My Gaol, my Torture—
Oh! I can't bear it.—I cannot bear the rushing
Of new Thoughts,—
Fancy expands my Senses to Distraction,
And my Soul stretches to that boundless Space,
35 To which I've sent my wretched, wretched Friend,
Oh! *Latine*! *Latine*! Is all our Mirth and Humour
Come to this?
Give me thy Bosom, close in thy Bosome hide me,
From thy Eyes, I cannot bear their Pity or Reproach—

40   *Latine.* Dear *Bookwit*, how heartily I love you.—I don't know what to say.—But pray have Patience.

   Young Bookwit. If you can't bear my Pain, that's but communicated by your Pity,—How shall I my proper inborn Woe, my wounded Mind?

45   *Latine.* In all Assaults of Fortune that shou'd be serene,
Not in the Power of Accident or Chance—

   Young Bookwit. Words! Words! all that is but mere Talk;

Perhaps indeed to undeserv'd Affliction
Reason and Argument may give Relief,
Or in the known Vicissitudes of Life, 50
We may feel Comfort by our Self-persuasion.
But oh! there is no talking away Guilt!
This divine Particle will ake for ever,
There is no help but whence I dare not ask;
When this material Organ's indispos'd, 55
Juleps can cool, and Anodines give rest,
But nothing mix with this celestial Drop,
But Dew from that high Heav'n of which 'tis part.
    Latine. May that high Heav'n compose your Mind
And reconcile you to your self. 60
    Young Bookwit. How can I hope it!—
No—I must descend from Man
Grovel on Earth, nor dare look up again!
Oh *Lovemore*! *Lovemore*! where is he now?
Oh! thinking, thinking, why didst thou not come sooner, 65
Or not now!—
My Thoughts do so confuse me now,—as my Folly and Pleasures
did before this fatal Accident,—that I cannot recollect whence
Lovemore was provok'd to challenge me.
    Latine. You know, dear *Bookwit*, I fear'd some Ill from 70
a careless way of talking—But, alas! I dreamt not of so
great—
    Young Bookwit. Ay there it was.—He was naturally a little
jealous! Heav'ns do I say he was! I talk'd to him of Ladies, Treats,
and he might possibly believe 'twas where he had engag'd.—I 75
remember his serious Behaviour on that Subject.—Oh this unhappy
Tongue of mine!
Thou lawless voluble destroying Foe
That still run'st on, nor waitest Command of Reason:
Oh! I cou'd tear thee from me— 80
    Latine. Did you not expostulate before the Action?
    Young Bookwit. He wou'd have don't; but I, flush'd with the
Thoughts of Duelling—press'd on—Thus for the empty Praise of
Fools, I'm solidly unhappy.

85   *Latine.* You take it too deeply.—Your Honour was concern'd.

   Young Bookwit. Honour! the horrid Application of that sacred Word, to a Revenge 'gainst Friendship, Law and Reason, is a damn'd last shift of the damn'd envious Foe of Human Race. The routed Fiend projected this but since th' expansive glorious Law
90 from Heav'n came down—Forgive.

Enter Turn-key.

   Turn-key. Gentlemen, I come to tell you that you have the Favour to be carried in Chairs to your Indictment, to which you must go immediately.

   Latine. We are ready, Sir.

95   *Young Bookwit.* How shall I bear the Eye-shot of the Crowd in Court?

Exeunt.

[Act V. Scene ii.]

Scene, Frederick's *Lodgings.*

Enter Lovemore *in a Serjeant's Gown,*
and Frederick.

   Lovemore. Mankind is infinitely beholden to this noble Stiptick, that cou'd produce such wonderful Effects so suddenly: But tho' my Wound was very slight, I'm weak by the Effusion of so much Blood—

5   *Frederick.* Yet after all you have not lost enough to cool your Passion. Your Heart still beats *Penelope, Penelope.*—But in this Disguise you have Opportunity for Observation; you'll see whether you ought still to value her or not: I'm glad you thought of being

brought hither as soon as you came to your self: I expect old *Bookwit*
every Moment here.—   10

Enter Old Bookwit.

There he is—

Old Bookwit. Oh! Mr. *Frederick.*—Too late, too late was our Care,
They met last Night, and then the fatal Act was done.—You'll
excuse, Sir, a Father's Sorrow.—I can't speak much, but you may
guess what I hope from you.   15

Frederick. You may depend upon ingenuous Usage in the Prosecu-
tion; I'm going instantly to *Penelope's* with this learned Gentleman,
to know what she can say to this matter.—I desir'd you in the Note
I sent you to purchase the Favour of your Son's being brought
thither, where he and you may be Witnesses of what shall pass.—I 20
seek not his Blood, nor wou'd neglect a Justice to my deceas'd
Friend.

Old Bookwit. I believe my Son and the rest are going thither e'er
this; and I desire this worthy Serjeant's Favour and Advice,—since
we both mean the same thing, only to act with Honour, if his Life 25
may be sav'd—

Lovemore. I'll do what's just to the Deceas'd and the Survivour.

Old Bookwit. I'll leave you, but will take care to come in just afore
the Criminals arrive—

Exit.

Lovemore. The poor old Gentleman.—Prithee let's go, I long to 30
see my lovely Torment *Penelope.*

Frederick. I'll but leave word within.

Exeunt.

27 *Lovemore.*] D2; *Lat.*

[Act V. Scene iii.]

Scene, Penelope's *Lodgings*.

Enter Penelope *and* Victoria.

Penelope. It seems *Simon* lay out all Night, and was carried away by the Watch with some Gentlemen in a Quarrel.

Victoria. I fancy the Men who are always for shewing their Valour, are like the Women who are always talking of their 5 Chastity, because they're conscious of their defect in't.

Penelope. Right,—for we are not apt to raise Arguments, but about what we think is disputable—

Victoria. Ay, ay, they whose Honour is a sore part, are more fearful of being touch'd, than they in whom 'tis only a tender one. 10 But tell me honestly, *Penelope*, shou'd poor *Lovemore* be in this Rencounter, and that for your sake, wou'd it have no effect upon you in his Favour?

Penelope. I don't know how to answer you; but I find something in that Reflexion, which acquaints me 'tis very hard for one to know 15 one's own Heart. (*Sighs.*)

Victoria. However, let your Heart answer me one question more, as well as it can.—Do's it love me as well as ever it did?

Penelope. Do's not, Madam, that question proceed from a change 20 in your own?

Victoria. It does, *Penelope*, I own it does.—I had a long conflict with my self on my Pillow, last Night.

Penelope. What were your thoughts there?

Victoria. That I ow'd it to our Friendship to acknowledge to you, 25 that all the Pleasure I once had in you, is vanished.— Ah *Penelope*! I'm sorry for every good Quality you have—

Penelope. Since you are so frank—I must confess to you something very like this.—But however I envy'd that sprightly ingenuous native Beauty of yours; I see it now so much the figure of your

Mind, that I can conquer, I think I can, any inclination in my self 30
that opposes the happiness of so sincere a Friend—

Victoria. Explain your self, my Dear.

Penelope. I'll discountenance this *Bookwit's* ambiguous Addresses.
—And if *Lovemore* can forgive my late ill usage,—I need say no
more—   35

Enter Servant.

Servant. Mr. *Frederick* below desires to see you on some extraordinary Business.

Victoria. I have not time, my dearest Friend, to applaud or thank
you—but must run in. He comes from *Lovemore*—remember.

Exit.

Penelope. Let him come up.—Now can't I for my Life forbear a 40
little Tyranny.

Enter Frederick *and* Lovemore.

Good morrow, Sir, I believe I know your Business—you're
officious for your Friend.—But I am deaf.

Frederick. I know you are, and have been, but I come only to do
him a last office.—He'll trouble you no more, but I must conjure you 45
to read this, and inform this learned Gentleman what you know of
this Misfortune.

Penelope. (*Reading.*) *Your cruelty provok'd me to desire the favour of
dying by Mr* Bookwit's *hand, since he had taken from me more than Life,
in robbing me of you—farewell for ever—I direct* Frederick, *not to give* 50
you this, 'till I am no more.—Writ in his Blood!—'Till I am no more!

Lovemore. No more!—Thou shalt not be no more.—Thou shalt live
here for ever. Here, thou dearest Paper, mingle with my Life's
Stream: Either the Paper bleeds anew, or my Eyes weep Blood.—So
let 'em do for ever.—Oh, my *Lovemore*! Did the Vanity of a prating 55
Boy banish thy solid Services and manly Love?

Frederick. This is no Reparation to him for his lost Life, nor me for
my lost Friend.—Yet when you please to receive 'em, I am oblig'd
to deliver you some Papers, wherein he has given you all the
Fortune he cou'd bestow; nor wou'd revoke it, ev'n thus injur'd 60
as he was—

Penelope. Curse on all Wealth and Fortune! he, he is gone who only deserv'd all, and whose Worth I know too late.

Lovemore. (*To* Frederick.) Oh Extasie! why was I angry at her 65 rejoicing in my Sorrow, when hers to me is such a perfect Bliss? 'Tis barbarous, not discover my self!

Frederick. Do, and be us'd barbarously.—But, Madam, you must be compos'd; your Life for ought I know's at stake, for there is no such thing as Accessaries in Murder; and it can be prov'd, you knew of 70 *Lovemore's* threatning to fight *Bookwit.*—You must either take your Trial your self, or be Mr. *Bookwit's* Witness.

Penelope. I his Witness!—No,—I'll swear any thing to hang him.

Frederick. Ah! Madam, you must consider your self however.— 75 Pray, Sir, read her Indictment to her.

Lovemore. (*Reading.*) *That on the said third Day of* April, *the said* Penelope, *of the Parish of St.* Martin's *in the Fields, Spinster, without Fear before her Eyes, but by the Instigation of the Devil, and through an evil Pride of Heart,*

80 *Penelope.* 'Tis too true—(*Weeping.*)

Lovemore. Did contrive, abett, and consent to the Death of John Love-more *Esquire, of the Age of twenty eight Years, or thereabouts.*

Frederick. I can't hear the mention of him without Tears. He was the sincerest Friend.

85 *Lovemore.* I think I have seen him.—He was, I've heard, a Man of Honesty, but of something a disagreeable Make.

Penelope. Oh! Sir, you never saw him if you think so.—His Person was as free as his Mind was honest, nor had he Imperfection but his Love of me. (*Weeps.*)

90 *Lovemore.* (*To* Frederick.) I tremble, I shall disoblige her too much.

Frederick. You shan't discover your self, you shall go through her Soul, now 'tis mov'd on our side.—Win her now, or see my Face no more.—I'll not have my Wine spoil'd every Night, with your 95 Recitals of Love and asking Advice, tho' you never mean to take it, like a true Lover.

Penelope. When did that best of Men expire, good Mr. *Frederick?*

Frederick. This Morning: But shou'd I speak the manner. With a faint dying Voice he call'd me to him.—I went in Tenderness 100 to take my long Farewel.—He in a last Effort of Nature prest me to his Breast, And with the softest Accent sigh'd in Death, *Penelope.*

Penelope. Oh the too generous Man! Ungrateful I! Curses on him first flatter'd with his Tongue, on her that first dissembled in her 105 Silence—
What Miseries have they entail'd on Life
To bring in Fraud, and Diffidence in Love!
Simplicity's the Dress of honest Passion,
Then why our Arts, why to a Man enamour'd,   110
That at her Feet effuses all his Soul,
Must Woman cold appear, false to her self and him?

Frederick. (*Aside to* Lovemore.) Do you see there!—You'd have spoke before she consider'd that—

Penelope. Oh! cou'd I see him now to press his liv'd Lips,   115
And call him back to Life with my Complaints,
His Eyes wou'd glare upon my Guilt with Horrour,
That us'd to glote and melt in Love before me—
Let mine for ever then be shut to Joy,
To all that's bright, and valuable in Man!   120

> *I'll to his sacred Ashes be a Wife,*
> *And to his Memory devote my Life.*

                                     Exit.

Lovemore. This is worth dying for indeed.—I'll follow her.

Frederick. No you shan't; let her go in,—throw her self upon her Bed, and hug, and call her Pillow *Lovemore.* 'Tis but what you've 125 done a thousand times for her.

Lovemore. That's true too.

Frederick. Let her contemplate on the Mischief of her Vanity, She shall lament 'till her Glass is of our side—Till its pretty Nies be all blubber'd, its Heart must heave and pant with perfect Anguish 130 before 'twill feel the Sorrow of another's; don't you know Pride, Scorn, Affectation, and a whole Train of Ils must be sob'd away before a great Beauty's mortify'd to purpose.

Enter Servant.

Servant. Old Mr. *Bookwit* enquires for you here, Mr. *Frederick.*
135   *Frederick.* Pray let him come up.

Enter Old Bookwit.

Lovemore. What's the matter? you seem more discompos'd than
you were at Mr. *Frederick's;* something still new?
    Old Bookwit. I saw the Boy a coming in a Chair, he looks so languid
and distress'd, poor Lad: He has all his Mother's Softness, by
140 nature of the sweetest Disposition—Oh! Gentlemen!—you know
not what it is to be a Father.—To see my only Child in that Condition.—My Grief quickned at the sight of him; I thought I could
have Patience till I saw him.

Enter Servant.

Servant. There are two or three in Chairs desire Admittance by
145 Appointment.
    Old Bookwit. 'Tis right, Sir:

Enter Young Bookwit, Latine, *and* Gaoler.

Oh, my dear Child, oh *Tom*! are all thy aged Father's Hopes then
come to this, that he can't see thee, his only Son, but guarded by a
Gaoler?—Thy Mother's happy that liv'd not to see this Day.—Is
150 all the Nurture that she gave thy Infancy—The Erudition she
bequeath'd thy Youth, thus answer'd?—Oh, my Son! my Son! rise
and support thy Father! I sink with Tenderness, my Child, come to
my Arms while thou art mine.
    Young Bookwit. Oh best of Fathers! Let me not see your Tears,
155 don't double my Afflictions by your Woe—There's Consolation
when a Friend laments us, but When a Parent grieves, the Anguish
is too native, Too much our own to be called Pity.

154–7 Oh . . . Pity.]   Decisions on what should be set as poetry and what as
prose are difficult with Steele, and no doubt the compositor met some problems, not
all of which he solved satisfactorily. I have changed to poetic lineation some passages
that appear as prose in Q (see Emendations of Accidentals). Certainly Steele intended
as blank verse some lines with a few extra syllables, and I have left those as poetry.
However, the reader would be hard put to find any metre in lines 154–7. They are,
therefore, set as prose.

Oh! Sir, consider, I was born to die.—
'Tis but expanding Thought, and Life is nothing;
Ages and Generations pass away,   160
And with resistless Force like Waves, o'er Waves,
Roul down the irrevocable Stream of Time.
Into the insatiate Ocean for ever—Thus we are gone.
But the erroneous Sense of Man—'tis the lamented that's at rest,
but the Survivour mourns—   165
All my sorrows vanish with that Thought,
But Heav'n grant my aged Father Patience.
 Old Bookwit. Oh Child? (*Turning away.*)
 Young Bookwit. Do not torment your self, you shall promise not
to grieve—   170
What if they do upbraid you with my Death—
Consider, Sir, in Death that our Relation ceases.
Nor, shall I want your Care, or know your Grief.
It matters not whether by Law, or Nature 'tis I dye.
What, won't my Father hear me plead to him?   175
Don't turn from me—
Yet don't look at me, with your Soul so full.
 Old Bookwit. Oh my Child, my Child!—I cou'd hear thee ever.
'Twas that I lov'd thee, that I turn'd away,
To hear my Son persuade me to resign him.   180
I can't, I can't. The Grief is insupportable.
 Young Bookwit. You make a Coward of me with your Anguish,
I grow an Infant, scarce can weep with Silence,
Let me keep some decency in my Distress.
 Old Bookwit. If we might be apart—(*Looking at the Company.*) But   185
that's too much to hope.
 Gaoler. No, no, we'll leave you to your selves.
          Exeunt.

 Old Bookwit. I have too much upon me, Child, to speak.—And
indeed, have nothing to say, but to feed my Eyes upon thee, e'er we
part for ever, if tears would let me.—When you have slept in your   190
Cradle, I have wak'd for you,—and was it to this end—Oh Child!
you've broke your Father's Heart. (*Swoons.*)

Young Bookwit. Good Heaven forbid it—guard him and protect him.

195 He faints, he's cold, he's gone. (*Running to him.*)
He's gone, and with his last Breath call'd me Parricide,
You've broke your Father's Heart! Oh killing Sound!
I'm all Contagion, to pitty me is Death.
My Griefs to all are mortal but my self,
200 You've broke your Father's Heart! If I did so,
Why thus serene in Death, thou smiling Clay,
Why that calm Aspect to thy Murderer?
Oh big unutterable Grief—merciful Heav'n,
I don't deserve this ease of Tears to melt,
205 With Penitence—Oh sweet, sweet Remorse,
Now all my Powers give way,
To my just sorrow, for the best of Fathers. (*Aloud.*)
Thou venerable Fountain of my Life,
Why don't I also die deriv'd from thee?
210 Sure you are not gone—Is the way out of Life, thus easy, which
you so much fear'd in me. (*Takes him by the Hand.*)
Why stay I after? But I deserve to stay,
To feel the quick remembrance of my Follies,
Yet if my Sighs, my Tears, my Anguish can atone—

Re-enter Frederick, Lovemore, Latine,
Gaoler, Victoria, Penelope.

215 *Frederick.* What is the matter?—What?—
Young Bookwit. Behold this sight, I am the guilty Wretch—
Frederick. Keep aside a little, Sir, he only swoons I hope, I think
he breaths,—yes he returns—you must compose your self.
Latine. Poor *Bookwit*, how utterly he seems distress'd.
220 *Old Bookwit.* I will be calm—resign to Heaven, and hear you
patiently.
Frederick. You, Sir, his Favourite Servant, pray speak honestly
the truth of what you know, to this learned Gentleman; who is
Council in this case.
225 *Young Bookwit.* Sir he is not—

Lovemore. Pray Sir, give the Servant leave first.

Latine. Know then, I am not what I seem, but a Gentleman of a
plentiful Fortune, I am thus dress'd to carry on such gay pursuits
as should offer in this Town.—Not to detain you, Mr. *Bookwit* sent
me late last Night, with a Letter to one of these Ladies—coming 230
from thence, as I cross'd, I saw *Lovemore* in the Garden, he stop'd
me, and after some Questions concerning my Message to this
House, to which he did not like my answers, he struck me, we
fought—I left him dead upon the Spot, of which this Gentleman
is guiltless—   235

Old Bookwit. How! was it you then that kill'd Mr. *Lovemore?*

Latine. 'Twas this unhappy Hand gave him his Death, but so
provok'd—

Young Bookwit. Who cou'd believe that any pleasing Passion
Cou'd touch a Breast loaded with Guilt like mine: 240
But all my Mind is seiz'd with Admiration
Of thy stupendious Friendship.—What then—
Cou'd'st thou hold thy innocent Hand up at a Bar
With Felons, to save thy Friend?
How shall I chide, or praise thy brave Imposture?   245
Ah! Sir! believe him not.—He cannot bear the Loss of me whom he
o'er values, therefore with highest Gallantry he offers a Benefit
which 'twere the meanest Baseness to receive,
But Death's more welcome than a Life so purchas'd.

Latine. We all know you can talk, and guild things as you please, 250
But the Lady's Servant knows I was taken near the Body when
you—.

Young Bookwit. Sir, do but hear me—(*Pushing away* Latine.)

Latine. I'll easily convince you. (*Pushing away Young* Bookwit.)

Young Bookwit. Pray mind him not, his Brain is touch'd—   255

Latine. I am the Man, he was not near the Place—

Lovemore. I can hold out no longer.—*Lovemore* still lives t'adore
your noble Friendship, and begs a Share in't. Be not amaz'd! but
let me grasp you both, who in an Age degenerate as this, have such
transcendent Virtue—   260

Young Bookwit. Oh *Lovemore! Lovemore!* How shall I speak my Joy
at thy Recovery—

I fail beneath the too extatick Pleasure—
What help has Human Nature from its Sorrows
265 When our Relief it self is such a Burthen.

   Old Bookwit. Oh, the best Burthen upon Earth! I beg your Pardon,
Sir.—I never was so taken with a Man in my Life at first Sight
(*Kisses* Lovemore.) (*To* Latine.) Let me be known to you too.

   Latine. Sir, you do me Honour—

270   *Old Bookwit.* But you, Ladies, are the first Cause of the many
Errors we have been in, and you only can extricate us with Satisfaction.—Such is the Force of Beauty.—The Wounds the Sword
gave this Gentleman were slight, but you've transfix'd a Vital, and
a noble part, his Heart.—Had I known his Pretences, I had not
275 interpos'd for my Son—

   Frederick. Come, Madam, no more of the Cruel.—Go on *Lovemore*;
o' my Conscience the Man's afraid; 'tis Impudence to be alive
again.—You see him now, Madam, now you may press his liv'd
Lips, And call him back to Life with your Complaints.

280   *Lovemore.* I stand, methinks, upon the Brink of Fate
In an ambiguous Interval of Life,
And doubt t'accept of being, till you smile.
In every human Incident besides,
I am superiour, and can chuse or leave,
285 But in minutest things that touch my Love,
My Bosom's seiz'd with Anguish, or with Transport.

   Penelope. You've shewn your Passion to me with such Honour,
that if I am confus'd, I know I should not be, to say I approve it.—
For I know no Rules shou'd make me insensible of generous Usage.
290 —My Person and my Mind are yours for ever.

   Lovemore. Then Doubts, and fears, and anxious Cares be gone,
All ye black Thoughts that did corrode my Breast,
Here enter Faith, and Confidence, and Love!
Love that can't live with Jealousie, but dwells
295 With sacred Marriage, Truth, and mutual Honour;
I knew not where you wou'd bestow your Vows,
But never doubted of your Faith when given. (*Kissing her
Hand.*)

   Old Bookwit. You see, my Son, how Constancy's rewarded.

You have from Nature every Quality,   300
To make you well become what Fortune gave you;
But neither Wit, or Beauty, Wealth or Courage,
Implicitly deserve the World's Esteem,
They're only in their Application, Goods—
How cou'd you fight a Man you knew not why,   305
You don't think that 'tis great, merely to dare?
'Tis that a Man is just he shou'd be bold.
Indeed you've err'd.

Latine. You give my Friend, methinks, too much Compunction
for a little Levity in his Actions,—When he is too severe in's own 310
Reflections on 'em.

Penelope. Well, *Victoria*, you see I take your Advice at last in
Choice of *Lovemore*.

Victoria. I congratulate your missing of the other.

Penelope. I heartily believe you, my dear Friend.   315

Old Bookwit. But we best guide our Actions by hopes of Reward.
(*To* Victoria.) Cou'd but my Son have such a glorious Prospect as
this Fair one, I doubt not but his future Carriage wou'd deserve
her.

Victoria. I believe I may safely promise to approve of all the truth 320
he tells me.

Young Bookwit. You've promis'd then to like all I shall say.

Old Bookwit. These unexpected good Events deserve our Celebration with some Mirth and Fiddles.

Frederick. I foresaw this happy Turn, therefore have prepar'd 'em. 325
—Call in the Dancers.

Song.

By Mr. *Leveridge.*

I.

The rolling Years the Joys restore,
Which happy happy Britain knew,
When in a Female Age before
Beauty the Sword of Justice drew.   330

II.

Nymphs, and Fauns, and Rural Powers
Of christal Floods, and shady Bowers
No more shall here preside:
The flowing Wave, and living Green
335 *Owe only to their present Queen*
Their Safety and their Pride.

III.

United Air, and Pleasures bring
Of tender Note, and tuneful String
All your Arts devoted are
340 *To move the Innocent and Fair*
While they receive the pleasing Wound,
Eccho repeats the dying Sound.

Young Bookwit. Since such deserv'd Misfortunes they must share
Who with gay Falshoods entertain the Fair:
345 Let all with this just Maxim guide their Youth,
There is no Gallantry in Love but Truth.

Exeunt.

[*The End of the Fifth Act.*]

EPILOGUE.

Our too advent'rous Author soar'd to Night
Above the little Praise, Mirth to excite,
And chose with Pity to chastise Delight.
For Laughter's a distorted Passion, born
Of sudden self Esteem, and sudden Scorn;   5
Which, when 'tis o'er, the Men in Pleasure wise,
Both him that mov'd it, and themselves despise,
While generous Pity of a painted Woe
Makes us our selves both more approve, and know.
What is that Touch within, which Nature gave   10
For Man to Man, e'er Fortune made a Slave?
Sure it descends from that dread Power alone,
Who levels Thunder from his awful Throne,
And shakes both Worlds,—yet hears the wretched Groan.
'Tis what the antient Sage could ne'er define,   15
Wonder'd—and call'd, part human, part divine:
'Tis that pure Joy, which guardian Angels know,
When timely they assist their Care below,
When they the good protect, the ill oppose,
'Tis what our Sovereign feels, when she bestows,   20
Which gives her glorious Cause such high Success,
That only on the Stage you see Distress.

[FINIS]

THE TENDER HUSBAND: OR, THE
ACCOMPLISH'D FOOLS

COMPOSITION AND SOURCES

LITTLE is known of the actual composition of *The Tender Husband*. Steele, stranded at Landguard Fort with mounting debts and little hope for professional advancement, reportedly retired periodically to a farmhouse at nearby Walton[1] to work on the manuscript that would become his most light-hearted and genuinely comic play. He never later referred publicly to his reason for abandoning an attempt at a play called *The Election of Gotham* or for now writing a comedy untouched by the sentimentalism of *The Funeral* and *The Lying Lover*.

For source material he turned to Molière. *Le Sicilien* (1667) provided the incident of the lover disguised as painter. Steele imitated the basic device and translated some lines in IV. ii, but he did not hesitate to change speeches and actions to meet the requirements of his own plot and characterizations. In the original, Adraste uses the ruse of the portrait painter to approach Isidore, Dom Pedro's beautiful Greek slave. He does not, however, reveal himself to her by anecdote as Captain Clerimont does; rather his valet provides a diversion to allow him to whisper with the girl. Isidore eludes her master later by a veil trick instead of eloping during the painting scene.

John Dennis claimed, probably accurately, that Biddy Tipkin was taken from Molière's *Les Précieuses ridicules* (1659).[2] But if Molière's girls evoked the idea of Biddy, Steele characteristically made the finished character distinct from the originals. His attitude is one of complaisant amusement toward his pretty young 'city nymph' rather than sharp satire. Cathos and Magdelon are ridiculous because they believe naïvely in all facets of contemporary culture and embrace preciosity for its own sake; Biddy is distracted by her literary tastes alone. Whereas Cathos and Magdelon are no more than targets for Molière's satire, Biddy remains amusing and likable. Steele attacks the romances and the English taste for them, but Biddy herself, a victim of contemporary taste, escapes unscathed; she is never cured or even

---

[1] *Gentleman's Magazine*, lx (1790), Part ii, 993.
[2] *Characters and Conduct of Sir John Edgar*, in Dennis, ii. 187.

criticized for her romanticism by any character except her old aunt, who is scarcely a spokesman for acceptable behaviour. In the final act she is rewarded, not humiliated, perhaps because, along with her affectation, she obviously embodies some of the old-fashioned earthy virtues of that long line of Bridgets and Alices and Joans from whom she descends.

Additional evidence of Steele's familiarity with Molière appears in parallels with a third play, *L'Avare*.[1] The plays imitated in *The Tender Husband* had all been translated into English: John Crowne adapted *Le Sicilien* as *The Countrey Wit* (London, 1675); Richard Flecknoe, *Les Précieuses ridicules* as *The Damoiselles a la Mode* (London, 1667, acted September 1668); and Thomas Shadwell, *L'Avare* as *The Miser* (London, 1672).[2] But there is no reason to believe Steele used the translations, most of which had not been performed since he had come to London and none of which had been reprinted. Comparison of the texts leaves no doubt that he turned to Molière rather than to his imitators. In a few speeches he obviously translated directly from the text with some care; in other instances, he adapted loosely, perhaps in some even unwittingly.

Steele also showed his usual familiarity with the English stage tradition. His characters were in general new renderings of Restoration stock figures, such as the doltish young squire and his haranguing father, the antiquated virgin, and the cast mistress. He introduced specific plot details which suggest knowledge of earlier plays. It is wrong to infer from the similarities that he 'borrowed' from antecedent plays, for some details, the duping of the country booby, for example, were traditional. But those comedies which were popular during Steele's early years in and around London must be considered part of the literary climate in which he wrote; they had at least an indirect effect on his own work, although relationships cannot be incontrovertibly proven. It is worth noting that seemingly strong parallels exist between his plays and unpopular ones which had not been performed in London or reprinted for so many years that he would not likely have known them. One must be wary, then, of

---

[1] See Paul E. Parnell, 'A New Molière Source for Steele's "The Tender Husband"', *NQ* cciv (1959), 218.

[2] Aphra Behn based Isabella in *The False Count* (1682) on Molière's *précieuses*. John Wilcox convincingly argues that Lady Fantast and her daughter Mrs. Fantast in Shadwell's *Bury Fair* (1689) derive from *Les Femmes savantes* rather than *Les Précieuses ridicules*. Other English writers, notably Thomas Betterton in *The Amorous Widow* (acted 1670, printed 1706) and Crowne in *Sir Courtly Nice* (1685), borrowed Mascarille but not Cathos and Magdelon. See John Wilcox, *The Relation of Molière to Restoration Comedy* (New York, 1938), pp. 180–1 and *passim*. Dates of first performances appear in Van Lennep, *passim*.

regarding too seriously even striking similarities unless lines are echoed or unique action or characterization is imitated.

Steele's titular plot, the entrapment of an erring woman by her husband, was prefigured in two plays that Steele probably knew, *Womans Wit: or, The Lady in Fashion* (1697) by his friend Colley Cibber and *The Ladies Visiting Day* (1701) by another friend, William Burnaby. Both satirize French affectations and 'innocent freedoms'. The latter particularly resembles Steele's work, with a *billet doux*, a husband's watching his wife approach a young 'man', and a man drawing a sword against his wife. Another play by Burnaby, *The Reform'd Wife* (1700), introduces a fortune-hunter named Clerimont —the name was not unusual—bent on winning a lady with a quirk by an unconventional courtship.

Lubberly dolts, predecessors to Humphry, appear in many Restoration plays, but notable resemblances occur in Thomas Wright's *The Female Vertuoso's* (1693), an adaptation of Molière's *Les Femmes savantes*; Thomas D'Urfey's *Madam Fickle: or the Witty False One* (acted 1676, published 1677, and revived 24 August 1704); and Thomas Shadwell's *The Lancashire Witches and Tegue O Divelly The Irish-Priest* (1682, performed six times between January 1703 and August 1704).[1] Wright's young Witless, a university fool dragged to town to marry the reluctant Mariana, like Humphry, performs an absurd dance and marries a girl named Lucy through the trickery of her brother. Mariana loves another Clerimont, who disguises himself, this time as a dancing master, to win her. Moreover, some of Steele's lines parallel Wright's, but whether they derive from him or Molière is incapable of proof. D'Urfey's Captain Tilbury introduces his boorish son Toby to an old friend in a scene strongly similar to Sir Harry's presentation of Humphry to Tipkin (I. ii). Shadwell's Young Hartford, ordered to marry his cousin or be disinherited, has little heart for the match and willingly allows himself to be deprived of his intended bride.[2]

Critics through the years have found resemblances to still other plays. A. W. Ward suggests that the moral was derived from Cibber's *The Careless Husband*,[3] first acted 7 December 1704 and published

---

[1] Dates of performance are taken from Van Lennep and Avery, *passim*.

[2] R. S. Forsythe is over-generous in attributing touches in Steele's play to Shadwell ('Shadwell's Contributions to *She Stoops to Conquer* and to *The Tender Husband*', *Journal of English and Germanic Philology*, xi (1912), 104–11). He gives Shadwell credit for characteristics shared by all the stage bumpkins and for numerous touches borrowed from Molière.

[3] A. W. Ward, *A History of English Dramatic Literature, to the Death of Queen Anne*, 3 vols. (London, 1875), ii. 604.

19 December. Subsequent critics have often echoed the suggestion; to find any connections between the two plays, however, demands feats of manipulation. George H. Nettleton calls Tipkin's insistence on being written down a rascal 'obviously reminiscent of Dogberry',[1] a more convincing claim. The scene in which Biddy and Humphry hurl insults at one another has been compared to the scene between Miss Prue and Ben in Congreve's *Love for Love* (1695).[2] Although the scenes are roughly comparable, there are no specifically parallel lines, and the characters are really quite different. Winton cites as a female francophile antecedent to Mrs. Clerimont Mrs. Fantast in Shadwell's *Bury Fair*, which was revived 11 July 1702.[3] Smith sees in Humphry's outdated suit an echo of Sir Credulous Easy in Aphra Behn's *Sir Patient Fancy*,[4] a play which bears some resemblance to *The Funeral* and contains a character named Fainlove.[5] Willard Connely finds in Steele's plot 'not a few devices from Congreve and Wycherley'.[6]

Besides his adaptation of materials from Molière and his perhaps unconscious absorption and remoulding of the materials of Restoration comedy, Steele also had the help of a successful acquaintance, Joseph Addison, only a year older than himself but already recognized in politics and literature. The two had known each other since schooldays at the Charterhouse and later at Oxford. When Richard Blackmore had attacked Addison in his *Satyr against Wit* in 1700, Steele had written in his defence. He had also published in *The Diverting Post* on 4 November 1704 'An Imitation of the Sixth Ode of Horace', puffing Addison's as yet unpublished poem *The Campaign*.[7] But never had the two collaborated until Addison came to Steele's aid on *The Tender Husband*. Years later Steele described his debt thus:

When the Play above-mentioned [*The Tender Husband*] was last Acted, there were so many applauded Stroaks in it which I had from the same Hand, that I thought very meanly of my self that I had never publickly acknowledged

---

[1] G. H. Nettleton, *English Drama of the Restoration and Eighteenth Century (1642–1780)* (New York, 1921), p. 162.

[2] John Harrington Smith, 'Tony Lumpkin and the Country Booby Type in Antecedent English Comedy', *PMLA* lviii (1943), p. 1041, n. 12.

[3] Calhoun Winton, ed., *The Tender Husband*, in Regents Restoration Drama Series (Lincoln, Neb., 1967), p. xii.

[4] 'Tony Lumpkin', p. 1040, n. 11. Smith also cites parallels with D'Urfey's *Madam Fickle* (1676), Crowne's *The Countrey Wit* (1676), and Shadwell's *The Squire of Alsatia* (1688).

[5] Steele used the name in *The Lying Lover*.

[6] Willard Connely, *Sir Richard Steele* (New York, 1934), p. 88.

[7] Winton, pp. 72–3. The poem is reprinted in *Verse*, pp. 14–15.

them. After I have put other Friends upon importuning him to publish Dramatick, as well as other Writings he has by him, I shall end what I think I am obliged to say on this Head, by giving my Reader this Hint for the better judging of my Productions, that the best Comment upon them would be an Account when the Patron to the *Tender Husband* was in *England*, or Abroad.[1]

Although Addison had been in Ireland on government business when Steele began the *Tatler*, his longest absence from English life began in September 1699, when he left for a grand tour of the continent, and lasted until he returned to English soil in late February or early March 1704.[2] Surely Steele refers in this remark to the tour, made during the years that *The Christian Hero* and the first two plays were published; and the comment, in that light, is revealing. Steele, having gained little reputation from his *Lying Lover*, and needing desperately to repair his fortunes through a new play against which he had already borrowed money, would have eagerly approached his highly esteemed friend for advice and help in composition.

Steele never mentioned which strokes he owed to Addison's pen, and scholars have speculated about it for more than 200 years. As early as 1721 Thomas Tickell, in the Preface to his edition of Addison's *Works*, enlarges upon Steele's statement, claiming that he 'owed some of the most taking scenes of it to Mr. *Addison*'. The extent of Steele's indebtedness has been variously interpreted and misinterpreted since then. Peter Smithers, for example, conservatively states that Addison had gone over the drafts and made 'a number of corrections and suggestions',[3] but Willard Connely interprets Steele's remark to mean that Addison's work had 'amounted almost to collaboration', although he considered Steele's estimate too generous.[4] Henry R. Montgomery believes Addison had revised the draft, touched it up, and helped to promote it.[5] Many critics attribute to Addison groups of scenes involving one set of characters rather than individual lines or phrases. John Forster, for example, believes Addison's hand can be traced in the scenes involving Sir Harry Gubbin and Humphry, and cites as evidence the 'heightened humour of these scenes'.[6] F. W. Bateson agrees that Addison might have created Sir Harry, 'a kind

---

[1] *Spectator*, no. 555.
[2] Peter Smithers, *The Life of Joseph Addison* (Oxford, 1954), pp. 45–87.
[3] Smithers, p. 88.
[4] Connely, p. 87.
[5] Henry R. Montgomery, *Memoirs of the Life and Writings of Sir Richard Steele*, 2 vols. (Edinburgh, 1865), i. 51.
[6] John Forster, *Biographical Essays* (London, 1860), p. 214.

of prototype of the Tory Foxhunter' in *The Freeholder*, and continues, '. . . it is tempting, remembering Leonora's library in *The Spectator*, with "The Grand Cyrus: With a Pin stuck in one of the middle Leaves", to assign Biddy Tipkin to the same hand.'[1] H. Hartmann, on the other hand, attributes the scenes between Clerimont Senior and his wife to Addison.[2]

Bibliographical evidence supports Hartmann. Discrepancies in speech prefixes, names, and details in two scenes suggest that the manuscript sent to the printer was actually the papers of two dramatists, and that a couple of scenes, III. i. III.I (or II6.I)–I50.I and v. i. 81.I–162.I, were undoubtedly Addison's.[3] Possibly his contributions extend beyond these two scenes and the prologue which bears his name, but no others have been detected or conclusively proved. It is unlikely, although not impossible, that he wrote other major portions or corrected the manuscript. From the bibliographical evidence several conclusions may be drawn about this first collaboration between Addison and Steele: Addison, probably brought into the project late, knew the comedy only vaguely. It was he rather than Steele who wrote the serious marital plot and introduced the conventional sword-drawing. Addison's scenes, because they were added shortly before the play opened, were never carefully integrated with the printer's copy of those parts written by Steele. In the promptbook, however, the inaccuracies must have been detected immediately and corrected.

STAGE HISTORY

Captain Steele, finding himself again in debt, came, probably in the winter of 1703–4, to Christopher Rich, chief patentee of the Drury Lane Theatre, with a play called *The Election of Gotham* allegedly near completion. Rich agreed to lend him £72 against it, taking as insurance a bond for £144. Steele soon applied the money to other debts, but he never delivered the completed comedy; instead, somewhat tardily, in late March of 1705, he brought Rich *The Tender Husband: Or, The Accomplish'd Fools*.[4] The date of the financial agreement

---

[1] F. W. Bateson, *English Comic Drama, 1700–1750* (Oxford, 1929), p. 50.

[2] H. Hartmann, *Steele als Dramatiker* (Königsberg, 1880), cited in Aitken, i. 110, n. 1.

[3] For a discussion of bibliographical evidence of authorship see my article, 'Two Scenes by Addison in Steele's *Tender Husband*', *SB* xix (1966), 217–26.

[4] Complainant's Bill, Public Record Office, Chancery Pleadings, B. & A. Hamilton, IV. before 1714, No. 642, *Steele* v. *Rich*. Quoted in Aitken, i. 113.

is conjectural: Steele said, in his Chancery suit against Rich in 1707, that the transaction occurred in or about December 1702, and he delivered *The Tender Husband* in or about April 1704.[1] Rich said the agreement was signed on or about 7 January 1703, *The Election of Gotham* was to be delivered 20 February, and the substitute comedy arrived in late March 1705.[2] Probably Steele miscalculated all the dates by a year, for he surely brought the play to Rich in the spring of 1705, when it was performed; the financial agreement would presumably have been signed after Rich accepted *The Lying Lover*, which ran in January 1703. Had the agreement been earlier than this run, *The Lying Lover* would have been offered; had his financial difficulties arisen in January 1703, presumably Steele would have borrowed against his third nights for the present play rather than project future ones, unless, of course, he had already done that. Curiously, *The Lying Lover* is never mentioned by either complainant or defendant in the legal proceedings.

Steele and Rich disagreed as to which of them urged immediate rehearsals when Steele finally delivered his play. April was a notably bad month for a *première* performance; nevertheless, the play opened on 23 April 1705.[3] In the light of Steele's financial necessities, his faith in the literary skill of Addison, and the genuine merit of the play, the first run must have been woefully disappointing. The comedy played five nights to small houses. The second night's receipts were a meagre £26. 14s.; on the third night, Steele's benefit, total receipts amounted to £61. 6s.; on the fourth to £26. 11s.[4] The author's profits from his benefit amounted to no more than £10. 8s. 2d., according to Rich's calculations, so by an elaborate agreement, Steele waived his second author's benefit, preferring profits from one or two performances in the autumn or winter (Steele and Rich differ on the number).[5] Out of the receipts of £64. 3s. 6d. for the performance on 20 November 1705, Rich was willing to add to Steele's third-night profit £2. 17s. 6d., a sum which Steele apparently construed as the final stroke in a gross injustice. He attempted to regain his bond and collect author's fees in a suit against Rich, but he ended up with nothing but costly legal obligations. As an escape from debt *The Tender Husband*, Steele's brightest comedy, proved a dismal failure.

---

[1] Aitken, i. 113.

[2] Defendant's answer in *Steele* v. *Rich*. Quoted in Aitken, i. 117–19.

[3] The comedy was advertised as late as Saturday, 21 April, two days before the opening, as *The City Nymph; Or, The Accomplish'd Fools* (*Daily Courant*, no. 941). Not until the day of performance did the advertisement read *The Tender Husband*. Perhaps Addison's scenes, which emphasized the plotline of the married Clerimonts, precipitated the change.

[4] Aitken, i. 119–20.

[5] Aitken, i. 114, 120.

The sparse houses during the first run are inexplicable. The taste for unsentimental comedies was not diminishing, as the playbills of the period amply illustrate. Admittedly the April timing was bad; on the other hand the cast was excellent and the play superior to much of the theatrical fare. Anne Oldfield and Robert Wilks, in their prime, played Biddy and Captain Clerimont, and the two comedians Bullock and Pinkethman took the roles of Sir Harry and Numps. Daniel Purcell set two of the songs, and the third was set by Lewis Ramondon;[1] Francis Hughes, a playhouse musician and opera singer, sang one of them.[2] The music must have embellished the play delicately. The initial rejection is particularly surprising because the comedy's popularity grew steadily for decades thereafter. Colley Cibber, in his Preface to *Zimena* published in 1719, attributed the failure to the 'low latent Malice' of audiences who praise a dramatist's first play, 'swelling him up to Rival the Reputation of others', only to dispraise the next so that he will know that 'they, who gave him Fame, can take it away'. He believed that 'after the Success of the *Funeral*, it was the same Caprice that deserted *The Tender Husband*'.

Whatever the cause, *The Tender Husband* did not long remain in obscurity. It was performed twice more during its first season and seven times the following season. In its early years it far surpassed *The Funeral* in performances; *The Funeral* was performed five times from autumn 1705 to summer 1710, but *The Tender Husband* played sixteen times in those years. Or, to look at the figures in a different way, *The Funeral* played once in its second season, twice in its third, and none in its fourth, but *The Tender Husband* played seven times in its second season, twice in its third, and four times in its fourth. Statistics for the first forty years of each play, exclusive of the opening season, for which there are no figures on *The Funeral*, show that *The Tender Husband* ran 127 times and *The Funeral* 109. Thereafter, however, the popularity of *The Tender Husband* declined abruptly, as a census of performances by decades, beginning with the second season, indicates:

1705–15	24 performances
1715–25	27 performances
1725–35	43 performances
1735–45	33 performances

---

[1] Ramondon's Christian name, usually listed in twentieth-century works as Lewis, was perhaps Littleton. I am indebted to Philip Highfill for information from legal documents on a musician of the period named Littleton Ramondon, who seems to be the same man.

[2] *Verse*, p. 84.

1745–55 9 performances (including 6 at Southwark Fair)
1755–65 2 performances[1]
1765–75 2 performances

In all, there was a total of 147 performances by 1776, of which 37 were benefits. Further, the play was acted by royal command on eight occasions. The play that barely topped £26 in receipts on its second night became very profitable. It brought in £246. 11s. 6d. as late as 17 March 1760 and £236. 19s. 6d. on 6 April 1772.[2] Nor was it forgotten outside London. It ran in Dublin and also on occasion, at least as late as 1774, in such cities as Canterbury, York, Norwich, Cork, and Limerick.[3]

REPUTATION AND INFLUENCE

Although at the time he wrote the Dedication to Addison, Steele felt the play was 'no improper Memorial of an Inviolable Friendship', and he mentioned it with some pleasure in the *Spectator*, no. 555, he never otherwise indicated that he thought very highly of it, perhaps because of its initial lack of success, perhaps because it was not exemplary comedy. He didn't quote from it or paraphrase it in his periodicals as he did *The Funeral* and *The Conscious Lovers*. When he referred to it in his 'Verses to the Author of the Tragedy of *Cato*', published in the seventh edition of Addison's *Cato* in 1713, it was disparagingly:

> To my light Scenes I once inscrib'd your Name,
> And impotently strove to borrow Fame:
> Soon will that die, which adds thy Name to mine,
> Let me, then, live, join'd to a Work of thine.

Underrating it as he apparently did, he could not have foreseen its continuing popularity on stage long after his death, its eighteen or more eighteenth-century editions, or its value to later and greater writers. For of his four plays, his only first-run failure proved second only to *The Conscious Lovers* in influence on later literature.

---

[1] On 16 January 1758 a two-act afterpiece 'taken from Sir Richard Steele's *Accomplished Fools*' played at the Little Theatre in the Haymarket (Stone, ii. 641).

[2] All statistics are based on facts in Avery, Scouten, and Stone, *passim*.

[3] La Tourette Stockwell, *Dublin Theatres and Theatre Customs (1637–1820)* (Kingsport, Tenn., 1938), p. 59; Sybil Rosenfeld, *Strolling Players and Drama in the Provinces, 1660–1765* (Cambridge, 1939), *passim*; William Smith Clark, *The Irish Stage in the County Towns 1720 to 1800* (Oxford, 1965), pp. 335–6.

In assessing the impact, there are, of course, dangers of claiming with too much assurance the indebtedness of later writers. Yet some resemblances to passages and devices original with Steele demand recognition. Steele's chief contribution was the creation of characters who are recognizably English and completely individual. Working with the stuff of Restoration comedy, the country booby, for example, he innovated and produced not Toby Tilbury or Young Hartford or Mass Johnny, but Humphry Gubbin, a new breed. And it is Numps that is the ancestor of Tony Lumpkin. That Oliver Goldsmith knew *The Tender Husband* is obvious from specific lines as well as details in *She Stoops to Conquer*.[1] Similarities between Humphry and Tony have been noticed by many scholars[2] and discussed at length by Smith.[3] The resemblances are indeed striking: both bumpkins have a scruple against marrying their cousins, and both help them marry someone else. Both couples hurl humorous insults at each other, the bumpkins employing the lowliest of images. In each play there is a scene in which the cousins deceive the girl's aunt, who is arranging the match, by pretending courtship while they actually plot to avoid matrimony. Neither booby is aware of having reached his majority until he is told by someone older and better informed; each, being of age, is entitled to £1,500 a year. Not only are the details similar, but several passages, all relating to Humphry and Tony in some way, are noticeably close in language.

In the thirties, when *The Tender Husband* was enjoying wide popularity, Henry Fielding was active in the theatre, and he owned a copy of the collected plays. Specific parallels between Mrs. Barsheba Tipkin and Mrs. Western in *Tom Jones* as well as between Sir Harry Gubbin and Squire Western suggest that he knew the comedy rather well. Mrs. Western is not an imitation of Mrs. Tipkin, although both are antiquated virgins and aunts of the heroines, but both aunts boast of former lovers of some position and breeding, and in Book XVII, Chapter 4 Mrs. Western explains her former cruelty to suitors to Sophia in almost exactly the language of Mrs. Tipkin speaking to Biddy. Finally, Mrs. Western claims she was called 'the cruel Parthenissa', echoing Biddy's choice of name.

---

[1] Arthur Friedman has pointed out that Steele's plays were not among the books in Goldsmith's library when it was auctioned (*Philological Quarterly*, xxiii (1944), 166). Goldsmith was in serious debt, and it is possible that some of his books were sold before his death. Also, of course, he could have known the play without owning a copy.

[2] See, for example, Bateson, pp. 51–2; Forster, p. 214; Aitken, i. 109; Nettleton, p. 162. [3] 'Tony Lumpkin', 1038–49.

Although the similarities of the two maiden aunts, except in this one passage, are not striking, those of Sir Harry and Squire Western call for some consideration, for the two squires are from the same stock. Fielding was familiar enough with *The Tender Husband* to write the 'cruel Parthenissa' passage and to name his opportunistic lawyer 'Pounce' as did Steele. He certainly knew Sir Harry, who more closely resembles Squire Western than any other squire in antecedent literature does. Of course, the two have many of the qualities of stereotyped country knights of the Restoration stage: they are irascible by nature and unreasonable as parents; they look on London with distaste and distrust, and they are helpless to deal with the intrigues of the Town. Both attempt to arrange their children's marriages according to pecuniary interests and to exert their wills by threats of physical violence. But both depart from the stereotyped, one-dimensional characters. They are men of some strength and determination, completely dedicated to the most reactionary of notions, refusing to accept the dictates of modern society, entirely impatient of such extravagances as French foods. Squire Western shares his predecessor's individuality and Englishness, but he is a much more fully developed character.

Biddy Tipkin to some extent influenced later romanticizing young ladies, notably Charlotte Lennox's popular Female Quixote, George Colman's Polly Honeycombe, and Richard Brinsley Sheridan's Lydia Languish in *The Rivals*. Arabella in Mrs. Lennox's novel, like Biddy, is governed by the nonsense in French romances, in fact, the same ones ('And what was still more unfortunate, not in the original *French*, but very bad translations').[1] Polly and Lydia react to novels, but the effect is comparable. All are courted, in the forms prescribed by the literature, by men who, like Captain Clerimont, have more or less unromantic matrimonial motives. Polly berates Ledger, her parents' choice of suitor, as Biddy does Humphry. Lydia, like Biddy, is a girl of middle-class stock pursued by a young captain despite 'an old tough aunt in the way'.[2] Mrs. Lennox, Colman, and Sheridan did not use lines similar to Steele's as Goldsmith did, but the direct descent of their heroines from Biddy is obvious.

Samuel Richardson, too, had a close acquaintance with Steele's play, as shown by Pamela's critique in Volume IV, Letter xv.[3] While the play was admirably designed for Pamela's critical ends, one

[1] *The Female Quixote; or, The Adventures of Arabella*, 2nd edn. (London, 1752), i. 5.
[2] *The Rivals*, I. i.   [3] *Pamela in Her Exalted Condition*.

wonders that Richardson should have chosen a thirty-five-year-old piece as his vehicle for expressing genteel notions of drama.[1] Pamela herself is priggishly disdainful of *The Tender Husband*; she is shocked by its lack of morality and disappointed by its improbability and the unnaturalness of the characters. That Richardson was as shocked as Pamela is doubtful. He referred to Biddy's conversation on living comfortably (II. ii. 85–7) in both *Clarissa* and *Sir Charles Grandison*, misquoting, as Leo Hughes says, 'just enough to show that he depended on his memory of a favorite passage'.[2] Finally, a copy of Steele's plays is found by Clarissa in Madame Sinclair's library. It is impossible to measure Steele's influence, if any, on Richardson's writing, however.[3]

As late as 1841 Richard Brinsley Peake, a nineteenth-century play-wright, chose to adapt Steele's play. Ignoring the titular plot, he combined the sub-plot of Biddy's romance with scenes from Frances Sheridan's *The Discovery* (1763) and brought the action forward to 1789, to create *Court and City*.

THE TEXT

Although originally Steele had agreed, according to Rich, not to publish *The Tender Husband* till a month after the *première* performance,[4] Jacob Tonson issued the first edition on 9 May 1705, sixteen days after the play opened. During Steele's lifetime, Tonson published three more, dated 1712, 1717, and 1723, all in collections of Steele's works, and the next followed in 1731. One edition was printed by Stephen Powell for George Risk in Dublin in 1725.

---

[1] Alan Dugald McKillop suggested that 'we probably have here Richardson's own theatrical reminiscences, such as they are' (*Samuel Richardson, Printer and Novelist*, 2nd edn. (Hamden, Conn., 1960), p. 143), but Richardson worked from a printed copy. Pamela talks of Wilks and Anne Oldfield in the roles of Captain Clerimont and Biddy, although they had both died long before and had not performed the parts since 1729. They belonged to the original cast, however, the list of which was faithfully repro-duced in new editions. While it is possible that Richardson saw a performance of the play with this cast, there is no reason to suppose it or assume that a theatrical experience of twelve or more years before inspired his critical remarks. The mention of the two actors rules out the possibility of his having seen a recent performance. Further, the exactness of the quotations in Pamela's letter can only mean that when he wrote the passage he sat with a copy of the play before him.

[2] Leo Hughes, 'Theatrical Convention in Richardson: Some Observations on a Novelist's Technique', in *Restoration and Eighteenth-Century Literature*, ed. Carroll Camden (Chicago, 1963), p. 246, n. 8.

[3] Hughes has demonstrated that Richardson's novels abound in theatrical gestures and 'stage business'; perhaps the novelist learned something about gesture from Steele. (Hughes, pp. 239–50.)

[4] Defendant's answer in *Steele v. Rich*, quoted in Aitken, i. 118.

The first edition is a quarto with the collational formula π^2 A–I^4. Steele was casual about the condition of the copy he brought Tonson, as Addison's poorly integrated passages demonstrate. An example of his carelessness in preparing copy is the treatment of the song celebrating the Battle of Blenheim. The song itself, not printed as intended in Act IV, since it was not sung in performance, was included instead in the prelims. However, at the end of Act II lines referring to it remained in the printer's copy, although they were no longer appropriate, and should have been excised in the prompt copy:

> *Pou.* . . . . You have seen her, the next Regular Approach is, that you cannot subsist a moment, without sending forth Musical Complaints of your misfortune by way of Serenade.
>
> *Capt.* I can nick you there, Sir—I have a Scribbling Army-Friend, that has Writ a triumphant, rare, noisy, Song, in Honour of our late Victory, that will hit the Nymph's Fantasque to a Hair. I'll get every thing ready as fast as possible.

Blatant errors such as the misuse of the name 'Jenny' for 'Lucy' in v. i were passed along to the compositors and printed.

One compositor set the type for sheets B–E, and a second for F–I. No definite assignment of the prelims can be made. The second compositor's work begins at III. i. 136. The first compositor's pages are, as a rule, several lines longer than those of the second, and there are other consistent differences in the work of the two.[1] Each compositor was reasonably consistent in the names and abbreviations used for speech prefixes, except for Clerimont Senior, who is designated 'Mr. Clerimont' in speech prefixes and stage directions in the two scenes presumably by Addison.

Sheets F–I were printed from two skeletons: one set of running-titles headed the outer formes of F, G, and I, and the inner forme of H; another set was used for the inner formes of F, G, and I, and outer H. Four more sets of running-titles can be recognized in gatherings B–E, one for inner B and outer C, a second for outer B and both formes of D, a third for inner C and inner E, and a fourth for outer E. Probably

---

[1] A few examples are:

First Compositor	*Second Compositor*
Neice [two exceptions]	Niece [one exception]
Mrs., *Mr.*, *Sir* [in speech prefixes]	Mrs., Mr., Sir
[Large type for act headings]	[Small type]
(*The*) End of the *Act*	[Omitted]
[Long dashes]	[Short dashes]
[Stage directions usually enclosed in parentheses]	[Square brackets always used]

the prelims, π^2 A^4, were printed with sheets B–E; the use of at least two presses for sheets B–E and the prelims would have adjusted the time necessary for getting the book in print. At least outer A was doubtless printed late, for it contains an erratum correcting 13^r. There are two states of sheet H, pages 50, 51, and 54 incorrectly numbered 58, 59, and 62 in the first. D3^r appears in two settings.[1] No corrections are made, and consequently no reason for the resetting is apparent; pied type seems the most likely explanation, even though there is no displacement of other type in the outer forme of D.

The first edition abounds in errors in speech prefixes. The most confusing arise from the use of 'Cler.' as an abbreviation for both Clerimont Senior and Captain Clerimont, probably a result of abbreviation in the manuscript. When both characters are on stage together in Acts I and V, '*Cler.*' several times prefixes lines which could be spoken by either. Further, '*Cle. S.*' heads some speeches obviously intended for Captain Clerimont, again probably because of a misleading manuscript. In the second edition, a duodecimo printed in 1711 but dated 1712 in the collection *The Funeral; and The Tender Husband: Comedies*, the only editorially significant change is the standardization of speech prefixes. The obviously miscast speeches are corrected. The older brother is consistently referred to as Clerimont Senior, the younger as Clerimont, Numps as Humphry; 'Gubbin' replaces the variant spellings 'Gobbin' and 'Gobbins'. The changes reflect a meticulous attempt at uniformity, although some speeches are assigned to the wrong speaker. Obviously a printing-house editor made the corrections; the mistakes in speech prefixes prove that he consulted neither Steele nor the promptbook. Although Steele revised *The Funeral* in the collection, he did not touch *The Tender Husband*. Therefore the second edition has no more authority than any other which has received attention only from an editor.

The third, fourth, and fifth editions introduce the usual compositorial improvements of books reprinted in the period, regularized

[1] They may be distinguished by the following characteristics:

		State A	State B
l.	1	Ladies	Ladies,
l.	4	those who	those, who
ll.	8–9	*Pa-|ladin*	*Pala-|din*
l.	12	*Hu.*	*Au.*
l.	12	Niece,	Neice,
l.	15	Opportunities	opportunities
l.	25	*Grey-Goose,*	*Grey-Goose,,*
l.	31	me)	me.)
l.	35	Cleri	Cler.

punctuation, standardized speech prefixes, and reduced capitalization. Obviously editors gave little if any attention to the copy, and, as a result, the compositors consistently retained some absurdly obvious errors, such as the spelling 'Pitkin' for 'Tipkin' (III. ii. 9). Nothing in these editions merits an editor's consideration.

The 1717 edition, printed in the second edition of *The Funeral; and The Tender Husband: Comedies*, is a line-for-line reprint of the second to p. 138; after that point, the pages are slightly crowded, apparently to save sheet H (H⁴ of the second edition is blank). There is no sign of editing in the printing-house; very few new errors creep in. It served as copy-text for the 1723 edition, in the *Dramatick Works*; again the number of changes is negligible. The 1731 edition derived from the second and introduced few new errors. George Risk's Dublin edition of 1725 appeared along with Steele's other plays; it is a careful imitation of the fourth, of no editorial significance.

I base the present text on the first edition, recognizing in the speech prefixes of the second no more than educated guesses, not to be considered authoritative. When context indicates that they are wrong, I do not hesitate to emend them. In a few cases there is no clear proof that either Clerimont Senior or Captain Clerimont should speak the lines; I do not necessarily follow the second edition in my choices.

The text is based on a collation of the following copies: first edition, Folger, Library of Congress, University of Texas (four copies); second edition, Folger, University of Texas (two copies), British Museum, Yale, Bodleian; third edition, Folger, University of Chicago; fourth edition, Folger, University of Texas; fifth edition, Folger (three copies); Dublin, 1725, Yale.

THE

TENDER HUSBAND;

OR, THE

ACCOMPLISH'D FOOLS.

A COMEDY.

Oportet ut is qui Audiat Cogitet plura quam Videat.
                    Cicero, *de Oratore.*

[motto] Cicero] ed.; Tull.

ABBREVIATIONS USED IN THE NOTES

The following abbreviations are used in reference to early editions of *The Tender Husband*:

Q First edition. London: Tonson, 1705.

D1 Second edition. In *The Funeral; and The Tender Husband: Comedies.* London: Tonson, 1712.

D2 Third edition. In *The Funeral; and The Tender Husband: Comedies.* London: Tonson, 1717.

D3 Fourth edition. In *The Dramatick Works of Sir Richard Steele.* London: Tonson, 1723.

D4 Fifth edition. London: Tonson, 1731.

Du First Dublin edition. Dublin: Risk, 1725.

TO

Mr. *ADDISON*.

SIR,

You'l be surpriz'd, in the midst of a daily and familiar Conversation, with an Address which bears so distant an Air as a publick Dedication: But to put You out of the Pain which I know this will give You, I assure You I do not design in it what would be very needless, 5 a Panegyrick on Your self, or what perhaps is very necessary, a Defence of the Play. In the one I should discover too much the Concern of an Author, in the other too little the Freedom of a Friend.

My Purpose, in this Application, is only to show the Esteem I 10 have for You, and that I look upon my Intimacy with You as one of the most valuable Enjoyments of my Life. At the same time I hope I make the Town no ill Compliment for their kind Acceptance of this Comedy, in acknowledging that it has so far rais'd my Opinion of it, as to make me think it no improper Memorial of an Inviolable 15 Friendship.

I should not offer it to You as such, had I not been very careful to avoid every thing that might look Ill-natur'd, Immoral, or prejudicial to what the Better Part of Mankind hold Sacred and Honourable. 20

Poetry, under such Restraints, is an obliging Service to Human Society; especially when 'tis us'd, like Your Admirable Vein, to recommend more useful Qualities in Your self, or Immortalize Characters truly Heroick in others. I am, here, in danger of breaking my Promise to You, therefore shall take the only Opportunity that 25 can offer it self of resisting my own Inclinations, by complying with Yours. I am,

SIR,

Your Most Faithful,

Humble Servant, 30

Richard Steele.

PROLOGUE,

Written by Mr. *ADDISON*.

Spoken by Mr. *Wilks*.

In the first Rise and Infancy of Farce,
When Fools were many, and when Plays were scarce,
The Raw unpractis'd Authors could with Ease
A young, and unexperienc'd Audience please:
No Single Character had e'er been shown,   5
But the whole Herd of Fops was all their Own;
Rich in Originals, they set to View,
In ev'ry Peice, a Coxcomb that was New.

  But now Our British Theatre can boast
Droles of all kinds, a Vast Unthinking Hoast!   10
Fruitful of Folly and of Vice, it shows
Cuckolds, and Citts, and Bawds, and Pimps, and Beaux;
Rough-Country Knights are found of ev'ry Shire,
Of ev'ry Fashion gentle Fops appear;
And Punks of diff'rent Characters we meet,   15
As frequent on the Stage as in the Pit:
Our Modern Wits are forc'd to pick and cull,
And here and there by Chance glean up a Fool:
Long e'er they find the necessary Spark;
They search the Town, and beat about the Park: 20
To all his most frequented Haunts resort,
Oft dog him to the Ring, and oft to Court;
As Love of Pleasure, or of Place invites:
And sometimes catch Him taking Snuff at White's.

  How e'er to do you Right, the present Age   25
Breeds very hopeful Monsters for the Stage;
That scorn the Paths their dull Forefathers trod,
And won't be Blockheads in the Common Road.

Do but survey this Crowded House to-Night:
30   *—Here's still Encouragement for those that write.*

Our Author, to divert his Freinds to-Day,
Stocks with Variety of Fools his Play;
And that there may be something Gay, and New,
Two Ladies Errant has expos'd to View:
35   *The First a Damsel, travail'd in Romance;*
The To'ther more refin'd; she comes from France:
Rescue, like Courteous Knights, the Nymph from Danger;
And kindly Treat, like Well-bred Men, the Stranger.

A SONG

Design'd for the Fourth ACT, but not Set.

I.

See, Britons, see with *Awful Eyes*,
Britannia *from her Seas arise!*
Ten Thousand Billows round Me roar,
    While Winds and Waves engage,
That break in Froth upon my Shoar,   5
    And impotently Rage.
Such were the Terrors, which of late
    Surrounded my afflicted State;
United Fury thus was bent
    On my Devoted Seats,   10
'Till all the Mighty Force was spent
    In Feeble Swells, and Empty Threats.

II.

But now with rising Glory Crown'd,
My Joys run high, they know no Bound;
    Tides of unruly Pleasure flow   15
    Through ev'ry Swelling Vein,
    New Raptures in my Bosom glow,
And warm me up to Youth again.
    Passing Pomps my Streets Adorn;
    Captive Spoils, in Triumph born,   20
Standards of Gauls, in Fight subdu'd,
Colours in Hostile Blood embru'd,
    Ensigns of Tyrannic Might,
    Foes to Equity and Right,
In Courts of British Justice wave on high,   25
    Sacred to Law, and Liberty.

My Crowded Theatres repeat,
In Songs of Triumph, the Defeat.
Did ever Joyful Mother see
So Bright, so Brave a Progeny!
Daughters with so much Beauty Crown'd,
Or Sons for Valour so renown'd!

III.

But oh I gaze and seek in vain
To find amidst this Warlike Train
My Absent Sons, that us'd to Grace
With decent Pride this Joyous Place:
Unhappy Youths! how do my Sorrows rise,
Swell my Breast, and melt my Eyes,
While I your mighty Loss deplore?
Wild, and raging with Distress,
I mourn, I mourn my own Success,
And boast my Victories no more.
Unhappy Youths! far from their native Sky,
On Danube's *Banks enterr'd they lye.*
Germania, *give me back my Slain,*
Give me my slaughter'd Sons again.
Was it for this they rang'd so far,
To free thee from oppressive War?
Germania *&c.*

IV.

Tears of Sorrow while I shed
O'er the Manes of my Dead,
Lasting Altars let me raise
To my living Heroes Praise;
Heav'n give them a longer Stay,
As Glorious Actions to Display,
Or perish on as Great a Day.

DRAMATIS PERSONAE.

MEN.

Sir *Harry Gubbin*.

Humphry Gubbin.

Mr. *Tipkin*.

Clerimont Senior.

Captain *Clerimont*.

Mr. *Pounce*.

Mr. *Bullock*.

Mr. *Pinkethman*.

Mr. *Norris*.

Mr. *Mills*.

Mr. *Wilks*.   5

Mr. *Eastcourt*.

WOMEN.

Mrs. *Clerimont*.

Aunt.

Niece.

Fainlove.

Jenny, Maid to Mrs. *Clerimont*.

Mrs. *Cross*.

Mrs. *Powell*.

Mrs. *Oldfield*.

Mrs. *Kent*.   10

Mrs. *Sapsford*.

THE TENDER HUSBAND:

OR,

The Accomplish'd Fools.

Act I. Scene i.

Enter Clerimont *Senior and* Fainlove.

Clerimont Senior. Well Mr. *Fainlove*, how do you go on in your
Amour with my Wife?

Fainlove. I am very civil, and very distant; If she smiles or speaks,
I Bow, and Gaze at her—Then throw down my Eyes, as if oppress'd
by fear of Offence, then steal a look again till she again sees me— 5
This is my general Method.

Clerimont Senior. And 'tis right—For such a fine Lady has no Guard
to her Virtue, but her Pride; therefore you must constantly apply
your self to that: But, Dear *Lucy*, as you have been a very faithful,
but a very costly Wench to me, so my Spouse also has been constant 10
to my Bed, but careless of my Fortune.

Fainlove. Ah! my dear, how could you leave your poor *Lucy*, and

---

1 *Clerimont Senior.*] Three speech prefixes for the title character appear in the first
edition: *Clerimont Senior*, *Clerimont*, and *Mr. Clerimont*, in various abbreviated forms.
Clerimont Senior was uniformly established as the speech prefix in D1. Steele must
have intended *Clerimont Senior*, for it appears in Act I and consistently in the pages set
by the first compositor except in the scene written by Addison. But Steele also
abbreviated to *Cler.* or perhaps merely *C.* in his manuscript for both Clerimont Senior
and Captain Clerimont, leading the compositor into considerable difficulty in I. i,
in which both characters appear. As a result, the compositor mistakenly assigned
four of the Captain's speeches (I. i. 198, 223, 228, 248) to Clerimont Senior, and pre-
fixed two of Clerimont Senior's lines (I. i. 94, 187) by *Cler.* The second compositor,
except in the Addisonian scene, set *Cler.* or *Cl.* as the speech prefix for Clerimont
Senior and used *Clerimont* in stage directions, giving a further indication of a shortened prefix in the manuscript. He had some difficulty in assigning speeches in V. ii
when both Clerimont Senior and Captain Clerimont are on stage. He used the
speech prefix *Cler.* for four speeches, two of which should be assigned to the Captain,
two to Clerimont Senior. In the present edition I have used *Clerimont Senior* in all his
speech prefixes and stage directions.

run into *France* to see Sights, and show your Gallantry with a Wife? Was not that unnatural?

15   *Clerimont Senior.* She brought me a noble Fortune, and I thought she had a right to share it: Therefore carry'd her to see the World, forsooth, and make the Tour of *France* and *Italy*, where she learn'd to lose her Money Gracefully, to admire every Vanity in our Sex, and contemn every Virtue in her own, which, with Ten Thousand
20 other Perfections, are the ordinary Improvements of a Travail'd Lady. Now I can neither Mortify her Vanity that I may Live at ease with her, or quite discard her, till I have catch'd her a little enlarging her Innocent Freedoms, as she calls 'em: For this end I am content to be a *French* Husband, tho' now and then with the secret Pangs of an *Italian*
25 One; and therefore, Sir, or Madam, you are thus Equip'd to attend and accost her Ladyship: It concerns you to be diligent: If we wholly part —I need say no more; if we do not—I'le see thee well provided for.

   Fainlove. I'le do all I can, I warrant you, but you are not to expect I'le go much among the Men.

30   *Clerimont Senior.* No, no, you must not go near Men, you are only (when my Wife goes to a Play) to sit in a side Box with pretty Fellows—I don't design you to personate a real Man, you are only to be a pretty Gentleman—Not to be of any Use or Consequence in the World, as to your self, but meerly as a property to others, such
35 as you see now and then have a Life in the Intail of a great Estate, that seem to have come into the World only to be Taggs in the Pedigree of a Wealthy House—You must have seen many of that Species.

   Fainlove. I apprehend you, such as stand in Assemblies, with an indolent Softness, and Contempt of all around 'em, who make a
40 figure in Publick, and are scorn'd in Private, I have seen such a One, with a Pocket-Glass to see his own Face, and an affected Perspective to know others. (*Imitates each.*)

   Clerimont Senior. Ay, Ay, that's my Man—Thou dear Rogue.

   Fainlove. Let me alone—I'll lay my Life I'll Horn you, that is, I'll
45 make it appear I might, if I could—

   Clerimont Senior. Ay, that will please Me quite as well.

   Fainlove. To show you the Progress I have made, I last night won of her Five Hundred Pounds, which I have brought you safe. (*Giving him Bills.*)

Clerimont Senior. Oh, the Damn'd Vice! That Women can imagine 50
all Houshold Care, regard to Posterity, and fear of Poverty, must
be Sacrific'd to a Game at Cards—Suppose she had not had it to
pay, and you had been capable of finding your Account another
Way—

Fainlove. That's but a Suppose—   55

Clerimont Senior. I say, she must have complied with every thing
you ask'd.—

Fainlove. But she knows you never limit her Expences—(*Aside.*)
I'll gain Him from Her for ever, if I can—

Clerimont Senior. With this you have repaid me two thousand 60
Pound, and if you did not refund thus Honestly, I could not have
supply'd Her—We must have parted.

Fainlove. (*Aside.*) Then you shall part—If t'other way fails. [*To*
Clerimont *Senior.*] However, I can't blame your fondness of Her, she
has so many entertaining Qualities with Her Vanity—Then she has 65
such a pretty unthinking Air, while she Saunters round a Room,
and prattles Sentences.—

Clerimont Senior. That was her Turn from her Infancy, she always
had a great Genius for knowing every thing, but what it was necessary she should—The Wits of the Age, the great Beauties, and 70
short-liv'd People of Vogue, were always her Discourse and Imitation.—Thus the Case stood when she went to *France*; but her fine
Follies improv'd so daily, that tho' I was then proud of her being
call'd Mr. *Clerimont's* Wife, I am now as much out of Countenance to
hear my self call'd Mrs. *Clerimont's* Husband, so much is the 75
Superiority of Her side.

Fainlove. I am sure if ever I gave myself a little Liberty, I never
found you so indulgent.

Clerimont Senior. I should have the whole Sex on my Back, should
I pretend to retrench a Lady so well Visited as mine is—Therefore 80
I must bring it about, that it shall appear her own Act, if she
reforms; or else I shall be pronounc'd Jealous, and have my Eyes
pull'd out for being open—But I hear my Brother *Jack* coming, who,
I hope, has brought yours with Him—Hist, not a Word.

72 she] D1; he

Enter Captain Clerimont *and* Pounce.

85 *Captain Clerimont.* I have found him out at last, Brother, and brought you the Obsequious Mr. *Pounce*, I saw Him at a distance in a Crowd, whispering in their Turns with all about Him—He is a Gentleman so Receiv'd, so Courted, and so Trusted—

Pounce. I am very glad if you saw any thing like that, if the 90 Approbation of Others can recommend me (where I much more desire it) to this Company—

Clerimont Senior. Oh, the Civil Person—But, Dear *Pounce*, you know I am your Professed Admirer; I always celebrated you for your excellent Skill, and Address for that happy Knowledge of the World, 95 which makes you seem Born for living with the Persons you are with, where-ever you come—Now, my Brother and I want your help, in a Business that requires a little more dexterity, than we our selves are Masters of.

Pounce. You know, Sir, my Character is helping the Distress'd, 100 which I do freely, and without reserve, while others are for distinguishing rigidly on the Justice of the Occasion, and so lose the Grace of the Benefit—Now, 'tis my Profession to assist a Free-hearted young Fellow against an unnatural long-liv'd Father—to disencumber Men of Pleasure of the Vexation of unweildly Estates, to sup- 105 port a Feeble Title to an Inheritance, to—

Clerimont Senior. I have been well acquainted with your Merits, ever since I saw you with so much compassion prompt a stammering Witness in *Westminster-hall*—that wanted Instruction—I love a Man that can venture his Ears with so much Bravery for his 110 Friend—

85 *Captain Clerimont*] ed.; *Cler.* The character is variously called *Captain Clerimont*, *Captain*, and *Clerimont*, usually in abbreviated form, in speech prefixes and stage directions. The most likely explanation is that Steele began writing the rather burdensome full name, then shortened to either *Cler.* or *C.*; otherwise there would be no reason for both compositors to have assigned to the older brother speeches of the younger. In the present edition, *Captain Clerimont* is consistently used.

92 *Clerimont Senior*] ed.; *Cle.* This speech was assigned to Captain Clerimont in all editions, including the Mermaid and Regents, following D1, but a close examination of the lines shows that it is, in fact, Clerimont Senior's. The Captain and Pounce arrive together, and the ceremonious ironies spoken here would have preceded their arrival had Captain Clerimont been the speaker. Further, Pounce, in reply to the speech, addresses his remarks to Clerimont Senior, as is evident by the fact that Clerimont Senior, not the Captain, interrupts him with further ironic compliments and Pounce next asks Cleremont Senior 'to what all this Panegyrick tends'.

Pounce. Dear Sir, spare my Modesty, and let me know to what all this Panegyrick tends.

Clerimont Senior. Why, Sir, what I would say is in behalf of my Brother the Captain here, whose Misfortune it is that I was born before him.   115

Pounce. I am confident he had rather you should have been so, than any other Man in *England*.

Captain Clerimont. You do me Justice, Mr. *Pounce*—But, tho' 'tis to that Gentleman, I am still a younger Brother, and you know We that are so, are generally Condemn'd to Shops, Colleges, or Inns 120 of Court.

Pounce. But you, Sir, have escap'd 'em, you have been Trading in the Noble Mart of Glory—

Captain Clerimont. That's true,—But the General makes such hast to finish the War, that We Red-coats may be soon out of Fashion,— 125 And then I am a Fellow of the most Easy indolent Disposition in the World! I hate all manner of Business.

Pounce. A Compos'd Temper, indeed!

Captain Clerimont. In such a Case I should have no way of Livelihood, but Calling over this Gentleman's Dogs in the Country, 130 Drinking his Stale-Beer to the Neighbourhood, or Marrying a Fortune.

Clerimont Senior. To be short, *Pounce*—I am putting *Jack* upon Marriage, and you are so publick an Envoy, or rather Plenipotentiary, from the very different Nations of *Cheapside*, *Covent-Garden*, and 135 *St. James's*; you have too the Mein, and Language of each Place so naturally, that you are the properest Instrument I know in the World, to help an honest young Fellow to Favour in one of 'em, by Credit in the other.

Pounce. By what I understand of your many Prefaces, Gentlemen, 140 the purpose of all this is—That it would not in the least discompose this Gentleman's easie indolent Disposition to fall into Twenty Thousand Pounds, tho' it came upon him never so suddenly.

Captain Clerimont. You are a very discerning Man—How could you see so far through Me, as to know I Love a fine Woman, pretty 145 Equipage, good Company, and a clean Habitation.

129 *Captain Clerimont*] ed.; *Cl.*

Pounce. Well, tho' I am so much a Conjurer—What then?

Clerimont Senior. You know a certain Person, into whose Hands you now and then recommend a young Heir, to be reliev'd from the
150 Vexation of Tenants, Taxes, and so forth—

Pounce. What! My Worthy Friend and City-Patron *Hezekiah Tipkin*, Banker in *Lombard Street*, would the noble Captain lay any Sums in his Hands?

Captain Clerimont. No—But the Noble Captain would have
155 Treasure out of his Hands—You know his Neice.

Pounce. To my knowledge Ten thousand Pounds in Money.

Captain Clerimont. Such a Stature, such a Blooming Countenance, so easy a Shape!

Pounce. In Jewels of her Grandmother's five Thousand—

160 *Captain Clerimont.* Her Wit so lively, her Mein so alluring!

Pounce. In Land a Thousand a Year.

Captain Clerimont. Her Lips have that certain Prominence, that Swelling softness, that they invite to a pressure; her Eyes that Languer, that they give Pain, tho' they look only inclin'd to rest—
165 Her whole Person that one Charm—

Pounce. Raptures! Raptures!

Captain Clerimont. How can it so insensibly to itself, lead us through cares it knows not, thro' such a Wilderness of Hopes, Fears, Joys, Sorrows, Desires, Despairs, Extasies and Torments, with so Sweet,
170 yet so Anxious Vicissitude.

Pounce. Why I thought you had never seen Her—

Captain Clerimont. No more I han't.

Pounce. Who told you then of her inviting Lips, her soft sleepy Eyes—

175 *Captain Clerimont.* You, yourself—

Pounce. Sure you rave, I never spoke of her afore to you.

Captain Clerimont. Why, you won't face me down—Did you not just now say, she had 10,000 *l.* in Money, five in Jewels, and a
180 Thousand a Year?—

Pounce. I confess my own Stupidity and Her Charms—Why, if you were to meet, you would certainly please Her, you have the

cant of Loving; but, pray, may we be free—That young Gentleman—

Clerimont Senior. A very honest, modest Gentleman of my Ac- 185
quaintance, one that has much more in him, than he appears to
have, you shall know him better, Sir, This is Mr. *Pounce*. Mr.
Pounce, this is Mr. *Fainlove*, I must desire you to let him be known
to you, and your Friends.

Pounce. I shall be proud—Well, then since we may be free, you 190
must understand, the young Lady by being kept from the World,
has made a World of her own—She has spent all her solitude in
Reading *Romances*, her Head is full of Shepherds, Knights, Flowery
Meads, Groves and Streams, so that if you talk like a Man of this
World to her, you do nothing.   195

Captain Clerimont. Oh, let me alone—I have been a great Traveller
in Fairy-land my self, I know *Oroondates*, *Cassandra*, *Astræa*, and
Clelia, are my intimate Acquaintance.

> *Go my Heart's Envoys, tender sighs make hast,*
> *And with your Breath swell the soft* Zephyr's *Blast;*   200
> *Then near that Fair One, if you chance to fly,*
> *Tell her in Whispers, 'tis for her I die.*

Pounce. That would do, That would do—Her very Language.

Clerimont Senior. Why then, dear *Pounce*, I know thou art the only
Man Living that can serve him.   205

Pounce. Gentlemen, you must pardon me, I am Solliciting the
Marriage Settlement between her, and a Country Booby, her
Cousin *Humphry Gubbin*, Sir *Harry's* Heir, who is come to Town to
take Possession of her.

Clerimont Senior. Well, all that I can say to the matter is, that a 210
thousand Pound on the Day of *Jack's* Marriage to her, is more than
you'l get by the dispatch of those Deeds.

Pounce. Why, a Thousand Pounds is a pretty thing, especially

---

183 be] D1; [om.]
185 *Clerimont Senior*] ed.; *Cler.* Again the compositor of Q set *Cler.* for the speech
prefix, and the compositors of later editions gave the speech to the Captain. Had
they been familiar with the play, they would have realized that the 'very honest,
modest Gentleman' of the speaker's acquaintance is Clerimont Senior's mistress
Fainlove. The duty of 'introducing' her, to her own brother, rests on him. Winton
in the Regents edition, corrected the speech prefix.
196 *Captain Clerimont*] D1 (*Cler.*); *Cle. S.*

when 'tis to take a Lady fair out of the Hands of an obstinate ill-bred
215 Clown, to give her to a gentle Swain, a dying enamour'd Knight.

Clerimont Senior. Ay, Dear *Pounce*—consider but that—the Justice
of the thing.

Pounce. Besides, he is just come from the Glorious *Bleinheim*! Look'y,
Captain; I hope you have learn'd an Implicit Obedience to your
220 Leaders.

Captain Clerimont. 'Tis all I know.

Pounce. Then, if I am to Command—make not one step without
me—And since we may be free—I am also to acquaint you, there
will be more Merit in bringing this matter to bear than you imagine
225 —Yet right Measures make all things possible.

Captain Clerimont. We'll follow yours exactly.

Pounce. But the great matter against us is want of Time, for the
Nymph's Uncle, and Squire's Father, this very Morning met, and
made an end of the matter—But the difficulty of a thing, Captain,
230 shall be no reason against attempting it.

Captain Clerimont. I have so great an Opinion of your Conduct,
that I warrant you we Conquer all.

Pounce. I am so intimately employ'd by old *Tipkin*, and so necessary to him,—that I may, perhaps, puzzle things yet.

235 *Clerimont Senior.* I have seen thee Cajole the Knave very dex-
terously.

Pounce. Why, really, Sir, generally speaking, 'tis but knowing
what a Man thinks of himself, and giving him that, to make him
what else you please—Now *Tipkin* is an absolute *Lombard-Street* Wit,
240 a Fellow that droles on the strength of Fifty Thousand Pounds: He
is call'd on Change Sly-Boots, and by the force of a very good
Credit, and very bad Conscience, he is a leading Person: But we
must be quick, or he'll sneer old Sir *Harry* out of his Senses, and
strike up the Sale of his Niece immediately.

245 *Captain Clerimont.* But my Rival, what's he—

Pounce. There's some hopes there, for I hear the Booby is as averse

---

221 *Captain Clerimont*] D1; (*Cler.*); *Cle. S.*
226 *Captain Clerimont*] D1 (*Cler.*); *Cle. S.*
231 *Captain Clerimont*] ed.; *Cle. S.* Winton also makes this emendation.
245 *Captain Clerimont*] D1 (*Cler.*); *Cle. S.*

as his Father is inclin'd to it—One is as Obstinate, as the other Cruel.

Clerimont Senior. He is, they say, a pert Blockhead, and very lively out of his Father's sight.   250

Pounce. He that gave me his Character, call'd him a docile Dunce, a Fellow rather absurd, than a direct Fool—When his Father's Absent, he'll pursue any thing he's put upon—But we must not lose time—Pray, be you two Brothers at home to wait for any Notice from me—While that pretty Gentleman, and I, whose Face 255 I have known, take a walk and look about for 'em—(*Aside to* Fainlove.) So, so—Young Lady—

Exeunt.

[Act I. Scene ii.]

Enter Sir Harry Gubbin *and* Tipkin.

Sir Harry Gubbin. Look y', Brother *Tipkin,* as I told you before, my Business in Town is to dispose of an Hundred Head of Cattle, and my Son.

Tipkin. Brother *Gubbin*; as I signified to you in my last, bearing Date *Semptember* 13th, My Neice has a Thousand Pound *per Annum* 5 and because I have found you a plain-dealing Man (particularly in the easy Pad you put into my Hands last Summer) I was willing you should have the Refusal of my Niece, provided that I have a Discharge from all retrospects while her Guardian, and One Thousand Pounds for my Care.   10

Sir Harry Gubbin. Ay, but Brother, you Rate her too high; the War has fetch'd down the Price of Women: The whole Nation is

---

0.1 Gubbin] Whether Sir Harry and Humphry were named 'Gobbin' or 'Gubbin' is not conclusively ascertainable. Historically the latter spelling has been accepted because it was used in D1. Either would have been proper, and it is quite possible that Steele used both. In Act III the name is consistently spelled 'Gubbin' by both compositors, three times by one and four times by the other; in Act I, it is consistently spelled 'Gobbin' (four times) with the exception of 'Gobbins' once and 'Gubbin' once in a stage direction. Lacking proof of Steele's intention, I have chosen the traditional 'Gubbin' for this text.

over-run with Petticoats; Our Daughters lye upon our Hands, Brother *Tipkin*; Girls are Drugs, Sir, mere Drugs.

15   *Tipkin.* Look y', Sir *Henry*—Let Girls be what they will—a Thousand Pound a Year, is a Thousand Pound a Year, and a Thousand Pound a Year is neither Girl nor Boy.

  Sir Harry Gubbin. Look y', Mr. *Tipkin*, the main Article with me, is, that Foundation of Wives Rebellion, and Husband's Cuckoldom,

20 that Cursed Pin-Money—500 *l. per Annum* Pin-Money.

  Tipkin. The Word Pin-Money, Sir *Harry*, is a Term—

  Sir Harry Gubbin. It is a Term, Brother, we never had in our Family, nor ever will—Make her Jointure in Widdowhood accordingly large, but 400 *l.* a Year is enough to give no account of.

25   *Tipkin.* Well, Sir *Harry*, since you can't Swallow these Pins, I will abate to 400 *l.*

  Sir Harry Gubbin. And to mollify the Article—as well as specify the Uses, we'll put in the Names of several Female Utensils as Needles, Knitting-Needles, Tape, Thread, Scissars, Bodkins, Fans, Play-

30 Books, with other Toys of that nature: And now, since we have as good as concluded on the Marriage, it will not be improper that the young People see each other.

  Tipkin. I do'nt think it prudent till the very Instant of Marriage, least they should not like one another.

35   *Sir Harry Gubbin.* They shall meet—As for the young Girl, she cannot dislike *Numps*; and for *Numps*, I never suffered him to have any thing he lik'd in his Life. He'll be here immediately; he has been train'd up from his Child-hood under such a Plant as this in my Hand—. I have taken pains in his Education.

40   *Tipkin.* Sir *Harry*, I approve your Method, for since you have left off Hunting, you might otherwise want Exercise, and this is a subtle expedient to preserve your own Health, and your Son's Good Manners.

  Sir Harry Gubbin. It has been the Custom of the *Gubbins* to pre-

45 serve Severity and Discipline in their Families—I my self was Caned the Day before my Wedding.

  Tipkin. Ay, Sir *Henry*, had you not been well Cudgelled in your Youth, you had never been the Man you are.

  Sir Harry Gubbin. You say right, Sir, now I feel the Benefit of it—

There's a Crab-Tree near our House which Flourishes for the good 50
of my Posterity, and has brush'd our Jackets from Father to Son for
several Generations—

Tipkin. I am glad to hear you have all things necessary for the
Family within your selves—

Sir Harry Gubbin. Oh, yonder, I see *Numps* is coming—I have 55
dress'd him in the very Suit I had on at my own Wedding; 'Tis a
most becoming Apparrel—

Enter Humphry.

Tipkin. Truly, the Youth makes a good Marrigeable Figure.

Sir Harry Gubbin. Come forward, *Numps*, this is your Unckle *Tipkin*,
your Mother's Brother, *Numps*, that is so kind as to bestow his Neice 60
upon you (*Apart.*) *Don't be so Glum, Sirrah, Don't bow to a Man with a
Face as if you'd knock him down, don't Sirrah!*

Tipkin. I am glad to see you, Cousin *Humphry*—he is not Talkative,
I observe already.

Sir Harry Gubbin. He is very shrowd, Sir, when he pleases; (*Apart.*) 65
do you see this Crab-stick, you Dog. [*Before* Tipkin.] Well *Numps*, don't
be out of humour: (*Apart.*) *Will you talk?* [*Before* Tipkin.] Come,
we're your Friends, *Numps*, come Lad.

Humphry. (*Apart to his Father.*) You are a pure fellow for a Father.
This is always your Tricks, to make a great Fool of one before 70
Company.

Sir Harry Gubbin. (*Apart.*) *Don't disgrace me, Sirrah: You grim Grace-
less Rogue*—[*To* Tipkin.] Brother, he has been bred up to respect and
silence before his Parents—Yet did you but hear what a noise he

57.1 Humphry] Steele began with the stage direction and speech prefix '*Numps*' in
the first scene in which Humphry appears, probably because the character is consistently addressed as Numps by his father. However, in the middle of the scene, and
in the middle of a page of type, the speech prefixes switch to '*Hum.*' (I. ii. 103), and
thereafter '*Hum.*' appears consistently. I have used the speech prefix '*Humphry*' in
this edition. There is no proof of whether Steele wrote 'Humphry' or Humphrey',
both of which are used at random by the two compositors of Q. Probably he, like the
compositors, used both. I have arbitrarily chosen the spelling which occurs more
frequently in Q.

61 *Don't . . . Sirrah,*] In the manuscript, Steele apparently put all the statements
Sir Harry speaks apart to Humphry in italics and enclosed at least some in parentheses to further differentiate them. The italics have been retained in this edition,
but parentheses, sporadically set by the first compositor, have been removed to
avoid confusion. Notations on the parentheses are listed in the Emendations of
Accidentals.

75 makes sometimes in the Kitchen, or the Kennel, he's the loudest
of 'em all.

Tipkin. Well, Sir *Harry*, since you assure me he can speak, I 'le take
your Word for it.

Humphry. I can speak when I see occasion, and I can hold my
80 Tongue when I see occasion.

Sir Harry Gubbin. Well said, *Numps*—, (*Apart.*) *Sirrah, I see you can
do well, if you will.*

Tipkin. Pray, walk up to me, Cousin *Humphry*.

Sir Harry Gubbin. Ay, walk too and fro between us with your Hat
85 under your Arm. (*Apart.*) *Clear up your Countenance.*

Tipkin. I see, Sir *Harry*, you han't set him a Capering under a
French Dancing-Master: He does not mince it: He has not learn't to
walk by a Courant, or a Boree—His Paces are natural—Sir *Harry*.

Humphry. I don't know, but 'tis so we walk in the West of
90 *England*.

Sir Harry Gubbin. Ay, right *Numps*, and so we do—ha! ha! ha!
Pray, Brother, observe his Make, none of your Lath-back'd wishy
washy Breed—Come hither, *Numps*, (*Apart.*) *can't you stand still.*
(*Measuring his Shoulders.*)

95   *Tipkin.* I presume this is not the first time, Sir *Harry*, you have
measured his Shoulders with your Cane.

Sir Harry Gubbin. Look y', Brother, two Foot and an half in the
Shoulders.

Tipkin. Two Foot and an Half? We must make some Settlement
100 on the younger Children.

Sir Harry Gubbin. Not like him, Quotha'!

Tipkin. He may see his Cousin when he pleases.

Humphry. But harke'e, Unkle, I have a Scruple I had better mention before Marriage than after.

105   *Tipkin.* What's that? What's that?

Humphry. My Cousin, you know, is a Kin to me, and I
don't think it Lawful for a young Man to Marry his own
Relations.

Sir Harry Gubbin. Harke'e, harke'e, *Numps*: We have got a Way to
110 solve all that, (*Apart.*) *Sirrah! Consider this Cudgel! Your Cousin! suppose
I'd have you Marry your Grand-mother: What then?*

Tipkin. Well, has your Father satisfy'd you in the Point, Mr.
Humphry?

Humphry. Ay, ay, Sir, very well: I have not the least scruple
remaining, No, no,—not in the least, Sir.   115

Tipkin. Then harke'e, Brother, we'll go take a Whet, and settle
the whole Affair.

Sir Harry Gubbin. Come, we'll leave *Numps* here—He knows the
Way. [*Apart.*] *Not Marry your own Relations, Sirrah.*

Exeunt [*Sir* Harry Gubbin *and* Tipkin.]

Humphry. Very fine, very fine! How prettily this Park is stock'd 120
with Soldiers, and Dear, and Ducks and Ladies—Ha! Where are the
old Fellows gone, where can they be?—tro—I'll ask these People—

Enter Pounce *and* Fainlove.

Humphry. Ha, you pretty young Gentleman, did you see my
Father?

Fainlove. Your Father, Sir?   125

Humphry. A Weezel-fac'd cross old Gentleman with Spindle-
Shanks?

Fainlove. No, Sir.

Humphry. A Crab-Tree stick in his Hand?

Pounce. We han't met any Body with these Marks, but sure I have 130
seen you before—Are not you Mr *Humphry Gubbin,* Son and Heir to
Sir *Henry Gubbin.*

Humphry. I am his Son and Heir—But how long I shall be so, I
can't tell, for he talks every day of Disinheriting me.

Pounce. Dear Sir, let me embrace you—Nay, don't be offended if 135
I take the Liberty to Kiss you, Mr *Fainlove,* pray Kiss the Gentleman (Fainlove *Kisses.*)—Nay, dear Sir, don't stare and be surpriz'd,
for I have had a desire to be better known to you ever since I saw
you one day Clinch your Fist at your Father, when his Back was
turn'd upon you—For I must own I very much admire a young 140
Gentleman of Spirit.

Humphry. Why, Sir, would it not vex a Man to the Heart, to have
an old Fool snubbing a Body every minute afore Company—

Pounce. Oh, Fie, he uses you like a Boy.

119 *your*] D1; *you*

145 *Humphry.* Like a Boy! He lays me on now and then, as if I were one of his Hounds,—You can't think what a Rage he was in this Morning, because I boggled a little at Marrying my Own Cousin.

Pounce. A Man can't be too Scrupulous, Mr. *Humphry*, a Man cannot be too Scrupulous.

150 *Humphry.* Sir, I could as soon Love my own Flesh and Blood; we should squabble like Brother and Sister; do you think we should not? Mr—Pray, Gentlemen, may I crave the favour of your Names?

Pounce. Sir, I am the very Person that have been employ'd to
155 draw up the Articles of Marriage between you and your Cousin.

Humphry. Ay, Say you so? Then you can inform me in some things concerning my self—Pray, Sir, what Estate am I Heir to?

Pounce. To 1500 *l.* a Year, an intail'd Estate—

Humphry. I am glad to hear it with all my Heart, and can you
160 satisfie me in another Question—Pray how Old am I at present?

Pounce. Three and twenty last *March*.

Humphry. Why, as sure as you are there, They have kept me back. I have been told by some of the Neighbourhood, that I was born the very year the Pidgeon-house was built, and every Body
165 knows the Pidgeon-house is three and twenty—Why? I find there have been tricks Play'd me. I have obey'd him all along, as if I had been oblig'd to it.

Pounce. Not at all, Sir, your Father can't cut you out of one Acre of 1500 *l.* a year.

170 *Humphry.* What a Fool have I been to give him his Head so long!

Pounce. A Man of your Beauty and Fortune may find out Ladies enough that are not akin to you.

Humphry. Looky', Mr. what de' call—As to my Beauty, I don't know but they may take a liking to that—But, Sir, mayn't I crave
175 your Name!

Pounce. My Name, Sir, is *Pounce*, at your Service.

Humphry. Pounce, with a *P*—!

Pounce. Yes, Sir, and *Samuel*, with an *S*—

Humphry. Why, then, Mr. *Samuel Pounce*, do you know any Gentle-
180 woman, that you think I could like? For to tell you truly, I took an Antipathy to my Cousin, ever since my Father propos'd Her to me

—And since every Body knows I came up to be Married, I don't
care to go down, and look balk'd.

Pounce. I have a Thought just come into my Head—Do you see
this young Gentleman? He has a Sister, a prodigious Fortune—Faith 185
you two shall be acquainted—

Fainlove. I can't pretend to expect so accomplish'd a Gentleman
as Mr. *Humphry* for my Sister, but being your Friend, I'le be at his
Service in the Affair.

Humphry. If I had your Sister, She and I should live like two 190
Turtles.

Pounce. Mr *Humphry*, you shan't be fool'd any longer, I'll carry
you into Company; Mr *Fainlove*, you shall introduce him to Mrs
Clerimont's Toilet.

Fainlove. She'll be highly taken with him—For she loves a Gentle- 195
man, whose manner is particular.

Pounce. What, Sir, a Person of your Pretensions, a clear Estate, no
Portions to pay! 'Tis Barbarous, your Treatment—Mr *Humphry*, I
am afraid you want Money—There's for you (*Giving a Purse.*)—
What a Man of your Accomplishments?   200

Humphry. And yet you see, Sir, how they use me—Dear Sir, you
are the best Friend I ever met with in all my Life—Now I am flush
of Money, bring me to your Sister, and I warrant you for my
Behaviour—A Man's quite another thing with Money in his
Pocket—You know.   205

Pounce. [*Aside.*] How little the Oaf wonders why I should give him
Money! [*To* Humphry.] You shall never want, Mr *Humphry*, while
I have it—Mr *Humphry*; but, dear Friend, I must take my leave of
you, I have some Extraordinary Business on my Hands. I can't stay:
But you must not say a Word—   210

Fainlove. But you must be in the way half an hour hence, and I'll
introduce you at Mrs *Clerimont's*.

Pounce. Make'm believe you are willing to have your Cousin
Bridget till opportunity serves; Farewel, dear Friend.

Exeunt Pounce *and* Fainlove.

Humphry. Farewel, good Mr *Samuel Pounce*—But let's see my 215
Cash—'Tis very true, the old Saying, a Man meets with more

Friendship from Strangers, than his own Relations—Let's see my Cash, 1, 2, 3, 4 there on that side—1, 2, 3, 4 on that side, 'tis a foolish thing to put all ones Money in one Pocket, 'tis like a Man's
220 whole Estate in one County—These five in my Fob—I'll keep these in my Hand, least I should have a present Occasion—But this Town's full of Pick-pockets—I'll go home again.

Exit Whistling.

The End of the First Act.

Act. II. Scene i.

Enter Pounce *and* Captain Clerimont,
with his Arm in a Scarf.

Pounce. You are now well enough instructed both in the Aunt and Neice to form your Behaviour.

Captain Clerimont. But to talk with her Apart is the great matter!

Pounce. The Antiquated Virgin has a mighty Affectation for
5 Youth, and is a great Lover of Men and Money—One of these, at least, I am sure I can gratifie Her in, by turning Her Pence in the Annuities, or the Stocks of one of the Companies; some way or other I'll find to entertain Her, and engage you with the young Lady.

10 *Captain Clerimont.* Since that is her Ladiships turn, so busy a fine Gentleman as Mr *Pounce*, must needs be in Her Good Graces.

Pounce. So shall you Too—But you must not be seen with me at first meeting—I'll Dog 'em, while you watch at a distance.

Exeunt.

[Act II. Scene ii.]

Enter Aunt *and* Niece.

Niece. Was it not my Gallant that Whistled so Charmingly in the Parlour, before he went out this Morning? He's a most accomplish'd Cavalier.

Aunt. Come, Neice, Come—You don't do well to make sport with your Relations, especially with a young Gentleman that has so much 5 kindness for you.

Niece. Kindness for me! What a Phrase is there to express the Darts and Flames, the Sighs and Languishings of an expecting Lover!

Aunt. Pray, Neice, forbear this Idle Trash, and talk like other 10 People. Your Cousin *Humphry* will be True and Hearty in what he says, and that's a great deal better than the Talk and Complement of Romances.

Niece. Good Madam, don't Wound my Ears with such Expressions; do you think I can ever Love a Man that's True and Hearty! 15 What a Peasant-like Amour do these course Words import? True and Hearty! Pray, Aunt, endeavour a little at the embellishment of your Stile.

Aunt. Alack a day, Cousin *Biddy*, these Idle Romances have quite turn'd your Head.   20

Niece. How often must I desire you, Madam, to lay aside that familiar Name, Cousin *Biddy*? I never hear it without Blushing—Did you ever meet with an Heroine in those Idle Romances as you call 'em, that was term'd *Biddy*?

Aunt. Ah! Cousin, Cousin,—These are meer Vapours, indeed— 25 Nothing but Vapours—

Niece. No, the Heroine has always something soft and engaging in Her Name—Something that gives us a notion of the sweetness

0.1 Niece] The first compositor as a rule set 'Neice' and the second 'Niece'. I have arbitrarily chosen the modern spelling.
23 with] D1; with of

of her Beauty and Behaviour. A Name that glides through half a
30 dozen Tender Syllables, as *Elismonda*, *Clidamira*, *Deidamia*, that runs
upon Vowels off the Tongue, not hissing through one's Teeth, or
breaking them with Consonants—'Tis strange Rudeness those
Familiar Names they give us, when there is *Aurelia*, *Sacharissa*,
Gloriana, for People of Condition; and *Celia*, *Chloris*, *Corinna*, *Mapsa*,
35 for their Maids, and those of Lower Rank.

Aunt. Looky', *Biddy*, this is not to be supported—I know not
where you learn'd this Nicety; but I can tell you, forsooth, as much
as you despise it, your Mother was a *Bridget* afore you, and an
excellent House-Wife.

40 *Niece.* Good Madam, don't upbraid me with my Mother *Bridget*,
and an Excellent House-Wife.

Aunt. Yes, I say, she was, and spent Her Time in better Learning
than you ever did—Not in Reading of Fights and Battles, of Dwarfs
and Giants: but in Writing out Receipts for Broaths, Possets,
45 Caudles and Surfeit-Waters, as became a good Country Gentlewoman.

Niece. My Mother, and a *Bridget*!

Aunt. Yes, Neice, I say again, your Mother, my Sister, was a
Bridget; the Daughter of her Mother *Margery*, of Her Mother *Sisly*,
50 of Her Mother *Alice*.

Niece. Have you no Mercy? Oh, the Barbarous Genealogy!

Aunt. Of Her Mother *Winifred*, of Her Mother *Joan*.

Niece. Since you will run on, then I must needs tell you I am not
satisfy'd in the point of my Nativity. Many an Infant has been
55 placed in a Cottage with Obscure Parents, till by chance some
Ancient Servant of the Family has known it by its Marks.

Aunt. Ay, you had best be search'd—That's like your calling the
Winds the Fanning Gales, before I don't know how much Company,
and the Tree that was blown by it, had, forsooth, a Spirit imprison'd
60 in the Trunk of it.

Niece. Ignorance!

Aunt. Then a Cloud this Morning had a flying Dragon in
it.

Niece. What Eyes had you, that you could see nothing? For my
65 part I look upon it to be a Prodigy, and expect something extra-

ordinary will happen to me before night—But you have a gross relish of things. What noble Descriptions in Romances had been lost, if the Writers had been Persons of your Goust?

Aunt. I wish the Authors had been Hang'd, and their Books burnt, before you had seen 'em.   70

Niece. Simplicity!

Aunt. A parcel of improbable Lyes.

Niece. Indeed, Madam, your Raillery is Course—

Aunt. Fit only to corrupt young Girls, and fill their Heads with a thousand foolish Dreams of I don't know what.   75

Niece. Nay, now, Madam, you grow extravagant.

Aunt. What I say to you is not to Vex, but advise you for your Good.

Niece. What to burn *Philocles, Artaxerxes, Oroondates,* and the rest of the Heroick Lovers, and take my Country-Booby, Cousin 80 *Humphry,* for an Husband!

Aunt. Oh Dear, Oh Dear, *Biddy*! Pray, good Dear, learn to Act and Speak like the rest of the World, Come, come, you shall Marry your Cousin, and live Comfortably.

Niece. Live Comfortably! What kind of Life is that? A great 85 Heiress live Comfortably! Pray, Aunt, learn to raise your Idea's— What is, I wonder, to live Comfortably?

Aunt. To live Comfortably, is to live with Prudence and Frugality, as we do in *Lombard-Street.*

Niece. As we do—That's a fine Life, indeed, with one Servant of 90 each Sex—Let's see how many things our Coachman is good for—He Rubs down his Horses, lays the Cloath, whets the Knives, and sometimes makes Beds.

Aunt. A good Servant should turn his Hand to every thing in a Family.   95

Niece. Nay, there's not a Creature in our Family, that has not two or three different Duties, as *John* is Butler, Footman and Coachman; so *Mary* is Cook, Laundress and Chamber Maid.

Aunt. Well, and do you laugh at that?

Niece. No,—Not I—Nor at the Coach Horses, tho' one has an 100 easy Trot for my Unkle's Riding, and t'other an easy pace for your Side-Saddle—

Aunt. And so you jeer at the good management of your Relations, do you?

105 *Niece.* No, I'm well satisfied that all the House are Creatures of Business, but, indeed, was in hopes that my poor little Lap-Dog might have liv'd with me upon my Fortune without an employment, but my Unkle threatens every day to make him a Turn-spit, that he too, in his Sphere, may help us to live Comfortably.—

110 *Aunt.* Hark y', Cousin *Biddy.*

Niece. I vow I'm out of Countenance, when our Butler, with his Careful Face, drives us all stowed in a Chariot, drawn by one Horse Ambling, and 'to'ther Trotting, with his Provisions behind for the Family, from *Saturday* Night till *Monday* Morning, bound for

115 *Hackney*—Then we make a comfortable Figure, indeed.

Aunt. So we do, and so will you always, if you marry your Cousin *Humphry*—

Niece. Name not the Creature.

Aunt. Creature! What your own Cousin a Creature!

120 *Niece.* Oh, let's be going, I see yonder another Creature that does my Unkle's Law-Business, and has, I believe, made ready the Deeds, those barbarous Deeds!

Aunt. What, Mr. *Pounce*, a Creature too! Nay, now I'm sure you're Ignorant—You shall stay, and you'l learn more Wit from him

125 in an hour, than in a Thousand of your Foolish Books in an Age—

Enter Pounce.

Your Servant Mr. *Pounce.*

Pounce. Ladies I hope I don't interrupt any private Discourse.

Aunt. Not in the least, Sir.

Pounce. I should be loath to be esteem'd one of those who think

130 they have a Privilege of mixing in all Companies, without any Business, but to bring forth a loud Laugh, or vain Jest.

Niece. (*Aside.*) He talks with the Mein and Gravity of a *Paladin.*

Pounce. Madam, I bought the other day at three and an half, and Sold at Seven—

135 *Aunt.* Then pray, Sir, sell for me in time; Niece, mind him. He has an infinite deal of Wit—

125.1 *Enter* Pounce.] D1; [om.]
135 *Aunt*] D1; *Hu.* [one state of Q; see p.204]

Pounce. This that I speak of was for you—I never neglect such Opportunities to serve my Friends.

Aunt. Indeed, Mr. *Pounce,* you are, I protest, without flattery, the wittiest Man in the World.   140

Pounce. I assure you, Madam, I said last Night before an Hundred Head of Citizens, that Mrs. *Barsheba Tipkin* was the most Ingenious young Lady in the Liberties.

Aunt. Well, Mr. *Pounce,* you are so facetious—But you are always among the Great Ones—'Tis no wonder you have it.   145

Niece. Idle! Idle!

Pounce. But, Madam, you know Alderman *Grey-Goose,* he's a notable Joking Man—Well, says he, here's Mrs. *Barsheba's* Health— She's my Mistress.

Aunt. That Man makes me split my Sides with Laughing, he's 150 such a Wagg—(*Aside.*) (Mr. *Pounce* pretends *Grey-Goose* said all this, but I know 'tis his own Wit, for he's in love with me.)

Pounce. (*Apart.*) But, Madam, there's a certain Affair I should Communicate to you.   155

Aunt. [*Aside.*] Ay, 'tis certainly so—He wants to break his Mind to me.

Captain Clerimont *passing.*

Pounce. Oh, Mr. *Clerimont,* Mr. *Clerimont*—Ladies, pray let me introduce this young Gentleman, he's my Friend, a Youth of great Virtue and Goodness, for all he's in a Red Coat.   160

Aunt. If he's your Friend, we need not doubt his Virtue.

Captain Clerimont. Ladies, you are taking the cool Breath of the Morning.

Niece. (*Aside.*) A pretty Phrase.

Aunt. That's the pleasantest time this warm Weather.   165

Captain Clerimont. Oh, 'tis the Season of the *Pearly Dews,* and gentle *Zephirs.*

Niece. (*Aside.*) Ay! pray mind that again, Aunt.

Pounce. Shan't we Repose our Selves on yonder Seat, I Love Improving Company, and to Communicate.   170

Aunt. [*Aside.*] 'Tis certainly so—He's in Love with me, and wants

Opportunity to tell me so—[*To* Pounce.] I don't care if we do—[*Aside.*] He's a most Ingenious Man.

Exeunt Aunt *and* Pounce.

Captain Clerimont. We enjoy here, Madam, all the pretty Landskips
175 of the Country, without the pains of going thither.

Niece. Art and Nature are in a Rivalry, or rather a Confederacy, to adorn this Beauteous Park with all the agreeable Variety of Water, Shade, Walks and Air. What can be more Charming than these Flowery Lawns?

180 *Captain Clerimont.* Or, these Gloomy Shades—

Niece. Or, these Embroider'd Vallies—

Captain Clerimont. Or, that Transparent Stream?

Niece. Or, these Bowing Branches on the Banks of it, that seem to admire their own Beauty in the Chrystial mirrour?

185 *Captain Clerimont.* I am surpris'd, Madam, at the delicacy of your Phrase—Can such Expressions come from *Lombard Street*?

Niece. Alass! Sir, What can be expected from an Innocent Virgin, that has been immur'd almost one and Twenty Years from the Conversation of Mankind, under the Care of an *Urganda* of an *Aunt*?

190 *Captain Clerimont.* Bless me, Madam, how have you been abus'd! Many a Lady before your Age has had an hundred Lances broken in her Service, and as many Dragons cut to pieces in Honour of her.

Niece. (*Aside.*) Oh, the Charming Man!

Captain Clerimont. Do you believe *Pamela* was One and Twenty
195 before she knew *Musidorus*?

Niece. (*Aside.*) I could hear him ever—

Captain Clerimont. A Lady of your Wit and Beauty might have given occasion for a whole Romance in Folio before that Age.

Niece. Oh, the Powers! Who can he be? Oh, youth unknown, But
200 let me, in the first place, know whom I talk to, for, Sir, I am wholly unacquainted both with your Person, and your History—You seem, indeed, by your Deportment, and the Distinguishing mark of your Bravery which you bear, to have been in a Conflict—May I not know what cruel Beauty oblig'd you to such Adventures, till she
205 pitied you?

Captain Clerimont. (*Aside.*) Oh, the pretty Coxcomb! [*To* Niece.] Oh, *Bleinheim, Blenheim*! Oh, *Cordelia, Cordelia*!

Niece. You mention the place of Battle—I would fain hear an exact Description of it—Our Publick Papers are so defective, they don't so much as tell us how the Sun Rose on that Glorious Day— 210 Were there not a great many flights of Vultures before the Battle began?

Captain Clerimont. Oh, Madam, they have eaten up half my Acquaintance.

Niece. Certainly never Birds of Prey were so feasted—By report, 215 they might have liv'd half a Year on the very Legs and Arms our Troops left behind 'em.

Captain Clerimont. Had we not fought near a Wood, we shou'd ne'er have got Legs enough to have come home upon. The Joyner of the Foot-Guards has made his Fortune by it.   220

Niece. I shall never forgive your General—He has put all my Antient Heroes out of Countenance. He has pull'd down *Cyrus* and *Alexander*, as much as *Louis-le-Grand*—But your own part in that Action?

Captain Clerimont. Only that slight hurt, for the Astrologer said at 225 my Nativity—Nor Fire, nor Sword, nor Pike, nor Musquet, shall destroy this Child, let him but avoid fair Eyes—But, Madam, mayn't I crave the Name of her that has captivated my Heart.

Niece. I cant guess whom you mean by that description; but if you ask my Name—I must confess you put me upon Revealing what I 230 always keep as the greatest Secret I have—For would you believe it—They have call'd me—I don't know how to own it, but they have called me—*Bridget*.

Captain Clerimont. Bridget?

Niece. Bridget.   235

Captain Clerimont. Bridget?

Niece. Spare my Confusion, I beseech you, Sir, and if you have occasion to mention me, let it be by *Parthenissa*, for that's the Name I have assum'd ever since I came to years of Discretion.

Captain Clerimont. The insupportable Tyranny of Parents, to fix 240 Names on helpless Infants, which they must blush at all their Lives after! I don't think there's a Sirname in the World to match it.

Niece. No! What do you think of *Tipkin*?

Captain Clerimont. Tipkin! Why, I think if I was a young Lady that
245 had it, I'd part with it immediately.

Niece. Pray, how would you get rid of it?

Captain Clerimont. I'd change it for another—I could recommend
to you three very pretty Sillables—What do you think of *Clerimont*?

Niece. Clerimont! *Clerimont*! Very well—But what right have I to it?

250 *Captain Clerimont.* If you'll give me leave, I'll put you in Possession
of it. By a very few Words I can make it over to you, and your
Children after you.

Niece. Oh, fie! Whither are you running! You know a Lover
should Sigh in private, and Languish whole Years before he Reveals
255 his Passion; he should retire into some Solitary Grove, and make the
Woods and Wild Beasts his Confidents—You should have told it to
the Eccho half a Year before you had discover'd it, even to my
Hand-maid. And yet besides—To talk to me of Children—Did you
ever hear of an *Heroine* with a Big-belly?

260 *Captain Clerimont.* What can a Lover do, Madam, now the Race of
Giants is extinct? Had I liv'd in those days, there had not been a
Mortal six foot high, but should have own'd *Parthenissa* for the
Paragon of Beauty, or measur'd his length on the Ground—*Par-
thenissa* should have been heard by the Brooks and Desarts at Mid-
265 night—The Eccho's Burden, and the Rivers Murmur.

Niece. That had been a Golden Age, indeed! But see my Aunt has
left her Grave Companion, and is coming towards Us—I Command
you to leave me.

Captain Clerimont. Thus *Oroondates* when *Statira* dismiss'd him her
270 Presence, threw himself at her Feet, and implor'd Permission but
to Live. (*Offering to Kneel.*)

Niece. And thus *Statira* raised him from the Earth, permitting
him to Live and Love.

Exit Captain Clerimont.

Enter Aunt.

Aunt. Is not Mr. *Pounce's* Conversation very improving, Neice?
275 *Niece.* Is not *Clerimont* a very pretty Name, Aunt?

Aunt. He has so much Prudence.

Niece. He has so much Gallantry.

Aunt. So Sententious in his Expressions.

Niece. So polish'd in his Language!

Aunt. All he says, is, methinks so like a Sermon.   280

Niece. All he speaks savours of Romance.

Aunt. Romance, Neice? Mr *Pounce*! what savours of Romance?

Niece. No, I mean his Friend, the Accomplish'd Mr. *Clerimont*.

Aunt. Fie, for one of your Years to commend a young Fellow!

Niece. One of my Years is mightily govern'd by Example! you 285
did not dislike Mr *Pounce*.

Aunt. What Censorious too? I find there is no trusting you out of
the House—A moments fresh Air does but make you still the more
in Love with Strangers, and despise your own Relations.

Niece. I am certainly by the power of an Enchantment plac'd 290
among you, but I hope I have this morning employed one to seek
Adventures, and break the Charm.

Aunt. Vapours, *Biddy*, indeed? Nothing but Vapours—Cousin
Humphry shall break the Charm.

Niece. Name him not—Call me still *Biddy*, rather than Name that 295
Brute.

                                  Exeunt Aunt *and* Niece.

[Act II. Scene iii.]

              Enter Captain Clerimont *and* Pounce.

Captain Clerimont. A perfect *Quixot* in Petticoats! I tell thee, *Pounce*,
she governs herself wholly by Romance—It has got into her very
Blood—She starts by Rule, and Blushes by Example—Could I but
have produc'd one instance of a Ladies complying at first sight, I
should have gain'd her Promise on the Spot—How am I bound to 5
Curse the cold Constitutions of the *Philocleas* and *Statiras*! I am
undone for want of Presidents.

          2967.1 *Exeunt*] D1 (*Exe.*); *Exit.*

Pounce. I am sure I labour'd hard to favour your Conference; and
ply'd the old Woman all the while with something that tickled
10 either her Vanity or her Covetuousness; I consider'd all the Stocks,
Old and New Company, her own Complexion and Youth, Partners
for Sword-Blades, Chamber of *London*, Banks for Charity, and Mine-
Adventures, till she told me I had the repute of the most
facetious Man that ever came to *Garaways*—For you must know
15 Publick Knaves and Stock-Jobbers pass for Wits at her end of the
Town, as common Cheats and Gamesters do at yours.

Captain Clerimont. I pitty the Drudgery you have gone through,
but what's next to be done towards getting my pretty *Heroine*?

Pounce. What should next be done, in ordinary method of things
20 —You have seen her, the next Regular Approach is, that you cannot
subsist a moment, without sending forth Musical Complaints of
your misfortune by way of Serenade.

Captain Clerimont. I can nick you there, Sir—I have a Scribbling-
Army-Friend, that has Writ a triumphant, rare, noisy, Song, in
25 Honour of our late Victory, that will hit the Nymph's Fantasque
to a Hair, I'll get every thing ready as fast as possible.

Pounce. While you are playing upon the Fort, I'll be within, and
observe what execution you do, and give you intelligence accordingly.

30 *Captain Clerimont.* You must have an Eye upon Mr *Humphry*, while
I feed the Vanity of *Parthenissa*—For I am so experienc'd in these
matters that I know none but Coxcombs think to win a Woman by
any desert of their own—No, it must be done rather by complying
with some prevailing Humour of your Mistress, than exerting any
35 Good Quality in your self.

> *'Tis not the Lover's Merit wins the Field,*
> *But to themselves alone the Beauteous yield.*

The End of the Second Act.

23–26 I . . . Hair] Since the 'triumphant, rare, noisy, Song, in Honour of our late
Victory' was omitted from the performance, these lines should have been deleted
from the hastily prepared printer's copy. The speech would more properly read,
'I can nick you there, Sir—I'll get every thing ready as fast as possible.' But whether
the passage was actually omitted even from performance is perhaps questionable,
considering the haste with which final preparations for the production were made.
The song itself was printed in the prelims of Q.

Act III. [Scene i.]

Enter Mrs. Clerimont, Fainlove (*carrying her Lap-Dog*) *and* Jenny.

Jenny. Madam, the Footman that's recommended to you is below, if your Ladiship will please to take him—

Mrs. Clerimont. Oh, fie; don't believe I'll think on't—It is impossible he should be good for any thing—The *English* are so Saucy with their Liberty—I'll have all my Lower Servants *French*—There 5 cannot be a good Footman born out of an Absolute Monarchy—

Jenny. I am beholden to your Ladiship, for believing so well of the Maid Servants in *England.*

Mrs. Clerimont. Indeed, *Jenny*, I could wish thou wer't really *French*; for thou art plain *English* in spite of Example—Your Arms 10 do but hang on, and you move perfectly upon Joints. Not with a Swim of the whole Person—But I am talking to you, and have not adjusted my self to day: What pretty Company a Glass is, to have another self! (*Kisses the Dog.*) To converse in Soliloquy! To have Company that never contradicts or displeases us! The pretty visible 15 Eccho of our Actions (*Kisses the Dog.*) How easy too it is to be disencumber'd with Stays, where a Woman has any thing like Shape, if no Shape, a good Air—But I look best when I'm talking. (*Kisses the Lap-Dog in* Fainlove's *Arms.*)

Jenny. You always look Well.   20

Mrs. Clerimont. For I'm always talking, you mean so, that disquiets thy Sullen *English* Temper, but I don't really look so well when I am Silent—If I do but offer to Speak—Then I may say that —Oh, Bless me, *Jenny*, I am so Pale, I am afraid of my self—I have not laid on half Red enough—What a Dough-bak'd thing was I 25 before I improv'd my self, and Travell'd for Beauty—However, my Face is very prettily design'd to day.

0.1 *Mrs.* Clerimont, Fainlove] D1; Clerimont, *Mr* Fainlove
21 *Mrs.*] D1; *Mr.*

Fainlove. Indeed, Madam, you begin to have so fine an Hand, that you are younger every day than other.

30 *Mrs. Clerimont.* The Ladies abroad us'd to call me *Madamoiselle Titian*, I was so famous for my Colouring; but prethee, Wench, bring me my Black Eye-brows out of the next Room.

Jenny. Madam, I have 'em in my Hand.

Fainlove. It would be happy for all that are to see you to day, if 35 you could change your Eyes too.

Mrs. Clerimont. Gallant enough—No, hang it, I'le wear these I have on, this Mode of Visage takes mightily, I had three Ladies last Week came over to my Complexion—I think to be a fair Woman this Fortnight, till I find I'm ap'd too much—I believe there are an 40 hundred Copies of me already.

Jenny. Dear Madam, won't your Ladyship please to let me be of the next Countenance you leave off.

Mrs. Clerimont. You may, *Jenny*—but I assure you—it is a very pretty piece of ill-nature, for a Woman that has any Genius for 45 Beauty, to observe the Servile Imitation of her Manner, her Motion, her Glances, and her Smiles.

Fainlove. Ay, indeed, Madam, nothing can be so Ridiculous as to imitate the Inimitable.

Mrs. Clerimont. Indeed, as you say, *Fainlove*, the *French* Mein is no 50 more to be learn'd, than the Language without going thither— Then again to see some poor Ladies who have Clownish, Penurious, *English* Husbands, turn and torture their old Cloaths into so many Forms, and Dye 'em into so many Colours, to follow me—What say'st, *Jenny*? What say'st? not a Word?

55 *Jenny.* Why, Madam, all that I can say—

Mrs. Clerimont. Nay, I believe, *Jenny*, thou hast nothing to say any more than the rest of thy Country-Women—The Splenaticks Speak just as the Weather lets 'em—They are mere talking Barometers— Abroad the People of Quality go on so eternally, and still go on, and 60 are Gay and Entertain—In *England* Discourse is made up of nothing but Question and Answer—I was t'other day at a Visit, where there was a profound Silence, for, I believe, the third part of a Minute.

Jenny. And your Ladyship there?

Mrs. Clerimont. They infected me with their Dulness, who can 65
keep up their good humour at an *English* Visit—They sit as at a
Funeral, silent in the midst of many Candles—One, perhaps, alarms
the Room—'Tis very cold Weather—then all the Mute play their
Fans—till some other Question happens, and then the Fans go off
again— 70

Boy. Madam, your Spinet-Master is come.

Mrs. Clerimont. Bring him in, he's very pretty Company.

Fainlove. His Spinet is, he never Speaks himself.

Mrs. Clerimont. Speak, *Simpleton*? What then, he keeps out silence,
does not he— 75

[*Enter Spinet-Master.*]

Oh, Sir, you must forgive me, I have been very Idle—Well, you
pardon me (*Master Bows*—) Did you think I was perfect in the Song
—(*Bows.*) but pray let me hear it once more. Let us see it—(*Reads.*)

SONG.

With Studied Airs, and practis'd Smiles,
Flavia *my Ravish'd Heart beguiles,* 80
The Charms we make, are Ours alone,
Nature's Works are not our own;
Her Skilful Hand gives every Grace,
And shows her fancy in her Face.
She Feeds with Art my Amorous Rage, 85
Nor fears the Force of Coming Age.

You Sing it very well; but, I confess, I wish you'd give more into
the *French* Manner. Observe me, Hum it *A-la-Françoise.*
With Studied Airs, &c.

The whole Person, every Limb, every Nerve Sings—The *English* 90
Way is only being for that time a mere Musical Instrument, just
sending forth a Sound without knowing they do so—Now, I'll give
you a little of it, like an *English* Woman—You are to suppose I've
deny'd you 20 times, look'd silly, and all that—Then with Hands
and Face insensible—I have a mighty Cold. 95
With Studied, &c.

Enter Servant.

Servant. Madam, Captain *Clerimont*, and a very strange Gentleman, are come to wait on you.

Mrs. Clerimont. Let him, and the very strange Gentleman come in.

100 *Fainlove.* Oh! Madam, that's the Country Gentleman I was telling you of.

Enter Humphry *and Captain* Clerimont.

Fainlove. Madam, may I do my self the Honour to Recommend Mr. *Gubbin*, Son and Heir to Sir *Harry Gubbin*, to your Ladyship's Notice.

105 *Mrs. Clerimont.* Mr. *Gubbin*, I am extreamly pleased with your Suit, 'tis Antique, and originally from *France*.

Humphry. It is always lock'd up, Madam, when I'm in the Country. My Father prizes it mightily.

Mrs. Clerimont. 'Twou'd make a very pretty Dancing Suit in a 110 Mask. Oh! Captain *Clerimont*, I have a Quarrel with you.

Enter Servant.

Servant. Madam, your Ladiship's Husband desires to know, whether you see Company to day or not?

Mrs. Clerimont. Who, you Clown?

Servant. Mr *Clerimont*, Madam.

115 *Mrs. Clerimont.* He may come in.

Enter Clerimont *Senior.*

Mrs. Clerimont. Your very humble Servant.

Clerimont Senior. I was going to take the Air this Morning in my Coach, and did my self the Honour before I went, to receive your Commands, finding you saw Company.

120 *Mrs. Clerimont.* At any time when you know I do, you may let me see you. Pray, how did you Sleep last night? (*Aside.*) If I had not ask'd him that Question, they might have thought we lay together. (*Here* Fainlove *looking thro' a Perspective, bows to* Clerimont *Senior.*) But Captain I have a quarrel to you—I have utterly forgot those 125 three Coupees you promis'd to come agen, and shew me.

115.1 Clerimont *Senior*] D1; *Mr*. Clerimont.
117, 126, 131 *Clerimont Senior*] (D1; Mr (*Mr.*) *Cl*.

Clerimont Senior. Then Madam, you have no Commands this Morning.

Mrs. Clerimont. Your humble Servant, Sir,—But, oh! (*As she is going to be led by the Captain.*) Have you sign'd that Mortgage, to pay off my Lady *Faddle's* Winnings at *Ombre*?   130

Clerimont Senior. Yes, Madam.

Mrs. Clerimont. Then all's well, my Honour's safe.

Exit Clerimont *Senior.*

Come, Captain—Lead me this Step—For I'm apt to make a false One—You shall shew me.

Captain Clerimont. I'll shew you, Madam, 'tis no matter for a 135 Fiddle; I'll give you 'em the *French* way, in a Teaching Tune. Pray more quick—*Oh Madamoiselle que faitez vous*—*A moy*—There again —Now slide as it were with and without Measure—There you out-did the Gipsy—And you have all the Smiles of the Dance to a tittle.

Mrs. Clerimont. Why truly I think that the greatest Part—I have 140 seen an *Englishwoman* dance a Jigg with the Severity of a Vestal Virgin—

Humphry. If this be *French* dancing and singing, I fancy I could do it—Haw! haw! (*Capers aside.*)

Mrs. Clerimont. I protest, Mr. *Gubbin*, you have almost the Step, 145 without any of our Country Bashfulness. Give me your Hand— Haw! haw! So, so, a little quicker—That's right Haw! Captain, your Brother delivered this Spark to me, to be diverted here till he calls for him.

Exit Captain Clerimont.

Humphry. This cutting so high makes one's Mony jingle con- 150 foundedly: I'm resolv'd I'll never carry above one Pocket full hereafter.

Mrs. Clerimont. You do it very readily—You amaze me.

Humphry. Are the Gentlemen in *France* generally so well bred as we are in *England*—Are they, Madam, ha! But young Gentleman, 155 when shall I see this Sister? Haw! haw! haw! Is not the higher one jumps the better?

Fainlove. She'll be mightily taken with you, I'm sure. One would not think 'twas in you—You're so gay—and dance so very high—

127 [om.] D1; (*Exeunt.*   132.1 Clerimont *Senior.*] D1; Clerimont

160   *Humphry.* What should ail me? Did you think I was Windgall'd?
I can sing too if I please—but I won't till I see your *Sister*—This is
a mighty pretty House.

    Mrs. Clerimont. Well, do you know that I like this Gentleman
extremely? I should be glad to 'form him—But were you never in
165 *France*, Mr. *Gubbin*?

    Humphry. No,—but I'm always thus pleasant, if my Father is not
by—I protest I'd advise your Sister to have me—I'm for marrying
her at once—Why should I stand shilly-shally, like a Country
Bumpkin?

170   *Fainlove.* Mr. *Gubbin*, I dare say, she'll be as forward as you; We'll
go in, and see her.

    Mrs. Clerimont. Then he has not yet seen the Lady he is in love
with. I protest very new and gallant—Mr. *Gubbin*, she must needs
believe you a frank Person—*Fainlove*, I must see this Sister too, I'm
175 resolv'd she shall like him.

> *There needs not time true Passion to discover;*
> *The most believing is the most a Lover.*

Exeunt Omnes.

[Act III. Scene ii.]

Enter Niece *sola.*

    Niece. Oh *Clerimont*! *Clerimont*! To be struck at first sight! I'm
asham'd of my Weakness; I find in my self all the Symptoms of a
raging Amour; I love Solitude, I grow pale, I sigh frequently, I call
upon the Name of *Clerimont* when I don't think of it—His Person is
5 ever in my Eyes, and his Voice in my Ears—Methinks I long to lose
my self in some pensive Grove, or to hang over the Head of some
warbling Fountain, with a Lute in my hand, softning the Murmurs
of the Water.

171 [om.] ed.; [apart.

Aunt *entring*.

Aunt. *Biddy*, *Biddy*, where's *Biddy Tipkin*?

Niece. Whom do you enquire for?   10

Aunt. Come, come, he's just a-coming at the Park Door.

Niece. Who is coming?

Aunt. Your Cousin *Humphry*—who shou'd be coming? Your
Lover, your Husband that is to be—Pray, my Dear, look well, and
be civil for your Credit, and mine too.   15

Niece. If he answers my Idea, I shall rally the Rustick to death.

Aunt. Hist—Here, he is.

Enter Humphry.

Humphry. Aunt, your humble Servant—Is that—Ha! Aunt?

Aunt. Yes, Cousin *Humphry*, that's your Cousin *Bridget*. Well, I'll
leave you together.   20

Exit Aunt. *They sit.*

Humphry. Aunt does as she'd be done by, Cousin *Bridget*, does not
she, Cousin? Ha! What are you a *Londoner*, and not speak to a
Gentleman? Look'y Cousin, the old Folks resolving to marry us, I
thought it would be proper to see how I lik'd you, as not caring to
buy a Pig in a Poke—for I love to look before I leap.   25

Niece. Sir, your Person and Address bring to my mind the whole
History of *Valentine* and *Orson*: What, would they marry me to a
wild Man? Pray answer me a Question or two.

Humphry. Ay, ay, as many as you please, Cousin *Bridget*.

Niece. What Wood were you taken in? How long have you been 30
caught?

Humphry. Caught!

Niece. Where were your Haunts?

Humphry. My Haunts!

Niece. Are not Cloaths very uneasy to you? Is this strange Dress 35
the first you ever wore?

Humphry. How!

Niece. Are not you a great Admirer of Roots, and raw Flesh?—Let
me look upon your Nails?—Don't you love Black-berries, Haws,
and Pignuts, mightily?   40

9 *Tipkin*] ed.; *Pitkin*   22 not] D1; [om.]

Humphry. How!

Niece. Canst thou deny that thou we'rt suckled by a Wolf? You ha'n't been so Barbarous I hope, since you came amongst Men, as to Hunt your Nurse—have you?

45   *Humphry.* Hunt my Nurse? Ay, 'tis so, she's distracted as sure as a Gun—Harke'e, Cousin, Pray will you let me ask you a Question, or two?

Niece. If thou hast yet learn'd the use of Language, Speak Monster.

50   *Humphry.* How long have you been thus?

Niece. Thus? What wouldst thou say.

Humphry. What's the cause of it. Tell me truly now—Did you never love any body before me?

Niece. Go, go, Thou'rt a Savage. (*Rises.*)

55   *Humphry.* They never let you go abroad, I suppose.

Niece. Thou'rt a Monster I tell thee.

Humphry. Indeed, Cousin, tho' 'tis a folly to tell thee so—I am afraid thou art a Mad-Woman.

Niece. I'le have thee carried into some Forrest.

60   *Humphry.* I'le take thee into a Dark Room.

Niece. I hate thee.

Humphry. I wish you did—There's no Hate lost I assure you, Cousin *Bridget*.

Niece. Cousin *Bridget*, Quoth a'—I'de assoon claim Kindred with
65 a Mountain-Bear—I detest thee.

Humphry. You never do any harm in these Fits, I hope—but do you hate me in earnest?

Niece. Dost thou ask it ungentle Forrester?

Humphry. Yes, for I've a reason looky', it happens very well If you
70 hate me, and are in your Senses, for to tell you truly—I don't much care for you, and there is another Fine Woman as I am inform'd, that is in some hopes of having me.

Niece. (*Aside.*) This merits my attention.

Humphry. Looky' d' see,—as I said, since I don't care for you—I
75 would not have you set your Heart on me—but if you like any body else let me know it—and I'le find out a way for us to get rid of one another, and deceive the Old Folks that would Couple us.

Niece. This wears the Face of an Amour—There is something in that Thought which makes thy presence less insupportable.

Humphry. Nay, nay, Now you're growing fond; If you come with 80 these Maids Tricks to say you hate at first, and afterwards like me —you'l spoil the whole Design.

Niece. Don't fear it—when I think of Consorting with thee, may the Wild-Boar defile the cleanly Ermin, may the Tyger be Wedded to the Kid.   85

Humphry. When I of thee, may the Pole-Cat Catterwaul with the Civet.

Niece. When I harbour the least thought of thee, may the Silver-Thames forget it's Course.

Humphry. When I like thee, may I be sows'd over Head and Ears 90 in a Horse-Pond—But do you hate me?

Enter Aunt.

Niece. For ever; and you me?

Humphry. Most heartily.

Aunt. (*Aside.*) Ha, I like this—They are come to Promises—and Protestations.   95

Humphry. I am very glad I have found a way to please you.

Niece. You promise to be constant.

Humphry. Till Death.

Niece. Thou best of Savages.

Humphry. Thou best of Savages! Poor *Biddy*.   100

Aunt. Oh the pretty Couple joking on one another. Well, How do you like your Cousin *Humphry*, now?

Niece. Much better than I thought I should—He's quite another thing than what I took him for—We have both the same Passion for one another.   105

Humphry. We wanted only an occasion to open our Hearts— Aunt.

Aunt. Oh, how this will rejoice my Brother, and Sir *Harry*, we'll go to them.

Humphry. No, I must fetch a walk with a new Acquaintance, Mr. 110 *Samuel Pounce.*

109 them] ed.; him

Aunt. An Excellent Acquaintance for your Husband; Come, Niece, come.

Niece. Farewell Rustick.

115 *Humphry.* Buy *Biddy.*

Aunt. Rustick! *Biddy*! Ha! ha! pretty Creatures.

Exeunt.

[*The End of the Third Act.*]

Act IV. Scene i.

Enter Captain Clerimont *and* Pounce.

Captain Clerimont. Do's she expect me then, at this very instant?

Pounce. I tell you, she order'd me to bring the Painter at this very Hour, precisely, to Draw her Niece—for to make her Picture 5 peculiarly charming, she has now that downcast pretty Shame, that warm Cheek, glowing with the Fear and Hope of to-Day's fate, with the inviting, coy-Affectation of a Bride, all in her Face at once. Now I know you are a pretender that way.

Captain Clerimont. Enough, I warrant, to personate the Character 10 on such an inspiring Occasion.

Pounce. You must have the Song I spoke of, perform'd at this Window—at the end of which I'le give you a Signal—Every thing is ready for you, your Pencil, your Canvas stretch'd—your—Be sure you play your part in Humour; to be a Painter for a Lady, you're to 15 have the excessive Flattery of a Lover; the ready Invention of a Poet; and the easie Gesture of a Player.

Captain Clerimont. Come, come, no more Instructions, my Imagination out-runs all you can say; Be gone, be gone!

Exit Pounce.

A SONG

I.

Why lovely Charmer, tell me why,
So very kind, and yet so shy? 20
Why does that cold forbidding Air
Give Damps of Sorrow and Despair?
Or why that Smile my Soul subdue,
And kindle up my Flames anew?

II.

In vain you strive with all your Art, 25
By turns to freeze and fire my Heart:
When I behold a Face so fair,
So sweet a Look, so soft an Air,
My ravish'd Soul is charm'd all o'er,
I cannot love thee less nor more. 30

After the Song Pounce *appears*
beckoning the Captain.

Pounce. Captain, Captain.

Exit Captain Clerimont.

[Act IV. Scene ii.]

Enter Aunt *and* Niece.

Niece's *Lodgings, two Chairs and Table.*

Aunt. Indeed, Niece, I am as much overjoy'd to see your Wedding day, as if it were my own.

Niece. But, Why must it be huddled up so?

Aunt. Oh, my Dear a private Wedding is much better, your Mother had such a bustle at hers with Feasting, and Fooling: 5 Besides, they did not go to Bed till Two in the Morning.

Niece. Since you understand things so well, I wonder you never married your self.

Aunt. My Dear, I was very cruel Thirty Years ago, and no body
10 has ask'd me since.

Niece. Alas! a Day!

Aunt. Yet I assure you, there were a great many Matches propos'd to me—There was Sir *Gilbert Jolly*, but he, forsooth, could not please; He drank Ale, and smoak'd Tobacco, and was no fine
15 Gentleman, forsooth—but, then again, there was Young Mr. *Peregrine Shapely*, who had travel'd and spoke *French*, and smil'd at all I said; He was a fine Gentleman—but then he was Consumptive; And yet again, to see how one may be mistaken; Sir *Jolly* dy'd in half a Year, and my Lady *Shapely* has by that Thin slip Eight Chil-
20 dren, that should have been mine; but here's the Bridegroom.

Enter Humphry.

So Cousin *Humphry*!

Humphry. Your Servant Ladies,—So, my Dear—

Niece. So my Savage—

Aunt. O, fie, no more of that to your Husband, *Biddy*.

25 *Humphry.* No matter, I like it as well as Duck or Love: I know my Cousin loves me as well as I do her.

Aunt. I'll leave you together; I must go and get ready an Enter-tainment for you when you come home.

Exit.

Humphry. Well, Cousin, are you constant?—Do you hate me still?
30 *Niece.* As much as ever.

Humphry. What an Happiness it is, when People's Inclinations jump? I wish I knew what to do with you: Can you get no body, d'ye think, to marry you.

Niece. (*Aside.*) Oh! *Clerimont, Clerimont*! Where art thou?

Enter Aunt *and Captain* Clerimont *disguis'd.*

35 *Aunt.* This, Sir, is the Lady, whom you are to draw,—You see, Sir, as good Flesh and Blood, as a Man wou'd desire to put in Colours,—I must have her Maiden-Picture.

Humphry. Then the Painter must make haste,—ha Cousin!

Niece. Hold thy Tongue, good Savage.

Captain Clerimont. Madam, I'm generally forced to new-mould 40
every Feature, and mend Nature's Handy-work; but here she has
made so finish'd an Original, that I despair of my Copy's coming
up to it.

Aunt. Do you hear that, Niece?

Niece. I don't desire you to make Graces where you find none.   45

Captain Clerimont. To see the difference of the Fair Sex!—I protest
to you, Madam, my Fancy is utterly exhausted with inventing
Faces for those that sit to me. The first Entertainment I generally
meet with, are Complaints for want of Sleep, They never look'd so
pale in their Lives, as when they sit for their Pictures—Then so 50
many Touches and Retouches, when the Face is finish'd—That
Wrincle ought not to have been, those Eyes are too languid, that
Colour's too weak, that Side-look hides the Mole on the left Cheek:
In short, the whole Likeness is struck out. But in you, Madam, the
Highest I can come up to will be but rigid Justice.   55

Humphry. A comical Dog, this!

Aunt. Truly the Gentleman seems to understand his Business.

Niece. Sir, if your Pencil flatters like your Tongue, you are going
to draw a Picture that won't be at all like me. (*Aside.*) Sure I have
heard that Voice somewhere.   60

Captain Clerimont. Madam, be pleas'd to place your self near me,
nearer still, Madam, here falls the best Light—You must know,
Madam, there are three kinds of Airs which the Ladies most delight
in—There is your Haughty—your Mild—And, your Pensive Air—
The Haughty may be express'd with the Head a little more erect 65
than ordinary, and the Countenance with a certain Disdain in it, so
as she may appear almost, but not quite inexorable: This kind of
Air is generally heightned with a little knitting of the Brows—I
gave my Lady *Scornwell* her Choice of a dozen Frowns, before she
cou'd find one to her liking.   70

Niece. But what is the mild Air?

Captain Clerimont. The Mild Air is compos'd of a Languish, and a
Smile—But if I might advise, I'd rather be a Pensive Beauty; the

52 not] D1; not not

Pensive usually feels her Pulse, leans on one Arm, or sits ruminating
75 with a Book in her hand—which Conversation she is suppos'd to
chuse, rather than the endless Importunities of Lovers.

Humphry. A Comical Dog—

Aunt. Upon my word he understands his Business well; I'll tell
you, Neice, how your Mother was drawn—She had an Orange in
80 her Hand, and a Nosegay in her Bosom, but a Look so pure and
fresh-colour'd, you'd have taken her for one of the Seasons.

Captain Clerimont. You seem indeed, Madam, most inclin'd to the
Pensive—The Pensive delights also in the fall of Waters, Pastoral
Figures, or any Rural View suitable to a fair Lady, who with a
85 delicate Spleen has retir'd from the World, as sick of its Flattery and
Admiration.

Niece. No—since there is room for Fancy in a Picture, I wou'd be
drawn like the Amazon *Thalestris*, with a Spear in my Hand, and an
Helmet on a Table before me—At a distance behind let there be a
90 Dwarf, holding by the Bridle a Milk-white Palfrey,—

Captain Clerimont. Madam, the Thought is full of Spirit, and if you
please, there shall be a *Cupid* stealing away your Helmet, to shew
that Love shou'd have a Part in all gallant Actions.

Niece. That Circumstance may be very Picturesque.

95 *Captain Clerimont.* Here, Madam, shall be your own Picture, here
the Palfrey, and here the Dwarf—The Dwarf must be very little,
or we shan't have room for him.

Niece. A Dwarf cannot be too little.

Captain Clerimont. I'll make him a Blackamore, to distinguish him
100 from the other too powerful Dwarf (*Sighs.*) the *Cupid*—I'll place
that beauteous Boy near you, 'twill look very natural—He'll
certainly take you for his Mother *Venus.*

Niece. I leave these Particulars to your own Fancy.

Captain Clerimont. Please, Madam, to uncover your Neck a little;
105 a little lower still—a little, little lower.

Niece. I'll be drawn thus, if you please, Sir.

Captain Clerimont. Ladies, have you heard the News of a late
Marriage between a young Lady of a great Fortune, and a younger
Brother of a good Family?

99 make him] D1; make him him

Aunt. Pray, Sir, how is it? 110

Captain Clerimont. This young Gentleman, Ladies, is a particular Acquaintance of mine, and much about my Age and Stature; (look me full in the Face, Madam) he accidentally met the young Lady, who had in her all the Perfections of her Sex; (hold up your Head, Madam, that's right) she let him know that his Person and Dis- 115 course were not altogether disagreeable to her—The Difficulty was how to gain a second Interview, (your Eyes full upon mine, Madam) for never was there such a Sigher in all the Valleys of *Arcadia*, as that unfortunate Youth, during the absence of her he lov'd—

Aunt. A-lack-a-day—Poor young Gentleman! 120

Niece. (*Aside.*) It must be he—what a charming Amour is this!

Captain Clerimont. At length, Ladies, he bethought himself of an Expedient; he dress'd himself just as I am now, and came to draw her Picture, (your Eyes full upon mine, pray Madam.) 125

Humphry. A subtile Dog, I warrant him.

Captain Clerimont. And by that means found an Opportunity of carrying her off, and marrying her.

Aunt. Indeed your Friend was a very vicious young Man.

Niece. Yet perhaps the young Lady was not displeas'd at what 130 he had done.

Captain Clerimont. But, Madam, what were the Transports of the Lover, when she made him that Confession?

Niece. I dare say she thought her self very happy, when she got out of her Guardians hands. 135

Aunt. 'Tis very true, Niece—There are abundance of those Head-strong young Baggages about Town.

Captain Clerimont. The Gentleman has often told me, he was strangely struck at first sight; but when she sat to him for her Picture, and assum'd all those Graces that are proper for the 140 occasion—his Torment was so exquisite, his Passion so violent, that he cou'd not have liv'd a day, had he not found means to make the Charmer of his Heart his own.

Humphry. 'Tis certainly the foolishest thing in the World to stand shilly-shally about a Woman, when one has a Mind to marry 145 her.

Captain Clerimont. The young Painter turn'd Poet on the Subject; I believe I have the Words by heart.

Niece. A Sonnet! pray repeat it.

[*Captain Clerimont.*]

I.

150
While Gentle Parthenissa *walks,*
And sweetly smiles, and gayly talks,
A thousand Shafts around her fly,
A thousand Swains unheeded die.

II.

If then she labours to be seen,
155
With all her killing Air and Mien;
From so much Beauty, so much Art,
What Mortal can secure his Heart?

Humphry. I fancy if 'twas sung, 'twou'd make a very pretty Catch.

Captain Clerimont. My Servant has a Voice, you shall hear it.

Here 'tis sung.

160 *Aunt.* Why this is pretty? I think a Painter should never be without a good Singer—It brightens the Features strangely—I profess I'm mightily pleas'd, I'll but just step in, and give some Orders, and be with you presently.

Exit Aunt.

Niece. Was not this Adventurous Painter call'd *Clerimont?*

165 *Captain Clerimont.* It was *Clerimont* the Servant of *Parthenissa;* but let me beseech that Beauteous Maid to resolve, and make the Incident I feign'd to her a real one—Consider, Madam, you are inviron'd by Cruel and Treacherous Guards, which would force you to a disagreeable Marriage, your case is exactly the same with the
170 Princess of the *Leontines* in *Clelia.*

Niece. How can we commit such a Solecism against all Rules! What in the first Leaf of our History to have the Marriage? You know it cannot be.

Captain Clerimont. The pleasantest part of the History will be
175 after Marriage.

Niece. No! I never yet read of a Knight that entred Tilt or Tournament after Wedlock—'tis not to be expected—when the Husband begins, the Heroe ends; all that noble impulse to Glory, all the Generous Passion for Adventures is consum'd in the Nuptial Torch; I don't know how it is, but *Mars* and *Hymen* never 180 hit it.

Humphry. (*Listning. Aside.*) Consum'd in the Nuptial Torch! *Mars* and *Hymen*! What can all this mean—I am very glad I can hardly read—They could never get these foolish Fancies into my Head—I had always a strong Brain. [*To* Niece.] Harky' Cousin, is not this 185 Painter a Commical Dog?

Niece. I think he's very agreeable Company—

Humphry. Why then I tell you what,—Marry him—A Painter's a very Genteel Calling—He's an Ingenious Fellow, and certainly Poor. I fancy he'd be glad on't; I'll keep my Aunt out of the Room 190 a Minute or two, that's all the Time you have to consider—

Exit Humphry.

Captain Clerimont. Fortune points out to us this only occasion of our Happiness: Love's of Cœlestial Origine, and needs no long Acquaintance to be manifest. Lovers like Angels speak by intuition —Their Souls are in their Eyes—   195

Niece. (*Aside.*) Then I fear he sees mine. [*To Captain* Clerimont.] But I can't think of abridging our Amours, and cutting off all farther decoration of Disguise, Serenade, and Adventure.

Captain Clerimont. Nor would I willingly lose the Merit of long Services, Midnight Sighs, and Plaintive Solitudes—Were there not 200 a necessity.

Niece. Then to be seiz'd by Stealth!

Captain Clerimont. Why Madam, you are a great Fortune, and should not be Married the common way. Indeed, Madam, you ought to be Stol'n, nay, in strictness, I don't know but you ought 205 to be Ravish'd.

Niece. But then our History will be so short.

Captain Clerimont. I grant it, but you don't consider there's a device in another's leading you instead of this Person that's to have you; and Madam, tho' our Amours can't furnish out a Romance, 210 they'l make a very pretty Novel—Why smiles my Fair?

Niece. I am almost of opinion, that had *Oroondates* been as pressing as *Clerimont, Cassandra* had been but a Pocket-Book: But it looks so ordinary, to go out at a Door to be Married—Indeed, I ought to be
215 taken out of a Window, and run away with.

Enter Humphry *and* Pounce.

Humphry. Well, Cousin, the Coach is at the Door. If you please I'le lead you.

Niece. I put my self into your Hands, good Savage; but you promise to leave me.
220 *Humphry.* I tell you plainly, you must not think of having me.

Pounce. (*To Captain* Clerimont.) You'l have opportunity enough to carry her off; The old Fellows will be busy with me—I'll gain all the Time I can, but be bold and prosper.

Niece. Clerimont, you follow us.
225 *Captain Clerimont.* Upon the Wings of Love.

[*The End of the Fourth Act.*]

Act V. [Scene i.]

Enter Clerimont *Senior and* Fainlove.

Clerimont Senior. Then she gave you this Letter, and bid you read it as a Paper of Verses?

Fainlove. This is the Place, the Hour, the lucky Minute—Now am I rubbing up my Memory, to recollect all you said to me when you
5 first ruin'd me, that I may attack her right.

Clerimont Senior. Your Eloquence would be needless—'tis so unmodish to need perswasion: Modesty makes a Lady embarras'd— But my Spouse is above that, as for Example, (*Reading her Letter.*)

0.1 Clerimont *Senior*] D1; Clerimont   The speech prefixes of lines 1, 6, 17, and
24 read '*Cler.*' in Q.

Fainlove,

You don't seem to want Wit—therefore I need say no more, then that 10
distance to a Woman of the World is becoming in no Man, but an
Husband: An hour hence come up the Back-stairs to my Closet.

Adieu Mon Mignon.

I am glad you are punctual, I'le conceal my self to observe your
Interview—(*Aside.*) Oh, Torture! but this Wench must not see it— 15
Fainlove. Be sure you come time enough to save my Reputation.
Clerimont Senior. Remember your Orders, distance becomes no
Man but an Husband.
Fainlove. I am glad you are in so good Humour on the occasion;
But you know me to be but a Bully in Love that can Bluster only 20
till the Minute of Engagement—But I'll top my part, and form my
Conduct by my own Sentiments—If she grows Coy, I'll grow more
Saucy—'Twas so I was won my self—
Clerimont Senior. Well, my Dear Rival—Your assignation draws
nigh—You are to put on your Transport, your Impatient Throb- 25
bing Heart won't let you wait her Arrival—Let the dull Family-thing
an Husband, who reckons his Moments by his Cares be content to
wait, but you are a Gallant, and measure Time by Extasies.
Fainlove. I hear her coming—To your Post—Good Husband know
your Duty, and don't be in the way when your Wife has a mind 30
to be in private—To your Post, into the Cole-hole. [Clerimont
Senior hides.]

Enter Mrs. Clerimont.

Welcome my Dear, my Tender Charmer—Oh! To my longing
Arms—Feel the Heart pant, that falls and rises as you smile or
frown—Oh, the Extatick Moment!— 35
(*Aside.*) I think that was something like what has been said to me.
Mrs. Clerimont. Very well—*Fainlove*—I protest I value my self for
my discerning—I knew you had Fire through all the respect you
shew'd me—But how came you to make no direct Advances, young
Gentleman?—Why was I forc'd to admonish your Gallantry?— 40
Fainlove. Why, Madam, I knew you a Woman of Breeding, and
above the senseless Niceties of an English Wife—The French way

is, you are to go so far, whether you are agreeable or not: If you are so happy as to please, no body that is not of a constrain'd Behaviour
45 is at a loss to let you know it—Besides, if the humble Servant makes the first Approaches, he has the Impudence of making a Request, but not the Honour of obeying a Command.

Mrs. Clerimont. Right—a Woman's Man should conceal Passion in a familiar Air of Indifference—now there's Mr. *Clerimont*; I can't
50 allow him the least Freedom, but the unfashionable Fool grows so fond of me, he cannot hide it in Publick—

Fainlove. Ay, Madam, I have often wonder'd at your Ladyships Choice of one that seems to have so little of the *beau monde* in his Carriage, but just what you force him to—while there were so many
55 pretty Gentlemen—(*Dancing.*)

Mrs. Clerimont. O young Gentleman, you are mightily mistaken, if you think such Animals as you, and pretty Beau *Titmouse*, and pert *Billy Butterfly*, tho' I suffer you to come in, and play about my Rooms, are any ways in competition with a Man whose Name one
60 would wear.

Fainlove. Oh Madam! then I find we are—

Mrs. Clerimont. A Woman of Sense must have respect for a Man of that Character; but alas! Respect—What is Respect? Respect is not the thing—Respect has something too solemn for soft Moments
65 —You things are more proper for Hours of Dalliance.

Clerimont Senior. (*Peeping.*) How have I wrong'd this fine Lady!— I find I am to be a Cuckold out of her pure esteem for me.

Mrs. Clerimont. Besides those Fellows for whom we have respect, have none for us: I warrant on such an occasion *Clerimont* would have
70 ruffled a Woman out of all Form, while you—

Clerimont Senior. (*Aside.*) A good hint—now my Cause comes on.

Fainlove. Since then you allow us fitter for soft Moments, why do we misemploy 'em? Let me kiss that beauteous Hand, and clasp that graceful Frame.

75 *Mrs. Clerimont.* How, *Fainlove*! What, you don't design to be impertinent—But my Lips have a certain roughness on 'em to-day, ha'n't they?

Fainlove. (*Kissing.*) No—they are all Softness—Their delicious Sweetness is inexpressible—Here Language fails—Let me applaud thy Lips not by the utterance, but the Touch of mine.　　　80

　　　　　Enter Clerimont *Senior, drawing his Sword.*

Clerimont Senior. Ha, Villain! Ravisher! Invader of my Bed and Honour! draw.

Mrs. Clerimont. What means this Insolence—this Intrusion into my Privacy? What, do you come into my very Closet without knocking? Who put this into your Head?—　　　85

Clerimont Senior. My Injuries have alarm'd me, and I'll bear no longer, but sacrifice your Bravado, the Author of 'em.

Mrs. Clerimont. Oh! poor Mr. *Fainlove*—Must he die for his Complaisance, and innocent Freedoms with me? How could you, if you might? Oh! the sweet Youth! What, fight Mr. *Fainlove*? What will　90 the Ladies say?

Fainlove. Let me come at the Intruder on Ladies private Hours— The Unfashionable Monster—I'll prevent all future Interruption from him—Let me come—(*Drawing his Sword.*)

Mrs. Clerimont. O the brave pretty Creature! Look at his Youth　95 and Innocence—He is not made for such rough Encounters—Stand behind me—Poor *Fainlove*!—There is not a Visit in Town, Sir, where you shall not be display'd at full length for this Intrusion—I banish you for ever from my Sight and Bed.

Clerimont Senior. I obey you, Madam, for Distance is becoming in　100 no Man but an Husband—(*Giving her the Letter which she reads, and falls into a Swoon.*) I've gone too far—(*Kissing her.*) The Impertinent was guilty of nothing but what my Indiscretion led her to—This is the first Kiss I've had these six Weeks—but she awakes.

Well, *Lucy*, you topp'd your part, indeed—Come to my Arms　105 thou ready willing fair one—Thou hast no Vanities, no Niceties; but art thankful for every Instant of Love that I bestow on thee— (*Embracing her.*)

80.1 Clerimont *Senior.*] D1; Clerimont
81 *Clerimont Senior*] D1; Mr. *Cl.*　Q uses 'Mr. *Cl.*' consistently for speech prefixes to the end of the scene.
104 six] D1; sick
105 *Lucy*] ed.; *Jenny*　Although all editions except the Regents retain the incorrect *Jenny*, Fainlove's name as it appears in I. i is Lucy.

Mrs. Clerimont. What am I then abus'd? Is it a Wench then of his?
110 Oh me! Was ever poor abus'd Wife, poor innocent Lady thus injur'd!
(*Runs and seizes* Fainlove's *Sword.*)

Clerimont Senior. Oh the brave pretty Creature—Hurt Mr. *Fain-love*! Look at his Youth, his Innocence—Ha! ha! (*Interposing.*)

Fainlove. Have a Care, have a Care, Dear Sir,—I know by my self
115 she'll have no Mercy.

Mrs. Clerimont. I'll be the death of her—Let me come on—Stand from between us, Mr. *Clerimont*—I wou'd not hurt you. (*Pushing and crying.*)

Clerimont Senior. Run, run *Lucy.*

Exit Fainlove.

120 (*Looks at her upbraidingly before he speaks.*) Well, Madam, are these the innocent Freedoms you claim'd of me? Have I deserv'd this? How has there been a Moment of yours ever interrupted with the real Pangs I suffer? The daily Importunities of Creditors, who become so by serving your profuse Vanities: Did I ever murmur at supplying
125 any of your Diversions, while I believ'd 'em (as you call'd 'em) harmless? Must then those Eyes that us'd to glad my heart with their familiar Brightness, hang down with Guilt? Guilt has transform'd thy whole Person; nay, the very memory of it—Fly from my growing Passion.

130   *Mrs. Clerimont.* I cannot fly, nor bear it—Oh! look not—

Clerimont Senior. What can you say? speak quickly. (*Offering to draw.*)

Mrs. Clerimont. I never saw you mov'd before—Don't murder me impenitent; I'm wholly in your Power as a Criminal, but remember
135 I have been so, in a tender Regard.

Clerimont Senior. But how have you consider'd that Regard?

Mrs. Clerimont. Is't possible you can forgive what you ensnar'd me into?—Oh, look at me kindly—You know I have only err'd in my Intention, nor saw my Danger, till, by this honest Art, you had
140 shown me what 'tis to venture to the utmost Limit of what is lawful. You laid that Train, I'm sure, to alarm, not to betray, my Innocence—Mr. *Clerimont* scorns such Baseness! Therefore I kneel—I weep—I am convinc'd. (*Kneels.*)

119 *Lucy*] ed.; *Jenny*   119.1 Fainlove] ed.; Jenny

Clerimont Senior. (*Takes her up embracing her.*) Then kneel, and weep no more—my Fairest—my Reconcil'd!—Be so in a Moment, for 145 know I cannot (without wringing my own Heart) give you the least Compunction—Be in Humour—It shall be your own Fault, if ever there's a serious Word more on this Subject.

Mrs. Clerimont. I must correct every Idea that rises in my Mind, and learn every Gesture of my Body a-new—I detest the thing I was. 150

Clerimont Senior. No, no—You must not do so—Our Joy and Grief, Honour and Reproach, are the same; you must slide out of your Foppery by degrees, so that it may appear your own Act.

Mrs. Clerimont. But this Wench!—

Clerimont Senior. She is already out of your Way—You shall see the 155 Catastrophe of her Fate your self—But still keep up the fine Lady 'till we go out of Town—You may return to it with as decent Airs as you please—And now I've shewn you your Error, I'm in so good Humour as to repeat you a Couplet on the Occasion—

> *They only who gain Minds, true Lawrels wear:*   160
> *'Tis less to conquer, than convince, the Fair.*

Exeunt.

[Act. V. Scene ii.]

Enter Pounce *with Papers.*

A Table, Chairs, Pen, Ink, and Paper.

Pounce. 'Tis a dear Delight to gall these old Rascals, and set 'em at variance about Stakes which I know neither of 'em will ever have Possession of.

Enter Tipkin *and Sir* Harry Gubbin.

Tipkin. Do you design, Sir *Harry*, that they shall have an Estate in their own Hands, and keep House themselves, poor Things?   5

Sir Harry Gubbin. No, no, Sir, I know better; they shall go down

161.1 *Exeunt*]] D1 (*Exe.*); *Exit*

into the Country, and live with me, not touch a Farthing of Money, but having all Things necessary provided, they shall go tame about the House, and Breed.

10   *Tipkin.* Well, Sir *Harry*, then considering that all Humane Things are subject to change, it behoves every Man that has a just Sense of Mortality, to take care of his Money.

Sir Harry Gubbin. I don't know what you mean, Brother.—What do you drive at, Brother?

15   *Tipkin.* This Instrument is executed by you, your Son, and my Niece, which discharges me of all Retrospects.

Sir Harry Gubbin. It is confess'd, Brother; but what then?—

Tipkin. All that remains is, That you pay me for the young Lady's Twelve Year's Board, as also all other Charges, as wearing Apparel,
20 *&c.*

Sir Harry Gubbin. What is this you say? Did I give you my Discharge from all Retrospects, as you call it, and after all do you come with this and t'other, and all that? I find you are, I tell you, Sir, to your Face, I find you are—

25   *Tipkin.* I find too what you are, Sir *Henry*.

Sir Harry Gubbin. What am I Sir? What am I?

Tipkin. Why, Sir, you are angry.

Sir Harry Gubbin. Sir, I scorn your Words, I am not angry—Mr. *Pounce* is my Witness, I am as gentle as a Lamb—Would it not make
30 any Flesh alive angry, to see a close Hunks come after all with a Demand of—?

Tipkin. Mr. *Pounce*, pray inform Sir *Harry* in this Point?

Pounce. Indeed, Sir *Harry*, I must tell you plainly, that Mr. *Tipkin*, in this, demands nothing but what he may recover—For tho' this
35 Case may be consider'd *Multifariam*, that is to say, as 'tis usually, commonly, *Vicatim*, or vulgarly express'd—Yet, I say, when we only observe, that the Power is settled as the Law requires, *Assensu Patris*, by the Consent of the Father—That Circumstance imports you are well acquainted with the Advantages which accrue to your
40 Family, by this Alliance, which corroborates Mr. *Tipkin's* Demand, and avoids all Objections that can be made.

Sir Harry Gubbin. Why then, I find, you are his Adviser in all this—

Pounce. Look'e, Sir *Harry*, to show you I love to promote among my Clients a good Understanding: Tho' Mr. *Tipkin* may claim Four Thousand Pounds, I'll engage for him, and I know him so well, 45 that he shall take Three Thousand Nine Hundred and Ninety eight Pounds, Four Shillings, and Eight-pence Farthing.

Tipkin. Indeed, Mr. *Pounce*, you are too hard upon me.

Pounce. You must consider a little, Sir *Harry* is your Brother.   50

Sir Harry Gubbin. Three Thousand Nine Hundred and Ninety eight Pound, Four Shillings, and Eight-pence Farthing! For what, I say? For what, Sir?

Pounce. For what, Sir! For what she wanted, Sir, a fine Lady is always in want, Sir—Her very Cloaths would come to that Money 55 in half the Time.

Sir Harry Gubbin. 3998 *l.* 4 *s.* 8 *d.* ¼. for Cloaths! Pray, how many Suits does she wear out in a Year?

Pounce. Oh, Dear Sir, A fine Lady's Cloaths are not old by being worn, but by being seen.   60

Sir Harry Gubbin. Well, I'll save her Cloaths for the future, after I have got her into the Country—I'll warrant her she shall not appear more in this wicked Town, where Cloaths are worn out by Sight— And as to what you demand, I tell you, Sir, 'tis Extortion.

Tipkin. Sir *Harry*, do you accuse me of Extortion?   65

Sir Harry Gubbin. Yes, I say Extortion.

Tipkin. Mr. *Pounce*, write down that—There are very good Laws provided against Scandal and Calumny—Loss of Reputation may tend to loss of Money—

Pounce. Item, For having accus'd Mr. *Tipkin* of Extortion.   70

Sir Harry Gubbin. Nay, if you come to your *Items*—Look'e, Mr. *Tipkin*, This is an Inventory of such Goods as were left to my Niece *Bridget* by her deceas'd Father, and which I expect shall be forth-coming at her Marriage to my Son—

Imprimis, A Golden Locket of her Mother's, with something very 75 ingenious in *Latin* on the in-side of it—

Item, A couple of Musquets with Two Shoulder-belts and Bandeliers—

Item, a large Silver Caudle-Cup, with a true Story engraven
80 on it.

Pounce. But, Sir *Harry*—

Sir Harry Gubbin. Item, a Base-Viol with almost all the Strings to
it, and only a small hole on the Back.

Pounce. But nevertheless, Sir—

85   *Sir Harry Gubbin.* This is the Furniture of my Brother's Bed-
Chamber that follows—A Suit of Tapestry Hangings, with the
Story of *Judith* and *Holofernes*, torn only where the Head should
have been off—an old Bedsted curiously wrought about the Posts,
consisting of two Load of Timber. A Hoan, a Basin, three Razors
90 and a Comb-Case—Look ye, Sir, you see I can *Item* it.

Pounce. Alas, Sir *Harry*, if you had ten Quire of *Items*, 'tis all
answer'd in the Word Retrospect.

Sir Harry Gubbin. Why then Mr. *Pounce*, and Mr. *Tipkin*, you are
both Rascals.

95   *Tipkin.* Do you call me Rascal, Sir *Harry*?

Sir Harry Gubbin. Yes Sir.

Tipkin. Write it down Mr. *Pounce*—at the end of the Leaf.

Sir Harry Gubbin. If you have room, Mr. *Pounce*—Put down Villain,
Son of a Whore, Curmudgeon, Hunks, and Scoundrel.

100   *Tipkin.* Not so fast, Sir *Harry*, He cannot write so fast, you are at
the Word Villain—Son of a Whore, I take it, was next—You may
make the account as large as you please, Sir *Harry*.

Sir Harry Gubbin. Come, come, I won't be us'd thus—Harky',
Sirrah, Draw—What do you do at this end of the Town without a
105 Sword?—Draw, I say—

Tipkin. Sir *Harry*, you are a Military Man, a Collonel of the
Militia.

Sir Harry Gubbin. I am so, Sirrah, and will run such an Extorting
Dog as you through the Guts, to show the Militia is use-
110 ful.

Pounce. Oh dear, oh dear!—How am I concern'd to see Persons of
your Figure thus mov'd?—The Wedding is coming in—We'll settle
these things afterwards.

Tipkin. I am Calm.

115   *Sir Harry Gubbin. Tipkin*, live these two Hours—but expect—

Enter Humphry *leading* Niece, *Mrs.* Clerimont
led by Fainlove, *Captain* Clerimont
and Clerimont *Senior.*

Pounce. Who are these? Hey-day, Who are these, Sir *Harry?* Ha!

Sir Harry Gubbin. Some Frolick, 'tis Wedding-day—no matter.

Humphry. Haw, haw; Father—Master Unkle—Come you must stir your stumps, you must Dance—Come, Old Lads Kiss the 120 Ladies—

Mrs. Clerimont. Mr. *Tipkin,* Sir *Harry*—I beg Pardon for an Introduction so *Mal-a-Propos*—I know suddain Familiarity is not the *English* way—Alas, Mr. *Gubbin,* this Father and Unckle of yours must be new modell'd—how they stare both of 'em!   125

Sir Harry Gubbin. Harky' *Numps,* Who is this you have brought hither? Is it not the famous fine Lady Mrs. *Clerimont?*—What a Pox did you let her come near your Wife?—

Humphry. Looky' don't expose your self, and play some mad Country prank to disgrace me before her—I shall be laugh'd at 130 because she knows I understand better.

Mrs. Clerimont. I congratulate, Madam, your coming out of the bondage of a Virgin State—A Woman can't do what she will properly till she's marry'd.

Sir Harry Gubbin. Did you hear what she said to your Wife?   135

Enter Aunt *before a Service of Dishes.*

Aunt. So, Mr. Bridegroom, pray take that Napkin, and serve your Spouse to Day according to Custom.

Humphry. Mrs. *Clerimont,* pray know my Aunt.

Mrs. Clerimont. Madam I must beg your pardon; I can't possibly like all that vast load of Meat, that you are sending in to Table— 140 besides, 'tis so offensively sweet, it wants that Haut-gout, we are so delighted with in *France.*

Aunt. You'l pardon it since we did not expect you. (*Aside.*) Who is this?

115.2–3 *Captain ... Senior*] D1; *Captain and* Clerimont.

145   *Mrs. Clerimont.* Oh Madam, I only speak for the future, little
Sawcers are so much more Polite—Looky' I'm perfectly for the
French way, where e're I'm admitted, I take the whole upon me.

　　Sir Harry Gubbin. The *French* Madam—I'd have you to
know—

150   *Mrs. Clerimont.* You'l not like it at first out of a natural *English*
Sullenness, but that will come upon you by degrees—When I first
went into *France*, I was mortally afraid of a Frog, but in a little time,
I cou'd eat nothing else except Sallads.

　　Aunt. Eat Frogs, Have I kiss'd one that has eat Froggs—Paw!
155 Paw!

　　Mrs. Clerimont. Oh Madam—A Frog and a Sallad are delicious
Fare—'tis not long come up in *France* it self, but their Glorious
Monarch has introduc'd the Diet which makes 'em so Spiritual—
He Eradicated all gross Food by Taxes, and for the Glory of the
160 Monarch sent the Subject a grazing; but I fear I defer the Entertain-
ment and Diversion of the Day.

　　Humphry. Now Father, Unckle—before we go any further, I think
'tis necessary we know who and who's together—then I give either
of you two Hours to guess which is my Wife—And 'tis not my
165 Cousin—so far I'll tell you.

　　Sir Harry Gubbin. How! What do you say? But oh—you mean she
is not your Cousin now—she's nearer a-kin, That's well enough—
Well said *Numps*—Ha, ha, ha.

　　Humphry. No, I don't mean so, I tell you, I don't mean so—My
170 Wife hides her Face under her Hatt.

All looking at Fainlove.

　　Tipkin. What does the Puppy mean? His Wife under a
Hatt.

　　Humphry. Ay, Ay, that's she, that's she—A good Jest
'faith—

175   *Sir Harry Gubbin.* Harky', *Numps*—What do'st mean Child—Is
that a Woman, and are you really marry'd to her?

　　Humphry. I am sure of both.

　　Sir Harry Gubbin. Are you so, Sirrah, then Sirrah this is your
Wedding-dinner, Sirrah—Do ye see, Sirrah, Here's Roast-Meat.

Humphry. Oh ho! What beat a marry'd Man! Hold him Mr. 180
Clerimont, Brother *Pounce*, Mr. Wife, No body stand by a young
marry'd Man! (*Runs behind* Fainlove.)

Sir Harry Gubbin. Did not the Dog say Brother *Pounce*, What is
this Mrs. *Ragou*—This Madam *Clerimont*; Who the Devil are you
all, but especially who the Devil are you two? (*Beats* Humphry *and* 185
Fainlove *off the Stage, following*.)

Tipkin. (*Aside*.) Master *Pounce*, all my Niece's Fortune will be
demanded now—For I suppose that Red-coat has her—Don't you
think you and I had better break?

Pounce. [*Apart to* Tipkin.] You may do as soon as you please, but 190
'tis my Interest to be Honest a little longer.

Tipkin. Well, *Biddy*, since you wou'd not accept of your Cousin,
I hope you han't dispos'd of your self elsewhere.

Niece. If you'l for a little while suspend your curiosity, you shall
have the whole History of my Amour to this my Nuptial-day, 195
under the Title of the Loves of *Clerimont* and *Parthenissa*.

Tipkin. Then, Madam, your Portion is in safe Hands—

Captain Clerimont. Come, come, old Gentleman, 'tis in vain to
contend, here's honest Mr. *Pounce* shall be my Ingineer, and I'll
warrant you, we beat you out of all your Holds—   200

Aunt. What then is Mr. *Pounce* a Rogue? (*Apart to* Tipkin.) he
must have some trick, Brother, it cannot be, He must have cheated
t'other side, for I'm sure he's honest.

Clerimont Senior. (*To* Pounce.) Mr. *Pounce*, All your Sister has won
of this Lady, she has honestly put into my Hands, and I'll return it 205
her, at this Lady's particular request.

Pounce. And the Thousand Pounds you promis'd in your Brother's
behalf, I'm willing shou'd be hers also.

Clerimont Senior. Then go in, and bring 'em all back to make the
best of an ill Game, we'll eat the Dinner, and have a Dance together, 210
or we shall transgress all form.

185 two?] D2; too.   I have changed the spelling and punctuation of Q so that
the modern reader will not have to pause over interpretation of the line.
198 *Captain Clerimont*] ed.; *Cler.*   204 *Clerimont Senior*] D1; *Cler.*
209 *Clerimont Senior*] ed.; *Cler.*   Following Q, later editions assigned the speech to
the younger Clerimont. However, it is surely the place of the older brother to give the
commands and make sure that the company does not 'transgress all form'. The
Mermaid and Regents editions properly assigned this speech to Clerimont Senior.

Re-enter Fainlove, Humphry, *and Sir* Harry Gubbin.

Sir Harry Gubbin. Well since you say you are worth something and the Boy has set his Heart upon you, I'll have Patience till I see further.

215 *Pounce.* Come, come, Sir *Harry*, you shall find my Alliance more considerable than you imagine, the *Pounce's* are a Family that will always have Money, if there's any in the World—Come Fiddles.

DANCE Here.

Captain Clerimont. You've seen th' extreams of the Domestick Life,
    A Son too much confin'd—too free a Wife;
220   *By generous bonds you either shou'd restrain,*
    And only on their Inclinations gain;
    Wives to Obey must Love, Children revere
    While only Slaves are govern'd by their fear.

[*The End of the Fifth Act*]

218 *Captain Clerimont*] ed.; *Cler.* With no clues from compositorial evidence in Q, one must arbitrarily assign the final couplets to either Clerimont Senior or the Captain. *Cler.*, the abbreviation used for the Captain, appears in D1–4 and Du, but Aitken and Winton both emend to Clerimont Senior. Genest writes of a performance at Crow Street, Dublin, in 1762, in which Captain Clerimont had the lines (vi. 396), but the prompt copy must have been a printed edition, so his anecdote casts no light on Steele's intentions. I have assigned the lines to Captain Clerimont as the more likely speaker; however, the speech would not be inappropriate to either character.

222 *Wives to Obey must Love, Children revere*] Q erratum; *Children and Wives obey whom they revere,*

EPILOGUE,

Spoken by Mr. EASTCOURT.

Britons, *who constant War, with factious Rage,*
For Liberty against each other wage,
From Foreign Insult save this English *Stage.*
*No more th'*Italian *squaling Tribe admit,*
5 *In Tongues unknown; 'tis Popery in Wit.*
The Songs (their selves confess) from Rome *they bring;*
And 'tis High-Mass, for ought you know, they Sing.
Husbands take Care, the Danger may come nigher,
The Women say their Eunuch is a Friar.

10   *But is it not a serious Ill to see*
Europe's *great Arbiters so mean can be;*
Passive, with an affected Joy to sit,
Suspend their native Taste of Manly Wit;
Neglect their Comic Humour, Tragic Rage,
15 *For known Defects of Nature, and of Age.*
Arise for shame, ye Conqu'ring Britons, *rise,*
Such unadorn'd Effeminacy despise;
Admire (if you will doat on Foreign Wit)
Not what Italians *Sing, but* Romans *Writ:*
20 *So shall less Works, such as to-Night's slight Play,*
At your Command, with Justice die away;
'Till then forgive your Writers, that can't bear
You shou'd such very Tramontanes *appear,*
The Nations, which contemn you, to revere.

25   *Let* Anna's *Soil be known for all its Charms;*
As Fam'd for Lib'ral Sciences, as Arms:
Let those Derision meet, who would Advance
Manners, or Speech, from Italy *or* France;
Let them learn You, who wou'd your Favour find,
30 *And* English *be the Language of Mankind.*

[FINIS.]

THE CONSCIOUS LOVERS

COMPOSITION AND SOURCES

S T E E L E had begun planning *The Conscious Lovers* reasonably soon after completion of *The Tender Husband*, perhaps by 1710, but surely by 1713.[1] Expelled from Parliament in March 1714, he remained in London as a Commissioner of Forfeited Estates in Scotland, a seeker of patronage, and an essayist and pamphleteer. His efforts to distinguish himself in public life were almost as fruitless as his earlier military ambitions. Moreover, he was mired in debt; as many as eight suits for non-payment came before the courts in Michaelmas term, 1716.[2] Unable to escape the pressures and responsibilities of London, he envisioned the new comedy as a way out of his financial troubles,[3] yet he postponed its completion for many months. Although there is no concrete evidence, it seems most likely that he finally finished the play or a draft of it in the autumn of 1719. A local tradition holds that it was written, at least in part, at Ty-Gwyn, a property of his wife's family, the Scurlocks, about a mile south of Carmarthen, Wales, and that it was first acted there by friends, some of whom came from London and elsewhere for the occasion.[4] After years of planning a trip to Wales, he did go in 1719.[5] Although he probably went again in the summer of 1722,[6] published references to the play before that time indicate the earlier date for completion.[7] Steele may also have taken the manuscript to Edinburgh, on one of his trips there for the Commission on Forfeited Estates in 1720 and 1721,[8] shortly before the comedy opened in London; John Dennis scoffed that he had trotted it to Edinburgh and Wales and read it 'to more Persons than will be

---

[1] For evidence of Steele's progress with the play see Loftis, pp. 183–9.

[2] Exchequer Pleas Judgment Roll, Mich. 3 Geo. I., 12, 16, 18; Index Judic. (Exchequer), Series B, Mich. 3 Geo. I., fol. 64; Exchequer Pleas Order Book, Hil. 3 Geo. I., fol. 6; Common Pleas Judgment Roll, Mich. 3 Geo. I., 386; King's Bench Judgment Roll, Mich. 3 Geo. I., 304. Cited in Aitken, ii. 109, n. 1.

[3] See, for example, his letter to his wife dated 16 July 1717, in which he says: '. . . I must keep my self to my self and have my Play ready this ensuing Winter, in Order to be quite out of Debt.' (British Museum, Add. MS. 5145, quoted in *Correspondence*, p. 361).

[4] *Correspondence*, p. 410, n. 2; Aitken, ii. 318.

[5] *Correspondence*, pp. 389–90, n. 2.   [6] *Correspondence*, p. 398, n.3.

[7] *Mist's Weekly Journal* in 1721 spoke of a delay of two years. *The Censor Censur'd* early in 1723 referred to Steele's three years' labour and industry in touching and retouching the play.   [8] Aitken, ii. 249, 265.

at the Representation of it, or vouchsafe to read it, when it is pub-lish'd'.[1]

In searching for a model for the play which was itself to be a model for English comedy,[2] Steele turned to Terence. Primarily revered as the greatest classical stylist, Terence was also defended by Augustan critics as a dramatist who created superior plots and charac-terizations.[3] Steele revealed his own view of Terence in the *Spectator*, no. 502, when he said he believed the *Self-Tormentor* (*Heautontimoru-menos*) is great because of its 'worthy Sentiments': 'It is from the Beginning to the End a perfect Picture of humane Life, but I did not observe in the Whole one Passage that could raise a Laugh. How well disposed must that People be, who could be entertained with Satisfaction by so sober and polite Mirth!' He later commended it for 'several Incidents which would draw Tears from any Man of Sense, and not one which would move his Laughter'.[4] Obviously Steele's response to Terence was affected by his own sensibility. Terence's comedy is, on the whole, relatively serious, but it is not devoid of humour, nor does it move the audience to tears. Steele drew from Terence sobriety and sententiousness as well as moral characters and a plot outline, but he read into the classical playwright the emotion-alism he himself believed should infuse comedy.

The *Andria*, on which he based his comedy, became a justification for his own dramatic theory rather than a model. Translation, indeed, ran no further than Act I, scene i of *The Conscious Lovers*, but Steele worked with the plot outline in some detail, embellishing it with the trimmings of fashionable eighteenth-century London life. He modern-ized the *Andria*, emphasized the graver aspects of the main plot by intensifying the moral and emotional tenor, and revamped the sub-plot for comicality. He cast his version with the sort of characters that populated his periodical essays, the gentlemanly merchant, the trusty servant, the impudent valet. He introduced such contemporary issues as duelling, arranged marriages, and snobbery toward the wealthy merchant class. He included talk of the opera and the theatre and cock-fighting. He substituted a masquerade for a funeral, on Colley Cibber's recommendation.[5] He emphasized the hero's exem-

[1] *A Defense of Sir Fopling Flutter*, in Dennis, ii. 241.
[2] Dedication, ll. 7–11.
[3] See, for example, the Preface to *Terence's Comedies: Made English with his Life; and Some Remarks at the End*. By Several Hands, 2nd edn., corrected (London, 1698); and Charles Gildon's 'Letter to Mr. D'Urfey, Occasioned by his Play, Called the Marriage-Hater Match'd', published with the play (London, 1692).
[4] Postcript, *Spectator*, no. 521.   [5] Preface, ll. 55–67.

plary behaviour and aggravated the quarrel between the two friends so that Bevil Junior could courageously reject a challenge and thereby instruct his audience. He replaced the mistress with an innocent virgin, and he brought the distressed heroine on stage, thereby greatly heightening the emotional quality which he believed to be Terence's. He gave the old servant rather than the young one the role of manipulator to make the main plot more sedate and decorous. Then, as in *The Lying Lover*, he also enlarged the comic aspects, perhaps at Cibber's instigation, but this time he confined them to the sub-plot. While the main plot remained serious and high-minded, Lucinda's marital arrangements, unstaged in the *Andria*, afforded ample opportunities for sight comedy, disguise scenes, and caricature. For comic effect he created Cimberton and Mrs. Sealand, not prefigured by Terence, and reworked other characters. For example, he chose to assign to Myrtle trickery reminiscent of Restoration comedy, although the construction of the plot did not require it. Further, in the disguise scenes Myrtle caricatures ridiculous type-characters, the lawyer and the solemn fool. Nor is the flirtation of Tom and Phillis, a parody of life above-stairs, essential, but their scenes brought applause from the earliest audiences[1] and they remain amusing. Arguing for comedy based on 'a joy too exquisite for laughter', Steele was careful to include conventional humour in his formula.

By 1721, when Steele, from all indications, had finished his adaptation, variously referred to in the press as 'The Gentleman', 'The Fine Gentleman', 'The Unfashionable Gentleman', and 'Sir John Edgar', it was not *The Conscious Lovers* in final form: revisions were to come. In the *Theatre*, no. 19, he referred to Bevil's evasion of the duel in Act III, although it occurs in Act IV; careless as Steele was in quotations and references to literary works, he may merely have named the wrong act, but perhaps the scene was shifted later. He showed in his Preface that some scenes were indeed rearranged, for he thanked Cibber for 'his care and application in instructing the Actors and altering the Disposition of the Scenes, when I was, through sickness, unable to cultivate such things myself'. The extent of Cibber's aid, however, seems to have been greater; it is probable that his suggestions led to sizable alterations directed toward

---

[1] For commentary on the audience's reaction to Phillis and Tom see the *St. James's Journal*, 18 November 1722; the *Freeholder's Journal*, 28 November 1722; *The Censor Censur'd; or, the Conscious Lovers Examin'd*. The *St. James's Journal* attributes Tom's success to Cibber's excellent acting; the *Freeholder's Journal* suggests that the 'frequent Kissing' between Tom and Phillis on stage obliged the galleries.

greater audience response. Cibber himself claimed he gave 'more Assistance . . . than becomes me to enlarge upon, of which Evidence has been given upon Oath by several of our Actors', and received for his labours no financial recompense;[1] he must have felt his alterations were substantial enough to warrant a fee. Cibber's son Theophilus, who played Daniel in the first run, estimated Steele's debt to his father as 'many additions' which 'greatly improved' the play. One, he related, was the recognition that the play was 'rather too grave for an English audience';[2] Steele allegedly took Cibber's advice to add comic characters and created Tom and Phillis, drawing materials from his *Guardian*, no. 87. It is probable that Steele in his Preface underestimated his debt, and Theophilus Cibber in his recollections thirty years later exaggerated it. Afterwards Steele grudgingly admitted that Cibber had helped him; in 1727, when they were involved in a legal tussle, he testified that Cibber had altered the play before it was acted, but to its disadvantage, and therefore he had not paid him for his meddling.[3] It is safe to assume that Cibber made his suggestions or alterations shortly before or during the period of rehearsal in 1722, about three years after Steele had finished the play. Paul E. Parnell has futher attributed to Cibber the source material for the duel scene in IV. i,[4] although neither Cibber nor Steele mentioned such a debt.[5]

One more revision, characteristic of Steele, was made after opening night. Cimberton's perusal of Lucinda's charms in III. i remains in the printed version the most suggestive passage in the play, although the lines seem mild enough to the modern reader lulled by knowledge of Steele's high moral purpose. However, in the version produced on

---

[1] Cibber, ii. 206.
[2] *The Lives of the Poets of Great Britain and Ireland*, 5 vols. (London, 1753), iv. 120.
[3] Chancery Decrees 1726B, 105; Chancery Proceedings, Reynardson, 1714–58, no. 2416. Cited in Aitken, ii. 314, n. 1.
[4] 'A Source for the Duel Scene in *The Conscious Lovers*', N*Q* ccvii (1962), 13–15.
[5] Parnell's argument is not completely convincing. Parallels in *The Tender Husband* suggest that Steele probably knew *Womans Wit*, the play Parnell cites, but the similarities between the two challenge scenes, when examined in the light of contemporary stage conventions, are not strong enough to arouse suspicions. Sword play and challenges were so common that their use shows nothing. Further, there is little in common between Cibber's device of the pistols and Steele's introduction of a letter as evidence of innocence. Moreover, Myrtle's anger and belief that he has been betrayed come straight from the *Andria*. And finally, that Cibber would not claim credit, were any due, is extremely improbable. Steele had been writing against duelling with great passion as early as *The Lying Lover* in 1703, and had deplored it many times in his periodicals; the theme was one that came easily to his pen. He was greatly indebted to the actor-manager, but there is no strong reason to assume as part of his obligation the one scene of all his theatrical work in which he took the greatest pride.

opening night, the lines were evidently more improper. Steele's consciousness of his role as moral censor of Great Britain, which earlier led him to chasten lines in *The Funeral*, must have dictated revision. Whether he received complaints about the passage or personally found it offensive, he cut questionable lines some time before the twelfth performance (21 November), for on 22 November the *St. James's Journal* commented on the deletion.

STAGE HISTORY

The comedy was expected in London in the season of 1719–20, but was delayed or prohibited. By 21 November 1719 *Applebee's Original Weekly Journal* announced that 'The Gentleman' by Steele would soon open at the Drury Lane Theatre.[1] However, *The Orphan Revived* of 13–20 February 1720 reported that the anticipated comedy probably would not be performed during the season, a rumour corroborated in a letter dated 24 March 1720 by Dr. Thomas Rundle, who indicated legal difficulties.[2] Steele himself wrote enigmatically in the *Theatre*, no. 19, dated 5 March 1720, that the play, 'had not some Accidents prevented, would have been performed before this time'. Loftis concludes that the apparently finished comedy was banned because of Steele's dispute with the Duke of Newcastle, the Lord Chamberlain, over other matters.[3]

Having lost the prospect of immediate production on stage, Steele adjusted his dramatic material to other purposes. First he dipped into it several times for his periodical, the *Theatre*. The fictitious editor of this publication was Sir John Edgar, the original name of the character who emerged on stage as Sir John Bevil.[4] In the *Theatre* Sir John has

[1] Loftis, p. 190. Avery, ii. 556.

[2] *Letters of the Late Thomas Rundle, L.L.D., to Mrs. Barbara Sandys*, ed. James Dallaway (Gloucester, 1789), cited in Loftis, p. 191.

[3] Steele had clashed with Newcastle on political issues, notably the Peerage Bill, and on matters pertaining to the theatre. On 23 January 1720 his royal theatrical licence was revoked. In a pamphlet entitled *The State of the Case Between the Lord-Chamberlain of His Majesty's Houshold and the Governor of the Royal Company of Comedians*, published in 1720, he counted as one of his losses due to the revocation of the licence £1,000 from 'The Profit of acting my own Plays already writ, or I may write' (*Tracts and Pamphlets*, p. 607), indicating that there was indeed some connection between Newcastle's actions and the postponement. For details of the dispute, see Loftis, pp. 121–49.

[4] Steele had originally chosen the name Sir John Edgar, as demonstrated by an early memorandum in his handwriting on the characters of Sir John, Mrs. Sealand (spelled Coeland), and Cimberton (Symberton) (British Museum, Add. MS. 5145C, f. 198, cited in Loftis, p. 191, n. 24). He fully intended to use it as late as the final issue of the *Theatre*, in which he announced that he would 'forthwith print a new

a young son Harry, for whom Bevil Junior must have served as prototype: his sobriety, filial devotion, good taste, and good nature bespeak the exemplary hero. The editor's old servant, like Humphrey, has served well for forty years. In the third issue, Edgar names candidates for 'Auditors', representatives of the British audience, again plundering the unacted comedy for names, characterizations, and even closely paraphrased lines. Highly recommended for the fictitious office is Mr. Sealand, the same grave and dignified merchant who was later to argue convincingly with Sir John Bevil the relative merits of the gentry and the merchant class. His daughter Lucinda, who despises coxcombs, mirrors the young lady contemptuous of Cimberton. A third candidate, Charles Myrtle, also taken from the play, is a young man basically good-natured but racked by unwarranted jealousies. Steele even printed Indiana's song 'The Lovesick Maid' in no. 18. There is no reason to believe that the *Theatre* was intended to puff the play; no mention was made of performance. In the last issue he announced plans to publish it although it had never been acted, 'To manifest further the Injury done me by robbing me of the Means of bringing on my own Performances in an advantageous Manner'. He must have believed a production to be impossible, or he would never have considered publication before performance, for a playwright's profits came largely from the theatre. However, by the autumn of 1721, there was again talk of a stage production. *Mist's Weekly Journal* announced on 18 November: 'Sir Richard Steele proposes to represent a character upon the stage this season that was never seen there yet: His *Gentleman* has been two years a dressing, and we wish he may make a good appearance at last.' But Bevil Junior had to wait in the wings another year.

'The Play of the *Conscious Lovers* had such a Reputation before it was known', one journalist commented, 'that a Man of no very great Curiosity would have ventur'd to squeeze into the Crowd that went to see it the first Night. The Reputation of the Author, who has wrote more, (at least has been read more, and that is writing to purpose), than any Man now amongst us, might, I believe, bring great Numbers there. . . .'[1] Steele's play had been so long expected, and for

Comedy, call'd *Sir John Edgar*'. He was not the first playwright to choose the name Bevil. A Lord Bevill appears in George Etherege's *The Comical Revenge* (1664). Bevil is a young rake in Thomas Shadwell's *Epsom Wells* (1672). Both plays remained popular in Steele's time, and he must have known them. Two *Spectators* by him, nos. 48 and 153, refer to *Epsom Wells*.

[1] *Freeholder's Journal*, 14 November 1722.

years had received so much notice in print, that when, in the autumn of 1722, it was finally brought to Drury Lane, public anticipation was keen.[1]

Production details were settled during rehearsals. The song of the love-sick maid, which had been set by Galliard,[2] was discarded, no doubt reluctantly on the part of Steele, who showed great pride in it earlier in the *Theatre* and later in the Preface to the published play. But since no suitable singer could be found, an instrumental interlude by an Italian violinist, Giovanno Steffano Carbonelli, was substituted. Sumptuous new costumes were prepared, and two new sets, one of Charing Cross and one of the Mall, were so elegantly executed that they themselves became attractions and drew newspaper commentary: '... you may see as far as from *White-Hall* to *Temple-Bar*, and the Shops and all: Then, there is the very Centry Box, the old Soldier, my Lord's Chair, and the Trees, just as tho' they were all alive.'[3] The expenditures for costumes and sets justified, or at any rate permitted, advanced prices for the first run.[4] The poet Leonard Welsted wrote a prologue for opening night, in which, ironically in the context of the elaborate production, he deplored authors who rely on 'gay Shew and costly Habits'. Young Benjamin Victor, ex-barber, would-be literary gentleman, and protégé of Steele, wrote an epilogue. Characteristic of its period, it was light and somewhat suggestive; in it Anne Oldfield, who played the virtuous Indiana, ridiculed the author's moral purpose in the first twenty-seven lines and defended it in the last seven.[5]

The publicity campaign and celebration of Steele proved too much for the temper of John Dennis, critic and enemy of the Drury Lane management. He was at odds with the governors for their

---

[1] For example, Vanbrugh wrote to Tonson on 18 June 1722: 'With all this encouragement from the Town, not a fresh Poet appears; they are forc'd to act round and round upon the old stock, tho' Cibber tells me, 'tis not to be conceiv'd, how many and how bad plays are brought to them. Steel however has one to come on at Winter, a Comedy; which they must commend.' Nichols reported that the newspapers of 2 October announced, 'Sir Richard Steele's excellent new comedy, called *The Unfashionable Lovers* will be acted on the 6th of next month. It is thought that this play is the best modern play that has been produced.'
The sniping also began before the play opened; a correspondent in the *Freeholder's Journal* for 31 October 1722 wrote: 'We flatter ourselves that the Drama we expect will ... afford a compleat Model to that leading Pattern of Life, *The Gentleman*. ...', and he then maliciously indicated that Steele himself did not have very great pretensions to that character by birth.   [2] *Theatre*, no. 18.
[3] *Freeholder's Journal*, 28 November 1722.
[4] *Remarks on a Play, Call'd The Conscious Lovers, A Comedy*, in Dennis, ii. 254.
[5] No doubt directed again by his responsibility to English morality, Steele rejected publication of this innocuous epilogue in favour of one by Welsted with no suggestive overtones.

treatment of his play; their mismanagement, he felt, had caused him personal and professional harm.[1] Now the adulation of Steele filled him with such ire that he published a venomous attack on *The Conscious Lovers* five days before the run opened.[2] Dennis's critical acumen was considerable, although marred by his hatred of Steele, but his ability to judge public reaction fell far below his literary judgement, for if he wanted to deter audiences, he failed completely; his attack, naturally, could only increase the curiosity of spectators who loved controversy as well as novelty.[3]

For this play, then, Steele had no need to pack the house on opening night. The *première* proved a truly remarkable one for the theatre; reportedly 'a greater Concourse of People was never known to be assembled'.[4] The audience was extremely receptive; in the printed Preface Steele graciously attributed the success to the actors' excellent performance. Indeed, he was fortunate in having a first-rate cast, for the most part those who had enlivened his earlier comedies: Robert Wilks, now in his late fifties but still handsome and youthful on stage, played Myrtle; Cibber took the role of Tom, and Anne Oldfield, Indiana. Barton Booth played Bevil Junior, John Mills his father, and Elizabeth Younger Phillis. Steele and a group of his friends sat in Burton's Box, an enclosed part of the first gallery; Steele was 'charmed' by all the actors except Griffin, who apparently played Cimberton too broadly. He was no doubt also pleased with the audience's response, which was, according to Victor, 'universal applause'.[5]

The play ran for eighteen nights, a remarkable number of performances for this period, and it might have continued, it was said, 'if, upon other Considerations, the Players had not thought proper to give it a violent Death without waiting for its natural Expiration'.[6] It played eight more times during the London season and ran five times in Dublin early in 1723.[7] Financially it had never been equalled in Steele's own career or in the annals of the Drury Lane Theatre, for it brought receipts of £2,536. 3s. 6d., more money than any play previously performed by the company.[8] Steele himself accumulated more

---

[1] *Correspondence*, pp. 143–5, n. 2.

[2] *A Defense of Sir Fopling Flutter*, in Dennis, ii. 241–50.

[3] Benjamin Victor, *An Epistle to Sir Richard Steele On his Play, call'd, The Conscious Lovers*, 2nd edn. (London, 1722), p. 6.

[4] *Daily Journal*, 8 November 1722, quoted in Avery, ii. 694.

[5] Benjamin Victor, *Original Letters, Dramatic Pieces, and Poems*, 3 vols. (London, 1776), i. 327–8.   [6] *St. James's Journal*, 8 December 1722.

[7] Avery, ii, *passim*; Stockwell, p. 59.

[8] Public Records Office, C11/2416/49, cited in Loftis, p. 193; Aitken, ii. 314.

than £1,100 profit: he received a sum later estimated as £329. 5s. for his three third-night benefits,[1] plus about £300 more for his share as a patentee of the theatre;[2] he got £40 and 'divers other good Causes and Considerations' from Jacob Tonson Jr. for publication rights;[3] and King George I, to whom the play was dedicated, granted him a gift of £500.[4] For the first time Steele found dramaturgy gratifyingly remunerative.

As maker and reflector of his era's taste also he was triumphant, for *The Conscious Lovers* remained one of the stage favourites of the century. It gained popularity with age, reaching its peak seasons in the 1730s and 1740s. After the first season the Drury Lane company performed it an average of three times a year for the next five years. Other theatres, which legally could have produced it the second season, surprisingly waited until 1730–1, when both the Goodman's Fields and Lincoln's Inn Fields companies gave performances and the Richmond company followed in August. Afterwards it ran without fail during every London season until 1775, and many times thereafter. Usually it was acted several times a season, as many as fifteen in 1735–6, thirteen in 1744–5, and twelve or thirteen as late as 1759–60.[5] A table of performances per decade for fifty years after the first season indicates the rise and gradual decline of its popularity:

1723–33	41 performances
1733–43	85 performances
1743–53	86 performances
1753–63	68 performances
1763–73	36 performances[6]

Although the number of performances began to diminish in the second half of the century, *The Conscious Lovers* was the sixth most frequently performed comedy at the Drury Lane in the years 1747–76; two tragedies, one opera, and one history play also ran more often. At Covent Garden it was the seventh comedy in popularity and was surpassed in frequency by only nine other pieces[7]—and this in the three

---

[1] Aitken, ii. 314.   [2] Cibber, ii. 206.

[3] Rodney M. Baine believes the sum was no greater than £40, although such legal terminology is commonly used to conceal actual amounts; see 'The Publication of Steele's *Conscious Lovers*', *SB* ii (1949–50), 170.

[4] British Museum, Add. MS. 34327, f. 6, *An Account of Treasury Expenditures from March 1721 to March 1725*, cited in *Correspondence*, p. 520, n. 1. The gift has sometimes been reported as 500 guineas. See, for example, Aitken, ii. 276, citing the *Daily Journal*, 18 December 1722.

[5] There is some question about whether it was performed 14 January 1760. See Stone, ii. 768.   [6] Performances listed in Avery, Scouten, Stone, *passim*.

[7] Stone, i. clxiii, clxv.

decades beginning with its twenty-fifth year. Prominent from the first in provincial repertoires, it long remained popular outside London. It was, for one example, the most frequently performed eighteenth-century play in the Norwich repertoire in the period 1721–50; only *Macbeth* ran more often.[1] In the second half of the century twenty-nine performances were given in Irish provincial towns, Cork, Belfast, Tralee, Kilkenny, Waterford, Limerick, and Wexford.[2] It continued to be acted in London and the provinces in the first decades of the nineteenth century.[3]

The occasions on which it was offered confirm great favour with audiences. It usually ran early in the season, when the management won spectators back to the theatres with old favourites. Actors and actresses often chose it for their benefits. Of 339 performances in its first fifty London seasons, 119 were benefits, a significantly large number. Particularly appropriate for charity benefits, with its emphasis on pity and benevolence, it was chosen once in 1741 and eleven times between 1751 and 1769 for relief of poor widows with children, other families in 'great distress', and public charities such as refurnishing the wards in Middlesex Hospital or supporting the lying-in hospitals at Aldersgate and Westminster. Charity benefits were relatively rare; the Drury Lane and Covent Garden theatres averaged about three or four a year during the third quarter of the century.[4] The recurrence of *The Conscious Lovers* is, then, impressive. The play was popular with the fashionable as well. It played at the 'particular desire' of various persons of quality, as the advertising formula ran, fifty times in these decades, almost all the requests coming within the first twenty-five years, and it played twelve times by royal command, nine of these performances in the 1730s.[5] Steele, pleased with its initial acceptance, would have been gratified indeed had he lived to witness its continuing success.

REPUTATION AND INFLUENCE

The enthusiastic audiences did not reflect the prevailing Grub Street opinion; the profits were not matched by universal critical acclaim. Steele himself had, in effect, drawn the battle lines. He had preached in his periodicals the functions of comedy, had conceived his play as an embodiment of his critical doctrines, had desired or a

[1] Rosenfeld, p. 72.   [2] Clark, *passim*.
[3] Nettleton, p. 163.   [4] Stone, i. cvii.
[5] Data are gathered from Scouten and Stone, *passim*.

least allowed it to be puffed as an entirely new and superior kind of comedy, and had even said in his Dedication that he hoped it would serve as a model for an improved English theatre. That neo-classical critics should attack his fundamental dramatic theory was inevitable; that political and literary enemies should attack Steele the man too was perhaps equally predictable. In essays and pamphlets they savagely ridiculed him and his work. Everything about the play was damned, the translation, diction, characterization, dialogue, incidents. Steele's advocates, Victor and others, rushed to his defence, and some critics attempted disinterested appraisals, but his enemies were sharper and louder. Only two scenes were consistently praised, the challenge (IV. i) and Indiana's recognition of her father (v. iii), a scene which also 'received the most reasonable and natural Applause of eighteen successive Audiences, their Silence and their Tears'.[1]

Privately Steele received accolades from friends and literary men who wrote numerous poems, some of which were printed, in praise of the salutary social effects of his writings. A single example will illustrate the adulatory tone and the quality of the verse:

Verses Written in the Summer-house Where Sir Richard
Steele Wrote His Conscious Lovers

Sure this is more than Classic ground I tread,
All Pindus seems to bloom around my head.
Wake then, my Muse; what lyre can lie unstrung,
In shades where Phoebus, or where Steele hath sung?
A Cymberton each gaudy tulip shows,
And each gay bed is throng'd with lacquey beaux.
In each fair plant young Bevil greets my eyes,
And Indiana in each whisper sighs.[2]

But even Steele's friends did not unanimously approve every line. One letter, oddly enough first printed in the *Gentleman's Magazine* in September 1762 although it had been written during the early run, praised the play and the character of Indiana, but condemned Bevil Junior as 'strained beyond all reason' and denounced the notion of absolute and unquestioned filial submission.[3]

All the critics, public and private, perceived the significance of Steele's use of exemplary characters, his substitution of tender

[1] *St. James's Journal*, 8 December 1722. For a thorough discussion of the critical controversy see Loftis, pp. 195–213.
[2] *A Select Collection of Poems*, vii. 313.
[3] Aitken identified the author, who signed himself 'X. Y.', as the painter Joseph Highmore (Aitken, ii. 282, n. 1).

emotionalism for humour in the main plot, his emphasis on virtue and benevolence, and his didacticism. Generally recognizing Bevil Junior as an alternative to Dorimant, they acknowledged and usually approved Steele's introduction of morality into the drama.[1] Despite the disdain of Dennis and his colleagues, people widely responded to Steele's play in the way he had intended.

The Conscious Lovers became an enduring model for dramatists and a part of the literary heritage of genteel Englishmen. Twentieth-century professors have exhibited it to students as a period piece, the pedagogically pleasing example of sentimental comedy, but have largely neglected its significance in its own century. The tendency in scholarship on sentimental comedy is to push back the date of the genesis of the mode in order to correct the notion that this play was the first of its kind. This valuable search for antecedents obscures another aspect of dramatic history, influence. Here Steele's final play stands unchallenged: it was so often played and published and so familiar to dramatists that it became, as James J. Lynch says, 'probably the most significant contribution of the age to drama' in terms of the number of imitations.[2]

Steele purposefully and effectively popularized his dramatic formula, although he was not successful in perpetuating his basically undramatic exemplary hero and preceptual dialogue, both of which he considered central; indeed it was Bevil and his maxims that finally buried *The Conscious Lovers*, because audiences began to find the whole thing a bore.[3] Steele was undoubtedly a force also in purifying the language and wit of subsequent comedy, but there is no means of measuring the negative effect, that is, what was not said because of his influence; he was, after all, not the only one advocating more

---

[1] For example, an epilogue given 7 March 1723 at a performance in Dublin reads, in part:

> *Your* fav'rite bard the Terence of the age,
> With antient virtue has adorn'd the Stage:
> *You* like another *Nation of the Gown*,
> With just applause his *matchless* merit Crown. . . .
> And thus some future bard will sing of you,
> 'In the Year Seventeen Hundred Twenty Two,
> 'Ireland at once was virtuous and polite
> 'The *Conscious Lovers* gave such just delight
> 'Thrice happy period when the learn'd and chaste
> 'Extoll'd the Poet that refin'd their taste. . . .'

Box, Pit and Gallery (Berkeley and Los Angeles, 1953), p. 39.

[3] The Foreword to Bell's 1791 edition indicates this by saying in part: '. . . an admirer of the old comedy rises fatigued from this piece as from a tedious lesson. It is as fine as Seneca, as profitable too, but weak humanity requires to be diverted into a sense of duty, and for risibility here is no food.'

refined language on the stage. There is little question, however, about the force of his concepts of characterization and plot not only on admittedly sentimental plays but on all later eighteenth-century comedy.

A multitude of pathetic heroines, generic daughters of Indiana, sighed and wept through intolerable situations in the comedies of the second half of the century, the period following the greatest stage popularity of *The Conscious Lovers*. Like Indiana, they believed themselves to be impoverished orphans, and they managed to protect their virtue in the most alarming circumstances. They shared with her a mournful history and the ability to discuss it with such exalted sorrow that the strongest of auditors, on stage or off, must presumably weep. Eventually, through improbable discoveries and sometimes the help of a young man, they found well-deserved happiness and often a long-lost parent as well. Although one cannot in good conscience credit Steele with the inspiration for all the heroines of eighteenth-century comedy who are preoccupied with their virtue and bereft of the wit of Millamant, one can with some assurance attribute to him the pattern of the distressed virgin. A few of the better-known principals of the tradition are Fidelia in Edward Moore's *The Foundling* (1748), Olivia in Goldsmith's unsentimental *The Good-Natured Man* (1768), and Augusta Aubrey in Richard Cumberland's *The Fashionable Lover* (1772). The tradition also found adherents on the continent; Voltaire, for example, modelled the discovery scene in *Zaire*, in which the heroine is recognized by the cross she wears, on Indiana's bracelet scene.[1]

Heroes, however, resembled Myrtle more closely than Bevil Junior. Errant but fundamentally meritorious, they, like their predecessor, repented, not usually of wantonness, as in some Restoration comedies, but of other faults such as jealousy or prodigality; however, they often shared with Bevil the necessity of proving their honour to loving but distrustful fathers. Charles Oakly gives up 'foolish riot and drinking' for Harriot in George Colman's *The Jealous Wife* (1761); Belcour forswears his impetuosity and his 'thousand flaws' in pursuit of the unfortunate Louisa Dudley in Cumberland's *The West Indian* (1771); Honeywood repents of his excessive generosity in *The Good-Natured Man*; Faulkland of his jealousy in Sheridan's *The Rivals* (1775); and Charles Surface of his prodigality in *The School for Scandal* (1777). Of the penitents, Charles Oakly, Belcour, Honeywood, and Charles

---

[1] Arthur Murphy, *The Life of David Garrick, Esq.*, 2 vols. (London, 1801), i. 243.

Surface all effect their cures under the watchful eye of a father, guardian, or uncle somewhat reminiscent of Sir John Bevil. These parents are typical of the estimable characters that fill eighteenth-century plays. From Steele's time derisible stock figures like the foolish old parents of Restoration comedy were replaced by characters in some way sympathetic; the shift was, of course, obvious in narrative writing as well.

Although his sub-plot was intentionally broad in humour, Steele reversed the order of many Restoration plays by giving the serious love story the first emphasis. This pattern was generally accepted in the sentimental comedies that followed. The new emphases in characterization all but dictated the earnest plot line and tearful denouement. Unexpected discovery of a long-lost parent and the solemn promise of repentance from a lover could, after all, wring tears from the audience. The sentimental plays among those listed above adhere to this pattern, and many other comedies, some as unsentimental as *The Clandestine Marriage* (1776), have a serious main plot and denouement.

It is not profitable to recount every play that bears a resemblance to the model Steele consciously provided, nor is it possible to calculate precisely his impact on playwrights. The brief mention of a few of the better-known comedies, sentimental and unsentimental, merely illustrates how deeply his techniques were embedded in the dramatic tradition for more than fifty years. Despite the disappearance of exemplary heroes and preceptual speeches from the comic formula, the innovations which were theatrically exciting became the stock material of several succeeding generations of playwrights.

The publication, at least forty-eight editions in the century, including translations into French, German, and Italian, testifies to the ubiquity of the play.[1] People were reading, or at least buying, *The Conscious Lovers* in the British Isles and on the Continent throughout the century. Frequency of publication suggests that the play was part of the library of the well-read gentleman and his emulators. That it was read as well as collected is amply demonstrated by the continuing familiarity of writers and their expectation that readers would know it. A few examples will suffice.

Henry Fielding knew *The Conscious Lovers*. In *Joseph Andrews* Parson Adams approaches startlingly close to the early critical commentary

[1] For details of forty-seven editions see my article 'Eighteenth-Century Editions of Steele's *Conscious Lovers*', *SB* xxi (1968), 253–61.

in his naïve remark, 'I never heard of any plays fit for a Christian to read, but *Cato* and the *Conscious Lovers*; and, I must own, in the latter there are some things almost solemn enough for a sermon.'[1]

In 1765 George Colman the Elder brought out a new two-volume translation of Terence's plays, the first of which is *The Andrian*. In eleven of his copious notes he compared Steele's adaptation at length with the original; his close criticism of Steele's work is reminiscent of the essays and pamphlets of 1722 and 1723. He condemned, for example, the flat characterizations, the awkward protasis, the dreariness of the denouement, and the inadequate development of the main plot; he praised the sub-plot and the modernization of Tom and Phillis. A brief notice of Steele's play might be expected in Colman's edition, but the translator's carefully considered critical commentary on the imitation suggests that he felt his readers would have some interest in it and knowledge of it.

Boswell and, we may presume, Johnson also knew it well enough to quote or paraphrase it. In a footnote to the *Life* Boswell recorded:

Mrs. Burney informs me that she heard Dr. Johnson say, 'An English Merchant is a new species of Gentleman.' He, perhaps, had in his mind the following ingenious passage in 'The Conscious Lovers,' Act IV. Scene ii, where Mr. Sealand thus addresses Sir John Bevil, 'Give me leave to say, that we merchants are a species of gentry that have grown into the world this last century, and are as honourable, and almost as useful as you landed-folks, that have always thought yourselves so much above us. . . .'[2]

Richard Brinsley Sheridan, whose comedies reflect some of the residual effects of Steele's campaign for moral comedy, revived *The Conscious Lovers* more than once during his tenure as manager of the Drury Lane Theatre. In a letter dated December 1796 he encouraged the temperamental actress Dorothy Jordan to take the role of Phillis. He had hopes for the play because of its 'novelty', he explained. A new performance was staged, with Harriot Mellon playing Phillis, on 20 December, but the novelty did not, it would seem, attract theatre-goers.[3]

Whether in the theatre or in printed texts, literary men throughout the eighteenth century knew the play. It is safe to conjecture that other reasonably well-educated men and women did too. With the

---

[1] Book III, Chapter xi.
[2] *Boswell's Life of Johnson*, ed. G. B. Hill, rev. L. F. Powell, 6 vols. (Oxford, 1934–50), i. 491–2, n. 3.
[3] *The Letters of Richard Brinsley Sheridan*, ed. Cecil Price, 3 vols. (Oxford, 1966), ii. 61–2.

passing years Steele's name and his work acquired a lustre that
his contemporary detractors and political enemies never allowed.
Through performances and imitations on the stage and through the
frequent editions which made it part of the literary climate for many
years, *The Conscious Lovers* was certainly, as Steele wished, 'the
Prelude' of what was attempted in later plays. It should be recognized
today not only as the best example of sentimental comedy but also as
the single work which most directly and successfully affected the
pattern of dramatic development in the eighteenth century.

THE TEXT

Jacob Tonson Jr. issued three editions of *The Conscious Lovers* in
rapid succession in a short period beginning 1 December 1722. All
were dated 1723, and no distinction was made on the title-page; there
was no way, in fact, for purchasers to differentiate between the
earliest copies marketed and those printed to bolster the diminishing
stock. Tonson successfully defeated one attempt at piracy in December, but two other publishers, safely outside the limits of English
copyright law, soon issued editions: a Dublin printer published at
least one and maybe three quick editions;[1] and T. Johnson, whose
operations were based at The Hague, also immediately printed one.
An Italian version appeared in London in 1724 and another Dublin
edition in 1725. Tonson, however, did not republish the play until
1730.

On 20 October 1722, eighteen days before the opening, Steele
assigned Tonson publication rights; Tonson reassigned half the rights
to Bernard Lintott on 26 October, according to a prior agreement
between the two booksellers.[2] With the play proving extremely
popular in performance and the critical controversy raging in pamphlets and newspapers, the booksellers found themselves possessed of a
valuable literary property. They proceeded therefore to an unusually
large edition, 'many thousand' according to Tonson,[3] issued on
1 December with the date 1723 on the title-page. When this printing
turned out to be insufficient, a second edition was quickly ordered
and then a third.[4]

---

[1] A copy at Princeton is marked 'The Third Edition'; I have seen none labelled
as the second.   [2] Nichols, *Literary Anecdotes*, viii. 303. Baine, 169–71.
[3] G. A. Aitken, 'Steele's *Conscious Lovers* and the Publishers', *Athenaeum*, 5 December 1891, p. 771, citing Chancery Pleadings, Winter 1714–58, no. 690.
[4] For a discussion of the order of these editions see 'Eighteenth-Century Editions'
253–61.

Steele must have prepared for publication with care: one can assume that compositors worked from reasonably clean copy, because the text lacks the muddled passages and misnamed characters that mar the printed versions of *The Funeral* and *The Tender Husband*. He wrote the Preface, which refers to an act passed nine days before publication, very shortly before the book was issued. It is conceivable, though not demonstrable, that he also read the proofs and requested the three substantive changes made in gathering E, 'plainly' for 'plain' on p. 52, 'his' for 'his own' and 'hence' for 'me' on p. 55.

The first edition is an octavo with the collational formula A–F^8 G^4. Although plays in this period were usually set by two or three compositors and imposed in two or three pairs of skeletons (therefore, presumably, run on two or three presses), the first edition of *The Conscious Lovers* has a far more complicated printing history. One setting of type was used throughout, but the compositors did not set type forme by forme and then distribute as printing occurred; instead, the printer's crew set all the type, ran off copies, tied and stored the type, then made another impression, and they stored and reimpressed several times.[1] One can deduce from the procedure the printer's initial recognition that the run would have to be both fast and large, and that it would therefore require a number of compositors and pressmen.

The evidence that is available, that of the presswork, demonstrates a multiplicity of running-titles, press-figures, and shifts in body type quite remarkable for plays printed in this period. Running-titles vary from copy to copy, one indication that several times the pressmen reinserted type pages in chases for press-runs. The only formes in which running-titles remained unchanged in the twelve copies I collated are A, G, and outer E, with the exception of E3, on which three variants appear in different copies. It seems probable that although the printer ordered the type of formes which reached the press earlier tied and stored, he extended the runs of outer E and G so that the type stayed in the chases. Shifts in the alignment of type in the two formes of A suggest that these pages were stored with their running-titles intact and then re-used.

The press-figures are equally suggestive of a printing-house rush. They occur in fifteen combinations in thirty-one examined copies.

---

[1] To discover how many compositors worked on the play is impossible, because the type was not distributed and re-used, and therefore such valuable evidence as recurring broken type is not available.

Some formes with the same press-figures vary in running-titles; some vary in press-figures but not in running-titles; some vary in both.

Finally, shifts in type reconfirm the removal and reinsertion of pages of type. For example, on p. 21 the words 'to me' and 'or taking' in ll. 30–1 become 'tome' and 'ortaking' in some copies. Again, one finds both 'andyou' and 'and you' on l. 27 in copies of p. 60. Ornaments were removed when the pages of type were stored, then reinserted when the run was extended. This is most obviously apparent from an examination of the factotum on A2, which appears with strapwork at top and bottom in some copies and at the sides in others. In those copies in which it is at the sides the initial appears in three different positions.

The type of this edition was corrected, and in most cases the order of the states is clear.[1] Normally in Steele's period type was corrected during a press-run. The press began printing, the proofs were read, and the run was then interrupted for corrections. With this kind of procedure, several states of a sheet could exist: both formes uncorrected, one forme corrected, or both corrected. Corrected states of some sheets were then sometimes gathered with uncorrected states of others. This, however, is not the case for the first edition of *The Conscious Lovers*. In the thirty-one examined copies one finds uniform gatherings of sheets, that is, either all first state or all second state. The most likely explanation is that the type was corrected between runs; otherwise no such sharp division between states would occur. It is possible, therefore, to distinguish early copies from late. Examples of early copies include Yale copy 1 and two in the Bodleian shelf-marked Malone B 109 and G.P. 63 (1); later examples are Bodleian 8° E66 (2) Jur., Yale copy 3, two at the Folger, and two at the University of Texas.

The second edition was not distinguished from the first by format or acknowledgement. The title-page is identical, except for one line division between the fourth and fifth lines of the motto (first, *Miseri- | cordiam*; second, *Misericor- | diam*), and the collational formula is also the same. Although there are differences in line divisions, there is only one variation in pagination: the last line of A5^v in the first edition is the first line of A6 in the second. There are ten substantive variants; three are corrections of obvious errors, four are introductions of new errors, and the other three are indifferent readings. There is no reason to suspect that Steele had anything to do with the variants.

[1] See 'Eighteenth-Century Editions', pp. 258–9.

The second edition, printed in smaller numbers than the first if survival is an indication of the size of the printing,[1] must have been ordered very soon, for type from seven formes of the first was incorporated into it. The re-used type, recognizable by broken letters, includes the outer forme of sheet C, the inner forme of E except E3^v (p. 54), and the following pages: A3^v, B1^v (p. 2), B8 (p. 15), E4^v (p. 56), E5 (p. 57), F5^v (p. 74), and G2^v (p. 84). It seems obvious that after the extended run of the first edition ended and compositors began distributing type, the printer, needing more copies, began a second edition, utilizing those pages of type which had not yet been distributed.

The third edition, not so labelled, is an unrevised reprint of the second with identical title-page and collation. It retains nine readings introduced in the second edition, corrects one obvious mistake, and adds seven new erroneous readings. Apparently printed at a more leisurely pace than the first two, it is a completely new setting with altogether regular press-work.[2]

The size and rapidity of production of these three editions, all probably printed within a few weeks or months, suggest that Steele's play strongly attracted readers as well as theatre-goers; the number of unauthorized editions supports this conclusion. Tonson stopped a piracy advertised for 8 December, one week after his own first edition appeared, by a restraining order and then an injunction issued on 11 December against Francis Clifton, Robert Tooke, John Lightbody, and Susanna Collins.[3] He was not able, however, to prevent the issue of two editions published outside England to which English copyright law did not apply. In Dublin A. Rhames printed a duodecimo dated 1722 for J. Hyde, R. Gunne, R. Owen, E. Dobson, and P. Dugan. T. Johnson's octavo, with the imprint 'London, 1723', was actually printed at The Hague, site of Johnson's extra-legal activities, probably in 1722. Both these editions used as copy-text the first state of Tonson's first edition; the incentive was to capitalize on the initial interest in the play. Neither has any authority.

Two other editions were published during Steele's lifetime, an

---

[1] Of thirty-six examined copies of the first three editions, thirty-one are of the first, two of the second, and three of the third.

[2] Running-titles show that one press printed the inner forme of B, both formes of C, the outer forme of F, and G by half-sheet imposition. A second press printed both formes of D and both formes of E. A third was used for the outer forme of B and the inner forme of F; it seems likely that this press also printed A, although lack of running-title evidence makes it impossible to be sure.

[3] Baine, 172–3. See also 'Steele's *Conscious Lovers* and the Publishers', p. 771.

Italian translation by Paolo Antonio Rolli (1687–1765), *Gli Amanti Interni*, published in London in 1724, and a reprint of the Dublin edition in 1725. Tonson did not publish another until 1730, the year after Steele's death. The first edition served as copy-text for this duodecimo, which was labelled 'The Third Edition'; Steele clearly had not revised his play for republication. The only notable change is the use of 'his' and 'me' for the variants on p. 55 of the first edition, a combination that could not have been derived from the copy-text, but there is no convincing reason to hold Steele responsible.

I use the corrected state of the first edition as copy text, basing the text on a collation of copies of the first edition in the Folger (two copies); Bodleian (three copies); British Museum; Library of Congress; University of Texas (two copies); Yale (two copies); Harvard. Other copies examined but not completely collated include Columbia University (two copies); Victoria and Albert Museum; Huntington Library (two copies); University of Pennsylvania; University of California, Berkeley; University of North Carolina; Richmond P. Bond's copy; Newberry Library; University of Chicago; University of California at Los Angeles; Princeton University; Williams College; University of Illinois (two copies); Temple University; Lehigh University. I have also collated copies of the second edition at Yale and in the Bodleian; copies of the third at the Folger and Harvard; the Folger copies of the 1730 edition, the Johnson edition of 1723, and the Dublin edition of 1722; and the Bodleian copy of the Dublin edition of 1725.

THE

CONSCIOUS LOVERS.

A COMEDY.

Illud Genus Narrationis, quod in Personis positum est,
debet habere Sermonis Festivitatem, Animorum Dissi-
militudinem, Gravitatem, Lenitatem, Spem, Metum,
Suspicionem, Desiderium, Dissimulationem, Miseri-
cordiam, Rerum Varietates, Fortunæ Commutationem,
Insperatum Incommodum, Subitam Letitiam, Jucundum
Exitum Rerum.   *Rhetorica ad Herennium,* Lib. I.

[motto] *Rhetorica ad Herennium,*] Cic. Rhetor. ad Herenn.

ABBREVIATIONS USED IN THE NOTES

The following abbreviations are used in reference to early editions of *The Conscious Lovers*:

O1   First edition. London: Tonson, 1723 (all copies).

O1(u) First edition (uncorrected).

O1(c) First edition (corrected).

O2   Second edition. London: Tonson, 1723.

O3   Third edition. London: Tonson, 1723.

D   Fourth edition. London: Tonson, 1730, 'Third Edition'.

TJ   Johnson edition. [The Hague]: T. Johnson, 1723.

Du 1 First Dublin edition. Dublin: Hyde, etc., 1722.

Du 2 Second Dublin edition. Dublin: Hyde, etc., 1725.

TO THE
KING.

May it please Your Majesty,

After having aspir'd to the Highest and most Laudable Ambition, that of following the Cause of Liberty, I should not have humbly petition'd Your Majesty for a Direction of the Theatre, had I not believ'd Success in that Province an Happiness much to be 5 wish'd by an Honest Man, and highly conducing to the Prosperity of the Common-wealth. It is in this View I lay before Your Majesty a Comedy, which the Audience, in Justice to themselves, has supported and encouraged, and is the Prelude of what, by Your Majesty's Influence and Favour, may be attempted in future 10 Representations.

The Imperial Mantle, the Royal Vestment, and the shining Diadem, are what strike ordinary Minds; But Your Majesty's Native Goodness, Your Passion for Justice, and Her constant Assessor Mercy, is what continually surrounds you, in the View of 15 intelligent Spirits, and gives Hope to the Suppliant, who sees he has more than succeeded in giving Your Majesty an Opportunity of doing Good. Our King is above the Greatness of Royalty, and every Act of His Will which makes another Man happy, has ten times more Charms in it, than one that makes Himself appear rais'd 20 above the Condition of others; but even this carries Unhappiness with it; for, Calm Dominion, Equal Grandeur and Familiar Greatness do not easily affect the Imagination of the Vulgar, who cannot see Power but in Terror; and as Fear moves mean Spirits, and Love prompts Great ones to obey, the Insinuations of Malecontents are 25 directed accordingly; and the unhappy People are insnar'd, from Want of Reflection, into Disrespectful Ideas of their Gracious and Amiable Sovereign; and then only begin to apprehend the Greatness of their Master, when they have incurr'd his Displeasure.

As Your Majesty was invited to the Throne of a Willing People, 30 for their own sakes, and has ever enjoy'd it with Contempt of the

Ostentation of it, we beseech You to Protect us who revere Your Title as we love Your Person. 'Tis to be a Savage to be a Rebel, and they who have fall'n from You have not so much forfeited their 35 Allegiance, as lost their Humanity. And therefore, if it were only to preserve my self from the Imputation of being amongst the Insensible and Abandon'd, I would beg Permission in the most publick manner possible, to profess my self, with the utmost Sincerity and Zeal,

40 *SIRE*,

Your MAJESTY'S
Most Devoted Subject
and Servant,
RICHARD STEELE.

THE
PREFACE.

THIS Comedy has been receiv'd with universal Acceptance, for it was in every Part excellently perform'd; and there needs no other Applause of the Actors, but that they excell'd according to the Dignity and Difficulty of the Character they represented. But this great Favour done to the Work in Acting, renders the Expectation 5 still the greater from the Author, to keep up the Spirit in the Representation of the Closet, or any other Circumstance of the Reader, whether alone or in Company: To which I can only say, that it must be remember'd a Play is to be Seen, and is made to be Represented with the Advantage of Action, nor can appear but with half the 10 Spirit, without it; for the greatest Effect of a Play in reading is to excite the Reader to go see it; and when he does so, it is then a Play has the Effect of Example and Precept.

The chief Design of this was to be an innocent Performance, and the Audience have abundantly show'd how ready they are to sup- 15 port what is visibly intended that way; nor do I make any Difficulty to acknowledge, that the whole was writ for the sake of the Scene of the Fourth Act, wherein Mr. *Bevil* evades the Quarrel with his Friend, and hope it may have some Effect upon the *Goths* and *Vandals* that frequent the Theatres, or a more polite Audience may 20 supply their Absence.

But this Incident, and the Case of the Father and Daughter, are esteem'd by some People no Subjects of Comedy; but I cannot be of their Mind; for any thing that has its Foundation in Happiness and Success, must be allow'd to be the Object of Comedy, and sure 25 it must be an Improvement of it, to introduce a Joy too exquisite for Laughter, that can have no Spring but in Delight, which is the Case of this young Lady. I must therefore contend, that the Tears which were shed on that Occasion flow'd from Reason and Good Sense, and that Men ought not to be laugh'd at for weeping, till we 30 are come to a more clear Notion of what is to be imputed to the

Hardness of the Head, and the Softness of the Heart; and I think it
was very politely said of Mr. *Wilks* to one who told him there was
a *General* weeping for *Indiana*, I'll warrant he'll fight ne'er the worse
35 for that. To be apt to give way to the Impressions of Humanity is
the Excellence of a right Disposition, and the natural Working of a
well-turn'd Spirit. But as I have suffer'd by Criticks who are got
no farther than to enquire whether they ought to be pleas'd or not,
I would willingly find them properer Matter for their Employment,
40 and revive here a Song which was omitted for want of a Performer,
and design'd for the Entertainment of *Indiana*; Sig. *Carbonelli* instead
of it play'd on the Fiddle, and it is for want of a Singer that such
advantageous things are said of an Instrument which were design'd
for a Voice. The Song is the Distress of a Love-sick Maid, and may
45 be a fit Entertainment for some small Criticks to examine whether
the Passion is just, or the Distress Male or Female.

I.

From Place to Place forlorn I go,
　　With downcast Eyes a silent Shade;
Forbidden to declare my Woe;
　　To speak, till spoken to, afraid.
50

II.

My inward Pangs, my secret Grief,
　　My soft consenting Looks betray:
He Loves, but gives me no Relief:
　　Why speaks not he who may?

55 It remains to say a Word concerning *Terence*, and I am extremely
surpris'd to find what Mr. *Cibber* told me, prove a Truth, That what
I valued my self so much upon, the Translation of him, should be
imputed to me as a Reproach. Mr. *Cibber's* Zeal for the Work, his
Care and Application in instructing the Actors, and altering the
60 Disposition of the Scenes, when I was, through Sickness, unable to
cultivate such Things my self, has been a very obliging Favour and
Friendship to me. For this Reason, I was very hardly persuaded to

throw away *Terence's* celebrated Funeral, and take only the bare Authority of the young Man's Character, and how I have work'd it into an *Englishman*, and made Use of the same Circumstances of 65 discovering a Daughter, when we least hop'd for one, is humbly submitted to the Learned Reader.

PROLOGUE,

By Mr. *Welsted*.

Spoken by Mr. *Wilks*.

To win your Hearts, and to secure your Praise,
The Comic-Writers strive by various Ways:
By subtil Stratagems they act their Game,
And leave untry'd no Avenue to Fame.
One writes the Spouse a beating from his Wife;   5
And says, Each stroke was Copy'd from the Life.
Some fix all Wit and Humour in Grimace,
And make a Livelyhood of Pinkey's *Face:*
Here, One gay Shew and costly Habits tries,
Confiding to the Judgment of your Eyes: 10
Another smuts his Scene (a cunning Shaver)
Sure of the Rakes and of the Wenches Favour.
Oft have these Arts prevail'd; and one may guess,
If practis'd o'er again, would find Success.
But the bold Sage, the Poet of To-night,   15
By new and desp'rate Rules resolv'd to Write;
Fain would he give more just Applauses Rise,
And please by Wit that scorns the Aids of Vice;
The Praise he seeks, from worthier Motives springs,
Such Praise, as Praise to those that give it, brings.   20
  Your Aid, most humbly sought, then Britons *lend,*
And Lib'ral Mirth, like Lib'ral Men, defend:
No more let Ribaldry, with Licence writ,
Usurp the Name of Eloquence or Wit;
No more let lawless Farce uncensur'd go,   25
The lewd dull Gleanings of a Smithfield *Show.*

'*Tis yours, with Breeding to refine the Age,*
To Chasten Wit, and Moralize the Stage.
   Ye Modest, Wise and Good, ye Fair, ye Brave,
To-night the Champion of your Virtues save,
Redeem from long Contempt the Comic Name,
And Judge Politely for your Countrey's Fame.

30

DRAMATIS PERSONAE.

MEN.

Sir *John Bevil*.

Mr. *Sealand*.

Bevil junior, in Love with *Indiana*.

Myrtle, in Love with *Lucinda*.

Cimberton, a Coxcomb.

Humphrey, an old Servant to Sir *John*.

Tom, Servant to *Bevil* junior.

[*Boy*] *Daniel*, a Country Boy, Servant to *Indiana*.

Mr. *Mills*.

Mr. *Williams*.

Mr. *Booth*.

Mr. *Wilks*.

Mr. *Griffin*.   5

Mr. *Shepard*.

Mr. *Cibber*.

Mr. *Theophilus Cibber*.

WOMEN.

Mrs. *Sealand*, second Wife to *Sealand*.

Isabella, Sister to *Sealand*.

Indiana, *Sealand's* Daughter by his first Wife.

Lucinda, *Sealand's* Daughter by his second Wife.

Phillis, Maid to *Lucinda*.

Mrs. *Moore*.

Mrs. *Thurmond*.

Mrs. *Oldfield*.   10

Mrs. *Booth*.

Mrs. *Younger*.

[Servants, Musick-Master.]   15

SCENE, *London*.

THE
CONSCIOUS LOVERS.

Act I. Scene i.

Scene, *Sir* John Bevil's *House.*

Enter Sir John Bevil, *and* Humphrey.

Sir John Bevil. Have you order'd that I should not be interrupted while I am dressing?

Humphrey. Yes, Sir: I believ'd you had something of Moment to say to me.

Sir John Bevil. Let me see, *Humphrey*; I think it is now full forty 5 Years since I first took thee, to be about my Self.

Humphrey. I thank you, Sir, it has been an easy forty Years; and I have pass'd 'em without much Sickness, Care, or Labour.

Sir John Bevil. Thou hast a brave Constitution; you are a Year or two older than I am, Sirrah. 10

Humphrey. You have ever been of that mind, Sir.

Sir John Bevil. You Knave, you know it; I took thee for thy Gravity and Sobriety, in my wild Years.

Humphrey. Ah Sir! our Manners were form'd from our different Fortunes, not our different Age. Wealth gave a Loose to your Youth, 15 and Poverty put a Restraint upon mine.

Sir John Bevil. Well, *Humphrey*, you know I have been a kind Master to you; I have us'd you, for the ingenuous Nature I observ'd in you from the beginning, more like an humble Friend than a Servant. 20

Humphrey. I humbly beg you'll be so tender of me, as to explain your Commands, Sir, without any farther Preparation.

Sir John Bevil. I'll tell thee then. In the first Place, this Wedding of my Son's, in all Probability, (shut the Door) will never be at all.

25   *Humphrey*. How, Sir! not be at all? for what reason is it carry'd
     on in Appearance?

        Sir John Bevil. Honest *Humphrey*, have patience; and I'll tell thee
     all in Order. I have my self, in some part of my Life, liv'd (indeed)
     with Freedom, but, I hope, without Reproach: Now, I thought
30   Liberty wou'd be as little injurious to my Son; therefore, as soon as
     he grew towards Man, I indulg'd him in living after his own manner:
     I knew not how, otherwise, to judge of his Inclination; for what can
     be concluded from a Behaviour under Restraint and Fear? But what
     charms me above all Expression is, that my Son has never in the
35   least Action, the most distant Hint or Word, valued himself upon
     that great Estate of his Mother's, which, according to our Marriage
     Settlement, he has had ever since he came to Age.

        Humphrey. No, Sir; on the contrary, he seems afraid of appearing
     to enjoy it, before you or any belonging to you—He is as dependant
40   and resign'd to your Will, as if he had not a Farthing but what must
     come from your immediate Bounty—You have ever acted like a
     good and generous Father, and he like an obedient and grateful
     Son.

        Sir John Bevil. Nay, his Carriage is so easy to all with whom he
45   converses, that he is never assuming, never prefers himself to
     others, nor ever is guilty of that rough Sincerity which a Man is not
     call'd to, and certainly disobliges most of his Acquaintance; to be
     short, *Humphrey*, his Reputation was so fair in the World, that Old
     Sealand, the great *India* Merchant, has offer'd his only Daughter, and
50   sole Heiress to that vast Estate of his, as a Wife for him; you may be
     sure I made no Difficulties, the Match was agreed on, and this very
     Day named for the Wedding.

        Humphrey. What hinders the Proceeding?

        Sir John Bevil. Don't interrupt me. You know, I was last *Thursday*
55   at the Masquerade; my Son, you may remember, soon found us out
     —He knew his Grandfather's Habit, which I then wore; and tho'
     it was the Mode, in the last Age, yet the Maskers, you know,
     follow'd us as if we had been the most monstrous Figures in that
     whole Assembly.

60   *Humphrey*. I remember indeed a young Man of Quality in the
     Habit of a Clown, that was particularly troublesome.

Sir John Bevil. Right—He was too much what he seem'd to be. You remember how impertinently he follow'd, and teiz'd us, and wou'd know who we were.

Humphrey. (*Aside*.) I know he has a mind to come into that Particular.

Sir John Bevil. Ay, he follow'd us, till the Gentleman who led the Lady in the *Indian* Mantle presented that gay Creature to the Rustick, and bid him (like *Cymon* in the Fable) grow Polite, by falling in Love, and let that worthy old Gentleman alone, meaning me: The Clown was not reform'd, but rudely persisted, and offer'd to force off my Mask; with that the Gentleman throwing off his own, appear'd to be my Son, and in his Concern for me, tore off that of the Nobleman; at this they seiz'd each other; the Company call'd the Guards: and in the Surprize, the Lady swoon'd away: Upon which my Son quitted his Adversary, and had now no Care but of the Lady,—when raising her in his Arms, Art thou gone, cry'd he, for ever—forbid it Heav'n!—She revives at his known Voice,—and with the most familiar tho' modest Gesture hangs in Safety over his Shoulder weeping, but wept as in the Arms of one before whom she could give her self a Loose, were she not under Observation: while she hides her Face in his Neck, he carefully conveys her from the Company.

Humphrey. I have observ'd this Accident has dwelt upon you very strongly.

Sir John Bevil. Her uncommon Air, her noble Modesty, the Dignity of her Person, and the Occasion it self, drew the whole Assembly together; and I soon heard it buzz'd about, she was the adopted Daughter of a famous Sea-Officer, who had serv'd in *France*. Now this unexpected and publick Discovery of my Son's so deep Concern for her—

Humphrey. Was what I suppose alarm'd Mr. *Sealand*, in behalf of his Daughter, to break off the Match.

Sir John Bevil. You are right—He came to me yesterday, and said, he thought himself disengag'd from the Bargain; being credibly informed my Son was already marry'd, or worse, to the Lady at the Masquerade. I palliated matters, and insisted on our Agreement; but we parted with little less than a direct Breach between us.

Humphrey. Well, Sir; and what Notice have you taken of all this
100 to my young Master?

Sir John Bevil. That's what I wanted to debate with you—I have
said nothing to him yet—But look you, *Humphrey*—if there is so
much in this Amour of his, that he denies upon my Summons to
marry, I have cause enough to be offended; and then by my insisting
105 upon his marrying to-day, I shall know how far he is engag'd to this
Lady in Masquerade, and from thence only shall be able to take my
Measures: in the mean time I would have you find out how far that
Rogue his Man is let into his Secret—He, I know, will play Tricks
as much to cross me, as to serve his Master.

110 *Humphrey.* Why do you think so of him, Sir? I believe he is no
worse than I was for you, at your Son's Age.

Sir John Bevil. I see it in the Rascal's Looks. But I have dwelt on
these things too long; I'll go to my Son immediately, and while I'm
gone, your Part is to convince his Rogue *Tom* that I am in
115 Earnest. I'll leave him to you.

Exit Sir John Bevil.

Humphrey. Well, tho' this Father and Son live as well together as
possible, yet their fear of giving each other Pain, is attended with
constant mutual Uneasiness. I'm sure I have enough to do to be
honest, and yet keep well with them both: But they know I love 'em,
120 and that makes the Task less painful however—Oh, here's the Prince
of poor Coxcombs, the Representative of All the better fed than
taught.—Ho! ho! *Tom*, whither so gay and so airy this Morning?

Enter Tom, *Singing.*

Tom. Sir, we Servants of Single Gentlemen are another kind of
People than you domestick ordinary Drudges that do Business: We
125 are rais'd above you: The Pleasures of Board-Wages, Tavern-Dinners,
and many a clear Gain; Vails, alas! you never heard or dreamt of.

Humphrey. Thou hast Follies and Vices enough for a Man of Ten
thousand a Year, tho' 'tis but as t'other Day that I sent for you to
Town, to put you into Mr. *Sealand's* Family, that you might learn
130 a little before I put you to my young Master, who is too gentle for
training such a rude Thing as you were into proper Obedience—
You then pull'd off your Hat to every one you met in the Street, like

a bashful great aukward Cub as you were. But your great Oaken Cudgel when you were a Booby, became you much better than that dangling Stick at your Button now you are a Fop. That's fit for nothing, except it hangs there to be ready for your Master's Hand when you are impertinent.

Tom. Uncle *Humphrey*, you know my Master scorns to strike his Servants. You talk as if the World was now, just as it was when my old Master and you were in your Youth—when you went to dinner because it was so much a Clock, when the great Blow was given in the Hall at the Pantrey-door, and all the Family came out of their Holes in such strange Dresses and formal Faces as you see in the Pictures in our long Gallery in the Country.

Humphrey. Why, you wild Rogue!

Tom. You could not fall to your Dinner till a formal Fellow in a black Gown said something over the Meat, as if the Cook had not made it ready enough.

Humphrey. Sirrah, who do you prate after?—Despising Men of Sacred Characters! I hope you never heard my good young Master talk so like a Profligate?

Tom. Sir, I say you put upon me, when I first came to Town, about being Orderly, and the Doctrine of wearing Shams to make Linnen last clean a Fortnight, keeping my Cloths fresh, and wearing a Frock within Doors.

Humphrey. Sirrah, I gave you those Lessons, because I suppos'd at that time your Master and you might have din'd at home every Day, and cost you nothing; then you might have made a good Family Servant. But the Gang you have frequented since at Chocolate Houses and Taverns, in a continual round of Noise and Extravagance—

Tom. I don't know what you heavy Inmates call Noise and Extravagance; but we Gentlemen, who are well fed, and cut a Figure, Sir, think it a fine Life, and that we must be very pretty Fellows who are kept only to be looked at.

Humphrey. Very well, Sir,—I hope the Fashion of being lewd and extravagant, despising of Decency and Order, is almost at an End, since it is arrived at Persons of your Quality.

Tom. Master *Humphrey*, Ha! Ha! you were an unhappy Lad to be

170 sent up to Town in such Queer Days as you were: Why now, Sir,
the Lacquies are the Men of Pleasure of the Age; the Top-Gamesters;
and many a lac'd Coat about Town have had their Education in our
Party-colour'd Regiment,—We are false Lovers; have a Taste of
Musick, Poetry, Billet-deux, Dress, Politicks, ruin Damsels, and
175 when we are weary of this lewd Town, and have a mind to take up,
whip into our Masters Wigs and Linnen, and marry Fortunes.

Humphrey. Hey-day!

Tom. Nay, Sir, our Order is carry'd up to the highest Dignities
and Distinctions; step but into the *Painted Chamber*—and by our
180 Titles you'd take us all for Men of Quality—then again come down
to the *Court of Requests*, and you see us all laying our broken Heads
together for the Good of the Nation: and tho' we never carry a
Question *Nemine Contradicente*, yet this I can say with a safe Conscience, (and I wish every Gentleman of our Cloth could lay his
185 Hand upon his Heart and say the same) that I never took so much
as a single Mug of Beer for my Vote in all my Life.

Humphrey. Sirrah, there is no enduring your Extravagance; I'll
hear you prate no longer. I wanted to see you, to enquire how things
go with your Master, as far as you understand them; I suppose he
190 knows he is to be married to-day.

Tom. Ay, Sir, he knows it, and is dress'd as gay as the Sun; but,
between you and I, my Dear, he has a very heavy Heart under all
that Gayety. As soon as he was dress'd I retir'd, but overheard him
sigh in the most heavy manner. He walk'd thoughtfully to and fro
195 in the Room, then went into his Closet; when he came out, he gave
me this for his Mistress, whose Maid you know—

Humphrey. Is passionately fond of your fine Person.

Tom. The poor Fool is so tender, and loves to hear me talk of the
World, and the Plays, Opera's, and *Ridotto's*, for the Winter; the
200 Parks and *Bellsize*, for our Summer Diversions; and Lard! say she,
you are so wild—but you have a world of Humour—

Humphrey. Coxcomb! Well, but why don't you run with your
Master's Letter to Mrs. *Lucinda*, as he order'd you?

Tom. Because Mrs. *Lucinda* is not so easily come at as you think
205 for.

Humphrey. Not easily come at? Why Sirrah, are not her Father

and my old Master agreed, that she and Mr. *Bevil* are to be One
Flesh before to-morrow Morning?

Tom. It's no Matter for that; her Mother, it seems, Mrs. *Sealand*,
has not agreed to it: and you must know, Mr. *Humphrey*, that in that 210
Family the Grey Mare is the better Horse.

Humphrey. What do'st thou mean?

Tom. In one Word, Mrs. *Sealand* pretends to have a Will of her
own, and has provided a Relation of hers, a stiff, starch'd Philosopher, and a wise Fool for her Daughter; for which Reason, for 215
these ten Days past, she has suffer'd no Message nor Letter from
my Master to come near her.

Humphrey. And where had you this Intelligence?

Tom. From a foolish fond Soul, that can keep nothing from me—
One that will deliver this Letter too, if she is rightly manag'd.   220

Humphrey. What! Her pretty Hand-maid, Mrs. *Phillis*?

Tom. Even she, Sir; this is the very Hour, you know, she usually
comes hither, under a Pretence of a Visit to your Housekeeper
forsooth, but in reality to have a Glance at—

Humphrey. Your sweet Face, I warrant you.   225

Tom. Nothing else in Nature; you must know, I love to fret, and
play with the little Wanton.—

Humphrey. Play with the little Wanton! What will this World
come to!

Tom. I met her, this Morning, in a new Manteau and Petticoat, 230
not a bit the worse for her Lady's wearing: and she has always new
Thoughts and new Airs with new Cloaths—then she never fails to
steal some Glance or Gesture from every Visitant at their House;
and is indeed the whole Town of Coquets at second hand. But here
she comes; in one Motion she speaks and describes herself better 235
than all the Words in the World can.

Humphrey. Then I hope, dear Sir, when your own Affair is over,
you will be so good as to mind your Master's with her.

Tom. Dear *Humphrey*, you know my Master is my Friend, and
those are People I never forget.—   240

Humphrey. Sawciness itself! but I'll leave you to do your best for
him.

                                                              Exit.

Enter Phillis.

Phillis. Oh, Mr. *Thomas*, is Mrs. *Sugar-key* at home?—Lard, one is almost asham'd to pass along the Streets. The Town is quite
245 empty, and no Body of Fashion left in it; and the ordinary People do so stare to see any thing (dress'd like a Woman of Condition) as it were on the same Floor with them pass by. Alas! Alas! it is a sad thing to walk. Oh Fortune! Fortune!

Tom. What! a sad thing to walk? Why, Madam *Phillis*, do you
250 wish your self lame?

Phillis. No, Mr. *Tom*, but I wish I were generally carry'd in a Coach or Chair, and of a Fortune neither to stand nor go, but to totter, or slide, to be short-sighted, or stare, to fleer in the Face, to look distant, to observe, to overlook, yet all become me; and, if I
255 was rich, I cou'd twire and loll as well as the best of them. Oh *Tom*! *Tom*! is it not a pity, that you shou'd be so great a Coxcomb, and I so great a Coquet, and yet be such poor Devils as we are?

Tom. Mrs. *Phillis*, I am your humble Servant for that—

Phillis. Yes, Mr. *Thomas*, I know how much you are my humble
260 Servant, and know what you said to Mrs. *Judy*, upon seeing her in one of her Lady's Cast Manteaus; That any one wou'd have thought her the Lady, and that she had ordered the other to wear it till it sat easy—for now only it was becoming:—To my Lady it was only a Covering, to Mrs. *Judy* it was a Habit. This you said, after some
265 Body or other. Oh, *Tom*! *Tom*! thou art as false and as base, as the best Gentleman of them all: but, you Wretch, talk to me no more on the old odious Subject. Don't, I say.

Tom. I know not how to resist your Commands, Madam. (*In a submissive Tone, retiring.*)
270 *Phillis.* Commands about Parting are grown mighty easy to you of late.

Tom. (*Aside.*) Oh, I have her; I have nettled and put her into the right Temper to be wrought upon, and set a prating.—[*To* Phillis.] Why truly, to be plain with you, Mrs. *Phillis*, I can take little
275 Comfort of late in frequenting your House.

Phillis. Pray, Mr. *Thomas*, what is it all of a sudden offends your Nicety at our House?

Tom. I don't care to speak Particulars, but I dislike the Whole.

Phillis. I thank you, Sir, I am a Part of that Whole.

Tom. Mistake me not, good *Phillis*.   280

Phillis. Good *Phillis*! Saucy enough. But however—

Tom. I say, it is that thou art a Part, which gives me Pain for the Disposition of the Whole. You must know, Madam, to be serious, I am a Man, at the Bottom, of prodigious nice Honour. You are too much expos'd to Company at your House: To be plain, I don't like 285 so many, that wou'd be your Mistress's Lovers, whispering to you.

Phillis. Don't think to put that upon me. You say this, because I wrung you to the Heart, when I touch'd your guilty Conscience about *Judy*.

Tom. Ah *Phillis*! *Phillis*! if you but knew my Heart!   290

Phillis. I know too much on't.

Tom. Nay then, poor *Crispo's* Fate and mine are one—Therefore give me Leave to say, or sing at least, as he does upon the same Occasion—(*Sings.*)

                       Se vedette, &c.   295

Phillis. What, do you think I'm to be fob'd off with a Song? I don't question but you have sung the same to Mrs. *Judy* too.

Tom. Don't disparage your Charms, good *Phillis*, with Jealousy of so worthless an Object; besides, she is a poor Hussey, and if you doubt the Sincerity of my Love, you will allow me true to my 300 Interest. You are a Fortune, *Phillis*—

Phillis. [*Aside.*] What wou'd the Fop be at now? [*To Tom.*] In good time indeed, you shall be setting up for a Fortune!

Tom. Dear Mrs. *Phillis*, you have such a Spirit that we shall never be dull in Marriage,when we come together. But I tell you, you are 305 a Fortune, and you have an Estate in my Hands.

           He pulls out a Purse, she eyes it.

Phillis. What Pretence have I to what is in your Hands, Mr. *Tom*?

Tom. As thus: there are Hours, you know, when a Lady is neither pleas'd or displeas'd, neither sick or well, when she lolls or loiters, when she's without Desires, from having more of every 310 thing than she knows what to do with.

Phillis. Well, what then?

Tom. When she has not Life enough to keep her bright Eyes quite open, to look at her own dear Image in the Glass.

315 *Phillis.* Explain thy self, and don't be so fond of thy own prating.

Tom. There are also prosperous and good-natur'd Moments, as when a Knot or a Patch is happily fix'd; when the Complexion particularly flourishes.

320 *Phillis.* Well, what then? I have not Patience!

Tom. Why then—or on the like Occasions—we Servants who have Skill to know how to time Business, see when such a pretty folded thing as this (*Shews a Letter.*) may be presented, laid, or dropp'd, as best suits the present Humour. And, Madam, because 325 it is a long wearisome Journey to run through all the several Stages of a Lady's Temper, my Master, who is the most reasonable Man in the World, presents you this to bear your Charges on the Road. (*Gives her the Purse.*)

Phillis. Now you think me a corrupt Hussey.

330 *Tom.* Oh fie, I only think you'll take the Letter.

Phillis. Nay, I know you do, but I know my own Innocence; I take it for my Mistress's Sake.

Tom. I know it, my Pretty One, I know it.

Phillis. Yes, I say I do it, because I wou'd not have my Mistress 335 deluded by one who gives no Proof of his Passion; but I'll talk more of this, as you see me on my Way home—No, *Tom*, I assure thee, I take this Trash of thy Master's, not for the Value of the thing, but as it convinces me he has a true Respect for my Mistress. I remember a Verse to the Purpose.

340
> *They may be false who Languish and Complain,*
> *But they who part with Money never feign.*

Exeunt.

[Act I.] Scene ii.

Bevil *junior's Lodgings.*

Bevil *junior, Reading.*

Bevil junior. These Moral Writers practise Virtue after Death: This charming Vision of *Mirza*! Such an Author consulted in a Morning, sets the Spirit for the Vicissitudes of the Day, better than the Glass does a Man's Person: But what a Day have I to go thro'! to put on an Easy Look with an Aking Heart.—If this Lady my 5 Father urges me to marry should not refuse me, my Dilemma is insupportable. But why should I fear it? is not she in equal Distress with me? has not the Letter, I have sent her this Morning, confest my Inclination to another? Nay, have I not moral Assurances of her Engagements too, to my Friend *Myrtle*? It's impossible but she 10 must give in to it: For, sure to be deny'd is a Favour any Man may pretend to. It must be so—Well then, with the Assurance of being rejected, I think I may confidently say to my Father, I am ready to marry her—Then let me resolve upon (what I am not very good at, tho' it is) an honest Dissimulation. 15

Enter Tom.

Tom. Sir *John Bevil*, Sir, is in the next Room.

Bevil junior. Dunce! Why did not you bring him in?

Tom. I told him, Sir, you were in your Closet.

Bevil junior. I thought you had known, Sir, it was my Duty to see my Father any where. (*Going himself to the Door.*) 20

Tom. (*Aside.*) The Devil's in my Master! he has always more Wit than I have.

Bevil *junior introducing Sir* John Bevil.

Bevil junior. Sir, you are the most Gallant, the most Complaisant of all Parents—Sure 'tis not a Compliment to say these Lodgings are yours—Why wou'd you not walk in, Sir? 25

Sir John Bevil. I was loth to interrupt you unseasonably on your Wedding-day.

Bevil junior. One to whom I am beholden for my Birth-day, might have used less Ceremony.

30 *Sir John Bevil.* Well, Son, I have Intelligence you have writ to your Mistress this Morning: It would please my Curiosity to know the Contents of a Wedding-day Letter; for Courtship must then be over.

Bevil junior. I assure you, Sir, there was no Insolence in it, upon
35 the Prospect of such a vast Fortune's being added to our Family; but much Acknowledgment of the Lady's greater Desert.

Sir John Bevil. But, dear *Jack*, are you in earnest in all this? And will you really marry her?

Bevil junior. Did I ever disobey any Command of yours, Sir? nay,
40 any Inclination that I saw you bent upon?

Sir John Bevil. Why, I can't say you have, Son; but methinks in this whole Business, you have not been so warm as I could have wish'd you: You have visited her, it's true, but you have not been particular. Every one knows you can say and do as handsome
45 Things as any Man; but you have done nothing, but liv'd in the General; been Complaisant only.

Bevil junior. As I am ever prepar'd to marry if you bid me, so I am ready to let it alone if you will have me.

Humphrey *enters unobserv'd.*

Sir John Bevil. Look you there now! why what am I to think of
50 this so absolute and so indifferent a Resignation?

Bevil junior. Think? that I am still your Son, Sir,—Sir—you have been married, and I have not. And you have, Sir, found the Inconvenience there is, when a Man weds with too much Love in his Head. I have been told, Sir, that at the Time you married, you made
55 a mighty Bustle on the Occasion. There was challenging and fighting, scaling Walls—locking up the Lady—and the Gallant under an Arrest for fear of killing all his Rivals—Now, Sir, I suppose you having found the ill Consequences of these strong Passions and Prejudices, in preference of one Woman to another, in Case of a
60 Man's becoming a Widower—

Sir John Bevil. How is this!

Bevil junior. I say Sir, Experience has made you wiser in your Care of me—for, Sir, since you lost my dear Mother, your time has been so heavy, so lonely, and so tasteless, that you are so good as to guard me against the like Unhappiness, by marrying me pruden- 65 tially by way of Bargain and Sale. For, as you well judge, a Woman that is espous'd for a Fortune, is yet a better Bargain, if she dies; for then a Man still enjoys what he did marry, the Money; and is disencumber'd of what he did not marry, the Woman.

Sir John Bevil. But pray, Sir, do you think *Lucinda* then a Woman 70 of such little Merrit?

Bevil junior. Pardon me, Sir, I don't carry it so far neither; I am rather afraid I shall like her too well; she has, for one of her Fortune, a great many needless and superfluous good Qualities. 75

Sir John Bevil. I am afraid, Son, there's something I don't see yet, something that's smother'd under all this Rallery.

Bevil junior. Not in the least, Sir: If the Lady is dress'd and ready, you see I am. I suppose the Lawyers are ready too.

Humphrey. (*Aside.*) This may grow warm, if I don't interpose. 80 [*To Sir* John Bevil.] Sir, Mr. *Sealand* is at the Coffee-house, and has sent to speak with you.

Sir John Bevil. Oh! that's well! Then I warrant the Lawyers are ready. Son, you'll be in the Way, you say—

Bevil junior. If you please, Sir, I'll take a Chair, and go to Mr. 85 *Sealand's*, where the young Lady and I will wait your Leisure.

Sir John Bevil. By no means—The old Fellow will be so vain, if he sees—

Bevil junior. Ay—But the young Lady, Sir, will think me so indifferent— 90

Humphrey. (*Aside to* Bevil *junior.*) Ay—there you are right—press your Readiness to go to the Bride—he won't let you.

Bevil junior. (*Aside to* Humphrey.) Are you sure of that?

Humphrey. (*Aside.*) How he likes being prevented.

Sir John Bevil. No, no: You are an Hour or two too early. (*Looking* 95 *on his Watch.*)

Bevil junior. You'll allow me, Sir, to think it too late to visit a

beautiful, virtuous young Woman, in the Pride and Bloom of Life,
ready to give her self to my Arms: and to place her Happiness or
100 Misery, for the future, in being agreeable or displeasing to me, is
a—Call a Chair.

Sir John Bevil. No, no, no, dear *Jack*; this *Sealand* is a moody old
Fellow: There's no dealing with some People, but by managing
with Indifference. We must leave to him the Conduct of this Day.
105 It is the last of his commanding his Daughter.

Bevil junior. Sir, he can't take it ill, that I am impatient to
be hers.

Sir John Bevil. Pray let me govern in this Matter: you can't tell
how humoursome old Fellows are:—There's no offering Reason to
110 some of 'em, especially when they are Rich—(*Aside.*) If my Son
should see him, before I've brought old *Sealand* into better Temper,
the Match would be impracticable.

Humphrey. Pray, Sir, let me beg you, to let Mr. *Bevil* go.—(*Aside
to Sir* John Bevil.) See, whether he will or not.—(*Then to* Bevil
115 *junior.*) Pray, Sir, command your self; since you see my Master is
positive, it is better you should not go.

Bevil junior. My Father commands me, as to the Object of my
Affections; but I hope he will not, as to the Warmth and Height
of them.

120 *Sir John Bevil.* [*Aside.*] So! I must even leave things as I found
them: And in the mean time, at least, keep Old *Sealand* out of his
sight.—[*To* Bevil *junior.*] Well, Son, I'll go my self and take orders
in your Affair—You'll be in the way, I suppose, if I send to you—
I'll leave your Old Friend with you.—[*Aside to* Humphrey.]
125 Humphrey—don't let him stir, d'ye hear: [*To* Bevil *junior.*] Your
Servant, your Servant.

Exit Sir John Bevil.

Humphrey. I have a sad time on't, Sir, between you and my
Master—I see you are unwilling, and I know his violent Inclinations
for the Match—I must betray neither, and yet deceive you both,
130 for your common Good—Heav'n grant a good End of this matter:
But there is a Lady, Sir, that gives your Father much Trouble and
Sorrow—You'll pardon me.

Bevil junior. Humphrey, I know thou art a Friend to both; and in

that Confidence, I dare tell thee—That Lady—is a Woman of
Honour and Virtue. You may assure your self, I never will Marry 135
without my Father's Consent: But give me leave to say too, this
Declaration does not come up to a Promise, that I will take whom-
soever he pleases.

Humphrey. Come Sir, I wholly understand you: You would engage
my Services to free you from this Woman, whom my Master intends 140
you, to make way, in time, for the Woman you have really a mind
to.

Bevil junior. Honest *Humphrey*, you have always been an useful
Friend to my Father, and my self; I beg you continue your good
Offices, and don't let us come to the Necessity of a Dispute; for, if 145
we should dispute, I must either part with more than Life, or lose
the best of Fathers.

Humphrey. My dear Master, were I but worthy to know this
Secret, that so near concerns you, my Life, my All should be engag'd
to serve you. This, Sir, I dare promise, that I am sure I will 150
and can be secret: your Trust, at worst, but leaves you where you
were; and if I cannot serve you, I will at once be plain, and tell
you so.

Bevil junior. That's all I ask: Thou hast made it now my Interest to trust thee—Be patient then, and hear the Story of my 155
Heart.

Humphrey. I am all Attention, Sir.

Bevil junior. You may remember, *Humphrey*, that in my last
Travels, my Father grew uneasy at my making so long a Stay at
Toulon.   160

Humphrey. I remember it; he was apprehensive some Woman had
laid hold of you.

Bevil junior. His Fears were just; for there I first saw this Lady:
She is of *English* Birth: Her Father's Name was *Danvers*, a Younger
Brother of an Ancient Family, and originally an Eminent Merchant 165
of *Bristol*; who, upon repeated Misfortunes, was reduced to go
privately to the *Indies*. In this Retreat Providence again grew
favourable to his Industry, and, in six Years time, restored him to
his former Fortunes: On this he sent Directions over, that his Wife
and little Family should follow him to the *Indies*. His Wife, impatient 170

to obey such welcome Orders, would not wait the leisure of a
Convoy, but took the first occasion of a single Ship, and with her
Husband's Sister only, and this Daughter, then scarce seven Years
old, undertook the fatal Voyage: For here, poor Creature, she lost
175 her Liberty, and Life; she, and her Family, with all they had, were
unfortunately taken by a Privateer from *Toulon*. Being thus made
a Prisoner, though, as such, not ill treated, yet the Fright, the
Shock, and cruel Disappointment, seiz'd with such Violence upon
her unhealthy Frame, she sicken'd, pined and died at Sea.
180 *Humphrey.* Poor Soul! O the helpless Infant!

Bevil junior. Her Sister yet surviv'd, and had the Care of her: The
Captain too proved to have Humanity, and became a Father to her;
for having himself married an *English* Woman, and being Childless,
he brought home into *Toulon* this her little Country-woman;
185 presenting her, with all her dead Mother's Moveables of Value, to
his Wife, to be educated as his own adopted Daughter.

Humphrey. Fortune here seem'd, again, to smile on her.

Bevil junior. Only to make her Frowns more terrible: For, in his
Height of Fortune, this Captain too, her Benefactor, unfortunately
190 was kill'd at Sea, and dying intestate, his Estate fell wholly to an
Advocate his Brother, who coming soon to take Possession, there
found (among his other Riches) this blooming Virgin, at his
Mercy.

Humphrey. He durst not, sure, abuse his Power!
195 *Bevil junior.* No wonder if his pamper'd Blood was fired at the
Sight of her—in short, he lov'd: but, when all Arts and gentle
Means had fail'd to move, he offer'd too his Menaces in vain,
denouncing Vengeance on her Cruelty; demanding her to account
for all her Maintenance, from her Childhood; seiz'd on her little
200 Fortune, as his own Inheritance, and was draging her by Violence
to Prison; when Providence at the Instant interpos'd, and sent me,
by Miracle, to relieve her.

Humphrey. 'Twas Providence indeed; But pray, Sir, after all this
Trouble, how came this Lady at last to *England*?
205 *Bevil junior.* The disappointed Advocate, finding she had so
unexpected a Support, on cooler Thoughts, descended to a Composition; which I, without her Knowledge, secretly discharg'd.

Humphrey. That generous Concealment made the Obligation double.

Bevil junior. Having thus obtain'd her Liberty, I prevail'd, not 210 without some Difficulty, to see her safe to *England*; where no sooner arrived, but my Father, jealous of my being imprudently engaged, immediately proposed this other fatal Match that hangs upon my Quiet.

Humphrey. I find, Sir, you are irrecoverably fix'd upon this 215 Lady.

Bevil junior. As my vital Life dwells in my Heart—and yet you see—what I do to please my Father: Walk in this Pageantry of Dress, this splendid Covering of Sorrow—But, *Humphrey* you have your Lesson. 220

Humphrey. Now, Sir, I have but one material Question—

Bevil junior. Ask it freely.

Humphrey. Is it, then, your own Passion for this secret Lady, or hers for you, that gives you this Aversion to the Match your Father has proposed you? 225

Bevil junior. I shall appear, *Humphrey*, more Romantick in my Answer, than in all the rest of my Story: For tho' I doat on her to death, and have no little Reason to believe she has the same Thoughts for me; yet in all my Acquaintance, and utmost Privacies with her, I never once directly told her, that 230 I loved.

Humphrey. How was it possible to avoid it?

Bevil junior. My tender Obligations to my Father have laid so inviolable a Restraint upon my Conduct, that 'till I have his Consent to speak, I am determin'd, on that Subject, to be dumb for 235 ever—

Humphrey. Well Sir, to your Praise be it spoken, you are certainly the most unfashionable Lover in *Great-Britain*.

Enter Tom.

Tom. Sir, Mr. *Myrtle*'s at the next door, and, if you are at Leisure, will be glad to wait on you. 240

Bevil junior. Whenever he pleases—hold, *Tom*! did you receive no Answer to my Letter?

Tom. Sir, I was desir'd to call again; for I was told, her Mother would not let her be out of her Sight; but about an Hour hence,
245 Mrs. *Phillis* said, I should certainly have one.

Bevil junior. Very well.

[*Exit* Tom.]

Humphrey. Sir, I will take another Opportunity: in the mean time, I only think it proper to tell you, that from a Secret I know, you may appear to your Father as forward as you please, to marry
250 *Lucinda*, without the least Hazard of its coming to a Conclusion— Sir, your most obedient Servant.

Bevil junior. Honest *Humphrey*, continue but my Friend, in this Exigence, and you shall always find me yours.

Exit Humphrey.

I long to hear how my Letter has succeeded with *Lucinda*—but I
255 think, it cannot fail: for, at worst, were it possible she could take it ill, her Resentment of my Indifference may as probably occasion a Delay, as her taking it right.—Poor *Myrtle*, what Terrors must he be in all this while?—Since he knows she is offer'd to me, and refused to him, there is no conversing, or taking any measures, with
260 him, for his own Service—But I ought to bear with my Friend, and use him as one in Adversity;

All his Disquiets by my own I prove,
The greatest Grief's Perplexity in Love.

Exit.

[*The*] *End of the First Act.*

245 *Phillis*] ed.; *Lettice*   Although all editions including twentieth-century ones, with the exception of the Regents edition, read '*Lettice*', it is obvious from the context that Steele intended '*Phillis*'. In I. i Tom convinces Phillis to take Bevil's letter to Lucinda; the scene ends before they say good-bye, and presumably they arrange to meet again. When Bevil Junior inquires about the letter in I. ii, Tom undoubtedly refers to Phillis rather than a second maid. The error could have arisen from an illegible manuscript or from a careless mistake on the part of Steele who created a maid named Lettice in *The Lying Lover*.
260 But] O2; But But
263.1 *Exit*] ed.; *Exeunt*

Act II. Scene i.

Scene *Continues.*

Enter Bevil *junior and* Tom.

Tom. Sir, Mr. *Myrtle.*

Bevil junior. Very well,—do you step again, and wait for an Answer to my Letter.

[*Exit* Tom.]

Enter Myrtle.

Bevil junior. Well *Charles,* why so much Care in thy Countenance? Is there any thing in this World deserves it? You, who used to be 5 so Gay, so Open, so Vacant!

Myrtle. I think we have of late chang'd Complexions. You, who us'd to be much the graver Man, are now all Air in your Behaviour —But the Cause of my Concern, may, for ought I know, be the same Object that gives you all this Satisfaction. In a word, I am told that 10 you are this very Day (and your Dress confirms me in it) to be married to *Lucinda.*

Bevil junior. You are not misinform'd.—Nay, put not on the Terrors of a Rival, till you hear me out. I shall disoblige the best of Fathers, if I don't seem ready to marry *Lucinda:* And you know I 15 have ever told you, you might make use of my secret Resolution never to marry her, for your own service, as you please. But I am now driven to the extremity of immediately refusing, or complying, unless you help me to escape the Match.

Myrtle. Escape? Sir, neither her Merit or her Fortune are below 20 your Acceptance.—Escaping, do you call it!

Bevil junior. Dear Sir, do you wish I should desire the Match?

Myrtle. No—but such is my humorous and sickly state of Mind, since it has been able to relish nothing but *Lucinda,* that tho' I must owe my Happiness to your Aversion to this Marriage, I can't bear 25 to hear her spoken of with Levity or Unconcern.

Bevil junior. Pardon me, Sir; I shall transgress that way no more. She has Understanding, Beauty, Shape, Complexion, Wit—

Myrtle. Nay, dear *Bevil*, don't speak of her as if you lov'd her,
30 neither.

Bevil junior. Why then, to give you Ease at once, tho' I allow *Lucinda* to have good Sense, Wit, Beauty and Virtue; I know another, in whom these Qualities appear to me more amiable than in her.

35 *Myrtle*. There you spoke like a reasonable and good-natur'd Friend. When you acknowledge her Merit, and own your Pre-possession for another, at once, you gratify my Fondness, and cure my Jealousie.

Bevil junior. But all this while you take no notice, you have no
40 Apprehension of another Man, that has twice the Fortune of either of us.

Myrtle. *Cimberton*! Hang him, a Formal, Philosophical, Pedantick Coxcomb—For the Sot, with all these crude notions of divers things, under the direction of great Vanity, and very little Judgment,
45 shews his strongest Biass is Avarice; which is so predominant in him, that he will examine the Limbs of his Mistress with the Caution of a Jockey, and pays no more Compliment to her personal Charms, than if she were a meer breeding Animal.

Bevil junior. Are you sure that is not affected? I have known some
50 Women sooner set on fire by that sort of Negligence, than by—

Myrtle. No, no; hang him, the Rogue has no Art, it is pure simple Insolence and Stupidity.

Bevil junior. Yet, with all this, I don't take him for a Fool.

Myrtle. I own the Man is not a Natural; he has a very quick Sense,
55 tho' very slow Understanding.—He says indeed many things, that want only the circumstances of Time and Place to be very just and agreeable.

Bevil junior. Well, you may be sure of me, if you can disappoint him; but my Intelligence says, the Mother has actually sent for the
60 Conveyancer, to draw Articles for his Marriage with *Lucinda*; tho' those for mine with her, are, by her Father's Order, ready for sign-ing: but it seems she has not thought fit to consult either him or his Daughter in the matter.

Myrtle. Pshaw! A poor troublesome Woman—Neither *Lucinda* nor her Father will ever be brought to comply with it,—besides, I 65 am sure *Cimberton* can make no Settlement upon her, without the Concurrence of his great Uncle Sir *Geoffry* in the West.

Bevil junior. Well Sir, and I can tell you, that's the very Point that is now laid before her Council; to know whether a firm Settlement can be made, without this Uncle's actual joyning in it.—Now pray 70 consider, Sir, when my affair with *Lucinda* comes, as it soon must, to an open Rupture, how are you sure that *Cimberton's* Fortune may not then tempt her Father too, to hear his Proposals?

Myrtle. There you are right indeed, that must be provided against.—Do you know who are her Council? 75

Bevil junior. Yes, for your Service I have found out that too, they are Serjeant *Bramble* and Old *Target*—by the way, they are neither of 'em known in the Family; now I was thinking why you might not put a couple of false Council upon her, to delay and confound matters a little—besides, it may probably let you into the bottom 80 of her whole Design against you.

Myrtle. As how pray?

Bevil junior. Why, can't you slip on a Black Whig and a Gown, and be Old *Bramble* your self?

Myrtle. Ha! I don't dislike it—but what shall I do for a Brother 85 in the Case?

Bevil junior. What think you of my Fellow, *Tom*? the Rogue's intelligent, and is a good Mimick; all his part will be but to stutter heartily, for that's Old *Target's* Case—Nay, it would be an immoral thing to mock him, were it not that his Impertinence is the 90 occasion of its breaking out to that degree—the Conduct of the Scene will chiefly lye upon you.

Myrtle. I like it of all things; if you'll send *Tom* to my Chambers, I will give him full Instructions: This will certainly give me occasion to raise Difficulties, to puzzle, or confound her Project for a while, 95 at least.

Bevil junior. I'll warrant you Success; so far we are right then: And now, *Charles*, your apprehension of my marrying her, is all you have to get over.

Myrtle. Dear *Bevil*! tho' I know you are my Friend, yet when I 100 abstract my self from my own interest in the thing, I know no Objection she can make to you, or you to her, and therefore hope—

Bevil junior. Dear *Myrtle*, I am as much obliged to you for the
105 Cause of your Suspicion, as I am offended at the Effect: but be assured, I am taking measures for your certain Security, and that all things with regard to me will end in your entire Satisfaction.

Myrtle. Well, I'll promise you to be as easy and as confident as I can; tho' I cannot but remember that I have more than Life at
110 stake on your Fidelity. (*Going.*)

Bevil junior. Then depend upon it, you have no Chance against you.

Myrtle. Nay, no Ceremony, you know I must be going.

Exit Myrtle.

Bevil junior. Well! this is another Instance of the Perplexities
115 which arise too, in faithful Friendship: We must often, in this Life, go on in our good Offices, even under the Displeasure of those to whom we do them, in Compassion to their Weaknesses and Mistakes—But all this while poor *Indiana* is tortured with the Doubt of me! she has no Support or Comfort, but in my Fidelity, yet sees
120 me daily press'd to Marriage with another! How painful, in such a Crisis, must be every Hour she thinks on me? I'll let her see, at least, my Conduct to her is not chang'd: I'll take this Opportunity to visit her; for tho' the Religious Vow, I have made to my Father, restrains me from ever marrying, without his Approbation, yet
125 that confines me not from seeing a virtuous Woman, that is the pure Delight of my Eyes, and the guiltless Joy of my Heart: But the best Condition of Human Life is but a gentler Misery.

> *To hope for perfect Happiness is vain,*
> *And Love has ever its Allays of Pain.*

Exit.

[Act II. Scene ii.]

Enter Isabella, *and* Indiana *in her own Lodgings.*

Isabella. Yes—I say 'tis Artifice, dear Child; I say to thee again and again, 'tis all Skill and Management.

Indiana. Will you persuade me there can be an ill Design, in supporting me in the Condition of a Woman of Quality? attended, dress'd, and lodg'd like one; in my Appearance abroad, and my 5 Furniture at home, every way in the most sumptuous manner, and he that does it has an Artifice, a Design in it?

Isabella. Yes, yes.

Indiana. And all this without so much as explaining to me, that all about me comes from him!   10

Isabella. Ay, Ay,—the more for that—that keeps the Title to all you have, the more in Him.

Indiana. The more in Him!—He scorns the Thought—

Isabella. Then He—He—He—

Indiana. Well, be not so eager.—If he is an ill Man, let us look 15 into his Stratagems. Here is another of them. (*Shewing a Letter.*) Here's two hundred and fifty Pound in Bank Notes, with these Words, 'To pay for the Set of Dressing-plate, which will be brought home To-morrow.' Why dear Aunt, now here's another Piece of Skill for you, which I own I cannot comprehend—and it is with a 20 bleeding Heart I hear you say any thing to the Disadvantage of Mr. *Bevil.* When he is present, I look upon him as one to whom I owe my Life, and the Support of it; Then again, as the Man who loves me with Sincerity and Honour. When his Eyes are cast another way, and I dare survey him, my Heart is painfully divided between 25 Shame and Love—Oh! cou'd I tell you:—

Isabella. Ah! You need not: I imagine all this for you.

Indiana. This is my State of Mind in his Presence; and when he is absent you are ever dinning my Ears with Notions of the Arts of Men; that his hidden Bounty, his respectful Conduct, his careful 30

Provision for me, after his preserving me from utmost Misery, are certain Signs he means nothing, but to make I know not what of me?

Isabella. Oh! You have a sweet Opinion of him, truly.

35   *Indiana.* I have, when I am with him, ten thousand Things, besides my Sex's natural Decency and Shame, to suppress my Heart, that yearns to thank, to praise, to say it loves him: I say, thus it is with me while I see him; and in his Absence I am entertain'd with nothing but your Endeavours to tear this amiable Image from my 40 Heart; and, in its stead, to place a base Dissembler, an artful Invader of my Happiness, my Innocence, my Honour.

Isabella. Ah poor Soul! has not his Plot taken? don't you die for him? has not the way he has taken, been the most proper with you? Oh! ho! He has Sense, and has judg'd the thing 45 right.

Indiana. Go on then, since nothing can answer you: say what you will of him. Heigh! ho!

Isabella. Heigh! ho! indeed. It is better to say so, as you are now, than as many others are. There are, among the Destroyers of 50 Women, the Gentle, the Generous, the Mild, the Affable, the Humble, who all, soon after their Success in their Designs, turn to the contrary of those Characters. I will own to you, Mr. *Bevil* carries his Hypocrisie the best of any Man living, but still he is a Man, and therefore a Hypocrite. They have usurp'd an Exemption 55 from Shame, for any Baseness, any Cruelty towards us. They embrace without Love; they make Vows, without Conscience of Obligation; they are Partners, nay, Seducers to the Crime, wherein they pretend to be less guilty.

Indiana. (*Aside.*) That's truly observ'd. [*To* Isabella.] But what's 60 all this to *Bevil*?

Isabella. This it is to *Bevil*, and all Mankind. Trust not those, who will think the worse of you for your Confidence in them. Serpents, who lie in wait for Doves. Won't you be on your Guard against those who would betray you? Won't you doubt those who would 65 contemn you for believing 'em? Take it from me: Fair and natural Dealing is to invite Injuries, 'tis bleating to escape Wolves who would devour you! Such is the World,—(*Aside.*) and such (since the

Behaviour of one Man to my self) have I believ'd all the rest of the Sex.

Indiana. I will not doubt the Truth of *Bevil*, I will not doubt it; He 70 has not spoke it by an Organ that is given to lying: His Eyes are all that have ever told me that he was mine: I know his Virtue, I know his filial Piety, and ought to trust his Management with a Father, to whom he has uncommon Obligations. What have I to be concern'd for? my Lesson is very short. If he takes me for ever, my 75 purpose of Life is only to please him. If he leaves me (which Heaven avert) I know he'll do it nobly; and I shall have nothing to do but to learn to die, after worse than Death has happen'd to me.

Isabella. Ay do, persist in your Credulity! flatter your self that a Man of his Figure and Fortune will make himself the Jest of the 80 Town, and marry a handsome Beggar for Love.

Indiana. The Town! I must tell you, Madam, the Fools that laugh at Mr. *Bevil*, will but make themselves more ridiculous; his Actions are the Result of Thinking, and he has Sense enough to make even Virtue fashionable.   85

Isabella. O' my Conscience he has turn'd her Head—Come, come; if he were the honest Fool you take him for, why has he kept you here these three Weeks, without sending you to *Bristol*, in search of your Father, your Family, and your Relations?

Indiana. I am convinc'd he still designs it; and that nothing keeps 90 him here but the Necessity of not coming to a Breach with his Father, in regard to the Match he has propos'd him: Beside, has he not writ to *Bristol*? and has not he Advice that my Father has not been heard of there, almost these twenty Years?

Isabella. All Sham, meer Evasion; he is afraid, if he should carry 95 you thither, your honest Relations may take you out of his hands, and so blow up all his wicked Hopes at once.

Indiana. Wicked Hopes! did I ever give him any such?

Isabella. Has he ever given you any honest ones? can you say, in your Conscience, he has ever once offer'd to marry you?   100

Indiana. No! but by his Behaviour I am convinc'd he will offer it, the Moment 'tis in his Power, or consistent with his Honour, to make such a Promise good to me.

Isabella. His Honour!

105   *Indiana.* I will rely upon it; therefore desire you will not make my
Life uneasie, by these ungrateful Jealousies of one, to whom I am,
and wish to be oblig'd: For from his Integrity alone, I have
resolv'd to hope for Happiness.

    Isabella. Nay, I have done my Duty; if you won't see, at your
110 Peril be it—

    Indiana. Let it be—This is his hour of visiting me.

    Isabella. Oh! to be sure, keep up your Form; don't see him in a
Bed-chamber: (*Apart.*) This is pure Prudence, when she is liable,
where-ever he meets her, to be convey'd where-e'er he pleases.

115   *Indiana.* All the rest of my Life is but waiting till he comes: I live
only when I'm with him.

Exit.

    Isabella. Well, go thy ways, thou willful Innocent! I once had
almost as much Love for a Man, who poorly left me, to marry an
Estate—And I am now, against my Will, what they call an Old
120 Maid—but I will not let the Peevishness of that Condition grow
upon me—only keep up the Suspicion of it, to prevent this
Creature's being any other than a Virgin, except upon proper
Terms.

Exit.

[Act II. Scene iii.]

Re-enter Indiana *speaking to a* Servant.

   Indiana. Desire Mr. *Bevil* to walk in—

[*Exit* Servant.]

Design! impossible! A base designing Mind could never think of
what he hourly puts in practice—And yet, since the late Rumour of
his Marriage, he seems more reserv'd than formerly—he sends in
5 too, before he sees me, to know if I am at leisure—such new Respect
may cover Coldness in the Heart—it certainly makes me thought-

ful—I'll know the worst, at once; I'll lay such fair Occasions in his
way, that it shall be impossible to avoid an Explanation—for these
Doubts are insupportable!—But see! he comes, and clears them all.

Enter Bevil *junior.*

Bevil junior. Madam, your most Obedient—I am afraid I broke in 10
upon your Rest last Night—'twas very late before we parted; but
'twas your own Fault: I never saw you in such agreeable Humour.

Indiana. I am extremely glad we were both pleas'd; for I thought
I never saw you better Company.

Bevil junior. Me, Madam! you rally; I said very little.   15

Indiana. But, I am afraid, you heard me say a great deal; and when
a Woman is in the talking Vein, the most agreeable thing a Man
can do, you know, is to have Patience, to hear her.

Bevil junior. Then it's pity, Madam, you should ever be silent,
that we might be always agreeable to one another.   20

Indiana. If I had your Talent, or Power, to make my Actions speak
for me, I might indeed be silent, and yet pretend to something more
than the Agreeable.

Bevil junior. If I might be vain of any thing, in my Power, Madam,
'tis that my Understanding, from all your Sex, has mark'd you out, 25
as the most deserving Object of my Esteem.

Indiana. Should I think I deserve this, 'twere enough to make my
Vanity forfeit the very Esteem you offer me.

Bevil junior. How so, Madam?

Indiana. Because Esteem is the Result of Reason, and to deserve 30
it from good Sense, the Height of Human Glory: Nay, I had rather
a Man of Honour should pay me that, than all the Homage of a
sincere and humble Love.

Bevil junior. You certainly distinguish right, Madam; Love often
kindles from external Merit only—   35

Indiana. But Esteem arises from a higher Source, the Merit of
the Soul—

Bevil junior. True—And great Souls only can deserve it. (*Bowing
respectfully.*)

Indiana. Now, I think, they are greater still, that can so charitably 40
part with it.

Bevil junior. Now, Madam, you make me vain, since the utmost Pride, and Pleasure of my Life is, that I esteem you—as I ought.

Indiana. (*Aside.*) As he ought! still more perplexing! he neither
45 saves, nor kills my Hope.

Bevil junior. But Madam, we grow grave methinks—Let's find some other Subject—Pray how did you like the Opera last Night?

Indiana. First give me leave to thank you, for my Tickets.

Bevil junior. O! your Servant, Madam—But pray tell me, you
50 now, who are never partial to the Fashion, I fancy, must be the properest Judge of a mighty Dispute among the Ladies, that is, whether *Crispo* or *Griselda* is the more agreeable Entertainment.

Indiana. With submission now, I cannot be a proper Judge of this Question.

55   *Bevil junior.* How so, Madam?

Indiana. Because I find I have a Partiality for one of them.

Bevil junior. Pray which is that?

Indiana. I do not know—there's something in that Rural Cottage of *Griselda*, her forlorn Condition, her Poverty, her Solitude, her
60 Resignation, her Innocent Slumbers, and that lulling *Dolce Sogno* that's sung over her; it had an Effect upon me, that—in short I never was so well deceiv'd, at any of them.

Bevil junior. Oh! Now then, I can account for the Dispute: *Griselda*, it seems, is the Distress of an injur'd Innocent Woman: *Crispo*, that
65 only of a Man in the same Condition; therefore the Men are mostly concern'd for *Crispo*, and, by a Natural Indulgence, both Sexes for *Griselda*.

Indiana. So that Judgment, you think, ought to be for one, tho' Fancy and Complaisance have got ground for the other. Well! I
70 believe you will never give me leave to dispute with you on any Subject; for I own, *Crispo* has its Charms for me too: Though in the main, all the Pleasure the best Opera gives us, is but meer Sensation.—Methinks it's Pity the Mind can't have a little more Share in the Entertainment.—The Musick's certainly fine; but, in
75 my Thoughts, there's none of your Composers come up to Old *Shakespear* and *Otway*.

Bevil junior. How, Madam! why if a Woman of your Sense were to say this in the Drawing-Room—

Enter a Servant.

Servant. Sir, here's Signior *Carbonelli* says he waits your Commands, in the next Room.   80

Bevil junior. A propos! You were saying Yesterday, Madam, you had a mind to hear him—will you give him leave to entertain you now?

Indiana. By all means: desire the Gentleman to walk in.

Exit Servant.

Bevil junior. I fancy you will find something in this Hand, that is 85 uncommon.

Indiana. You are always finding ways, Mr. *Bevil*, to make Life seem less tedious to me.—

Enter Musick Master.

When the Gentleman pleases.

After a Sonata is play'd Bevil *junior waits on
the Master to the Door*, &c.

Bevil junior. You smile, Madam, to see me so Complaisant to one, 90 whom I pay for his Visit: Now, I own, I think it is not enough barely to pay those, whose Talents are superior to our own (I mean such Talents, as would become our Condition, if we had them.) Methinks we ought to do something more, than barely gratify them, for what they do at our Command, only because their Fortune is 95 below us.

Indiana. You say I smile: I assure you it was a Smile of Approbation; for indeed, I cannot but think it the distinguishing part of a Gentleman, to make his Superiority of Fortune as easy to his Inferiors, as he can.—(*Aside.*) Now once more to try him.—[*To* 100 Bevil *junior.*] I was saying just now, I believed you would never let me dispute with you, and I dare say, it will always be so: However I must have your Opinion upon a Subject, which created a Debate between my Aunt and me, just before you came hither; she would needs have it, that no Man ever does any extraordinary Kindness 105 or Service for a Woman, but for his own sake.

Bevil junior. Well Madam! Indeed I can't but be of her Mind.

Indiana. What, tho' he should maintain, and support her, without demanding any thing of her, on her part?

110 *Bevil junior.* Why, Madam, is making an Expence, in the Service of a Valuable Woman (for such I must suppose her) though she should never do him any Favour, nay, though she should never know who did her such Service, such a mighty Heroick Business?

115 *Indiana.* Certainly! I should think he must be a Man of an uncommon Mold.

Bevil junior. Dear Madam, why so? 'tis but, at best, a better Taste in Expence: To bestow upon one, whom he may think one of the Ornaments of the whole Creation, to be conscious, that from his 120 Superfluity, an Innocent, a Virtuous Spirit is supported above the Temptations and Sorrows of Life! That he sees Satisfaction, Health and Gladness in her Countenance, while he enjoys the Happiness of seeing her (as that I will suppose too, or he must be too abstracted, too insensible) I say, if he is allowed to delight in that 125 Prospect; alas! what mighty matter is there, in all this?

Indiana. No mighty matter, in so disinterested a Friendship!

Bevil junior. Disinterested! I can't think him so; your Hero, Madam, is no more, than what every Gentleman ought to be, and 130 I believe very many are—He is only one, who takes more delight in Reflections, than in Sensations: He is more pleased with Thinking, than Eating; that's the utmost you can say of him—Why, Madam, a greater Expence, than all this, Men lay out upon an unnecessary Stable of Horses.

135 *Indiana.* Can you be sincere, in what you say?

Bevil junior. You may depend upon it, if you know any such Man, he does not love Dogs inordinately.

Indiana. No, that he does not.

Bevil junior. Nor Cards, nor Dice.

140 *Indiana.* No.

Bevil junior. Nor Bottle Companions.

Indiana. No.

Bevil junior. Nor loose Women.

Indiana. No, I'm sure he does not.

Bevil junior. Take my Word then, if your admired Hero is not 145
liable to any of these kind of Demands, there's no such Preheminence
in this, as you imagine: Nay this way of Expence you speak of,
is what exalts and raises him, that has a Taste for it: And, at
the same time, his Delight is incapable of Satiety, Disgust, or
Penitence.   150

Indiana. But still I insist his having no private Interest in the
Action, makes it Prodigious, almost Incredible.

Bevil junior. Dear Madam, I never knew you more mistaken: Why,
who can be more an Usurer, than he, who lays out his Money in
such Valuable Purchases? If Pleasure be worth purchasing, how 155
great a Pleasure is it to him, who has a true Taste of Life, to ease an
Aking Heart, to see the humane Countenance lighted up, into
Smiles of Joy, on the Receipt of a Bit of Oar, which is superfluous,
and otherwise useless in a Man's own Pocket? What could a Man do
better with his Cash? This is the Effect of an humane Disposition, 160
where there is only a general Tye of Nature, and common Necessity.
What then must it be, when we serve an Object of Merit, of
Admiration!

Indiana. Well! the more you argue against it, the more I shall
admire the Generosity.   165

Bevil junior. Nay, nay—Then, Madam, 'tis time to fly, after a
Declaration, that my Opinion strengthens my Adversary's Argument—I had best hasten to my Appointment with Mr. *Myrtle*, and
begone, while we are Friends, and—before things are brought to
an Extremity—   170

Exit carelesly.

Enter Isabella.

Isabella. Well, Madam, what think you of him now pray?

Indiana. I protest, I begin to fear he is wholly disinterested, in
what he does for me. On my Heart, he has no other View, but the
meer Pleasure of doing it, and has neither Good or Bad Designs
upon me.   175

Isabella. Ah! dear Neice! don't be in fear of both! I'll warrant you,
you will know time enough, that he is not indifferent.

Indiana. You please me, when you tell me so: For, if he has any

Wishes towards me, I know he will not pursue them, but with
180 Honour.

Isabella. I wish, I were as confident of one, as t'other—I saw the
respectful Downcast of his Eye, when you catcht him gazing at
you during the Musick: He, I warrant, was surpriz'd, as if he
had been taken stealing your Watch. O! the undissembled Guilty
185 Look!

Indiana. But did you observe any such thing, Really? I thought he
look'd most Charmingly Graceful! How engaging is Modesty, in
a Man, when one knows there is a great Mind within—So tender a
Confusion! and yet, in other Respects, so much himself, so col-
190 lected, so dauntless, so determin'd!

Isabella. Ah! Neice! there is a sort of Bashfulness, which is the
best Engine to carry on a shameless Purpose: some Men's Modesty
serves their Wickedness, as Hypocrisy gains the Respect due to
Piety: But I will own to you, there is one hopeful Symptom, if there
195 could be such a thing, as a disinterested Lover; But it's all a Perplexity, till—till—till—

Indiana. Till what?

Isabella. Till I know whether Mr. *Myrtle* and Mr. *Bevil* are really
Friends, or Foes—And that I will be convinced of, before I sleep:
200 For you shall not be deceiv'd.

Indiana. I'm sure, I never shall, if your Fears can guard me: In the
mean time, I'll wrap my self up, in the Integrity of my own Heart,
nor dare to doubt of his.

> *As Conscious Honour all his Actions steers:*
205 > *So Conscious Innocence dispels my Fears.*

Exeunt.

[*The*] *End of the Second Act.*

Act III.

Scene, Sealand's *House.*

Enter Tom *meeting* Phillis.

Tom. Well, *Phillis!*—what, with a Face, as if you had never seen me before—(*Aside.*) What a Work have I to do now? She has seen some new Visitant, at their House, whose Airs she has catch'd, and is resolv'd to practise them upon me. Numberless are the Changes she'll dance thro', before she'll answer this plain Question; *videlicet,* 5 Have you deliver'd my Master's Letter to your Lady? Nay, I know her too well, to ask an Account of it, in an ordinary Way; I'll be in my Airs as well as she.—[*To* Phillis.] Well, Madam, as unhappy as you are, at present, pleased to make me, I would not, in the general, be any other than what I am; I would not be a bit wiser, a bit 10 richer, a bit taller, a bit shorter, than I am at this Instant. (*Looking stedfastly at her.*)

Phillis. Did ever any body doubt, Master *Thomas,* but that you were extremely satisfied with your sweet self?

Tom. I am indeed—The thing I have least reason to be satisfied 15 with, is my Fortune, and I am glad of my Poverty; Perhaps, if I were rich, I should overlook the finest Woman in the World, that wants nothing but Riches, to be thought so.

Phillis. (*Aside.*) How prettily was that said? But, I'll have a great deal more, before I'll say one Word. 20

Tom. I should, perhaps, have been stupidly above her, had I not been her Equal; and by not being her Equal, never had Opportunity of being her Slave. I am my Master's Servant, for Hire; I am my Mistress's, from Choice; wou'd she but approve my Passion.

Phillis. I think, it's the first Time I ever heard you speak of it, 25 with any Sense of the Anguish, if you really do suffer any.

Tom. Ah! *Phillis,* can you doubt, after what you have seen?

Phillis. I know not what I have seen, nor what I have heard; but since I'm at Leisure, you may tell me, When you fell in Love with

30 me; How you fell in Love with me; and what you have suffer'd, or
are ready to suffer for me.

Tom. (*Aside.*) Oh! the unmerciful Jade! when I'm in haste about
my Master's Letter—But, I must go thro' it.—[*To* Phillis.] Ah! too
well I remember when, and how, and on what Occasion I was first
35 surpriz'd. It was on the first of *April*, one thousand seven hundred
and fifteen, I came into Mr. *Sealand's* Service; I was then a Hobble-
de-Hoy, and you a pretty little tight Girl, a favourite Handmaid of
the Housekeeper.—At that Time, we neither of us knew what was
in us: I remember, I was order'd to get out of the Window, one pair
40 of Stairs, to rub the Sashes clean,—the Person employ'd, on the
innerside, was your Charming self, whom I had never seen before.

Phillis. I think, I remember the silly Accident: What made ye, you
Oaf, ready to fall down into the Street?

Tom. You know not, I warrant you—You could not guess what
45 surpriz'd me. You took no Delight, when you immediately grew
wanton, in your Conquest, and put your Lips close, and breath'd
upon the Glass, and when my Lips approach'd, a dirty Cloth you
rubb'd against my Face, and hid your beauteous Form; when I
again drew near, you spit, and rubb'd, and smil'd at my Undoing.
50 *Phillis.* What silly Thoughts you Men have!

Tom. We were *Pyramus* and *Thisbe*—but ten times harder was my
Fate; *Pyramus* could peep only through a Wall, I saw her, saw my
Thisbe in all her Beauty, but as much kept from her as if a hundred
Walls between, for there was more, there was her Will against me—
55 Would she but yet relent!—Oh, *Phillis! Phillis!* shorten my Torment,
and declare you pity me.

Phillis. I believe, it's very sufferable; the Pain is not so exquisite,
but that you may bear it, a little longer.

Tom. Oh! my charming *Phillis*, if all depended on my Fair One's
60 Will, I could with Glory suffer—But, dearest Creature, consider
our miserable State.

Phillis. How! Miserable!

Tom. We are miserable to be in Love, and under the Command of
others than those we love—with that generous Passion in the
65 Heart, to be sent to and fro on Errands, call'd, check'd and rated for
the meanest Trifles. Oh, *Phillis!* you don't know how many *China*

Cups, and Glasses, my Passion for you has made me break: You
have broke my Fortune, as well as my Heart.

Phillis. Well, Mr. *Thomas*, I cannot but own to you, that I believe,
your Master writes and you speak the best of any Men in the 70
World. Never was Woman so well pleas'd with a Letter, as my
young Lady was with his, and this is an Answer to it. (*Gives him a
Letter.*)

Tom. This was well done, my Dearest; consider, we must strike
out some pretty Livelyhood for our selves, by closing their Affairs: 75
It will be nothing for them to give us a little Being of our own, some
small Tenement, out of their large Possessions: whatever they give
us, 'twill be more than what they keep for themselves: one Acre,
with *Phillis*, wou'd be worth a whole County without her.

Phillis. O, could I but believe you!   80

Tom. If not the Utterance, believe the Touch of my Lips. (*Kisses
her.*)

Phillis. There's no contradicting you; how closely you argue,
Tom!

Tom. And will closer, in due time. But I must hasten with this 85
Letter, to hasten towards the Possession of you.—Then, *Phillis*,
consider, how I must be reveng'd, look to it, of all your Skittish-
ness, shy Looks, and at best but coy Compliances.

Phillis. Oh! *Tom*, you grow wanton, and sensual, as my Lady calls
it, I must not endure it; Oh! Foh! you are a Man, an odious filthy 90
Male Creature; you should behave, if you had a right Sense, or were
a Man of Sense, like Mr. *Cimberton*, with Distance, and Indifference;
or let me see, some other becoming hard Word, with seeming in-
in-inadvertency, and not rush on one as if you were seizing a Prey.
But Hush—the Ladies are coming—Good *Tom*, don't kiss me above 95
once, and be gone—Lard, we have been Fooling and Toying, and
not consider'd the main Business of our Masters and Mistresses.

Tom. Why, their Business is to be Fooling and Toying, as soon
as the Parchments are ready.

Phillis. Well remember'd—Parchments—my Lady, to my Know- 100
ledge, is preparing Writings between her Coxcomb Cousin
Cimberton, and my Mistress; though my Master has an Eye to the

95 Good] O2; God

Parchments already prepar'd between your Master Mr. *Bevil*, and
my Mistress; and I believe, my Mistress herself has sign'd, and seal'd,
105 in her Heart, to Mr. *Myrtle*.—Did I not bid you kiss me but once,
and be gone? but I know you won't be satisfy'd.

Tom. No, you smooth Creature, how should I! (*Kissing her
Hand.*)

Phillis. Well, since you are so humble, or so cool, as to ravish my
110 Hand only, I'll take my Leave of you like a great Lady, and you a
Man of Quality. (*They Salute formally.*)

Tom. Pox of all this State. (*Offers to kiss her more closely.*)

Phillis. No, pr'ythee, *Tom*, mind your Business. We must follow
that Interest which will take; but endeavour at that which will be
115 most for us, and we like most—O here's my young Mistress! (Tom
taps her Neck behind, and kisses his Fingers.) Go, ye liquorish Fool.

Exit Tom.

Enter Lucinda.

Lucinda. Who was that you was hurrying away?

Phillis. One that I had no mind to part with.

Lucinda. Why did you turn him away then?

120   *Phillis.* For your Ladyship's Service, to carry your Ladyship's
Letter to his Master: I could hardly get the Rogue away.

Lucinda. Why, has he so little Love for his Master?

Phillis. No; but he has so much Love for his Mistress.

Lucinda. But, I thought, I heard him kiss you. Why do you suffer
125 that?

Phillis. Why, Madam, we Vulgar take it to be a Sign of Love; we
Servants, we poor People, that have nothing but our Persons to
bestow, or treat for, are forc'd to deal, and bargain by way of
Sample; and therefore, as we have no Parchments, or Wax necessary
130 in our Agreements, we squeeze with our Hands, and seal with our
Lips, to ratifie Vows and Promises.

Lucinda. But can't you trust one another, without such Earnest
down?

Phillis. We don't think it safe, any more than you Gentry, to come
135 together without Deeds executed.

Lucinda. Thou art a pert merry Hussy.

Phillis. I wish, Madam, your Lover and you were as happy, as *Tom* and your Servant are.

Lucinda. You grow impertinent.

Phillis. I have done, Madam; and I won't ask you, what you intend 140 to do with Mr. *Myrtle*, what your Father will do with Mr. *Bevil*, nor what you all, especially my Lady, mean by admitting Mr. *Cimberton* as particularly here, as if he were married to you already; nay, you are married actually as far as People of Quality are.

Lucinda. How's that? 145

Phillis. You have different Beds in the same House.

Lucinda. Pshaw! I have a very great Value for Mr. *Bevil*, but have absolutely put an End to his Pretensions, in the Letter I gave you for him: But, my Father, in his Heart, still has a mind to him, were it not for this Woman they talk of; and, I am apt to imagine he is 150 married to her, or never designs to marry at all.

Phillis. Then Mr. *Myrtle*—

Lucinda. He had my Parents Leave to apply to me, and by that has won me, and my Affections: who is to have this Body of mine, without 'em, it seems, is nothing to me; my Mother says, it's 155 indecent for me to let my Thoughts stray about the Person of my Husband: nay, she says, a Maid, rigidly Virtuous, tho' she may have been where her Lover was a thousand times, should not have made Observations enough, to know him from another Man, when she sees him in a third Place. 160

Phillis. That is more than the Severity of a Nun, for not to see, when one may, is hardly possible; not to see when one can't, is very easy: at this rate, Madam, there are a great many whom you have not seen who—

Lucinda. Mamma says, the first time you see your Husband should 165 be at that Instant he is made so; when your Father, with the help of the Minister, gives you to him; then you are to see him, then you are to Observe and take Notice of him, because then you are to Obey him.

Phillis. But does not my Lady remember, you are to Love, as 170 well as Obey?

Lucinda. To Love is a Passion, 'tis a Desire, and we must have no Desires. Oh! I cannot endure the Reflection! With what Insensibility

on my Part, with what more than Patience, have I been expos'd, and
175 offer'd to some aukward Booby or other, in every County of *Great
Britain*?

Phillis. Indeed, Madam, I wonder, I never heard you speak of it
before, with this Indignation.

Lucinda. Every Corner of the Land has presented me with a
180 wealthy Coxcomb. As fast as one Treaty has gone off, another has
come on, till my Name and Person have been the Tittle Tattle of
the whole Town: What is this World come to! No Shame left! To
be barter'd for, like the Beasts of the Fields, and that, in such an
Instance, as coming together, to an intire Familiarity, and Union
185 of Soul and Body; Oh! and this, without being so much as Well-
wishers to each other, but for encrease of Fortune.

Phillis. But, Madam, all these Vexations will end, very soon, in
one for all: Mr. *Cimberton* is your Mother's Kinsman, and three
hundred Years an older Gentleman than any Lover you ever had;
190 for which Reason, with that of his prodigious large Estate, she is
resolved on him, and has sent to consult the Lawyers accordingly.
Nay, has (whether you know it or no) been in Treaty with Sir
Geoffry, who, to join in the Settlement, has accepted of a Sum to do
it, and is every Moment expected in Town for that Purpose.

195 *Lucinda.* How do you get all this Intelligence?

Phillis. By an Art I have, I thank my Stars, beyond all the Waiting-
maids in *Great-Britain*; the Art of List'ning, Madam, for your
Ladyship's Service.

Lucinda. I shall soon know as much as you do; leave me, leave me,
200 *Phillis*, be gone: Here, here, I'll turn you out. My Mother says I
must not converse with my Servants; tho' I must converse with
no one else.

Exit Phillis.

How unhappy are we, who are born to great Fortunes! No one
looks at us, with Indifference, or acts towards us on the Foot of
205 Plain Dealing; yet, by all I have been heretofore offer'd to, or
treated for, I have been us'd with the most agreeable of all Abuses,
Flattery; but now, by this Flegmatick Fool, I am us'd as nothing,
or a meer Thing; He, forsooth! is too wise, too learned to have any
regard to Desires, and, I know not what the learned Oaf calls

Sentiments of Love and Passion—Here he comes with my Mother— 210
It's much if he looks at me; or if he does, takes no more Notice of
me, than of any other Moveable in the Room.

Enter Mrs. Sealand, *and Mr.* Cimberton.

Mrs. Sealand. How do I admire this noble, this learned Taste of
yours, and the worthy Regard you have to our own ancient and
honourable House, in consulting a Means, to keep the Blood as pure, 215
and as regularly descended as may be.

Cimberton. Why, really Madam, the young Women of this Age are
treated with Discourses of such a Tendency, and their Imaginations
so bewilder'd in Flesh and Blood, that a Man of Reason can't talk
to be understood: They have no Ideas of Happiness, but what are 220
more gross than the Gratification of Hunger and Thirst.

Lucinda. (*Aside.*) With how much Reflection he is a Coxcomb?

Cimberton. And in Truth, Madam, I have consider'd it, as a most
brutal Custom, that Persons, of the first Character in the World, 225
should go as ordinarily, and with as little Shame, to Bed, as to
Dinner with one another. They proceed to the Propagation of the
Species, as openly, as to the Preservation of the Individual.

Lucinda. (*Aside.*) She that willingly goes to Bed to thee, must
have no Shame, I'm sure.   230

Mrs. Sealand. Oh Cousin *Cimberton*! Cousin *Cimberton*! how ab-
stracted, how refin'd, is your Sense of Things! But, indeed, it is
too true, there is nothing so ordinary as to say, in the best govern'd
Families, my Master and Lady are gone to Bed; one does not know
but it might have been said of one's self. (*Hiding her Face with her* 235
Fan.)

Cimberton. Lycurgus, Madam, instituted otherwise; among the
Lacedemonians, the whole Female World was pregnant, but none, but
the Mothers themselves, knew by whom; their Meetings were
secret, and the Amorous Congress always by Stealth; and no such 240
professed Doings between the Sexes, as are tolerated among us,
under the audacious Word, Marriage.

Mrs. Sealand. Oh! had I liv'd, in those Days, and been a Matron
of *Sparta,* one might, with less Indecency, have had ten Children,

245 according to that modest Institution, than one, under the Confusion of our modern, barefac'd manner.

Lucinda. (*Aside.*) And yet, poor Woman, she has gone thro' the whole Ceremony, and here I stand a melancholy Proof of it.

Mrs. Sealand. We will talk then of Business. That Girl walking
250 about the Room there is to be your Wife. She has, I confess, no Ideas, no Sentiments, that speak her born of a thinking Mother.

Cimberton. I have observ'd her; her lively Look, free Air, and disengag'd Countenance speak her very—

Lucinda. Very, What?

255 *Cimberton.* If you please, Madam—to set her a little that way.

Mrs. Sealand. *Lucinda*, say nothing to him, you are not a Match for him; when you are married, you may speak to such a Husband, when you're spoken to. But, I am disposing of you, above your self, every way.

260 *Cimberton.* Madam, you cannot but observe the Inconveniences I expose my self to, in hopes that your Ladyship will be the Consort of my better Part: As for the young Woman, she is rather an Impediment, than a Help, to a Man of Letters and Speculation. Madam, there is no Reflection, no Philosophy, can, at all times,
265 subdue the Sensitive Life, but the Animal shall sometimes carry away the Man: Ha! ay, the Vermilion of her Lips.

Lucinda. Pray, don't talk of me thus.

Cimberton. The pretty enough—Pant of her Bosom.

Lucinda. Sir; Madam, don't you hear him?

270 *Cimberton.* Her forward Chest.

Lucinda. Intollerable!

Cimberton. High Health.

Lucinda. The grave, easy Impudence of him!

Cimberton. Proud Heart.

275 *Lucinda.* Stupid Coxcomb!

Cimberton. I say, Madam, her Impatience, while we are looking at her, throws out all Attractions—her Arms—her Neck—what a Spring in her Step!

Lucinda. Don't you run me over thus, you strange Unaccount-
280 able!

Cimberton. What an Elasticity in her Veins and Arteries!

Lucinda. I have no Veins, no Arteries.

Mrs. Sealand. Oh, Child, hear him, he talks finely, he's a Scholar, he knows what you have.

Cimberton. The speaking Invitation of her Shape, the Gathering 285 of her self up, and the Indignation you see in the pretty little thing —now, I am considering her, on this Occasion, but as one that is to be pregnant.

Lucinda. (*Aside.*) The familiar, learned, unseasonable Puppy!

Cimberton. And pregnant undoubtedly she will be yearly. I fear, 290 I shan't, for many Years, have Discretion enough to give her one fallow Season.

Lucinda. Monster! there's no bearing it. The hideous Sot!— there's no enduring it, to be thus survey'd like a Steed at Sale.

Cimberton. At Sale! she's very illiterate—But she's very well 295 limb'd too; turn her in; I see what she is.

Exit Lucinda *in a Rage.*

Mrs. Sealand. Go, you Creature, I am asham'd of you.

Cimberton. No harm done—you know, Madam, the better sort of People, as I observ'd to you, treat by their Lawyers of Weddings (*Adjusting himself at the Glass.*) and the Woman in the Bargain, like 300 the Mansion-House in the Sale of the Estate, is thrown in, and what that is, whether good or bad, is not at all consider'd.

Mrs. Sealand. I grant it, and therefore make no Demand for her Youth, and Beauty, and every other Accomplishment, as the common World think 'em, because she is not Polite. 305

Cimberton. Madam, I know, your exalted Understanding, ab-stracted, as it is, from vulgar Prejudices, will not be offended, when I declare to you, I Marry to have an Heir to my Estate, and not to beget a Colony, or a Plantation: This young Woman's Beauty, and Constitution, will demand Provision for a tenth Child at least. 310

Mrs. Sealand. (*Aside.*) With all that Wit, and Learning, how con-siderate! What an Oeconomist!—[*To* Cimberton.] Sir, I cannot make her any other than she is; or say she is much better than the other young Women of this Age, or fit for much, besides being a Mother; but I have given Directions for the Marriage Settlements, 315 and Sir *Geoffry Cimberton's* Council is to meet ours here, at this Hour, concerning his joyning in the Deed, which when executed, makes you capable of settling what is due to *Lucinda's* Fortune: Her self, as I told you, I say nothing of.

320　*Cimberton.* No, no, no, indeed, Madam, it is not usual, and I must depend upon my own Reflection, and Philosophy, not to overstock my Family.

Mrs. Sealand. I cannot help her, Cousin *Cimberton*; but she is, for ought I see, as well as the Daughter of any body else.

325　*Cimberton.* That is very true, Madam.

Enter a Servant, who whispers Mrs. Sealand.

Mrs. Sealand. The Lawyers are come, and now we are to hear what they have resolv'd as to the point whether it's necessary that Sir *Geoffry* should join in the Settlement, as being what they call in the Remainder. But, good Cousin, you must have Patience with 'em.
330　These Lawyers, I am told, are of a different kind, one is what they call a Chamber-Council, the other a Pleader: The Conveyancer is slow, from an Imperfection in his Speech, and therefore shun'd the Bar, but extremely Passionate, and impatient of Contradiction: The other is as warm as he; but has a Tongue so voluble, and a Head so
335　conceited, he will suffer no body to speak but himself.

Cimberton. You mean old Serjeant *Target*, and Counsellor *Bramble*? I have heard of 'em.

Mrs. Sealand. The same: shew in the Gentlemen.

Exit Servant.

Re-enter Servant, introducing Myrtle *and* Tom, *disguis'd as* Bramble *and* Target.

Mrs. Sealand. Gentlemen, this is the Party concern'd, Mr. *Cimber-*
340　*ton*; and I hope you have consider'd of the matter.

Tom. Yes, Madam, we have agreed that it must be by Indent—dent—dent—dent—

Myrtle. Yes, Madam, Mr. Serjeant and my self have agreed, as he is pleas'd to inform you, that it must be an Indenture Tripartite,
345　and Tripartite let it be, for Sir *Geoffry* must needs be a Party; old *Cimberton*, in the Year 1619, says, in that ancient Roll, in Mr.

341–413 *Tom . . . Myrtle*] ed.; speech prefixes and stage directions read *Tar.* and *Bram.* throughout.

Serjeant's Hands, as recourse thereto being had, will more at large
appear—

Tom. Yes, and by the Deeds in your Hands, it appears, that—

Myrtle. Mr. Serjeant, I beg of you to make no Inferences upon 350
what is in our Custody; but speak to the Titles in your own Deeds
—I shall not show that Deed till my Client is in Town.

Cimberton. You know best your own Methods.

Mrs. Sealand. The single Question is, whether the Intail is such,
that my Cousin Sir *Geoffry* is necessary in this Affair?   355

Myrtle. Yes, as to the Lordship of *Tretriplet*, but not as to the
Messuage of *Grimgribber*.

Tom. I say that *Gr—Gr—*that *Gr—Gr—Grimgribber*, *Grimgribber*
is in us. That is to say the remainder thereof, as well as that of
Tr—tr—Triplet.   360

Myrtle. You go upon the Deed of Sir *Ralph*, made in the middle of
the last Century, precedent to that in which old *Cimberton* made
over the Remainder, and made it pass to the Heirs general, by
which your Client comes in; and I question whether the Remainder
even of *Tretriplet* is in him—But we are willing to wave that, and 365
give him a valuable Consideration. But we shall not purchase what
is in us for ever, as *Grimgribber* is, at the rate as we guard against the
Contingent of Mr. *Cimberton* having no Son—Then we know Sir
Geoffry is the first of the Collateral Male Line in this Family—
Yet—   370

Tom. Sir, *Gr—gr—ber* is—

Myrtle. I apprehend you very well, and your Argument might be
of Force, and we would be inclin'd to hear that in all its Parts—But,
Sir, I see very plainly what you are going into—I tell you, it is as
probable a Contingent that Sir *Geoffry* may die before Mr. *Cimberton*, 375
as that he may outlive him.

Tom. Sir, we are not ripe for that yet, but I must say—

Myrtle. Sir, I allow you the whole extent of that Argument; but
that will go no farther than as to the Claimants under old *Cimberton*,
—I am of Opinion, that according to the Instruction of Sir *Ralph*, he 380
could not dock the Entail, and then create a new Estate for the
Heirs General.

Tom. Sir, I have not patience to be told that, when *Gr—gr—ber—*

Myrtle. I will allow it you, Mr. Serjeant; but there must be the
385 word Heirs for ever, to make such an Estate as you pretend.

Cimberton. I must be impartial, tho' you are Council for my side of
the Question—Were it not that you are so good as to allow him
what he has not said, I should think it very hard you should answer
him without hearing him—But Gentlemen, I believe you have both
390 consider'd this matter, and are firm in your different Opinions:
'Twere better therefore you proceeded according to the particular
Sense of each of you, and gave your Thoughts distinctly in Writing
—And do you see, Sirs, pray let me have a Copy of what you say,
in *English*.

395 *Myrtle.* Why, what is all we have been saying?—In *English*! Oh!
but I forgot my self, you're a Wit—But however, to please you, Sir,
you shall have it, in as plain terms, as the Law will admit of.

Cimberton. But I would have it, Sir, without delay.

Myrtle. That, Sir, the Law will not admit of: the Courts are
400 sitting at *Westminster*, and I am this moment oblig'd to be at every
one of them, and 'twould be wrong if I should not be in the Hall to
attend one of 'em at least, the rest would take it ill else—Therefore,
I must leave what I have said to Mr. Serjeant's Consideration, and
I will digest his Arguments on my part, and you shall hear from
405 me again, Sir.

Exit Myrtle.

Tom. Agreed, agreed.

Cimberton. Mr. *Bramble* is very quick—He parted a little abruptly.

Tom. He could not bear my Argument, I pincht him to the quick
about that *Gr—gr—ber.*

410 *Mrs. Sealand.* I saw that, for he durst not so much as hear you—I
shall send to you, Mr. Serjeant, as soon as Sir *Geoffry* comes to Town,
and then I hope all may be adjusted.

Tom. I shall be at my Chambers, at my usual Hours.

Exit.

Cimberton. Madam, if you please, I'll now attend you to the Tea-
415 Table, where I shall hear from your Ladyship, Reason, and good
Sense, after all this Law and Gibberish.

Mrs. Sealand. 'Tis a wonderful thing, Sir, that Men of Professions
do not study to talk the Substance of what they have to say, in the

Language of the rest of the World: Sure, they'd find their Account
in it.   420

Cimberton. They might, perhaps, Madam, with People of your
good Sense; but, with the generality 'twould never do: The Vulgar
would have no respect for Truth and Knowledge, if they were
exposed to naked View.

> *Truth is too simple, of all Art bereav'd:*   425
> *Since the World will—why let it be deceiv'd.*

Exeunt.

[*The*] *End of the Third Act.*

Act IV. Scene i.

Scene, Bevil *junior's Lodgings.*

Bevil *junior with a Letter in his Hand,*
follow'd by Tom.

Tom. Upon my Life, Sir, I know nothing of the matter: I never
open'd my Lips to Mr. *Myrtle,* about any thing of your Honour's
Letter to Madam *Lucinda.*

Bevil junior. [*Aside.*] What's the Fool in such a fright for? [*To*
Tom.] I don't suppose you did: What I would know is, whether Mr.   5
Myrtle shew'd any Suspicion, or ask'd you any Questions, to lead
you to say casually, that you had carry'd any such Letter, for me,
this Morning.

Tom. Why, Sir, if he did ask me any Questions, how could I
help it?   10

Bevil junior. I don't say you could, Oaf! I am not questioning you,
but him: What did he say to you?

Tom. Why, Sir, when I came to his Chambers, to be dress'd for
the Lawyer's Part, your Honour was pleas'd to put me upon, he

15 ask'd me, if I had been at Mr. *Sealand's* this Morning?—So I told
him, Sir, I often went thither—because, Sir, if I had not said that,
he might have thought, there was something more, in my going
now, than at another time.

    Bevil junior. Very well!—(*Aside.*) The Fellow's Caution, I find,
20 has given him this Jealousy. [*To* Tom.] Did he ask you no other
Questions?

    Tom. Yes, Sir—now I remember, as we came away in the Hackney
Coach, from Mr. *Sealand's, Tom,* says he, as I came in to your Master,
this Morning, he bad you go for an Answer to a Letter he had sent.
25 Pray did you bring him any? says he—Ah! says I, Sir, your Honour
is pleas'd to joke with me, you have a mind to know whether I can
keep a Secret, or no?

    Bevil junior. And so, by shewing him you could, you told him you
had one?

30   *Tom.* Sir—(*Confus'd.*)

    Bevil junior. [*Aside.*] What mean Actions does Jealousy make a
Man stoop to? How poorly has he us'd Art, with a Servant, to make
him betray his Master? [*To* Tom.] Well! and when did he give you
this Letter for me?

35   *Tom.* Sir, he writ it, before he pull'd off his Lawyer's Gown, at
his own Chambers.

    Bevil junior. Very well; and what did he say, when you brought
him my Answer to it?

    Tom. He look'd a little out of Humour, Sir, and said, It was very
40 well.

    Bevil junior. I knew he would be grave upon't,—wait with-
out.

    Tom. Humh! 'gad, I don't like this; I am afraid we are all in the
wrong Box here.—

                               Exit Tom.

45   *Bevil junior.* I put on a Serenity, while my Fellow was present:
But I have never been more thoroughly disturb'd; This hot Man!
to write me a Challenge, on supposed artificial Dealing, when I
profess'd my self his Friend! I can live contented without Glory;
but I cannot suffer Shame. What's to be done? But first, let me
50 consider *Lucinda's* Letter again. (*Reads.*)

SIR,

I Hope it is consistent with the Laws a Woman ought to impose upon
her self, to acknowledge, that your manner of declining a Treaty of
Marriage, in our Family, and desiring the Refusal may come from
hence, has something more engaging in it, than the Courtship of him, 55
who, I fear, will fall to my Lot; except your Friend exerts himself, for
our common Safety, and Happiness: I have Reasons for desiring Mr.
Myrtle *may not know of this Letter, till hereafter, and am your most*
oblig'd humble Servant,

Lucinda Sealand. 60

Well, but the Postscript. (*Reads.*)

I won't, upon second Thoughts, hide any thing from you. But, my
Reason for concealing this is, that Mr. Myrtle *has a Jealousy in his*
Temper, which gives me some Terrors; but my Esteem for him inclines
me to hope that only an ill Effect, which sometimes accompanies a 65
Tender Love; and what may be cur'd, by a careful and unblameable
Conduct.

Thus has this Lady made me her Friend and Confident, and put
her self, in a kind, under my Protection: I cannot tell him immediately the Purport of her Letter, except I could cure him of the 70
violent and untractable Passion of Jealousy, and so serve him, and
her, by disobeying her, in the Article of Secrecy, more than I should
by complying with her Directions—But then this Duelling, which
Custom has impos'd upon every Man, who would live with Reputation and Honour in the World:—How must I preserve my self 75
from Imputations there? He'll, forsooth, call it, or think it Fear,
if I explain without Fighting—But his Letter—I'll read it
again.—

SIR,

You have us'd me basely, in corresponding, and carrying on a Treaty, 80
where you told me you were indifferent: I have chang'd my Sword, since
I saw you; which Advertisement I thought proper to send you against
the next Meeting, between you, and the injur'd

Charles Myrtle.

Enter Tom.

85   *Tom.* Mr. *Myrtle*, Sir: would your Honour please to see him?
    Bevil junior. Why you stupid Creature! Let Mr. *Myrtle* wait at my
    Lodgings! Shew him up.

                                                           Exit Tom.

    Well! I am resolv'd upon my Carriage to him—He is in Love, and
    in every circumstance of Life a little distrustful, which I must allow
90 for—but here he is.

Enter Tom *introducing* Myrtle.

    Sir, I am extremely oblig'd to you for this Honour,—But, Sir,
    You, with your very discerning Face, leave the Room.

                                                           Exit Tom.

    Well, Mr. *Myrtle*, your Commands with me?
    Myrtle. The Time, the Place, our long Acquaintance, and many
95 other Circumstances, which affect me on this Occasion, oblige me,
    without farther Ceremony, or Conference, to desire you would not
    only, as you already have, acknowledge the Receipt of my Letter,
    but also comply with the Request in it. I must have farther Notice
    taken of my Message than these half Lines,—I have yours,—I shall
100 be at home.—
    Bevil junior. Sir, I own, I have received a Letter from you, in a very
    unusual Style; But as I design every thing, in this Matter, shall
    be your own Action, your own Seeking, I shall understand nothing,
    but what you are pleas'd to confirm, Face to Face, and I have
105 already forgot the Contents of your Epistle.
    Myrtle. This cool Manner is very agreeable to the Abuse you
    have already made of my Simplicity and Frankness; and I see your
    Moderation tends to your own Advantage, and not mine; to your
    own Safety, not Consideration of your Friend.
110 *Bevil junior.* My own Safety, Mr. *Myrtle*!
    Myrtle. Your own Safety, Mr. *Bevil*.
    Bevil junior. Look you, Mr. *Myrtle*, there's no disguising that I
    understand what you would be at—But, Sir, you know, I have often
    dared to disapprove of the Decisions a Tyrant Custom has intro-
115 duc'd, to the Breach of all Laws, both Divine and Human.

Myrtle. Mr. *Bevil*, Mr. *Bevil*, it would be a good first Principle, in those who have so tender a Conscience that way, to have as much Abhorrence of doing Injuries, as—

Bevil junior. As what?

Myrtle. As Fear of answering for 'em.   120

Bevil junior. As Fear of answering for 'em! But that Apprehension is Just or Blameable, according to the Object of that Fear.—I have often told you in Confidence of Heart, I abhorr'd the Daring to offend the Author of Life, and rushing into his Presence.—I say, by the very same Act, to commit the Crime against him, and immedi- 125 ately to urge on to his Tribunal.

Myrtle. Mr. *Bevil*, I must tell you, this Coolness, this Gravity, this Shew of Conscience, shall never cheat me of my Mistress. You have, indeed, the best Excuse for Life, the Hopes of possessing *Lucinda*: But consider, Sir, I have as much Reason to be weary of it, 130 if I am to lose her; and my first Attempt to recover her, shall be to let her see the Dauntless Man, who is to be her Guardian and Protector.

Bevil junior. Sir, shew me but the least Glimpse of Argument, that I am authoriz'd, by my own Hand, to vindicate any lawless 135 Insult of this nature, and I will shew thee—to chastize thee—hardly deserves the Name of Courage—slight, inconsiderate Man!—There is, Mr. *Myrtle*, no such Terror in quick Anger; and you shall, you know not why, be cool, as you have, you know not why, been warm.   140

Myrtle. Is the Woman one loves, so little an Occasion of Anger? You perhaps, who know not what it is to love, who have your Ready, your Commodious, your Foreign Trinket, for your loose Hours; and from your Fortune, your specious outward Carriage, and other lucky Circumstances, as easie a Way to the Possession of 145 a Woman of Honour; you know nothing of what it is to be alarm'd, to be distracted, with Anxiety and Terror of losing more than Life: Your Marriage, happy Man! goes on like common Business, and in the interim, you have your Rambling Captive, your *Indian* Princess, for your soft Moments of Dalliance, your Convenient, your Ready 150 *Indiana.*

Bevil junior. You have touch'd me beyond the Patience of a Man;

and I'm excusable, in the Guard of Innocence (or from the Infirmity of Human Nature, which can bear no more) to accept your Invita-
155 tion, and observe your Letter—Sir, I'll attend you.

Enter Tom.

Tom. Did you call, Sir? I thought you did: I heard you speak aloud.

Bevil junior. Yes, go call a Coach.

Tom. Sir,—Master—Mr. *Myrtle,*—Friends—Gentlemen—what
160 d'ye mean? I am but a Servant, or—

Bevil junior. Call a Coach.

Exit Tom.

A long Pause, walking sullenly by each other.

(*Aside.*) Shall I (though provok'd to the Uttermost) recover my self at the Entrance of a third Person, and that my Servant too, and not have Respect enough to all I have ever been receiving from Infancy,
165 the Obligation to the best of Fathers, to an unhappy Virgin too, whose Life depends on mine. (*Shutting the Door.*)

(*To* Myrtle.) I have, thank Heaven, had time to recollect my self, and shall not, for fear of what such a rash Man as you think of me, keep longer unexplain'd the false Appearances, under which your
170 Infirmity of Temper makes you suffer; when, perhaps, too much Regard to a false Point of Honour, makes me prolong that Suffering.

Myrtle. I am sure, Mr. *Bevil* cannot doubt, but I had rather have Satisfaction from his Innocence, than his Sword.

Bevil junior. Why then would you ask it first that Way?
175 *Myrtle.* Consider, you kept your Temper your self no longer than till I spoke to the Disadvantage of her you lov'd.

Bevil junior. True. But let me tell you, I have sav'd you from the most exquisite Distress, even tho' you had succeeded in the Dispute: I know you so well, that I am sure, to have found this Letter about
180 a Man you had kill'd, would have been worse than Death to your self—Read it—.[*Aside.*] When he is thoroughly mortify'd, and Shame has got the better of Jealousie, when he has seen himself throughly, he will deserve to be assisted towards obtaining *Lucinda.*

Myrtle. [*Aside.*] With what a Superiority has he turn'd the Injury 185
on me, as the Aggressor? I begin to fear, I have been too far transported—*A Treaty in our Family*! is not that saying too much? I shall
relapse—But, I find (on the Postscript) *something like Jealousie*—with
what Face can I see my Benefactor? my Advocate? whom I have
treated like a Betrayer.—[*To* Bevil *junior.*] Oh! *Bevil*, with what 190
Words shall I—

Bevil junior. There needs none; to convince, is much more than
to conquer.

Myrtle. But can you—

Bevil junior. You have o'erpaid the Inquietude you gave me, in 195
the Change I see in you towards me: Alas! what Machines are we!
thy Face is alter'd to that of another Man; to that of my Companion,
my Friend.

Myrtle. That I could be such a precipitant Wretch!

Bevil junior. Pray no more.   200

Myrtle. Let me reflect how many Friends have died, by the Hands
of Friends, for want of Temper; and you must give me Leave to say
again, and again, how much I am beholden to that Superior Spirit you
have subdu'd me with—what had become of one of us, or perhaps
both, had you been as weak as I was, and as incapable of Reason? 205

Bevil junior. I congratulate to us both the Escape from our selves,
and hope the Memory of it will make us Dearer Friends than
ever.

Myrtle. Dear *Bevil*, your Friendly Conduct has convinc'd me that
there is nothing manly, but what is conducted by Reason, and 210
agreeable to the Practice of Virtue and Justice. And yet, how many
have been sacrific'd to that Idol, the Unreasonable Opinion of Men!
Nay, they are so ridiculous in it, that they often use their Swords
against each other, with Dissembled Anger, and Real Fear.

> *Betray'd by Honour, and compell'd by Shame,*   215
> *They hazard Being, to preserve a Name:*
> *Nor dare enquire into the dread Mistake,*
> *'Till plung'd in sad Eternity they Wake.*

Exeunt.

[Act IV. Scene ii.]

Scene *St.* James's *Park.*

Enter Sir John Bevil, *and Mr.* Sealand.

Sir John Bevil. Give me leave, however, Mr. *Sealand*, as we are upon a Treaty for Uniting our Families, to mention only the Business of an ancient House—Genealogy and Descent are to be of some Consideration, in an Affair of this sort—

5 *Mr. Sealand.* Genealogy, and Descent!—Sir, there has been in our Family a very large one. There was *Galfrid* the Father of *Edward*, the Father of *Ptolomey*, the Father of *Crassus*, the Father of Earl *Richard*, the Father of *Henry* the Marquis, the Father of Duke *John*—

Sir John Bevil. What, do you rave, Mr. *Sealand*? all these great 10 Names in your Family?

Mr. Sealand. These? yes, Sir—I have heard my Father name 'em all, and more.

Sir John Bevil. Ay, Sir?—and did he say they were all in your Family?

15 *Mr. Sealand.* Yes, Sir, he kept 'em all—he was the greatest Cocker in *England*—he said, Duke *John* won him many Battles, and never lost one.

Sir John Bevil. Oh Sir, your Servant, you are laughing at my laying any Stress upon Descent—But I must tell you Sir, I never 20 knew any one, but he that wanted that Advantage, turn it into Ridicule.

Mr. Sealand. And I never knew any one, who had many better Advantages, put that into his Account—But, Sir *John*, value your self as you please upon your ancient House, I am to talk freely of 25 every thing, you are pleas'd to put into your Bill of Rates, on this Occasion—yet, Sir, I have made no Objections to your Son's Family —'Tis his Morals, that I doubt.

Sir John Bevil. Sir, I can't help saying, that what might injure a Citizen's Credit, may be no Stain to a Gentleman's Honour.

Mr. Sealand. Sir *John,* the Honour of a Gentleman is liable to be 30
tainted, by as small a matter as the Credit of a Trader; we are
talking of a Marriage, and in such a Case, the Father of a young
Woman will not think it an Addition, to the Honour, or Credit of
her Lover—that he is a Keeper—

Sir John Bevil. Mr. *Sealand,* don't take upon you, to spoil my Son's 35
Marriage, with any Woman else.

Mr. Sealand. Sir *John,* let him apply to any Woman else, and have
as many Mistresses as he pleases—

Sir John Bevil. My Son, Sir, is a discreet and sober Gentle-
man—   40

Mr. Sealand. Sir, I never saw a Man that wench'd soberly and
discreetly, that ever left it off—the Decency observ'd in the Practice, hides, even from the Sinner, the Iniquity of it. They pursue
it, not that their Appetites hurry 'em away; but, I warrant you,
because, 'tis their Opinion, they may do it.   45

Sir John Bevil. Were what you suspect a Truth—do you design
to keep your Daughter a Virgin, 'till you find a Man unblemish'd
that way?

Mr. Sealand. Sir, as much a Cit as you take me for—I know the
Town, and the World—and give me leave to say, that we Merchants 50
are a Species of Gentry, that have grown into the World this last
Century, and are as honourable, and almost as useful, as you landed
Folks, that have always thought your selves so much above us; For
your trading, forsooth! is extended no farther, than a Load of Hay,
or a fat Ox—You are pleasant People, indeed; because you are 55
generally bred up to be lazy, therefore, I warrant you, Industry
is dishonourable.

Sir John Bevil. Be not offended, Sir; let us go back to our
Point.

Mr. Sealand. Oh! not at all offended—but I don't love to leave any 60
part of the Account unclos'd—look you, Sir *John,* Comparisons are
odious, and more particularly so, on Occasions of this Kind, when
we are projecting Races, that are to be made out of both Sides of
the Comparisons.

Sir John Bevil. But, my Son, Sir, is, in the Eye of the World, a 65
Gentleman of Merit.

Mr. Sealand. I own to you, I think him so.—But, Sir *John*, I am a Man exercis'd, and experienc'd in Chances, and Disasters; I lost, in my earlier Years, a very fine Wife, and with her a poor little Infant; 70 this makes me, perhaps, over cautious, to preserve the second Bounty of Providence to me, and be as careful, as I can, of this Child—you'll pardon me, my poor Girl, Sir, is as valuable to me, as your boasted Son, to you.

Sir John Bevil. Why, that's one very good Reason, Mr. *Sealand*, 75 why I wish my Son had her.

Mr. Sealand. There is nothing, but this strange Lady here, this *Incognita*, that can be objected to him—here and there a Man falls in Love with an artful Creature, and gives up all the Motives of Life, to that one Passion.

80   *Sir John Bevil.* A Man of my Son's Understanding, cannot be suppos'd to be one of them.

Mr. Sealand. Very wise Men have been so enslav'd; and, when a Man marries with one of them upon his Hands, whether mov'd from the Demand of the World, or slighter Reasons; such a Husband 85 soils with his Wife for a Month perhaps—then Good B'w'y' Madam —the Show's over—ah! *John Dryden* points out such a Husband to a Hair, where he says,

> ' *And while abroad so prodigal the Dolt is,*
> ' *Poor Spouse at home as ragged as a Colt is.*

90 Now in plain Terms, Sir, I shall not care to have my poor Girl turn'd a grazing, and that must be the Case, when—

Sir John Bevil. But pray consider, Sir, my Son—

Mr. Sealand. Look you Sir, I'll make the Matter short: This unknown Lady, as I told you, is all the Objection I have to him: 95 But, one way or other, he is, or has been, certainly engag'd to her— I am therefore resolv'd, this very Afternoon, to visit her: Now from her Behaviour, or Appearance, I shall soon be let into, what I may fear, or hope for.

Sir John Bevil. Sir, I am very confident, there can be Nothing 100 enquir'd into, relating to my Son, that will not, upon being understood, turn to his Advantage.

Mr. Sealand. I hope that, as sincerely, as you believe it—Sir *John*

Bevil, when I am satisfied, in this great Point, if your Son's Conduct answers the Character you give him, I shall wish your Alliance more than that of any Gentleman in *Great Britain*, and so your 105 Servant.

Exit.

Sir John Bevil. He is gone, in a Way but barely Civil; but his great Wealth, and the Merit of his only Child, the Heiress of it, are not to be lost for a little Peevishness—

Enter Humphrey.

Oh! *Humphrey*, you are come in a seasonable Minute; I want to talk 110 to thee, and to tell thee, that my Head and Heart are on the Rack, about my Son.

Humphrey. Sir, you may trust his Discretion, I am sure you may.

Sir John Bevil. Why, I do believe I may, and yet I'm in a thousand 115 Fears, when I lay this vast Wealth before me: When I consider his Prepossessions, either generous, to a Folly, in an honourable Love; or abandon'd, past Redemption, in a vicious One; and, from the one or the other, his Insensibility to the fairest Prospect, towards doubling our Estate: a Father, who knows how useful Wealth is, 120 and how necessary, even to those who despise it, I say a Father, *Humphrey*, a Father cannot bear it.

Humphrey. Be not transported, Sir; you will grow incapable of taking any Resolution, in your perplexity.

Sir John Bevil. Yet, as angry as I am with him, I would not have 125 him surpriz'd in any thing—This Mercantile rough Man may go grosly into the Examination of this matter, and talk to the Gentlewoman so as to—

Humphrey. No, I hope, not in an abrupt manner.

Sir John Bevil. No, I hope not! Why, dost thou know any thing 130 of her, or of him, or of any thing of it, or all of it?

Humphrey. My dear Master, I know so much; that I told him this very Day, you had Reason to be secretly out of Humour about her.

Sir John Bevil. Did you go so far? Well, what said he to that?

Humphrey. His Words were, looking upon me stedfastly: *Hum-* 135 *phrey*, says he, That Woman is a Woman of Honour.

Sir John Bevil. How! Do you think he is married to her, or designs to marry her?

Humphrey. I can say nothing to the latter—But he says, he can
140 marry no one without your Consent, while you are living.

Sir John Bevil. If he said so much, I know he scorns to break his Word with me.

Humphrey. I am sure of that.

Sir John Bevil. You are sure of that—Well! that's some Comfort—
145 Then I have nothing to do but to see the bottom of this matter, during this present Ruffle—Oh, *Humphrey*—

Humphrey. You are not ill, I hope, Sir.

Sir John Bevil. Yes, a Man is very ill, that's in a very ill Humour: To be a Father, is to be in Care for one, whom you oftner disoblige,
150 than please, by that very Care—Oh! that Sons could know the Duty to a Father, before they themselves are Fathers—But, perhaps, you'll say now, that I am one of the happiest Fathers in the World; but, I assure you, that of the very happiest is not a Condition to be envied.

155 *Humphrey.* Sir, your Pain arises, not from the Thing it self, but your particular Sense of it—You are over-fond, nay, give me leave to say, you are unjustly apprehensive from your Fondness: My Master *Bevil* never disoblig'd you, and he will, I know he will, do every thing you ought to expect.

160 *Sir John Bevil.* He won't take all this Money with this Girl—For ought I know, he will, forsooth, have so much Moderation, as to think he ought not to force his Liking for any Consideration.

Humphrey. He is to marry her, not you; he is to live with her, not you, Sir.

165 *Sir John Bevil.* I know not what to think: But, I know, nothing can be more miserable than to be in this Doubt.—Follow me; I must come to some Resolution.

Exeunt.

[Act IV. Scene iii.]

Scene, Bevil *junior's Lodgings*.

Enter Tom *and* Phillis.

Tom. Well, Madam, if you must speak with Mr. *Myrtle*, you shall; he is now with my Master in the Library.

Phillis. But you must leave me alone with him, for he can't make me a Present, nor I so handsomly take any thing from him, before you; it would not be decent.   5

Tom. It will be very decent, indeed, for me to retire, and leave my Mistress with another Man.

Phillis. He is a Gentleman, and will treat one properly—

Tom. I believe so—but, however, I won't be far off, and therefore will venture to trust you: I'll call him to you.   10

Exit Tom.

Phillis. What a deal of Pother, and Sputter here is, between my Mistress, and Mr. *Myrtle*, from meer Punctilio? I could any hour of the Day get her to her Lover, and would do it—But she, forsooth, will allow no Plot to get him; but, if he can come to her, I know she would be glad of it: I must therefore do her an acceptable 15 Violence, and surprize her into his Arms. I am sure I go by the best Rule imaginable: If she were my Maid, I should think her the best Servant in the World for doing so by me.

Enter Myrtle *and* Tom.

Oh Sir! You and Mr. *Bevil* are fine Gentlemen, to let a Lady remain under such Difficulties as my poor Mistress, and no Attempt to set 20 her at Liberty, or release her from the Danger of being instantly married to *Cimberton*.

Myrtle. *Tom* has been telling—But what is to be done?

Phillis. What is to be done—when a Man can't come at his Mistress!—Why, can't you fire our House, or the next House to 25 us, to make us run out and you take us?

Myrtle. How, Mrs. *Phillis*—

Phillis. Ay—let me see that Rogue deny to fire a House, make a
Riot, or any other little thing, when there were no other Way to
30 come at me.

Tom. I am oblig'd to you, Madam.

Phillis. Why, don't we hear every day of People's hanging themselves for Love, and won't they venture the Hazard of being hang'd
for Love?—Oh! were I a Man—

35 *Myrtle.* What manly thing would you have me undertake?
according to your Ladyship's Notion of a Man.

Phillis. Only be at once, what, one Time or other, you may be,
and wish to be, or must be.

Myrtle. Dear Girl, talk plainly to me, and consider, I, in my
40 Condition, can't be in very good Humour—you say, to be at once
what I must be.

Phillis. Ay, ay,—I mean no more than to be an old Man; I saw
you do it very well at the Masquerade: In a Word, old Sir
Geoffry Cimberton is every Hour expected in Town, to join in
45 the Deeds and Settlements for marrying Mr. *Cimberton*—He is half
blind, half lame, half deaf, half dumb; tho', as to his Passions
and Desires, he is as warm and ridiculous as when in the Heat
of Youth.—

Tom. Come to the Business, and don't keep the Gentleman
50 in Suspence for the Pleasure of being courted, as you serve
me.

Phillis. I saw you at the Masquerade act such a one to Perfection;
Go, and put on that very Habit, and come to our House as Sir
Geoffry. There is not one there, but my self, knows his Person; I was
55 born in the Parish where he is Lord of the Manor. I have seen him
often and often at Church in the Country. Do not hesitate; but
come thither; they will think you bring a certain Security against
Mr. *Myrtle*, and you bring Mr. *Myrtle*; leave the rest to me, I leave
this with you, and expect—They don't, I told you, know you; they
60 think you out of Town, which you had as good be for ever, if you
lose this Opportunity.—I must be gone; I know I am wanted at
home.

Myrtle. My dear *Phillis*!

Catches and kisses her, and gives her Money.

Phillis. O Fie! my Kisses are not my own; you have committed Violence; but I'll carry 'em to the right Owner. (Tom *kisses her*.) (*To* 65 Tom.) Come, see me down Stairs, and leave the Lover to think of his last Game for the Prize.

Exeunt Tom and Phillis.

Myrtle. I think I will instantly attempt this wild Expedient—The Extravagance of it will make me less suspected, and it will give me Opportunity to assert my own Right to *Lucinda*, without whom I 70 cannot live: But I am so mortify'd at this Conduct of mine, towards poor *Bevil*; He must think meanly of me—I know not how to reassume my self, and be in Spirit enough, for such an Adventure as this—Yet I must attempt it, if it be only to be near *Lucinda*, under Her present Perplexities; and sure—   75

> *The next Delight to Transport, with the Fair,*
> *Is to relieve her, in her hours of Care.*

Exit.

The End of the Fourth Act.

Act V. Scene i.

Scene, Sealand's House.

Enter Phillis, *with Lights, before* Myrtle, *disguis'd like old Sir* Geoffry, *supported by Mrs.* Sealand, Lucinda, *and* Cimberton.

Mrs. Sealand. Now I have seen you thus far, Sir *Geoffry*, will you excuse me a Moment, while I give my necessary Orders for your Accommodation?

Exit Mrs. Sealand.

Myrtle. I have not seen you, Cousin *Cimberton*, since you were ten Years old; and as it is incumbent on you, to keep up our Name 5 and Family, I shall, upon very reasonable Terms, join with you, in a Settlement to that purpose. Tho' I must tell you, Cousin this is the first Merchant that has married into our House.

Lucinda. (*Aside.*) Deuce on 'em! am I a Merchant, because my
10 Father is?

Myrtle. But is he directly a Trader, at this time?

Cimberton. There's no hiding the Disgrace, Sir; he trades to all parts of the World.

Myrtle. We never had one of our Family before, who descended
15 from Persons that did any thing.

Cimberton. Sir, since it is a Girl that they have, I am, for the Honour of my Family, willing to take it in again; and to sink her into our Name, and no harm done.

Myrtle. 'Tis prudently, and generously resolv'd—Is this the
20 young thing?

Cimberton. Yes, Sir.

Phillis. [*Aside to* Lucinda.] Good Madam, don't be out of Humour, but let them run to the utmost of their Extravagance—Hear them out.

25 *Myrtle.* Can't I see her nearer? My Eyes are but weak.

Phillis. [*Aside to* Lucinda.] Beside, I am sure the Unkle has some-thing worth your Notice. I'll take care to get off the young one, and leave you to observe what may be wrought out of the old one, for your good.

Exit.

30 *Cimberton.* Madam, this old Gentleman, your Great Unkle, desires to be introduced to you, and to see you nearer!—Approach, Sir.

Myrtle. By your leave, young Lady—(*Puts on Spectacles.*)—Cousin *Cimberton!* She has exactly that sort of Neck, and Bosom, for which my Sister *Gertrude* was so much admired, in the Year sixty one,
35 before the *French* Dresses first discovered any thing in Women, below the Chin.

Lucinda. (*Aside.*) What a very odd Situation am I in? Tho' I cannot but be diverted, at the extravagance of their Humours, equally unsuitable to their Age—Chin, quotha—I don't believe my pas-
40 sionate Lover there knows whether I have one or not. Ha! ha!

Myrtle. Madam, I would not willingly offend, but I have a better Glass—(*Pulls out a large one.*)

Enter Phillis *to* Cimberton.

Phillis. Sir, my Lady desires to shew the Apartment to you, that she intends for Sir *Geoffry.*

Cimberton. Well Sir! by that time you have sufficiently gazed, and 45 sunned your self in the Beauties of my Spouse there, I will wait on you again.

Exeunt Cimberton *and* Phillis.

Myrtle. Were it not, Madam, that I might be troublesome, there is something of Importance, tho' we are alone, which I would say more safe from being heard.   50

Lucinda. [*Aside.*] There is something, in this old Fellow methinks, that raises my Curiosity.

Myrtle. To be free, Madam, I as heartily contemn this Kinsman of mine, as you do, and am sorry to see so much Beauty and Merit devoted, by your Parents, to so insensible a Possessor.   55

Lucinda. Surprizing!—I hope then, Sir, you will not contribute to the Wrong you are so generous as to pity, whatever may be the Interest of your Family.

Myrtle. This Hand of mine shall never be employ'd, to sign any thing, against your Good and Happiness.   60

Lucinda. I am sorry, Sir, it is not in my Power to make you proper Acknowledgments; but there is a Gentleman in the World, whose Gratitude will, I am sure, be worthy of the Favour.

Myrtle. All the Thanks I desire, Madam, are in your Power to 65 give.

Lucinda. Name them, and Command them.

Myrtle. Only, Madam, that the first time you are alone with your Lover, you will, with open Arms, receive him.

Lucinda. As willingly as his Heart could wish it.   70

Myrtle. Thus then he claims your Promise! O *Lucinda!*

Lucinda. O! a Cheat! a Cheat! a Cheat!

Myrtle. Hush! 'tis I, tis I, your Lover, *Myrtle* himself, Madam.

Lucinda. O bless me! what a Rashness, and Folly to surprize me so—But hush—my Mother—   75

44 Sir] O2; [om.]

Enter Mrs. Sealand, Cimberton, *and* Phillis.

Mrs. Sealand. How now! what's the matter?

Lucinda. O Madam! as soon as you left the Room, my Uncle fell into a sudden Fit, and—and—so I cry'd out for help, to support him, and conduct him to his Chamber.

80   *Mrs. Sealand.* That was kindly done! Alas! Sir, how do you find your self?

Myrtle. Never was taken, in so odd a way in my Life—pray lead me! Oh! I was talking here—(*pray carry me*) to my Cousin *Cimberton's* young Lady—

85   *Mrs. Sealand.* (*Aside.*) My Cousin *Cimberton's* young Lady! How zealous he is, even in his Extremity, for the Match! a right *Cimberton.*

Cimberton *and* Lucinda *lead him, as one*
in Pain, &c.

Cimberton. Pox! Uncle, you will pull my Ear off.

Lucinda. Pray Uncle! you will squeeze me to Death.

90   *Mrs. Sealand.* No matter, no matter—he knows not what he does. Come, Sir, shall I help you out?

Myrtle. By no means; I'll trouble no body, but my young Cousins here.

They lead him off.

Phillis. But pray, Madam, does your Ladyship intend that Mr. 95 *Cimberton* shall really marry my young Mistress at last? I don't think he likes her.

Mrs. Sealand. That's not material! Men of his Speculation are above Desires—but be it as it may; now I have given old Sir *Geoffry* the Trouble of coming up to Sign and Seal, with what Countenance 100 can I be off?

Phillis. As well as with twenty others, Madam; It is the Glory and Honour of a Great Fortune, to live in continual Treaties, and still to break off: it looks Great, Madam.

Mrs. Sealand. True, *Phillis*—yet to return our Blood again into the 105 *Cimberton's,* is an Honour not to be rejected—but were not you saying, that Sir *John Bevil's* Creature *Humphrey* has been with Mr. *Sealand*?

Phillis. Yes, Madam; I overheard them agree, that Mr. *Sealand* should go himself, and visit this unknown Lady that Mr. *Bevil* is so great with; and if he found nothing there to fright him, that Mr. *Bevil* should still marry my young Mistress.   110

Mrs. Sealand. How! nay then he shall find she is my Daughter, as well as his: I'll follow him this Instant, and take the whole Family along with me: The disputed Power of Disposing of my own Daughter shall be at an end this very Night—I'll live no longer in Anxiety for a little Hussey, that hurts my Appearance, wherever I 115 carry her: and, for whose sake, I seem to be not at all regarded, and that in the best of my Days.

Phillis. Indeed, Madam, if she were married, your Ladyship might very well be taken for Mr. *Sealand's* Daughter.

Mrs. Sealand. Nay, when the Chit has not been with me, I have 120 heard the Men say as much—I'll no longer cut off the greatest Pleasure of a Woman's Life, (the shining in Assemblies) by her Forward Anticipation of the Respect, that's due to her Superior— she shall down to *Cimberton-Hall*—she shall—she shall.

Phillis. I hope, Madam, I shall stay with your Ladyship.   125

Mrs. Sealand. Thou shalt, *Phillis*, and I'll place thee then more about me.—But order Chairs immediately—I'll be gone this Minute.

Exeunt.

[Act V. Scene ii.]

Scene, Charing-Cross.

Enter Mr. Sealand, *and* Humphrey.

Mr. Sealand. I am very glad, Mr. *Humphrey*, that you agree with me, that it is for our Common Good, I should look thoroughly into this Matter.

116 not] Du 1; [om.]   The omission of 'not', later corrected in the Dublin editions but not in Tonson's, renders the sentence meaningless. Mrs. Sealand objects to the lack of attention forced on her by competition with her daughter. Whether the phrase should have read 'not to be at all regarded' or 'to be not at all regarded' is disputable.

Humphrey. I am, indeed, of that Opinion; for there is no Artifice,
5 nothing concealed, in our Family, which ought in Justice to be
known; I need not desire you, Sir, to treat the Lady with Care and
Respect.

Mr. Sealand. Master *Humphrey*—I shall not be rude, tho' I design
to be a little abrupt, and come into the Matter at once, to see how
10 she will bear, upon a Surprize.

Humphrey. That's the Door, Sir I wish you Success—(*While*
Humphrey *speaks,* Sealand *consults his Table-Book.*) [*Aside.*] I am less
concern'd what happens there, because I hear Mr. *Myrtle* is well
lodg'd, as old Sir *Geoffry,* so I am willing to let this Gentleman
15 employ himself here, to give them time at home: for I am sure, 'tis
necessary for the Quiet of our Family, *Lucinda* were disposed of, out
of it, since Mr. *Bevil's* Inclination is so much otherwise engaged.

                                                          Exit.

Mr. Sealand. I think this is the Door—(*Knocks.*) I'll carry this
Matter with an Air of Authority, to enquire, tho' I make an Errand,
20 to begin Discourse.

              Knocks again, and Enter a Foot-Boy.

So young Man! is your Lady within?

Boy. Alack, Sir! I am but a Country Boy—I dant know, whether
she is, or noa: but an you'll stay a bit, I'll goa, and ask the Gentlewoman that's with her.

25 *Mr. Sealand.* Why, Sirrah, tho' you are a Country Boy, you can
see, can't you? you know whether she is at home, when you see
her, don't you?

Boy. Nay, nay, I'm not such a Country Lad neither, Master, to
think she's at home, because I see her: I have been in Town but a
30 Month, and I lost one Place already, for believing my own Eyes.

Mr. Sealand. Why, Sirrah! have you learnt to lie already?

Boy. Ah! Master! things that are Lies in the Country, are not
Lies at *London*—I begin to know my Business a little better thanso
so—but an you please to walk in, I'll call a Gentlewoman to you,
35 that can tell you for certain—she can make bold to ask my Lady
her self.

Mr. Sealand. O! then, she is within, I find, tho' you dare not say so.

Boy. Nay, nay! that's neither here, nor there: what's matter, whether she is within or no, if she has not a mind to see any Body.

Mr. Sealand. I can't tell, Sirrah, whether you are Arch, or Simple, 40
but however get me a direct Answer, and here's a Shilling for
you.

Boy. Will you please to walk in, I'll see what I can do for
you.

Mr. Sealand. I see you will be fit for your Business, in time, Child. 45
But I expect to meet with nothing but Extraordinaries, in such a
House.

Boy. Such a House! Sir, you han't seen it yet: Pray walk
in.

Mr. Sealand. Sir, I'll wait upon you.   50

Exeunt.

[Act V. Scene iii.]

Scene, Indiana's *House.*

Enter Isabella.

Isabella. What Anxiety do I feel for this poor Creature! What will
be the End of her? Such a languishing unreserv'd Passion, for a
Man, that at last must certainly leave, or ruin her! and perhaps
both! then the Aggravation of the Distress is, that she does
not believe he will—not but, I must own, if they are both 5
what they would seem, they are made for one another, as much
as *Adam* and *Eve* were, for there is no other, of their Kind, but
themselves.

Enter Boy.

So *Daniel!* what News with you?

Boy. Madam, there's a Gentleman below would speak with my 10
Lady.

Isabella. Sirrah! don't you know Mr. *Bevil* yet?

Boy. Madam, 'tis not the Gentleman who comes every Day, and

asks for you, and won't go in till he knows whether you are with
15 her or no.

Isabella. [*Aside.*] Ha! that's a Particular I did not know before:
[*To* Boy.] Well! be it who it will, let him come up to me.

Exit Boy; *and re-enters with Mr.* Sealand.

Isabella *looks amaz'd!*

Mr. Sealand. Madam, I can't blame your being a little surpriz'd,
to see a perfect Stranger make a Visit, and—
20 *Isabella.* I am indeed surpriz'd—[*Aside.*] I see he does not know
me.

Mr. Sealand. You are very prettily lodg'd here, Madam; in troth
you seem to have every thing in Plenty—(*Aside, and looking about.*)
a Thousand a Year, I warrant you, upon this pretty Nest of Rooms,
25 and the dainty One within them.

Isabella. (*Apart.*) Twenty Years, it seems, have less Effect in the
Alteration of a Man of Thirty, than of a Girl of Fourteen—he's
almost still the same; but alas! I find, by other Men, as well as
himself, I am not what I was—As soon as he spoke, I was convinc'd
30 'twas He—How shall I contain my Surprize and Satisfaction! he
must not know me yet.

Mr. Sealand. Madam, I hope I don't give you any Disturbance;
But there is a young Lady here, with whom I have a particular
Business to discourse, and I hope she will admit me to that
35 Favour.

Isabella. Why, Sir, have you had any Notice concerning her? I
wonder who could give it you.

Mr. Sealand. That, Madam, is fit only to be communicated to
herself.

40 *Isabella.* Well, Sir! you shall see her:—[*Aside.*] I find he knows
nothing yet, nor shall from me: I am resolv'd, I will observe this
Interlude, this Sport of Nature, and of Fortune.—[*To Mr.* Sealand.]
You shall see her presently, Sir; For now I am as a Mother, and will
trust her with you.

Exit.

45 *Mr. Sealand.* As a Mother! right; that's the old Phrase, for one of
those Commode Ladies, who lend out Beauty, for Hire, to young

Gentlemen that have pressing Occasions. But here comes the
precious Lady herself. In troth a very sightly Woman—

Enter Indiana.

Indiana. I am told, Sir, you have some Affair that requires your
speaking with me.   50
Mr. Sealand. Yes, Madam: There came to my Hands a Bill drawn
by Mr. *Bevil*, which is payable tomorrow; and he, in the Intercourse
of Business, sent it to me, who have Cash of his, and desired me to
send a Servant with it; but I have made bold to bring you the
Money my self.   55
Indiana. Sir! was that necessary?
Mr. Sealand. No, Madam; but, to be free with you, the Fame of
your Beauty, and the Regard, which Mr. *Bevil* is a little too well
known to have for you, excited my Curiosity.
Indiana. Too well known to have for me! Your sober Appearance, 60
Sir, which my Friend describ'd, made me expect no Rudeness, or
Absurdity, at least—Who's there? Sir, if you pay the Money to a
Servant, 'twill be as well.
Mr. Sealand. Pray, Madam, be not offended; I came hither on an
Innocent, nay a Virtuous Design; and, if you will have Patience to 65
hear me, it may be as useful to you, as you are in a Friendship with
Mr. *Bevil*, as to my only Daughter, whom I was this Day disposing
of.
Indiana. You make me hope, Sir, I have mistaken you; I am com-
posed again; be free, say on—(*Aside.*) what I am afraid to hear— 70
Mr. Sealand. I fear'd, indeed, an unwarranted Passion here, but I
did not think it was in Abuse of so worthy an Object, so accomplish'd a Lady, as your Sense and Mien bespeak—but the Youth of
our Age care not what Merit and Virtue they bring to Shame, so
they gratify—   75
Indiana. Sir—you are going into very great Errors—but, as you
are pleas'd to say you see something in me that has chang'd, at least,
the Colour of your Suspicions; so has your Appearance alter'd mine,
and made me earnestly attentive to what has any way concern'd
you, to enquire into my Affairs, and Character.   80
Mr. Sealand. [*Aside.*] How sensibly! with what an Air she Talks!

Indiana. Good Sir, be seated—and tell me tenderly—keep all
your Suspicions concerning me alive, that you may in a proper and
prepared way—acquaint me why the Care of your Daughter
85 obliges a Person of your seeming Worth and Fortune, to be thus
inquisitive about a wretched, helpless, friendless—(*Weeping.*) But
I beg your Pardon—tho' I am an Orphan, your Child is not; and
your Concern for her, it seems, has brought you hither—I'll be
composed—pray go on, Sir.

90 *Mr. Sealand.* How could Mr. *Bevil* be such a Monster, to injure
such a Woman?

Indiana. No, Sir—you wrong him—he has not injur'd me—my
Support is from his Bounty.

Mr. Sealand. Bounty! when Gluttons give high Prices for Deli-
95 cates, they are prodigious Bountiful.

Indiana. Still, still you will persist in that Error—But my own
Fears tell me all—You are the Gentleman, I suppose, for whose
happy Daughter he is design'd a Husband, by his good Father; and
he has, perhaps, consented to the Overture: He was here this
100 Morning, dress'd beyond his usual Plainness, nay most sumptuously
—and he is to be, perhaps, this Night a Bridegroom.

Mr. Sealand. I own he was intended such: But, Madam, on your
Account, I have determin'd to defer my Daughter's Marriage, till
I am satisfied from your own Mouth, of what Nature are the
105 Obligations you are under to him.

Indiana. His Actions, Sir, his Eyes have only made me think, he
design'd to make me the Partner of his Heart. The Goodness and
Gentleness of his Demeanour made me misinterpret all—'Twas my
own Hope, my own Passion, that deluded me—he never made one
110 Amorous Advance to me—His large Heart, and bestowing Hand,
have only helpt the Miserable: Nor know I why, but from his mere
Delight in Virtue, that I have been his Care, the Object on which
to indulge and please himself, with pouring Favours.

Mr. Sealand. Madam, I know not why it is, but I, as well as you,
115 am methinks afraid of entring into the Matter I came about; but 'tis
the same thing, as if we had talk'd never so distinctly—he ne'er
shall have a Daughter of mine.

Indiana. If you say this from what you think of me, you wrong

your self and him—Let not me, miserable tho' I may be, do Injury
to my Benefactor—No, Sir, my Treatment ought rather to reconcile 120
you to his Virtues—If to bestow, without a Prospect of Return; if
to delight in supporting, what might, perhaps, be thought an
Object of Desire, with no other View than to be her Guard against
those who would not be so disinterested; if these Actions, Sir, can
in a careful Parent's Eye commend him to a Daughter, give yours, 125
Sir, give her to my honest, generous *Bevil*—What have I to do, but
sigh, and weep, to rave, run wild, a Lunatick in Chains, or hid in
Darkness, mutter in distracted Starts, and broken Accents, my
strange, strange Story!

Mr. Sealand. Take Comfort, Madam.   130

Indiana. All my Comfort must be to expostulate in Madness, to
relieve with Frenzy my Despair, and shrieking to demand of Fate,
why—why was I born to such Variety of Sorrows?

Mr. Sealand. If I have been the least Occasion—

Indiana. No—'twas Heaven's high Will, I should be such—to be 135
plunder'd in my Cradle! Toss'd on the Seas! and even there, an
Infant Captive! to lose my Mother, hear but of my Father—To be
adopted! lose my Adopter! then plung'd again in worse Calamities!

Mr. Sealand. An Infant Captive!

Indiana. Yet then! to find the most Charming of Mankind, once 140
more to set me free, (from what I thought the last Distress) to load
me with his Services, his Bounties, and his Favours; to support my
very Life, in a way, that stole, at the same time, my very Soul it
self from me.

Mr. Sealand. And has young *Bevil* been this worthy Man?   145

Indiana. Yet then again, this very Man to take another! without
leaving me the Right, the Pretence of easing my fond Heart with
Tears! For oh! I can't reproach him, though the same Hand that
rais'd me to this Height, now throws me down the Precipice.

Mr. Sealand. Dear Lady! O yet one Moment's Patience: my Heart 150
grows full with your Affliction: But yet, there's something in your
Story that—

Indiana. My Portion here is Bitterness, and Sorrow.

Mr. Sealand. Do not think so: Pray answer me: Does *Bevil* know
your Name, and Family?   155

Indiana. Alas! too well! O, could I be any other Thing, than what I am—I'll tear away all Traces of my former Self, my little Ornaments, the Remains of my first State, the Hints of what I ought to have been—

In her Disorder she throws away a Bracelet, which Sealand takes up, and looks earnestly on it.

160 *Mr. Sealand.* Ha! what's this? my Eyes are not deceiv'd? It is, it is the same! the very Bracelet which I bequeath'd my Wife, at our last mournful Parting.

Indiana. What said you, Sir! Your Wife! Whither does my Fancy carry me? What means this unfelt Motion at my Heart? And yet 165 again my Fortune but deludes me; for if I err not, Sir, your Name is *Sealand:* But my lost Father's Name was—

Mr. Sealand. Danvers! was it not?

Indiana. What new Amazement! That is indeed my Family.

Mr. Sealand. Know then, when my Misfortunes drove me to the 170 *Indies,* for Reasons too tedious now to mention, I chang'd my Name of *Danvers* into *Sealand.*

Enter Isabella.

Isabella. If yet there wants an Explanation of your Wonder, examine well this Face, (yours, Sir, I well remember) gaze on, and read, in me, your Sister *Isabella!*
175 *Mr. Sealand.* My Sister!

Isabella. But here's a Claim more tender yet—your *Indiana,* Sir, your long lost Daughter.

Mr. Sealand. O my Child! my Child!

Indiana. All-Gracious Heaven! is it Possible! do I embrace my 180 Father!

Mr. Sealand. And do I hold thee—These Passions are too strong for Utterance—Rise, rise, my Child, and give my Tears their Way —O my Sister! (*Embracing her.*)

Isabella. Now, dearest Neice, my groundless Fears, my painful 185 Cares no more shall vex thee. If I have wrong'd thy noble Lover with too hard Suspicions, my just Concern for thee, I hope, will plead my Pardon.

Mr. Sealand. O! make him then the full Amends, and be your self
the Messenger of Joy: Fly this Instant! tell him all these wondrous
Turns of Providence in his Favour! Tell him I have now a Daughter 190
to bestow, which he no longer will decline: that this Day he still
shall be a Bridegroom: nor shall a Fortune, the Merit which his
Father seeks, be wanting: tell him the Reward of all his Virtues
waits on his Acceptance.

Exit Isabella.

My dearest *Indiana!* (*Turns, and embraces her.*)   195

Indiana. Have I than at last a Father's Sanction on my Love! His
bounteous Hand to give, and make my Heart a Present worthy of
Bevil's Generosity?

Mr. Sealand. O my Child! how are our Sorrows past o'erpaid by
such a Meeting! Though I have lost so many Years of soft paternal 200
Dalliance with thee, Yet, in one Day, to find thee thus, and thus
bestow thee, in such perfect Happiness! is ample! ample Reparation! And yet again the Merit of thy Lover.

Indiana. O! had I Spirits left to tell you of his Actions! how
strongly Filial Duty has suppressed his Love; and how Concealment 205
still has doubled all his Obligations; the Pride, the Joy of his
Alliance, Sir, would warm your Heart, as he has conquer'd mine.

Mr. Sealand. How laudable is Love, when born of Virtue! I burn
to embrace him—

Indiana. See, Sir, my Aunt already has succeeded, and brought him 210
to your Wishes.

Enter Isabella, *with Sir* John Bevil, Bevil *junior, Mrs.* Sealand,
Cimberton, Myrtle, *and* Lucinda.

Sir John Bevil. (*Entring.*) Where! where's this Scene of Wonder!—
Mr. *Sealand*, I congratulate, on this Occasion, our mutual Happiness
—Your good Sister, Sir, has, with the Story of your Daughter's
Fortune, fill'd us with Surprize and Joy! Now all Exceptions are 215
remov'd; my Son has now avow'd his Love, and turn'd all former
Jealousies and Doubts to Approbation, and, I am told, your Good-
ness has consented to reward him.

Mr. Sealand. If, Sir, a Fortune equal to his Father's Hopes, can
make this Object worthy his Acceptance.   220

Bevil junior. I hear your Mention, Sir, of Fortune, with Pleasure only as it may prove the Means to reconcile the best of Fathers to my Love—Let him be Provident, but let me be Happy—My ever-destin'd, my acknowledg'd Wife! (*Embracing* Indiana.)

225   *Indiana.* Wife!—O! my ever loved! my Lord! my Master!

Sir John Bevil. I congratulate my self, as well as you, that I had a Son, who could, under such Disadvantages, discover your great Merit.

Mr. Sealand. O! Sir *John*! how vain, how weak is Humane
230 Prudence? What Care, what Foresight, what Imagination could contrive such blest Events, to make our Children happy, as Providence in one short Hour has laid before us?

Cimberton. (*To Mrs.* Sealand.) I am afraid, Madam, Mr. *Sealand* is a little too busy for our Affair, if you please we'll take another
235 Opportunity.

Mrs. Sealand. Let us have patience, Sir.

Cimberton. But we make Sir *Geoffry* wait, Madam.

Myrtle. O Sir! I am not in haste.

                                   During this, Bevil *junior presents* Lucinda *to* Indiana.

240   *Mr. Sealand.* But here! here's our general Benefactor! Excellent young Man, that could be, at once, a Lover to her Beauty, and a Parent to her Virtue.

Bevil junior. If you think That an Obligation, Sir, give me leave to overpay my self, in the only Instance, that can now add to my
245 Felicity, by begging you to bestow this Lady on Mr. *Myrtle.*

Mr. Sealand. She is his without reserve, (I beg he may be sent for) —Mr. *Cimberton*, notwithstanding you never had my Consent, yet there is, since I last saw you, another Objection to your Marriage with my Daughter.

250   *Cimberton.* I hope, Sir, your Lady has conceal'd nothing from me?

Mr. Sealand. Troth, Sir! nothing but what was conceal'd from my self; another Daughter, who has an undoubted Title to half my Estate.

Cimberton. How! Mr. *Sealand*! why then if half Mrs. *Lucinda's*
255 Fortune is gone, you can't say, that any of my Estate is settled upon her: I was in Treaty for the whole; but if that is not to be come at, to be sure, there can be no Bargain,—Sir,—I have nothing to do but

to take my leave of your good Lady, my Cousin, and beg Pardon
for the Trouble I have given this Old Gentleman.

Myrtle. That you have, Mr. *Cimberton*, with all my Heart. (*Dis-* 260
covers himself.)

Omnes. Mr. *Myrtle!*

Myrtle. And I beg Pardon of the whole Company, that I assumed
the Person of Sir *Geoffry*, only to be present at the Danger of this
Lady's being disposed of, and in her utmost Exigence to assert my 265
Right to her: Which if her Parents will ratifie, as they once favour'd
my Pretensions, no Abatement of Fortune shall lessen her Value
to me.

Lucinda. Generous Man!

Mr. Sealand. If, Sir, you can overlook the Injury of being in 270
Treaty with one, who as meanly left her, as you have generously
asserted your Right in her, she is Yours.

Lucinda. Mr. *Myrtle*, tho' you have ever had my Heart, yet now
I find I love you more, because I bring you less.

Myrtle. We have much more than we want, and I am glad any 275
Event has contributed to the Discovery of our real Inclinations to
each other.

Mrs. Sealand. (*Aside.*) Well! however I'm glad the Girl's disposed
of any way.

Bevil junior. *Myrtle!* no longer Rivals now, but Brothers.   280

Myrtle. Dear *Bevil!* you are born to triumph over me! but now
our Competition ceases: I rejoyce in the Preheminence of your
Virtue, and your Alliance adds Charms to *Lucinda*.

Sir John Bevil. Now, Ladies and Gentlemen, you have set the
World a fair Example: Your Happiness is owing to your Constancy 285
and Merit: And the several Difficulties you have struggled with,
evidently shew

> *Whate'er the generous Mind it self denies,*
> *The secret Care of Providence supplies.*

Exeunt.

The End of the Fifth Act.

EPILOGUE,

Spoken by Mrs. *Oldfield* to the CONSCIOUS LOVERS.

Now, I presume, our moralizing Knight,
Is heartily convinc'd my Sense was right:
I told him, flat, his Conscious Lovers Passion,
Had, many Ages past, been out of Fashion:
5   *That all Attempts to mend the Mode were shallow,*
Our Man, in Favour, now's a pretty Fellow
That talks, and laughs, and sings, fights, dances, dresses,
Rakes with an Air, and keeps his String of Misses.
Then to his Fame, such Courage too belongs,
10   *That when, by Rivals, call'd to Account for Wrongs,*
Ne'er stands to talk, but—Hah—whips 'em thro' the Lungs.

   Not like his Bevil*—cooly waits his Season,*
And traps determin'd Courage into Reason:
Nor loves like him (poor Soul) confin'd to one!
15   *And is at vast Expence—for nothing done!*
To pass whole Days alone, and never meddle,
Treat her with senseless Solo*—on the Fiddle!*
And all this chast Restraint, forsooth, to flow
From strait Obedience to a Father due!
20   *T'have shewn his modern Breeding, he should rather*
Not have obey'd, but bit *the* PUT *his Father;*
Or, in Compliance to his Daddy's Courting,
Have starv'd his Dear, and fairly took the Fortune.
But to maintain her, and not let her know it—
O! the wild—crack-brain'd Notions of a Poet!
25   *What tho' his Hero never lov'd before,*
He might have, sure, done less for her—or more.

   With Scenes of this course Kind, he owns, that Plays,
Too often, have beguil'd you of your Praise:

Where Sense, and Virtue, were allow'd no Part, 30
That only touch'd the loose, and wanton Heart.
If then, a diff'rent Way of Thinking might
Incline the Chast to hear,—the Learn'd to write,
On you it rests—to make your Profit your Delight.

EPILOGUE,

By Mr. *WELSTED.*

Intended to be Spoken by *Indiana.*

Our *Author, whom Intreaties cannot move,*
Spight of the Dear Coquetry that you love,
Swears he'll not frustrate (so he plainly means)
By a loose Epilogue, his decent Scenes.
5 *Is it not, Sirs, hard Fate I meet To-day,*
To keep me Rigid Still beyond the Play?
And yet I'm sav'd a World of Pains that way.
I now can look, I now can move at Ease,
Nor need I torture these poor Limbs, to please;
10 *Nor with the Hand or Foot attempt Surprize,*
Nor wrest my Features, nor fatigue my Eyes:
Bless me! What freakish Gambols have I play'd!
What Motions try'd, and wanton Looks betray'd!
Out of pure Kindness all! to Over-rule
15 *The threaten'd Hiss, and screen some scribling Fool.*
With more Respect I'm entertain'd To-night:
Our Author thinks, I can with Ease delight.
My Artless Looks while modest Graces arm,
He says, I need but to appear; and charm.
20 *A Wife so form'd, by these Examples bred,*
Pours Joy and Gladness 'round the Marriage Bed;
Soft Source of Comfort, kind Relief from Care,
And 'tis her least Perfection to be Fair.
The Nymph with Indiana's *Worth who vies,*
25 *A Nation will behold with* Bevil's *Eyes.*

FINIS.

COMMENTARY

THE FUNERAL

[motto]. Horace, *Ars Poetica*, ll. 431–3. As hired mourners say and do more than those who truly grieve, so false admirers appear more moved than real ones.

Dedication

[title]. The Countess of Albemarle] The former Geertriud Johanna Quirina van der Duyn (*d.* 1741) had married the first Earl of Albemarle, King William III's Dutch friend Arnold Joost van Keppel, a few months before *The Funeral* was published. This Dedication has been held to be largely responsible for Steele's securing the favour of King William (*Correspondence*, p. 445, n. 1; Winton, p. 63).

17. Daughter of Mr. *Scravenmore*] The Countess was the daughter of another Dutchman, the Lord of St. Gravenmoer, General of the Forces to the States General. The name was variously spelt by his contemporaries.

Preface

2. the Duke of *Devonshire*] William Cavendish (1673–1729) had served in Flanders in 1692, as had Steele. In 1701, when *The Funeral* was in rehearsal, he was a member of Parliament, and thus 'a very great Man', as Steele wrote in his first Preface. He succeeded as second Duke of Devonshire in 1707 at the death of his father, so that in 1711 Steele was able to name his admirer with pride.

13. my Fellow-Soldiers] When the play opened, Captain Steele was serving with the Coldstream Guards. Critics have assumed from this statement and the Prologue (ll. 25–8) that Steele packed the house in order to ensure his play's success.

23–29. a Great Artist thus informs Us of his Cures upon the Dead. . .] A reference to an actual advertisement published by William Willkins in the *Post Boy*, no. 956, 3 July 1701. The wording of Willkins's advertisement is almost identical with Steele's, except that the undertaker named the gentle people whom he had so successfully embalmed:

William Willkins over against the Mewes at Chearing Cross, well known and approved for his Art of Embalming; having preserv'd the Body of a Gentlewoman sweet and entire Thirteen Years without Emboweling, now to be shewn: And he hath taken up the Corps of Sir Edward Deering and Colonel Wharton in Ireland, after Nine Months putrefaction in the Ground. The Body of Colonel Corthope at Namure, and a Merchant at Brussells, which he reduced to Sweetness without Emboweling, and their whole Bodies were seen and known by their Friends when brought to England. No Man performeth the like. . . (R. A. Aubin, 'Beyond Steele's Satire on Undertakers', *PMLA* lxiv (1949), 1022).

41. the Mourners should be in Earnest] Undertakers provided hired mourners for a fee.

51. a Man in a Gown] a lawyer.

68. so Clear a Mind in being] Aitken suggests that Steele may refer to Charles Montagu, Lord Halifax (1661–1715) (Mermaid, p. 7, n. 1). There is no evidence to support this opinion or suggest an alternative. Although Addison knew Halifax at this time, there is no proof that Steele did.

71–2. *Seu . . . carmen.*] adapted from Horace, Epistle 1. iii, ll. 23–4:

> *seu linguam causis acuis seu civica iura*
> *respondere paras seu condis amabile carmen,*

Whether he sharpens his tongue for causes, or prepares to give advice on civil law, or composes lovely poetry. . .

Prologue

1–7. *Nature's . . . Player*] Steele is referring to the elaborate stage sets, costumes, and machines that became an important element in the theatre of the last part of the seventeenth century. In Steele's time the lavish productions of English plays were designed effectively to rival the imported French dancers, Italian opera singers, rope-dancers, ladder-dancers, acrobats, and other oddities who intrigued audiences. The first words of the Prologue should be understood to mean 'Nature is deserted'.

8–15. *Old. . . . Please*] For information on the state of theatrical productions in London in the early part of the century see Avery, i. xvii–clxxvii.

1. i

1. *Cabinet*] private, secret (*OED*).

23. Absurd] illogical (*OED*).

31. pudder] obsolete or dialectal form of pother (*OED*).

60. she hir'd my Mourning Furniture] Undertakers rented the formal trappings of mourning, such as black hangings for rooms.

95. Wanscoat] Frequently applied to tanned or hardened visages, the term was taken from wainscot, a superior quality of imported oak (*OED*).

105. St. *Timothie's* in the Fields] The church did not exist; the subject matter forbade naming an actual church. The parish church in Covent Garden was St. Martin's in the Fields.

115. *Passeport*] The name implies a passport to heaven, a recognized usage (see *OED*).

116–7. our Country-Farm at *Kensington Gravel-Pits*] The area around the Gravel-Pits, a district bordering on Uxbridge Road, was known for its salubrity. Because the sick went there, Sable considered it a source of business.

117. our City-house in *Warwick-lane*] the Royal College of Physicians, which had moved to Warwick-Lane in 1674.

119–20. that Young Fellow came last from *Oxford*] a compliment to an un-identified doctor lately graduated from Oxford, one of the two English sources of medical degrees acceptable to the Royal College of Physicians.

127. your Bagg of Brick-dust and your Whiting] Goody Trash sells her goods while collecting intelligence of illnesses and impending deaths for Sable, information for which footmen, coachmen, and others were paid. Brickdust or powdered brick was hawked by peddlers (see *Tatler*, no. 9, and *Spectator*, no. 251) and was used for loosening soil, perhaps here for the kitchen garden. Whiting or powdered chalk was used for scouring plate.

I. ii

50. a Play] Steele had spoken of the widow in the theatre in his poem 'To Mr. *Congreve*, Occasion'd by his Comedy, call'd, *The Way of the World*', pub-lished early in 1701:

> The Widow, who impatient of Delay,
> From the Town-joys must Mask it to the Play,
> Joins with your *Mourning-Bride's* resistless Moan,
> And weeps a Loss she slighted, when her own;
>
> (*Verse*, p. 13)

106–7. the Cruelty . . . together] Dryden's description, in his translation of the *Aeneis*, The Eighth Book, reads:

> 'Till curs'd *Mezentius*, in a fatal Hour,
> Assum'd the Crown, with Arbitrary Pow'r.
> What Words can paint those execrable Times;
> The Subjects Suff'rings, and the Tyrant's Crimes!
> That Blood, those Murthers, O ye Gods replace
> On his own Head, and on his impious Race!
> The living, and the Dead, at his Command
> Were coupled, Face to Face, and Hand to Hand:
> 'Till choak'd with Stench, in loath'd Embraces ty'd,
> The ling'ring Wretches pin'd away, and dy'd.
>
> (Dryden, iii. 1279, ll. 630–9)

140. *Puzzle*] confound (*OED*).

188. every Inn in *Holborn* an Inn of Court] The numerous inns of Holborn were the usual stopping-places for long stages and were also the inns fre-quented by country gentlemen. Holborn was, however, long famous also as a law quarter of London. Gray's Inn, one of the four Inns of Court, was there, as well as Staple Inn and Barnard's Inn, two Inns of Chancery attached to it. Thavie's Inn and Furnival's Inn, Inns of Chancery attached to Lincoln's Inn, were also in Holborn.

203–20. [the deed] The redundancy in this instrument is not exaggerated; Steele may well have copied an actual document, for the wording accurately reflects the legal language. In fact, he omitted a few synonymous terms commonly included. Sample documents are printed by George Billinghurst in *Arcana Clericalia, Or, The Mysteries of Clarkship: Being a sure way of Setling Estates by Deeds, Fines, and Recoveries* (London, 1674).

II. i

1. *Lord Hardy*] Lord Hardy was probably an idealization of the author himself (see Winton, p. 62). Although Steele did not share Lord Hardy's ability to exist on a lofty moral plane, he did share many biographical details. Both were former Christ Church men who had become army captains. Knowing the meaning of debt, each had chosen the sword as a means of improving his lot, but each also felt patriotic fervour for the 'Brave Prince on the Throne' and the 'Glorious War in an Honest Cause'. As a captain Steele was thoroughly familiar with the desperate state of the army and the difficulties of recruiting reflected in this scene and IV. iii.

18. the Agent] Army pay agents profited by charging exorbitant percentages to advance pay, which was commonly well in arrears (J. W. Fortescue, *A History of the British Army*, 13 vols. in 14 (London, 1899), i. 383).

22. Subsistence] 'Money paid Weekly, or Monthly or otherwise, to Soldiers, for them to subsist on till the general Paydays, when their Accounts are made, and then receive what more is due to them, for the Subsistence is always less than the Pay' (*Military Dictionary*).

31–2. now Your Father's dead and they can't Arrest you] As a peer, Lord Hardy would no longer be subject to arrest for debt.

87. Gum, and Balm] that is, perfumed fragrance.

91. Granadier] 'Soldiers arm'd with a good Sword, a Hatchet, Fire-lock slung, and a Pouch full of Hand-Granadoes. Every Batalion of Foot, of late Years, has generally a Company of Granadeers belonging to it, or else four or five Granadeers belong to each Company of the Batalion, and upon occasion form a Company of themselves. There are Horse and Foot Granadeers, and they have often been found very serviceable' (*Military Dictionary*).

123. Fardingale] an outdated version of the whalebone circle worn under skirts; the name is indicative of the character, an outmoded old maid.

137. Tom's] Tom's Coffee-house in Russell Street, Covent Garden.

164. Serviture] an obsolete form of 'servitor', an undergraduate at Oxford who was excused from fees by acting as a servant.

205. Pactolian Guineas] golden guineas. The River Pactolus in ancient Lydia was famous for the gold washed from its sands. Trim's use of the phrase can be explained by his introduction to classical literature when he was a servitor.

II. ii

4. the Charges I have been at] Although Sable exaggerates, fees were paid for news of deaths and illnesses. Aubin quotes an advertisement by undertaker Azariah Reynolds, which refers to funeral specialists 'who are at great

Expence in procuring Intelligence of dying Persons, and watching their Death, and in bribing either the Relations, Pretended Friends, or Servants of the Deceased' (*The Flying Post*, 15 January 1698, quoted in Aubin, 1019–20).

II. iii

3. Good Dr. *Lucas*] Richard Lucas, D.D. (1648–1715) published numerous religious tracts and sermons, including 'An Enquiry After Happiness', 'Humane Life', 'Practical Christianity', and 'Religious Perfection'.

60–1. Tringham Trangham] trivial. A slang and dialectal form from the word 'trinket' (*OED*).

66–73. [Song] This is the first of four songs in *The Funeral* set by Daniel Purcell (1660?–1717). He set all the songs except 'Cynderaxa' in IV. ii (*Verse*, p. 80).

92. Old Mr. *Laws*] Henry Lawes (1596–1662), who had been Milton's associate in the production of *Comus*.

189. out of my Pantofles] descended from my high dignity. 'To stand upon one's pantofles' meant to 'carry it high' or 'stand upon high Terms' (*OED*; *A New English Dictionary*, By J. K. (London, 1702)).

208–9. those parts of *Italy* where the Armies Are] Prince Eugene of Savoy, having defeated Catinat, who had occupied Mantua, and repulsed Villeroi, settled his troops in Lombardy for the winter (Churchill, i. 537–8).

299–300. Morning Lectures, your self-examination] The Widow's terminology suggests a Puritan stance behind her hypocrisy.

306. a Leiger Lady] a camp follower.

III. i

21. Manto'es] open robes worn over petticoats (Cunnington, *Eighteenth*, p. 116). Dressmakers were called mantoe- or mantua-makers.

25. the latest French Cut] The interchange of fashions between France and England was continuous despite the political and military animosities between the two countries.

30. *D'Epingle*] 'Madam D'Epingle' was a common expression for a dressmaker.

III. ii

5. the Porter's Paper of How Dee's] It was fashionable in London for footmen to call on their mistress's acquaintances to inquire 'How do ye?' rather than leaving a card as later became usual (John Ashton, *Social Life in the Reign of Queen Anne* (London, 1904), p. 60).

37–141. [visiting scene] The author of the *Comparison Between the Two Stages* wrote, 'The Visiting Scene is a Master-piece; I prefer it to that in *The Lady's visiting Day* by great odds' (*Comparison*, p. 91). It is difficult to believe the 'compliment' was not an accusation of plagiarism, for there is a strong resemblance between the talk of the widows in the two scenes (see Burnaby, pp. 263–4).

46. Wottoo] wilt thou. *The Funeral* is the only reference listed in the *OED*.

66. *Fleer*] a sneer or 'deceitful grin of civility' (*OED*).

90. *Fusse*] a fat, frowzy woman. The term was a dialectal or slang form of fussock or fustilugs, both of which had this meaning (*OED*).

101. Tits] nags.

105. Gentile] an accepted spelling of 'genteel' (*OED*).

III. iii

24–8. The English . . . like] French affectations had been satirized similarly in *The Ladies Visiting-Day*. See Burnaby, p. 234.

65. *Leau D'Hongrie*] Hungary Water or Queen of Hungary Water was a popular perfume described in Phillips' *Dictionary* (London, 1708) as 'A Spirit of Wine fill'd with the more essential part of Rosemary-flowers'.

81–95. [discussion of undressing] Eustace Budgell made full use of this passage in the *Spectator*, no. 506, quoting carefully:

. . . in one of our Modern Comedies, where a *Frenchwoman* offering to undress and dress her self before the Lover of the Play, and assuring his Mistress that it was very usual in *France*, the Lady tells her, that's a Secret in Dress she never knew before, and that she was so unpolished an *Englishwoman*, as to resolve never to learn even to dress before her Husband.

There is something so gross in the Carriage of some Wives, that they lose their Husbands Hearts for Faults, which, if a Man has either good-Nature, or good-Breeding, he knows not how to tell them of.

IV. ii

45–56. [Song] The composer may have been William Croft. See *Verse*, p. 81.

122. under the Rose] *sub rosa*.

IV. iii

0.2. *a Cane*] a fashionable affectation of beaux. See the *Tatler*, no. 103.

8. *Steinkirk*] During the campaign in Flanders in August 1692 the English had attacked the French at Steinkirk, but had been repulsed and forced to retreat. Although losses on both sides were about equal, France claimed a victory (Churchill, i. 412–13). There is no documentary proof, but Winton believes that Steele left Oxford in June 1692 to join the Life Guards in Flanders (Winton, p. 41). If this is true, Steele himself would have participated in the battle.

19. right *French* Brandy] Trim is wise to doubt Kate's word. Duties on French wines and brandies increased drastically in the 1690s, and the quantity imported became very limited. There were clandestine shipments, but

the prices were exorbitant. (André L. Simon, *The History of the Wine Trade in England*, 3 vols. (London, 1909), iii. 130). Rich merchants might sip these superior brandies, but it is unlikely that Kate could afford them.

36. all Men are for a War] Trim's statement is not as broadly ironic as it at first seems. The plight of disbanded soldiers and half-pay officers was desperate at the turn of the century, until the dispatch of troops to the Low Countries in 1701 again supplied them employment. Petitions were pouring into Parliament for payment of arrears. Many of the officers themselves were on half-pay, and paying their men proved impossible (Fortescue, i. 389–92). Lord Hardy's tender concern for his men's welfare and their respect and love for him must have been rare phenomena in 1701; Steele not only demonstrates his views on the responsibilities of an officer but also shows that Lord Hardy is a man of superior qualities.

45–9. to cry . . . Hats] Trim imitates actual street cries of London. See Ashton, p. 365; *Spectator*, no. 251.

46–7. whip . . . *Flanders*] that is, bring the war news. 'A Bloody Battel alarms the Town from one end to another in an Instant. Every Motion of the *French* is Published in so great an hurry, that one would think the Enemy were at our Gates' (*Spectator*, no. 251).

74–5. in and about . . . *Drury-Lane*] Lord Hardy's soldiers were quartered directly by the Theatre-Royal where Steele's play was performed. To the southeast of the theatre, Russell Court and Vinegar Yard, the latter a disreputable haunt of thieves and prostitutes in *The Beggar's Opera*, were linked by Cross Court. Guys Court, immediately northeast of the theatre, joined Vinegar Yard to Play-House Passage, the chief entrance to the theatre from Drury Lane (John Rocque, *A Plan of the Cities of London and Westminster, and Borough of Southwark; with the Contiguous Buildings* (London, 1746)).

84. *Tattoo*] 'Sometimes call'd, The Retreat; the Beat of Drum at Night for all Soldiers in Garrison to repair to their Quarters, and to their Tents in the Field. After which, in Frontier Towns, and where the Inhabitants are suspected, they are not permitted to stir abroad, or, at least not without a Light' (*Military Dictionary*).

85. tight] in this case, neat in appearance.

90. *Matchlock*] 'a Musket that is fir'd with a Match fix'd on the Cock opening the Pan; now much out of use, Fire-Locks being altogether prefer'd before them' (*Military Dictionary*). These muskets were becoming obsolete by 1701. The tag name is appropriate to Steele's faithful, rusty soldier.

95. Halbert] The weapon was the mark of a sergeant.

103. an Act] The Act, passed in 1698, permitted officers and soldiers to enter trades regardless of whether they had served their full terms as apprentices. The law circumvented by-laws and customs of cities and corporations and an Elizabethan statute prohibiting the practice of some trades without apprenticeships of seven years (*The Statutes of the Realm* (London, 1820), vii. 528–9).

116. our last Cloathing] The problem of clothing for the regiment was a grave one. In 1697 a regulation ordered that the colonels were to provide clothing, the allowance for it being deducted from the men's pay. In December of that year, however, many regiments were disbanded, and the soldiers took their clothing as they left. In April 1698, when payment was due, the colonels were able to collect only for those men actually on the regimental rolls; consequently they could not pay for all of it (Fortescue, i. 392).

125. the Hospital] Chelsea Hospital for old and disabled soldiers was built at the end of the seventeenth century. Much of the money for its construction was deducted from the pay of the military forces (Wheatley, i. 383–5).

140. Priggish] dandified (OED).

149–54. an *Alexander . . . way*] Trim quotes the tag of Act IV of Nathaniel Lee's *The Rival Queens; or the Death of Alexander the Great*, changing 'shews' to 'leads'. The lines in *The Funeral* date from Steele's sojourn in Wandsworth in 1701 to work on the play. In a letter to Colonel Edmund Revett, dated 2 September 1701 (*Correspondence*, pp. 10–11), he speaks of 'my man Will repeating to her [his landlady] out of Alexander the Great', as Will Trim does here. In the letter he also misquotes Lee's line as ' ''Tis Beauty calls and Glory leads the way'.

v. i

17. Devil Incarnate] In Shadwell's *The Volunteers* (1692) Colonel Hackwell is turned off by his father at the instigation of a second wife. Mrs. Hackwell, like the Widow, has a man, 'Cozin' Nickum. The Colonel overhears them and calls her 'Devil Incarnate'.

v. ii

16–17. the same Disposition *Villeroy* and *Catinat* made at *Chiari*] After driving Marshal Catinat's French forces back in Italy to the River Oglio near Chiari in the spring of 1701, Prince Eugene, entrenched at Chiari, repulsed an attack by Marshal Villeroi, Catinat's successor, in September, but the allies sustained heavy losses (Churchill, i. 536–8). Trim's disposition of troops, needless to say, is less complex but more successful than those of Villeroi and Catinat.

v. iii

7. a Frock] at this time, a loose coat worn by men of the working class to keep their other clothes clean (Cunnington, *Eighteenth*, pp. 57–8).

42–4. But I . . . Face] Genest says this line is adapted from Cicero, '*Cato mirari se aiebat quod non rideret haruspex haruspicem cum vidisset*' (Genest, ii. 254).

60. Flannen] flannel. This is a reference to the Act of 1678 to stimulate the wool industry by requiring English citizens to be buried in wool rather than foreign linen. Anne Oldfield, who played Lady Sharlot, reflected the Widow's

sentiments when she was buried in Westminster Abbey in Brussels lace and Holland linen.

v. iv

152. Oh *Tattleaid*—His and our Hour is come] a mocking repetition of Lady Brumpton's own words (I. ii. 40) overheard by Lord Brumpton and Trusty.

233–4. supererogatory . . . thou] Steele re-used this line almost two decades later in the *Theatre*, no. 13: '. . . It [the petition which follows] is address'd to Persons of Supererogatory Virtue; and who, as Lord *Brumpton* says in *The Funeral*, should be generous, where others are only requir'd to be just.'

268.4 and 280.1. *Jemmie Bowin*, Mr. *Pate*] Jemmie Bowen and William Pate were two popular singers with the Drury Lane company.

Epilogue

10–33. *To his . . . Smile*.] Steele's chauvinistic epilogue reflected his military fervour and doubtless appealed to his audience, which consisted largely of 'Fellow-Soldiers'. William's armies had not, on the whole, been successful, and the call to arms sprang from genuine patriotism on Steele's part.

15. Roman *Eagle*] the emblem of the Roman army.

21. Paris *has the* Brittish *Yoke confess'd*] in the time of Henry VI.

27. Namure] The battle of Namur in the summer of 1695 was the only major military victory of William III against France.

31. *Bright Circle*] the royal family.

Dedication of *The Funeral; and The Tender Husband: Comedies*

0.4–7. the Dutchess of Hamilton] Elizabeth (1682–1744), only child and heiress of Digby, Lord Gerard, became the second wife of James Douglas in 1698. Douglas, a Scotch lord, was made one of the sixteen Scotch representative peers in 1708. He was first a Whig, then a Tory (*DNB*). Rae Blanchard comments: 'It is odd that Steele should have selected as patroness the wife of a Tory Scotch peer with Jacobite tendencies. . . . Perhaps it was because she looked with kindness upon authors and the stage' (*Correspondence*, pp. 458–9, n. 1).

10. had not these Plays been acted at Your Request] *The Funeral* ran three nights in the 1710–11 season, on 14 December, 9 February, and 26 April; *The Tender Husband* played twice, on 11 January and 10 May. The last four performances were all arranged 'At the Desire of several Ladies of Quality'. However, both plays had run at least once in each of the previous three seasons, and *The Tender Husband* had not missed a season since its opening (Avery, *passim*). Steele's gratitude, therefore, seems a bit excessive, particularly since he would have had no profit from the theatre for these performances.

THE LYING LOVER

[motto] Terence, *Eunuchus*, v. iv. To have seen this is salvation to the young. As usual, Steele adapted the quotation for his play; the source reads '*nosse omnia haec salutist adulescentulis*'.

Dedication

0.4. Duke of Ormond] James Butler (1665–1745), second Duke of Ormonde, to whose family Steele had strong ties of gratitude, was raising a new regiment of dragoons in the winter of 1703–4. The Dedication was probably a fruitless move on Steele's part to get a troop in the regiment (see Winton, p. 70; *Correspondence*, p. 447, n. 1). Steele had served in Ormonde's troop of Life Guards from 1692 to 1695.

3. Your Grace's Grandfather] James Butler (1610–88), the first Duke of Ormonde, for whom Steele's father had sometimes served as private secretary, had secured Steele a place in the Charterhouse (*Correspondence*, p. 447, n. 1).

19. the Son of an Ossory] Thomas Butler (1634–80), Earl of Ossory, was son of the first Duke of Ormonde and father of the second. Steele's compliment reflects general opinion of Ossory. He was a successful admiral and general, a courtier who served in many capacities, including the Privy Council, and, according to John Evelyn's account, 'a sincere friend, a brave souldier, a virtuous courtier, a loyal subject, an honest man, a bountifull master, and good christian' (*DNB*).

32. the Wealth of the *Indies*] The second Duke of Ormonde with Sir George Rooke, after an unsuccessful attack on Cadiz in 1702, defeated twenty-five galleons in Vigo Bay, bringing home a treasure worth £1 million sterling (Churchill, ii. 162, 164).

Preface

11. as He brought with Him from *France*] Young Bookwit's character is based on that of Dorante in Corneille's *Le Menteur* (1642).

30–1. Her Most Excellent Majesty has taken the Stage into Her Consideration] In January 1704, slightly more than a week before *The Lying Lover* was published, Queen Anne issued a proclamation to ban immorality from the theatres:

WHEREAS. We have already given Orders to the Master of Our Revels, and also to Both the Companies of Comedians, Acting in *Drury Lane*, and *Lincolns Inn Fields*, to take Special Care that Nothing be Acted in either of the Theatres contrary to Religion or Good Manners, upon Pain of our High Displeasure, and of being Silenc'd from further Acting; And being further desirous to Reform all other Indecencies, and Abuses of the Stage, which have Occasion'd great Disorders, and Justly give Offence; Our Will and Pleasure therefore is, and We do hereby strictly Command, That no Person of what Quality soever, Presume to go Behind the Scenes, or come upon the Stage, either before, or during the Acting of any Play. That no Woman be

Allow'd or Presume to wear a Vizard Mask in either of the Theatres. And that no Person come into either House without Paying the Prices Establish'd for their Respective Places. . . . (Quoted in Ashton, pp. 255–6).

Prologue

16. *Pleasure must still have something that's severe*] adapted from the fourth line of Steele's *The Procession* (1695), 'Pleasure it self has something that's *severe*'.

I. i

1–4. But . . . Choice] translated from *Le Menteur*, I. i. 1–3. Because of the great number of lines Steele borrowed, I do not quote the French passages in these notes.

5. *Maudlin*] Magdalen College, Oxford.

6–7. We agreed . . . Expedition] Steele introduced the device of friend serving as valet into Corneille's plot. Farquhar later used a similar arrangement between Aimwell and Archer in *The Beaux' Stratagem* (1707).

12–26. Has . . . ignorant] loosely adapted from *Le Menteur*, I. i. 7–14.

102–3. *Villeroy, Catinat,* and *Bouffleurs*] three marshals of France with armies in 1702 in the Italian theatre, the Rhine country, and the Low Countries respectively (Churchill, ii. 119–20).

120. high Mall] the time when the greatest number of promenaders thronged the Mall, a fashionable gravel walk in St. James's Park (*OED*).

127–49. Are . . . Footman] translated from *Le Menteur*, I. i. 84–104.

152–4. Do . . . Domesticks] The gossip of servants is described again by Steele in the *Spectator*, no. 88: 'Hither [the entrance of Hyde Park] People bring their Lacqueys out of State, and here it is that all they say at their Tables and act in their Houses is communicated to the whole Town.'

177–91. (*Stumbling . . . pleasing*] translated from *Le Menteur*, I. ii. 105–28.

222–36. nor . . . Gazette] translated from *Le Menteur*, I. iii. 153–67.

236. *Gazette*] the *London Gazette*, the official newspaper.

238. Tro] a parenthetical expression, the meaning of which, when used in questions, is not clear (*OED*).

240. *Ruremonde, Keyserwart,* and *Leige*] Ruremonde and Liége on the Meuse fell to Marlborough in October 1702; Kaiserwerth, in the Rhine country had been taken by the Allies in June (Churchill, ii. 121–3, 148, 150–1). Steele's mention of these battles reflects his usual pride in Marlborough's victories.

241. *Venlo*] Venloo, a strong French fort on the Meuse, capitulated to the Allies in September 1702. Commanded by Lord Cutts, Steele's former superior officer, to whom he had dedicated *The Procession* and *The Christian Hero*, the Royal Regiment of Ireland reached the ramparts of Fort St. Michael and waged a fierce hand-to-hand battle with the French inside the fort (Churchill, ii. 143–7). Steele's talk about a young gentleman on a parapet shows some familiarity with the siege.

244–6. Don't . . . away] translated from *Le Menteur*, I. iii. 180–2.

254–5. last Summer's Campaign with the renowned Prince *Eugene*] In the summer of 1703 Prince Eugene of Savoy, one of the Allied commanders, was in Hungary trying to deal with a rebellion against the Emperor (Churchill, ii. 241). There was also military activity in Holland in the summer of 1703. Steele allegedly named his son Eugene for the Prince (Winton, p. 147).

265–72. I . . . fit] translated from *Le Menteur*, I. iii. 175–85.

273–460. Rob . . . Troubles] translated from *Le Menteur*, I. iii. 191–I. vi. 370.

299. *Lovemore*] The name Lovemore had been used in other plays, for example Thomas Southerne's *The Wives Excuse* (1691) and Colley Cibber's *Womans Wit* (1697). Paul Bunyan Anderson suggests that John Tidcomb, a friend of Steele whose father's estate was near Landguard Fort, may have been the 'archetype' for this sentimental character. As with Lovemore, Anderson points out, Tidcomb's first name was John, and his father lived in Suffolk. Mary Delariviere Manley's *Adventures of Rivella* (1714) had Tidcomb for its narrator, under the name Sir Charles Lovemore ('Mistress Delariviere Manley's Biography', *Modern Philology*, xxxiii (1935–6), 265, n. 19). Anderson believes she perhaps borrowed the name from *The Lying Lover*.

354. Theorbo] a large lute with a double neck and two sets of tuning-pegs (*OED*).

400. Squibbs] a common kind of fireworks (*OED*).

407–10. Which . . . reported] When Jupiter went to Alcmena in the form of her husband Amphitryon, Phoebus the sun was told not to rise, so that the nocturnal pleasures could be prolonged. Dryden had adapted the myth in a comedy, *Amphitryon* (1690).

444. *Pontack*] the proprietor of Pontack's, a highly reputed French eating-place in London where one could dine very sumptuously at a high charge (*M. Misson's Memoirs and Observations in his Travels over England*, trans. John Ozell (London, 1719), p. 146; Wheatley, iii. 102).

II. i

7–11. I . . . you] translated from *Le Menteur*, II. i. 393–9.

15–16. my Hat, my Feather, Pantaloons, and Jerkin] Old Bookwit describes clothing fashionable no later than the 1670s, which would seem absurd in 1703. For an illustration of the costume he describes see C. Willett and Phillis Cunnington, *Handbook of English Costume in the Seventeenth Century* (London, 1955), p. 151.

56–72. To *Celia's* Spinet] This song, as well as a number of act-tunes used for special effects, was set by William Croft (*Verse*, p. 82).

110. Vails] tips.

140. Ah . . . *Penelope*] translated from *Le Menteur*, II. iii. 469.

173–200. Very . . . Fireworks] a loose translation of *Le Menteur*, II. iii. 474–97.

212. glote] gloat; cast amorous or admiring glances (*OED*).

223. Quartan Agues] fevers or agues with a paroxysm every fourth (in modern reckoning, third) day (*OED*).

226–54. What . . . ha] a loose translation of *Le Menteur*, II. iii. 497–534.

291–9.1 I'll . . . Exit] loosely translated from *Le Menteur*, II. ii. 450–68.

310. *Bohee* Tea] Bohea, a fine black tea, was associated with the luxury of the idle rich.

II. ii

1–6. Well . . . been] Geronte and Dorante, the forerunners of Old Bookwit and his son, discuss the growth and architecture of Paris (II. v. 551–64), but their remarks are different from the Bookwits'.

7. New Exchange] a bazaar on the south side of the Strand, frequented by the gentry and nobility. In the *Spectator*, no. 155, Steele condemned flirtatious gentlemen for wasting the time of the 'pretty merchants' without buying more than a trinket.

39–166. Your . . . Victoria] translated from *Le Menteur*, II. v. 567–II. vii. 712.

144. Privado] intimate private friend (*OED*).

156–7 she *Ganimede* . . . *Hæbe*] servants to the gods. Ganymede was the cup-bearer to Zeus; Hæbe, the handmaiden who poured for the gods the nectar associated with perpetual youth.

165. Rosomond's *Pond*] a pond in the south-west corner of St. James's Park, often the place of lovers' rendezvous in the plays of the period (Wheatley, iii. 168).

184.2–202. *Enter* . . . Letters] a loose translation of *Le Menteur*, V. iii. 717–26.

206. Gentleman Usher] 'a gentleman acting as usher to a person of superior rank' (*OED*). An usher was an attendant, an officer at court or in a dignitary's household.

207–8. wrap'd in ones Mother's Smock to be thus lucky] that is, successful with the ladies. The old superstition is frequently mentioned in plays, for example, Farquhar's *Love and a Bottle* (1699) and Burnaby's *The Modish Husband* (1702).

218. Mr. *Bays*] In Buckingham's *The Rehearsal* (1671) Bayes says 'Ay, now the Plot thickens very much upon us' (III. iv, but III. ii in the first edition).

III. i

8. nestled] fidgeted (*OED*).

30–3. But . . . Dear] The same kind of malicious gossip about a friend, followed by a warm greeting extended to her, occurs several times in

Burnaby's *The Ladies Visiting-Day*. For examples see Burnaby, pp. 251–2, 260–1, 264.

42. fetch] trick (*OED*).

65–6. That . . . are] Addison wrote a *Spectator* paper, no. 86, on this subject.

84. Hack] a hackney coach or carriage. The line is the first example of this usage cited in the *OED*.

III. ii

4. *Formosam . . . Sylvas*] Virgil, *Eclogue*, I, l. 5. You teach the woods to re-echo 'fair Amaryllis'.

27. *Aristippus*] a philosopher of Cyrene who taught that man should strive for the maximum of pleasure and minimum of pain in life.

28. Hermetical Chymist] that is, alchemist. Steele's own loss of money on an alchemical scheme had no doubt convinced him that alchemists 'are good only at making Fires'.

32. Commons] at Oxford, food served from the college kitchen at a regular charge.

50.1–60. [Song] The song was written by Richard Leveridge (1670?–1758), song-writer, composer, and singer in the Drury Lane company, who, according to Miss Blanchard, also sang it in the first run (*Verse*, p. 82–3). It was set by Daniel Purcell.

92. my Opinion in the Use of Pikes] The English army had changed from the use of pikes that screwed into the muzzle of the old matchlock weapons to ring-bayonets which fit around the barrel of flintlocks. France continued to use the old kind of weapon until it was suppressed in 1703 at Marshal Sebastien de Vauban's instance (Churchill, ii. 108–10; Fortescue, i. 586; C. T. Atkinson, *Marlborough and the Rise of the British Army* (New York, 1921), p. 507).

123. hanging-sleves] that is, his academic gown.

136–41. Ha . . . greater] a loose translation of *Le Menteur*, III. v. 1010–12.

138. gravell'd] perplexed or puzzled (*OED*).

145–60. Then . . . her] loosely translated from *Le Menteur*, III. v. 1034–50.

178–86. No . . . you] translated from *Le Menteur*, III. v. 1021–31.

183. *Greys-Inn*] one of the inns of court.

184. *Landen*] a disastrous battle in July 1693 in which the Allies lost nearly 20,000 men (Churchill, i. 416).

IV. ii

3–5. *Well . . .* Parthenia] The tale of Argalus and Parthenia occurs in Sir Phillip Sidney's *Arcadia*, not, of course, in the words read here. Steele was to laugh again at the reading of romances in *The Tender Husband*. The *Arcadia* was among the volumes in Leonora's library, described by Addison in the *Spectator*, no. 37.

60. bright Cook-maid] The malicious Mrs. Manley, in *The New Atalantis*, used this phrase to describe the mother of one of Steele's illegitimate children.

IV. iii

32. *Piazza*] an open arcade on the north and east sides of Covent Garden market-place, built by Inigo Jones, *c.* 1633–4.

38–47. [Song] In *The Monthly Masks of Vocal Musick*, July 1707, this song was described as 'Set and Sung by Mr. Leveridge' (*Verse*, p. 83). However, in the original production, Robert Wilkes obviously sang it. The play was not again run until 1746, so Leveridge's singing must have been in concerts or other entertainments.

69. Round House] the headquarters of the parish watchmen at the south end of St. Martin's Lane, where overnight cases were brought to await judgement the next morning.

IV. iv

5–42. You ... what] translated from *Le Menteur*, v. i. 1445–80.

IV. v

1. *Storm*] to attack or assault (*OED*).

11. *Faggot*] to bind hand and foot (*OED*).

15. Barter on the Change] that is, stoop to business. The Change is the Royal Exchange, where business was conducted.

24. *Charcole*] Charcoal was one of the fuels used by alchemists.

25. Correspondent] accomplice (*OED*).

29. *Raimundus Lullius*] Raymond Lully or Ramon Lull was reputedly the author of many important medieval tracts on alchemy. Many legends surrounded him, including one that he came to London to transmute metal into the purest gold for the king. The name, that of a Catalan mystic, philosopher, and poet, is probably not the right one for the alchemist. (See Arthur Edward Waite, *Lives of Alchemystical Philosophers* (London, 1888), pp. 81–7; F. Sherwood Taylor, *The Alchemists, Founders of Modern Chemistry* (London, 1951), pp. 110–11.)

34. Coining] Counterfeiting was quite prevalent in these times, and the laws had been made very strong in order to combat it. Male coiners were hanged, drawn, and quartered; females were burned (Arthur Griffiths, *The Chronicles of Newgate*, 2 vols. (London, 1884), i. 166).

43–5. I can shew ... so] Charcole uses the jargon of the alchemist. Sol was associated with gold and sophic sulphur, the quintessential sulphur necessary for the philosopher's stone (John Read, *The Alchemist in Life, Literature, and Art* (London, 1947), p. 9).

55. Garnish] The practice of garnish, a fee charged on entering prison, either for the gaoler or for drinks for the prisoners, was notoriously prevalent.

55-6. we . . . hither] Felons were incarcerated on one side of Newgate, debtors on the other.

79. the Keeper's side] For fees, prisoners could get better accommodation. The best lodgings were in the Press-yard, sometimes called the governor's or keeper's house (Griffiths, i. 159–60; *The History of the Press-Yard* (London, 1717), pp. 11–12).

87. the Tap-house] the south-west part of the Stone Room of the common side of Newgate, where beer, ale, wine, brandy, pipes, and tobacco were sold to both felons and debtors (Griffiths, i. 154).

v. i

86–90. Honour . . . Forgive] Steele had fought a duel with Henry or Harry Kelly in June 1700 (Winton, p. 54). His remorse at having almost killed a man apparently led to his many attacks on the generally accepted practice, the first of which appears here.

v. ii

0.2 *Enter* Lovemore *in a Serjeant's Gown*] Wisemore in Fielding's *Love in Several Masques* comes to Lady Matchless disguised 'in a Sergeant's Gown, his Hat over his Ears' (v. xii). A serjeant was a barrister of superior rank and a member of the Order of the Coif.

v. iii

101–3. He . . . *Penelope*] In Fielding's *Love in Several Masques* (v. xiii) Malvil tells Lady Matchless, who has refused Wisemore's attentions, that he has fought a duel and killed her suitor, 'whose dying Sighs were loaded with your Name—Yes, the last Words your *Wisemore* uttered, were to implore eternal Blessings on you. . . .'

119–22. Let . . . *Life*] Lady Matchless says, 'But now farewell Content, Greatness, Happiness, and all the Sweets of Life—I'll study to be miserable' (*Love in Several Masques*, v. xiii).

129. Nies] eyes.

326.1–42. [Song] The setting and composer are unknown.

335. *their present Queen*] Queen Anne.

THE TENDER HUSBAND

[title] Steele first used the phrase 'accomplish'd Fools' in *The Lying Lover*, III. ii. 15.

[motto] The auditor ought to think about more than meets the eye. Steele adapted his motto from Cicero's *De Oratore* II. lix: '*Orator surripiat oportet*

imitationem ut is qui audiet, cogitet plura, quam videat, praestet idem ingenuitatem et ruborem suum, verborum turpitudine et rerum obscenitate vitanda.' Steele's purpose in choosing this motto is lost on the modern reader.

Dedication

0.2. Mr. Addison] In the seventh edition of Addison's *Cato*, published 26 June 1713, Steele's 'Verses to the Author of the Tragedy of Cato' included these lines:

> To my light Scenes I once inscrib'd your Name,
> And impotently strove to borrow Fame:
> Soon will that die, which adds thy Name to mine,
> Let me, then, live, join'd to a Work of thine.

Prologue

20. *the Park*] St. James's Park.

22. *the Ring*] a circle in Hyde Park in which the fashionable rode and promenaded. 'In a pretty high Place, which lies very open, they have surrounded a Circumference of two or three hundred Paces Diameter with a sorry Kind of Ballustrade, or rather with Poles plac'd upon Stakes, but three Foot from the Ground; and the Coaches drive round and round this. When they have turn'd for some Time round one Way, they face about and turn t'other: So rowls the World' (Misson, p. 126).

24. *taking Snuff*] The practice became fashionable in 1702 after an immense quantity captured in Ormonde and Rooke's attack on Vigo Bay was dumped on the London market (Ashton, pp. 158–9).

24. *White's*] White's Chocolate-house, established *c.* 1698 on St. James's Street, soon became a gaming-house where aristocrats were gulled and corrupted by gamblers and profligates. See *The Rake's Progress*, Part vi.

Song

This song celebrates the resounding victory of the Grand Alliance led by Marlborough over the Franco-Bavarian army at Blenheim 13 August 1704, a few months before *The Tender Husband* was first performed. Allied casualties, mourned in the third and fourth stanzas, numbered more than 4,500 (Atkinson, pp. 235–6). Churchill sums up the importance of the victory: 'Blenheim is immortal as a battle not only because of . . . the overwhelming character of the victory, but because it changed the political axis of the world. This only gradually became apparent. Even a month after all the facts were known, measured, and discounted, scarcely any one understood what transformations had been wrought' (ii. 478). In the first two stanzas of his song Steele gives some indications of realizing the transformations.

51. *Manes*] Usually meaning the deified souls or reverenced spirits of departed persons, here it is taken in the sense of mortal remains. The earliest citation of this usage in the *OED* is 1707.

I. i

1. *Fainlove*] The role of Clerimont Senior's 'dear Lucy', who dresses as a young spark to trap Mrs. Clerimont in an indiscretion, is the only 'breeches part' in any of Steele's plays.

23. Innocent Freedoms] This expression was a stock phrase for fashionable women's flirtations, gambling, and other minor offences. It was identically used, for example, by Burnaby in *The Ladies Visiting-Day* (Burnaby, pp. 219–20).

41. Perspective] an optical instrument to make objects or people appear larger, nearer, or clearer (*OED*). Perspectives were at this period, apparently, like spy-glasses; Steele describes one in the *Tatler*, no. 103, as a 'Glass-Tube'. The fad is described in the *Tatler*, no. 77: 'About five Years ago, I remember it was the Fashion to be short-sighted: A Man would not own an Acquaintance 'till he had first examin'd him with his Glass. At a Lady's Entrance into the Play-house, you might see Tubes immediately levell'd at her from every Quarter of the Pit and Side-Boxes.'

85. *Clerimont*] The name Clerimont was also used in Thomas Wright's *The Female Vertuoso's* (1693). In Burnaby's *The Reform'd Wife* (1700) a Cleremont, usually spelt Clerimont, 'the Spirit of Mirth and Wickedness', is a fortune-hunter who seeks Lady Dainty for her £2,000 a year despite the fact that she is a hypochondriac. He is told to humour her, but, like Steele's Clerimont, believes 'the best way to gain her' is 'at her own Weapon', in this case contradiction (Burnaby, pp. 128–30).

108. *Westminster-hall*] Law courts were held in the open hall at Westminster, but the name 'Westminster Hall' was frequently used to refer to the law itself (Wheatley, iii. 483).

124–5. the General . . . War] a compliment to Marlborough, who was being celebrated in London for the triumph of Blenheim in 1704. Although the campaign of 1705 did not live up to the promise of Blenheim, Marlborough himself was honoured early in 1705 by a triumphal procession and state entertainment by the Lord Mayor and Aldermen of London, and he received the formal grant of Woodstock where Blenheim Palace was to be built. Additional supplies and six new battalions were voted for the army (Atkinson, p. 248).

125–7. We Red-coats . . . Business] Clerimont, the amiable fortune-hunter, mirrors many of the traits of his creator. Steele, a young captain and 'a Fellow of the most Easy indolent Disposition in the World', left the army in the spring of 1705. He, like the younger Clerimont, pursued an heiress, undoubtedly with the same motives. After the manuscript of *The Tender Husband* was delivered to Rich in March or April of 1705, Steele and his ageing but wealthy widow, Margaret Ford Stretch, were wed in April or May (Winton, pp. 76–7).

135–6. the very . . . St. James's] i.e. the worlds of business, pleasure, and fashion.

152. *Lombard Street*] a street inhabited by bankers, goldsmiths, and merchants, extending from the Mansion House to Gracechurch Street (Wheatley,
ii. 415–16).

197–8. *Oroondates, Cassandra, Astræa,* and *Clelia*] *Cassandra, Astraea,* and *Clelia*
are three seventeenth-century French romances translated in many-volumed
English editions. *Cassandra,* which contains the adventures of Oroondates, a
Scythian prince, was written by Gautier de Costes, Seigneur de la Cal-
prenède, published in Paris in 1642–5, translated into English in 1652, 1661,
1664, 1667, 1673, and abridged in 1703. *Astraea,* by Honoré d'Urfé, was
published in Paris in 1607–19 and translated into English in 1620 and 1657–8.
Clelia, by Madeleine de Scudéry, was published in Paris in 1654–61 and
translated in 1655–61 and again in 1677–8 (publication dates compiled from
Charles C. Mish, *English Prose Fiction, 1600–1700* (Charlottesville, 1967);
Donald Wing, *Short-Title Catalogue, 1641–1700* (New York, 1945–51); and
Arundell Esdaile, *A List of English Tales and Prose Romances Printed Before 1740*
(London, 1912)). All three romances were included by Addison in Leonora's
library, *Spectator,* no. 37, in which *Clelia* opened 'of it self in the Place that
describes two Lovers in a Bower'.

I. ii

0.1. *Sir* Harry Gubbin] The dialectal 'gobbin', used in Lancashire, Cheshire,
Derbyshire, and Suffolk, meant an ignorant or clownish person or a country
fellow. The word 'gubbins', also spelled 'gubbings', was used contemptuously
in reference to the inhabitants of a district near Brent Tor on the edge of
Dartmoor, who were said to be almost savages as late as the fourth quarter
of the century; Biddy capitalizes on this meaning when she deplores
Humphry's savagery in III. ii. 'Gubbin' or 'gobbin' is also a mining term
meaning the action of packing an excavated area with waste rock, as well as the
material—ironstone—used for this. It is noteworthy that the name Trelooby,
used for the Cornish bumpkin in the English translation of Molière's *Monsieur
de Pourceaugnac,* comes from the Cornish mining term 'treloobing' (*The English
Dialect Dictionary,* ed. Joseph Wright, 6 vols. (London, 1900–5); *OED*).

9. retrospects] Laws that have retrospects are designed to extend to
things already past (*OED*).

20. Pin-Money] According to the *Spectator,* no. 295, written by Addison,
pin-money, the allowance settled on a wife by the marriage contract for her
private expenditure on dress and other personal items, was often £400–600
per annum in Queen Anne's time. The Spectator saw the money as a serious
threat to marriages, contributing to extra-marital love affairs for example;
but he also felt it served as a kind of alimony in case husbands turned out
poorly.

84–5. your Hat under your Arm] It was fashionable, particularly for beaux,
to carry hats thus (Cunnington, *Eighteenth,* p. 87).

88. a Courant, or a Boree] two dances taken over from the French.

116. Whet] drink.

145–6. He . . . Hounds] In *She Stoops to Conquer*, Tony Lumpkin says 'Father-in-law has been calling me whelp, and hound, this half year'.

160–3. Pray . . . back] A similar revelation occurs in *She Stoops to Conquer*, Act V:

Hardcastle. While I thought concealing your age boy was likely to conduce to your improvement, I concurred with your mother's desire to keep it secret. But since I find she turns it to a wrong use, I must now declare, you have been of age these three months.
Tony. Of age! Am I of age, father?
Hardcastle. Above three months.

II. i

6. turning Her Pence] employing her money profitably.

7. Annuities] investments 'whereby the investor becomes entitled to receive a series of equal annual payments, which, except in the case of perpetual annuities, includes the ultimate return of both principal and interest' (*OED*).

II. ii

30. *Elismonda, Clidamira, Deidamia*] All are names from seventeenth-century romances. Elismonda and Clidamira are beautiful maidens of royal descent whose romantic adventures are described in *Clelia*; Deidamia, another princess, is wooed and won by Demetrius in *Cassandra*.

33–4. *Aurelia, Sacharissa, Gloriana*] *The Most Excellent History of Antonius and Aurelia: or, The Two Incomparable Lovers* was published in 1682. Another Aurelia appears in *Clelia*, and she too possesses the requisite beauty, virtue, and merit. Sacharissa is celebrated in Edmund Waller's poems. Gloriana is the Faerie Queene.

34. *Celia, Chloris, Corinna, Mapsa*] names standard in the romantic literature and pastorals. Mopsa in Sidney's *Arcadia* is the daughter of 'the most arrant doltish clowne Dametas', with whose family Pamela resides in a lodge in the forest.

44–5. Possets, Caudles and Surfeit-Waters] home remedies. Possets were made of hot milk curdled with ale or wine and seasoned with sugar and spices. A caudle was a warm drink composed of a thin gruel with wine or ale, also sweetened and spiced. According to the *OED*, these drinks were served to visitors as well as sick people, but in the *Spectator*, no. 143, Steele refers to them strictly as curatives: 'If a Man laments in Company, where the rest are in Humour enough to enjoy themselves, he should not take it ill if a Servant is order'd to present him with a Porringer of Cawdle or Posset-Drink, by way of Admonition that he go Home to Bed.' Surfeit-waters were given to cure over-indulgence in food and drink.

53–4. I . . . Nativity] Magdelon in *Les Précieuses ridicules* says, 'J'ai peine à me persuader que je puisse être véritablement sa fille, et je crois que quelque aventure, un jour, me viendra développer une naissance plus illustre.'

79. *Philocles, Artaxerxes*] Philocles describes his pursuit of Philista in the third volume of *Artamenes: Or, the Grand Cyrus* by Madeleine de Scudéry, published in Paris in 1649–53 and translated into English in 1653–5 and again in 1690 or 1691. This romance was the basis of Dryden's *Secret Love*, first acted in 1667 and published in 1668. Artaxerxes is a young hero in *Cassandra*.

115. *Hackney*] The suburb of Hackney, once frequented by the aristocracy, fell into the hands of the merchant class in the eighteenth century. Biddy's scornful reference indicates that the transition was well under way as early as 1705. John Strype, in his revised and enlarged edition of John Stow's *Survey of the Cities of London and Westminster* (1720), styled Hackney a 'pleasant and healthful Town . . . where divers Nobles in former Times had their Country Seats' (vi. 122). By 1774 the *Ambulator* described it as a large village inhabited by merchants and wealthy persons.

143. the Liberties] the district, extending beyond the London city boundaries, which is subject to the control of municipal authorities.

189. *Urganda*] an enchantress in the Amadis and Palmerin romances.

194–5. *Pamela . . . Musidorus*] young lovers in the *Arcadia*.

238. *Parthenissa*] Biddy's embarrassment at her name, so unsuitable for romances, and her decision to change it to a more mellifluous one, parallel the feelings of Cathos and Magdelon in *Les Précieuses ridicules*, who change their names to Aminta and Polyxena. Parthenissa is the heroine of Roger Boyle's romance *Parthenissa*, which was published in parts in 1651, 1654–6, and 1669, and the complete work again in 1676 (Mish, *passim*).

253–8. Oh . . . Hand-maid] Biddy's conception of courtship on the pattern set by the French romances is another echo from *Les Précieuses ridicules*.

269. *Statira*] the widow of Alexander, who married Oroondates after many difficulties, in *Cassandra*.

II. iii

6. *Philocleas*] Philoclea is Pamela's sister, the younger daughter of the Prince of Arcadia in Sidney's romance.

10–11. all the Stocks, Old and New Company] that is, the old and new East India Companies. Fierce rivalry between the old or London East India Company and the new or English East India Company raged from 1698, when the new company was formed, to 1702, bringing both to the brink of ruin. Attempts at a truce produced a pseudo-alliance in 1702, but animosities continued until 1708, when the two companies finally united (Beckles Willson, *Ledger and Sword, or the Honourable Company of Merchants of England Trading to the East Indies (1599–1874)*, 2 vols. (London, 1903), ii. 20–37).

12. Sword-Blades] The Sword Blade Company, originally founded in 1691 to manufacture blades, became a land company involved in buying Irish forfeited estates. Sword Blades stock reached its highest price in 1704, and in

April 1705, when the play opened, it was still quite high. Thereafter the price fell (W. R. Scott, *The Constitution and Finance of English, Scottish, and Irish Joint-Stock Companies to 1720*, 3 vols. (Cambridge, 1911), iii. 435–9).

12. Chamber of *London*] the city treasury, where the city funds were kept and all moneys due to it were received.

12. Banks for Charity] 'Banks of Piety and Charity' or 'Lumbards' were glorified pawnshops, where credit could be gained on the strength of goods of any sort. By the end of the seventeenth century, it became quite usual for Lumbard-bank activities to be suggested as part of the function of any new bank, regardless of the nature of its major operations. In arguing the desirability of a new bank, the eleemosynary aspect—to save the poor from usurers—was often introduced (Keith Horsefield, *British Monetary Experiments 1650–1710* (Cambridge, Massachusetts, 1960), pp. 95, 104–6, 111). Biddy's aunt was obviously interested in financial gain rather than helping the poor; it is possible that Steele intended to dispraise the banks of charity.

12–13. Mine-Adventures] speculations in mines.

14. *Garaways*] a coffee-house in Exchange Alley, which served as one of the chief auction rooms in the City as well as a retreat for businessmen and bankers (Wheatley, ii. 187). In *A Journey through England*, published in 1722, Defoe said that it was the haunt of 'the People of Quality, who have business in the City, and the most considerable and wealthy citizens' (i. 174).

III. i

78.1–86 [Song] set and sung by Ramondon (*The Monthly Masks of Vocal Musick*, May 1706, cited in *Verse*, p. 84). Ramondon had first performed on the London stage only ten days earlier (Avery, i. 92).

125. Coupees] a dance step in which the dancer puts one foot either forward or backward in a kind of bow or salutation (*OED*).

144. [Humphry's dance] A letter appeared in the *Weekly Journal or Saturday's Post* of 20 January 1722, complaining that in the performance of 8 January at Drury Lane, 'That filthy Brute, Mr Penkethman, who by his Part, was obliged to dance, [took] in the Galleries with an idle Jest, by pretending that his Activity had shuffled down his Breeches. In short, Mr Mist, this Indecorum fill'd me with such gross Ideas, that the Thoughts of them hinder'd me from sleeping all that Night' (quoted in Avery, ii. 657).

164. 'form] train, shape his conduct. Steele may have intended either 'form' or 'inform', both of which carried this meaning.

III. ii

27. *Valentine* and *Orson*] Characters in a French romance, translated into English as *The Hystory of the two valyaunte brethren Valentyne and Orson, sonnes unto the Emperour of Greece* in the middle of the sixteenth century, and republished, sometimes in abridged form, in 1637, 1649, 1664(?), 1671, 1673, 1682,

1683, 1685, 1688, 1694, 1696, and 1700 (Mish, *passim*). The wild man who precipitates Biddy's questions is Orson, who has been carried off by a bear and reared in the wilds. His brother Valentine, brought up as a knight, brings Orson to court and tames him.

90–116. When . . . Creatures] Goldsmith parallels this scene when Tony Lumpkin and Miss Neville deceive Mrs. Hardcastle similarly in IV. i.

IV. i

13. Pencil] an artist's paint brush.

18.1–30. [Song] The song was set by Daniel Purcell and sung by Francis Hughes, according to *The Monthly Masks of Vocal Musick*, May 1705 (cited in *Verse*, p. 84).

IV. ii

7–10. Since . . . since] Mrs. Western echoes Miss Tipkin in *Tom Jones*, Book XVII, Chapter 4, when she tells Sophia, 'I have been formerly thought cruel; by the Men I mean. I was called the cruel *Parthenissa*.'

12–20. Yet . . . mine] Mrs. Western says:

'I have had Lovers formerly, not so long ago neither; several Lovers, tho' I never would consent to Marriage. . . . I have refused the Offer of a Title; but it was not so good an Offer; that is, not so very, very good an Offer.'—'Yes, Madam,' said *Sophia*; 'but you have had very great Proposals from Men of vast Fortunes. It was not the first, nor the second, nor the third advantageous Match that offered itself.' 'I own it was not,' said she.

34.1–170. Enter . . . Clelia] This scene is derived largely from Scene xi of *Le Sicilien* by Molière (1667). Steele translated some lines, but he adapted the material to his own purpose.

40–3. Madam . . . it] In *Le Sicilien* Adraste says, 'Le Ciel, qui fit l'original, nous ôte le moyen d'en faire un portrait qui puisse flatter.'

45. I . . . none] Isidore tells Adraste: 'Je ne suis pas comme ces femmes qui veulent, en se faisant peindre, des portraits qui ne sont point elles, et ne sont point satisfaites du peintre s'il ne les fait toujours plus belles que le jour.'

58–9. Sir . . . me] Isidore says, 'Si votre pinceau flatte autant que votre langue, vous allez me faire un portrait qui ne me ressemblera pas.'

61–2. Madam . . . Light] In *Le Sicilien* the lines read:

Isidore. Où voulez-vous que je me place?
Adraste. Ici. Voici le lieu le plus avantageux, et qui reçoit le mieux les vues favorables de la lumière que nous cherchons.

62–102. You . . . *Venus*] The comments on art, satirizing the state of English portrait painting as well as the ladies' romantic notions in Steele's time, owe nothing to Molière.

88. *Thalestris*] The Queen of the Amazons enjoys an unbelievably complicated romance with Orontes, the history of which she repeats to Oroondates in *Cassandra*.

107–28. Ladies . . . her] The painter's repetition of his own story for the sake of his lady is new with Steele. In *Le Sicilien* Adraste tells of Apelles, who fell in love with one of Alexander's mistresses as he painted her and almost lost his life consequently before the generous Alexander gave the girl to him. The painter's directions to his subject for her pose are, however, parallel to those in the earlier play:

. . . Levez-vous un peu, s'il vous plaît. Un peu plus de ce côté-là; le corps tourné ainsi; la tête un peu levée, afin que la beauté du cou paraisse. Ceci un peu plus découvert. (*Il parle de sa gorge.*) Bon. Là, un peu davantage. Encore tant soit peu. . . . Un peu plus de ce côté; vos yeux toujours tournés vers moi, je vous en prie; vos regards attachés aux miens.

Again, however, there is a difference. Steele uses the painter's instructions as a means of informing Biddy of the artist's true identity, whereas Molière permits Adraste to reveal himself while Dom Pedro is otherwise occupied. Further, Isidore elopes after slipping out in the veil of Climène; Biddy leaves on the arm of Humphry, pretending that it is he she will wed.

150–7. [Song] set by Daniel Purcell (*The Monthly Masks of Vocal Musick*, April 1705, cited in *Verse*, p. 85).

170. Princess of the *Leontines*] Lysimena, the Princess of the Leontines in *Clelia*, is harrassed by her brother and her supposed friend Amarintha, who wish her to marry Meleontus although she prefers Zenocrates.

171–2. How . . . Marriage] In *The Female Vertuoso's*, Act 1, Catchat says to Clerimont, 'What! Would you come to a Conclusion so very quick? Fye, *Clerimont*, 'tis against the Rules.'

197–215. But . . . with] Magdelon, in *Les Précieuses ridicules*, spells out the procedure of courtship in greater detail:

. . . le mariage ne doit jamais arriver qu'après les autres aventures. Il faut qu'un amant, pour être agréable, sache débiter les beaux sentiments, pousser le doux, le tendre et le passionné, et que sa recherche soit dans les formes. Premièrement, il doit voir au temple, ou à la promenade, ou dans quelque cérémonie publique, la personne dont il devient amoureux; ou bien être conduit fatalement chez elle par un parent ou un ami, et sortir de là tout rêveur et mélancolique. Il cache un temps sa passion à l'objet aimé, et cependant lui rend plusieurs visites, où l'on ne manque jamais de mettre sur le tapis une question galante qui exerce les esprits de l'assemblée. Le jour de la déclaration arrive, qui se doit faire ordinairement dans une allée de quelque jardin, tandis que la compagnie s'est un peu éloignée; et cette déclaration est suivie d'un prompt courroux, qui paraît à notre rougeur, et qui, pour un temps, bannit l'amant de notre présence. Ensuite il trouve moyen de nous apaiser, de nous accoutumer insensiblement au discours de sa passion, et de tirer de nous cet aveu qui fait tant de peine. Après cela viennent les aventures, les rivaux qui se jettent à la traverse d'une inclination établie, les persécutions des pères, les jalousies conçues sur de fausses apparences, les plaintes, les désespoirs, les enlèvements, et ce qui s'ensuit.

212–13. I . . . Pocket-Book] taken from *Les Précieuses ridicules*, Scene iv: 'Mon Dieu, que, si tout le monde vous ressemblait, un roman serait bientôt fini! La belle chose que ce serait, si d'abord Cyrus épousait Mandane, et qu'Aronce de plain-pied fût marié à Clélie!' Catchat echoes in *The Female Vertuoso's*: 'What had become of the rest of the Romance had *Mandana* yielded presently to *Grand Cyrus*; or, *Clælia* fled into the Arms of *Aronces* at the first intimation of his Love?' (Act 1).

v. i

13. Mignon] darling, dear.

v. ii

75–90. *Imprimis . . . it*] Paul E. Parnell has pointed out that the list of items closely parallels Harpagon's inventory in Molière's *L'Avare* (II. i) in the following points:

(1) trois gros mousquets tout garnis de nacre de perles, avec les . . . fourchettes assertissantes
(2) un luth de Bologne, garni de toutes ses cordes, ou peu s'en faut
(3) une tenture de tapisserie des amours de Gombaut et de Macée
(4) un lit de quatre pieds, à bandes de points de Hongrie, appliquées sur un drap de couleur d'olive

('A New Molière Source for Steele's *The Tender Husband*', *NQ* cciv, N.S. vi (1959), 218).

87. *Judith* and *Holofernes*] the Apocryphal tale of a widow who, when Nebuchadnezzar's army descended on her town, went to the tent of the enemy general Holofernes and beheaded him.

157–8. their Glorious Monarch] Louis XIV.

159–60. He . . . grazing] The harsh and inequitable taxation in France and the hardships caused by the war and poor monetary administration had brought the French to a very serious financial situation by 1705. (See A. Cheruel, *Histoire de l'administration monarchique en France*, 3 vols. (Paris, 1885), ii. 421–4.)

179. Roast-Meat] To make roast meat of someone meant figuratively to burn him, destroy him, finish him off (*OED*).

218–23. *You've . . . fear*] The virtuous Pamela in Richardson's novel disapproved of the tag: '. . . the author seems to have forgotten the moral all the way; and being put in mind of it by some kind friend (Mr. Addison, perhaps), was at a loss to draw one from such characters and plots as he had produced; and so put down what came uppermost, for the sake of custom, without much regard to propriety.'

Epilogue

4. Italian *squaling Tribe*] Steele and other men of the theatre fought to protect their stronghold from invaders like Nicolini and his band of eunuchs, but the struggle was hopeless. As early as the seventh performance of *The Tender Husband* 'Songs . . . from Rome' (l. 6) were advertised to encourage attendance (Avery, i. 96).

23. Tramontanes] foreigners, outsiders. The word specifically means those who live beyond the mountains, i.e. the Alps.

25. Anna] Queen Anne.

THE CONSCIOUS LOVERS

[motto] *Rhetorica ad Herennium*, I. viii, a work no longer attributed to Cicero. The kind of narration based on characters ought to have pleasantry of discourse, diversity of spirits, gravity, gentleness, hope, fear, suspicion, desire, hypocrisy, compassion, variety of events, changes of fortune, unexpected misfortune, sudden joy, and a happy outcome.

Dedication

0.1–2. the King] George I.

4. Direction of the Theatre] Steele was appointed governor of Drury Lane Theatre in 1714 (Loftis, p. 37).

25–35. the Insinuations . . . Humanity] In April 1722 word of a Jacobite plot reached Robert Walpole, who collected evidence and called up the Guards to stay in Hyde Park. By May arrests began, and in a few months Bishop Atterbury, Christopher Layer, Lord North and Grey, Lord Orrery, the Duke of Norfolk, and others were in the Tower. In November, only weeks before Steele's play opened, Layer's trial revealed the outlines of the plot, which included Steele's friend, the Duke of Ormonde. Reprisals followed, including the suspension of habeas corpus for one year and taxes on Catholics and non-jurors (Basil Williams, *The Whig Supremacy 1714–1760* (Oxford, 1949), pp. 174–5).

Preface

8–11. To which . . . without it] In the *Theatre*, no. 28, Steele, speaking of the comedy he was writing, commented, 'a Play is not designed so much for the Reader as the Spectator.'

14–21. The chief . . . Absence] Aitken records rough notes for a preface from the Blenheim papers: 'The fourth act was the business of the play. The case of duelling. I have fought, nor shall I ever fight again. . . . Addison told me I had a faculty of drawing tears. . . . Be that as it will, I shall endeavour to do what I can to promote noble things which I will do as well as I can' (Mermaid, p. 269, n. 1).

19. and] According to Aitken, 'the stupid and diabolical custom of duelling' followed in the manuscript of the Preface in the Blenheim papers, but was erased (Mermaid, p. 270, n. 1).

33. Mr. *Wilks*] Robert Wilks, one of the actor-managers, played Myrtle.

34. a *General*] the Honourable Brigadier-General Charles Churchill, according to William Egerton (*Faithful Memoirs of the Life . . . of . . . Mrs. Anne*

Oldfield (London, 1731), p. 67 n.). If he was indeed the officer mentioned by Steele, he was watching his mistress, Anne Oldfield, play Indiana as he wept.

38. whether . . . not] Aitken gives the manuscript version as 'to enquire what should not which does please' (Mermaid, p. 270, n. 3).

41. Sig. *Carbonelli*] Giovanno Steffano Carbonelli (1700?–72), a virtuoso violinist who came from Italy in 1719 (E. Van der Straaten, *The History of the Violin*, 2 vols. (London, 1933), ii. 13).

42. play'd] 'played admirably well' in the manuscript version (Mermaid, p. 270, n. 5).

45. small] 'great' in the manuscript (Mermaid, p. 271, n. 1).

47–54. [Song] An earlier version entitled 'The Love-Sick Maid' appeared in the *Theatre*, no. 18. Lines 5–6 differed from the song printed with the play:

> Me to the Youth, who caus'd my Grief,
> My too consenting Looks betray:

'The Love-Sick Maid' was set by John Ernest Gallaird (1687?–1749), and Galliard's music was, presumably, to have been used in performance. In *Verse*, Miss Blanchard identifies four settings, including an unpublished one by Venanzio Rauzzini, and surmises that the one printed in *The Musical Miscellany* of 1729 (i. 104–5) is Galliard's (pp. 86–8). However, it is more probable that a broadside version was the original one, published soon after the *première* to capitalize on the play's success. Thomas Cross, John Walsh, and others engraved broadside songs during this period (for Walsh's rivalry with Cross, see *Grove's Dictionary of Music and Musicians*, ed. Eric Blom, 5th edn., 9 vols. (London, 1954), ii. 543). Miss Blanchard lists one broadside, engraved by Cross, and suggests that it was the version composed by Samuel Howard for a performance at Covent Garden 17 March 1737. Since the latest work by Cross was issued in 1733 (*Grove*, ii. 542), the identification seems extremely unlikely. Further, a second broadside of the same setting (copy in the Folger Shakespeare Library) suggests competition consistent with the early interest in the play. The broadsides and *The Musical Miscellany* reprint the lyrics as they appear in the play instead of the *Theatre*, but *The Musical Miscellany* misprints 'Pang' for 'Pangs' in line 5.

56. Mr. *Cibber*] Colley Cibber, who played Tom.

57. the Translation of him] 'the imitation of Pamphilus' in the manuscript (Mermaid, p. 271, n. 3).

62. persuaded] 'by him' followed in the manuscript (Mermaid, p. 271, n. 4).

63. *Terence's* celebrated Funeral] In the *Andria* the young lovers Pamphilus and Glycerium inadvertently reveal their love before the mourners at a funeral. Steele substituted a masquerade at Cibber's insistence.

Prologue

0.2. Mr. *Welsted*] Leonard Welsted, the poet (1688–1747), was a friend of Steele.

8. Pinkey] William Pinkethman, the comedian.

26. *a* Smithfield *Show*] one of the 'low' entertainments of Bartholomew Fair.

I. i

5–6. full forty Years] Steele characterized Humphrey in the servant of Sir John Edgar in the *Theatre*, no. 3: 'My Man *Humphrey*, who has liv'd with me for many Years, . . . is a diligent, careful, sensible Man, and has had a Right in all that comes off my Person these forty Years; for so long has he been my *Valet de Chambre*, or Gentleman, as they call it.'

17–20. Well . . . Servant] The opening dialogue between master and servant is loosely based on the opening scene of the *Andria*. Lines 20–3 parallel it closely:

Simo. ego postquam te emi, a parvolo ut semper tibi
   apud me iusta et clemens fuerit servitus
   scis.

23–33. I'll . . . Fear] This dialogue also parallels the *Andria*:

Simo. ita faciam. hoc primum in hac re praedico tibi:
   quas credis esse has non sunt verae nuptiae.
Sosia. quor simulas igitur?
Simo.   rem omnem a principio audies:
   eo pacto et gnati vitam et consilium meum
   cognosces et quid facere in hac re te velim.
   nam is postquam excessit ex ephebis, Sosia, et
   libera vivendi fuit potestas,—nam antea
   qui scire posses aut ingenium noscere,
   dum aetas metus magister prohibebant?

29–30. Now . . . Son] In the *Theatre*, no. I, Sir John Edgar speaks of his son Harry: 'I have always abhor'd living at Distance with him, and ever gave him his Freedom in all his Words and Actions, so that I have seldom expostulated with him concerning them; . . .'.

69. *Cymon*] a dull-witted clod who, seeing Iphigenia asleep, fell in love and consequently began his polite education. The tale from the *Decameron* (v. i) appears among Dryden's *Fables*.

94–115. You are . . . to you] These speeches are based on the *Andria*:

Simo. venit Chremes postridie ad me clamitans:
   indignum facinus; comperisse Pamphilum
   pro uxore habere hanc peregrinam. ego illud sedulo
   negare factum. ille instat factum. denique
   ita tum discedo ab illo, ut qui se filiam
   neget daturum.
Sosia.   non tu ibi gnatum . . .?
Simo.   ne haec quidem
   satis vemens causa ad obiurgandum.
Sosia.   qui? cedo.
Simo. 'tute ipse his rebus finem praescripsti, pater:
   prope adest quom alieno more vivendumst mihi:
   sine nunc meo me vivere interea modo.'
Sosia. qui igitur relictus est obiurgandi locus?

Simo. si propter amorem uxorem nolet ducere.
ea primum ab illo animum advortenda iniuriast;
et nunc id operam do, ut per falsas nuptias
vera obiurgandi causa sit, si deneget;
simul sceleratus Davos si quid consili
habet, ut consumat nunc quom nil obsint doli;
quem ego credo manibus pedibusque obnixe omnia
facturum, magis id adeo mihi ut incommodet,
quam ut obsequatur gnato.
Sosia.   quapropter?
Simo.   rogas?
mala mens, malus animus. quem quidem ego si sensero . . .
sed quid opust verbis? sin eveniat quod volo,
in Pamphilo ut nil sit morae, restat Chremes
qui mi exorandus est: et spero confore.
nunc tuomst officium has bene ut adsimules nuptias,
perterrefacias Davom, observes filium,
quid agat, quid cum illo consili captet.

125. Board-Wages] Steele attacked the practice of giving these wages as an allowance for servants' food in the *Spectator*, no. 88: '. . . I can attribute the Licentiousness which has at present prevailed among them [i.e. men servants] to nothing but what an hundred before me have ascribed it to, The Custom of giving Board-Wages: This one Instance of false Oeconomy is sufficient to debauch the whole Nation of Servants, and makes them as it were but for some Part of their Time in that Quality.'

133–4. Oaken Cudgel] the unfashionable walking stick of labourers (Cunnington, *Eighteenth*, p. 101).

135. that dangling Stick at your Button] Fashionable servants wore a walking stick attached to a coat button (Rolli, p. (151), n. 1).

159–60. Chocolate Houses and Taverns] Steele had complained of this practice in the *Spectator*, no. 88:

They are either attending in Places where they meet and run into Clubs, or else, if they wait at Taverns, they eat after their Masters, and reserve their Wages for other Occasions. From hence it arises, That they are but in a lower Degree what their Masters themselves are; and usually affect an Imitation of their Manners: And you have in Liveries Beaux, Fops, and Coxcombs in as high Perfection, as among People that keep Equipages.

171. the Lacquies] In the *Spectator*, no. 88, Steele commented: 'It is a general Observation, That all Dependants run in some Measure into the Manners and Behaviour of those whom they serve: You shall frequently meet with Lovers and Men of Intrigue among the Lacqueys, as well as at *White's* or in the Side-boxes.'

175. take up] mend our ways.

178–9. the highest Dignities and Distinctions] Steele also wrote of this practice in the *Spectator*, no. 88:

It is a common Humour among the Retinue of People of Quality, when they are in their Revels, that is when they are out of their Masters Sight, to assume in an humourous Way the Names and Titles of those whose Liveries they wear. . . . It is a thing too notorious to mention the Crowds of Servants, and their Insolence, near the Courts of Justice, and the Stairs towards the supreme Assembly; where there is an universal Mockery of all Order, such riotous Clamour and licentious Confusion, that one would think the whole Nation lived in jest, and there were no such thing as Rule and Distinction among us.

179. *Painted Chamber*] a room in the House of Parliament where servants of Members waited for their patrons. While there, they referred to each other by the names of their masters (Rolli, p. (151), n. 2).

181. the *Court of Requests*] the ancient building in which the House of Lords met. Here servants debated politics, sometimes coming to blows (Rolli, p. (151), n. 3).

199. *Ridotto's*] a new kind of musical entertainment introduced at the Opera House in the Haymarket in 1722, the year *The Conscious Lovers* opened.

200. *Bellsize*] an estate less than two miles from London whose gardens, refreshments, and amusements predated those of Vauxhall and Ranelagh for public entertainment in the summer.

230. Manteau and Petticoat] a gown open in front to display an under-skirt (Cunnington, *Eighteenth*, p. 116).

292. poor *Crispo's* fate] Crispo, the hero of an Italian opera by Giovanni Battista Bononcini with a text by Paolo Antonio Rolli, is falsely accused of deceit and sings '*Se vedette*': 'If you see | My Thoughts | Ye just Gods, defend | The Innocence of my Heart. | No one hears me, | And you are silent: | Wicked Malice | Condemns me, and | Deceives my Father' (translation from the English edition of the opera printed by Thomas Wood (London, 1721)).

I. ii

1–2. These . . . *Mirza*] In the *Spectator*, no. 159, Addison created a philosophical oriental tale, claiming it was the first part of *The Visions of Mirzah*, an imaginary manuscript acquired in Grand Cairo. Addison's fable remained well-known after his death in 1719.

206–7. descended to a Composition] agreed upon a smaller sum to satisfy his alleged claim on Indiana.

238. unfashionable Lover] 'The Unfashionable Lovers' was one of the early names attached to the play.

II. i

7. *Myrtle*] In the *Theatre*, no. 3, Myrtle's character is described:

Mr. *Charles Myrtle* . . . is a Gentleman of a very plentiful Fortune; a Student, or rather an Inhabitant of the *Temple*; he has a fine Taste of Letters, and from thence bears some Reputation of a Scholar, which makes him much more valuable in that of a Gentleman. He has many agreeable Qualities, besides the Distinction of a good Understanding, and more good Nature. But he has little Imperfections, that frequently indispose his Temper; and when Jealousy takes hold of him, he becomes untractable, and unhappily positive in his Opinions and Resolutions. . . .

Marmaduke Myrtle was the pseudonym chosen by Steele for *The Lover*, a periodical of forty numbers in 1714.

45. his strongest Biass is Avarice] In a letter printed in the *Spectator*, no. 190, attributed to Steele, Rebecca Nettletop says of old Sir Jeoffrey Foible, '. . . his Covetousness was his strongest Passion.' This paper includes a scene similar to Cimberton's examination of Lucinda in III. i.

54. Natural] half-wit.

60. Conveyancer] a lawyer who prepares documents for the conveyance of property (*OED*).

II. ii

18. Dressing-plate] a silver toilet service (*OED*).

II. iii

52. *Crispo* or *Griselda*] These two operas by Bononcini with libretti by Rolli opened at the King's Theatre in 1722. *Crispus* ran for eighteen nights, *Griselda* for sixteen before *The Conscious Lovers* opened in November.

60. *Dolce Sogno*] 'Sweet Dream'. Griselda, a shepherdess who has married the King of Sicily, finds herself persecuted by evil-wishers and hides in a rural cottage where her husband discovers her sleeping and sings this song.

89.1. [*Sonata*] During the musical interlude, Bevil and Indiana exchanged glances in the original production, as Isabella indicates (II. iii. 181–4). The scene is described disparagingly in the *Freeholder's Journal*, 28 November 1722:

> But we justly admire, That in this Dialogue, an Opera, which is painted here as a dull and empty Pleasure, should be imagin'd to be so very grateful at second-hand, should be followed by an insipid length of dumb Show, fill'd up by an Air of Seignior *Carbonelli*; which is, during the Time, a Resemblance of an Opera; is useful indeed to supply a Blank of Discourse, but suspends our Attention to the main Point, and lulls the Audience.

III. i

39–56. I . . . me] This incident is first described in the *Guardian*, no. 87:

> I happened the other Day to pass by a Gentleman's House, and saw the most flippant Scene of low Love that I have ever observed. The Maid was rubbing the Windows within side of the House, and her humble Servant the Footman was so happy a Man as to be employed in cleaning the same Glass on the side toward the Street. The Wench began with the greatest Severity of Aspect imaginable, and breathing on the Glass, followed it with a dry Cloth; her Opposite observed her, and fetching a deep Sigh, as if it were his last, with a very disconsolate Air did the same on his side of the Window. He still worked on and languished, 'till at last his Fair one smiled, but covered her self, and spreading the Napkin in her Hand, concealed her self from her Admirer, while he took Pains, as it were, to work through all that intercepted their Meeting. This pretty Contest held for four or five large

Panes of Glass, 'till at last the Waggery was turned to an humourous way of Breathing in each others Faces, and catching the Impression. The gay Creatures were thus Loving, and pleasing their Imaginations with their Nearness and Distance, till the Windows were so transparent that the Beauty of the Female made the Man-Servant impatient of beholding it, and the whole House besides being abroad, he ran in, and they romped out of my Sight.

(Quoted from the first collected edition, dated 1714, ii. 26–7.) The motto of the *Guardian* paper, a quotation from Ovid's *Metamorphoses*, iv. 71–2, was also echoed in this scene:

> —*Constiterant hinc Thisbe, Pyramus illinc,*
> *Inque vicem fuerat jactatus anhelitus oris.*

This may be translated:

> Here Pyramus, there gentle Thisbe, strove
> To catch each other's breath, the balmy breeze of love.

(Translation from *The British Essayists*, ed. Alexander Chalmers (New York, 1810), xvii. 182.)

77. Tenement] property (*OED*).

83. closely] pithily (*OED*). There is a pun on Tom's physical proximity.

114. take] succeed (*OED*).

116. liquorish] lustful (*OED*).

117. *Lucinda*] Lucinda was characterized in the *Theatre*, no. 3: '*Lucinda* is the Daughter of Mr. *Sealand*, an eminent Merchant; she is a young Woman of a most unaffected, easy, and engaging Behaviour, which has brought her much into Fashion among all the great Families she visits: She is conversant in Books, and no Stranger to Houshold Affairs, of a discerning and quick Spirit in Conversation, and has a mortal Aversion to all Coxcombs. . . .'

212.1. *Mrs.* Sealand, *and Mr.* Cimberton] Steele's manuscript memorandum on the play, now in the British Museum, describes these two characters:

. . . [And let M^rs. Cœland, the March', Wife have the Same Sort of Pride, rejoicing in her own high Blood, Dispising her husbands Pedigree, and Effecting to Marry her Daughter to a Relation of her Own, to take of the Stain of the lowe Birth of her husbands Side, it is Objected, that in the Reign of Edwd the 3^d A relation of her's was a Packer & lord Mayor of London.

The only Scandal to her Family which She Ownes & Cant help,] make M^r. Symberton, Such A Sort of Coxcomb as at first Designd Still more Rediculous & Unsufferable from his talents & Improvements.

(British Museum, Add. MS. 5145C, fol. 198, cited in the *Theatre*, pp. 126–7.)

237. *Lycurgus*] the famous law-giver of Lacedemonia or Sparta.

255–96. If . . . is] 'Dorimant', in a letter published in the *St. James's Journal*, no. 30, 22 November 1722, protested: 'I can't, however, reconcile myself to great part of Squire *Simberton*'s Conversation; some of which has since been omitted: nor did I think it at all of a piece with those Rules, which our Knight has frequently laid down, relating to the Entertainment of a polite Audience, and Circle of Women of Honour.' The lines, obviously omitted in publication as well as performance, occurred in this scene, which is the only one which could be construed as offensive to the ladies.

294. to be thus survey'd like a Steed at Sale] A similar scene, occurring to a young girl abandoned in a house of prostitution, is described in the *Spectator*, no. 190: 'With that the Gentlewoman, who was making her Market of me, in all the Turn of my Person, the Heaves of my Passion, and the suitable Changes of my Posture, took Occasion to commend my Neck, my Shape, my Eyes, my Limbs. All this was accompanied with such Speeches as you may have heard Horse-coursers make in the Sale of Nags when they are warranted for their Soundness.' It is noteworthy that Steele can turn the pathetic into the comic as he does in this scene.

329. Remainder] 'The residual or further interest remaining over from a particular estate, coming into effect when this has determined, and created by the same conveyance by which the estate itself was granted' (*OED*).

331. Chamber-Council] a lawyer who gives opinions in private but does not bring cases to court (*OED*).

331. Pleader] a trial lawyer (*OED*).

341–413. Yes . . . Hours] The *Freeholder's Journal*, 28 November 1722, commented:

The two Lawyers are not to be match'd in all the Inns, or the Courts at *Westminster*. The stammering of one is expos'd in a very barbarous and unnatural manner; for it is not the meer Effect of Passion, but unavoidable; and what is so, is not the Object of Ridicule, but of Pity. The Vehemence of the other is, like all the rest, over-done. But the Author has reason; the Lawyers are a *Butt* to him; he may have been sensible of their Power; and if the Bottom of it was found, these might appear to be strain'd Copies of two Originals in Life, by whom he has suffer'd.

Steele in his personal life was repeatedly unfortunate in litigation and had cause to find lawyers distasteful (see Aitken, *passim*). He had previously satirized them in his periodicals, in *The Funeral*, and with some good nature in *The Tender Husband*.

344. Indenture Tripartite] a deed, sealed agreement, or contract between three parties.

357. *Grimgribber*] According to the *OED*, this term was taken over from the comedy to mean legal or technical jargon. References as late as 1835 are recorded.

381. dock the Entail] change the legal succession to the estate.

IV. i

43–4. in the wrong Box] out of place.

114–15. Tyrant . . . Human] Steele earlier wrote of this 'Tyrant Custom, which is misnamed a Point of Honour', in the *Spectator*, no. 84, and in no. 97 issued '*Pharamond*'s Edict against Duels', outlawing the practice which exists 'in Contempt of all Laws, Divine and Human . . .'.

134-5. Sir, . . . authoriz'd] Steele wrote in the *Theatre*, no. 19:

A Friend of mine, who was lately preparing a Comedy, according to just Laws of the Stage, had formed a Character of a Gentleman very patient of Injuries, where he did not think himself authorized to resent them, but equally impatient, upon Occasions, wherein it is his Duty to exert Anger and Resentment. The third Act of this Comedy, which, had not some Accidents prevented, would have been performed before this time, has a Scene in it, wherein the first Character bears unprovok'd Wrongs, denies a Duel, and still appears a Man of Honour and Courage. This Example would have been of great Service; for since we see young Men are hardly able to forbear Imitation of Fopperies on the Stage, from a Desire of Praise, how warmly would they pursue true Gallantries, when accompanied with the Beauties with which a Poet represents them, when he has a Mind to make them amiable? But this Incident of the Play is between two Men, cool and sober, and, when not under any Emotion of Spirit, of exact Characters.

The reference, obviously, is to what was to become the fourth act of *The Conscious Lovers*.

iv. ii

1-4. Give . . . sort] In the manuscript memorandum in the British Museum, Steele instructed himself 'That the Character of S! John Edgar [Sir John Bevil in the final version] be Enlivened with a Secret vanity About Family'.

50-1. we Merchants are a Species of Gentry] The character and sentiments of Mr. Sealand were earlier published in the *Theatre*, no. 3:

Mr. *Sealand*, Father of *Lucinda* . . . is a true Pattern of that kind of third Gentry, which has arose in the World this last Century: I mean the great, and rich Families of Merchants, and eminent Traders, who in their Furniture, their Equipage, their Manner of Living, and especially their Oeconomy, are so far from being below the Gentry, that many of them are now the best Representatives of the ancient ones, and deserve the Imitation of the modern Nobility. . . . He is a Man that does Business with the Candour of a Gentleman, and performs his Engagements with the Exactness of a Citizen.

85. soils] cohabits (*OED*).

88-9. '*And while . . . is*] A quotation from Dryden's Epilogue to Vanbrugh's *The Pilgrim* (1700), ll. 41-2, but 'For' is changed to 'And'. A similar couplet in Dryden's Prologue to Southerne's *The Disappointment* (1684), ll. 59-60, reads 'liberal' rather than 'prodigal'. Steele obviously knew the line from *The Pilgrim*, which was frequently performed during his years in London; *The Disappointment* had not been performed since 1685.

v. ii

12. *Table-Book*] pocket notebook or memorandum-book (*OED*).

Epilogues

The Epilogue by Benjamin Victor, spoken during the first run, was not published with the play. One early critic suggested that Steele later found it too bawdy to suit his inclinations (*The Censor Censur'd: or, The Conscious Lovers Examin'd* (London, 1723)). While Welsted's Epilogue appeared in the printed version, Victor's was published in the second edition of his *Epistle to Sir Richard Steele, On his Play, call'd, The Conscious Lovers*, which was sold with the play, and later reprinted in Victor's *Original Letters, Dramatic Pieces, and Poems*, 3 vols. (London, 1776).

EMENDATIONS OF ACCIDENTALS

ALL changes in accidentals other than the silent alterations noted in the Introduction (pp. xiv–xv) are listed below. The reading in the present text is printed first, followed by the source of that reading, either the siglum for one of the early editions or 'ed.', with the exact reading in parentheses if it differs at all from the present text in accidentals. The copy-text reading, sometimes replaced by explanatory matter in square brackets, concludes the entry. Punctuation, capitalization, and spelling changes are included, as are obvious mis-spellings of words ('Pin-momey' for 'Pin-money'), turned *u*'s and *n*'s, compositors' erroneous repetitions of words, and expansions of abbreviations other than characters' names. To prevent misunderstanding of the original accidentals, I include hyphenations of compound words at the ends of lines in both the copy-text and the present edition unless the second part of the compound is capitalized.

THE FUNERAL

Preface

22	by,] D1; ~ₐ
35	mentions.] D1; ~ₐ
36	downright] D1; down-|right

Prologue

1	Deserted,] D1; ~ₐ

I. i

[title]	A-la-Mode] D2; Ala-Mode
10	'em.] D1; ~:
21–2	Under-|taker] ed.; Undertaker
23	Absurd] D1; Absur'd
31	Court.] D1; Court,
56	look'd] D1; lookₐd
112	'em] D1; e'm
113	longer.] D1; ~:
127	Brick-dust] ed.; Brick-|dust

I. ii

3–4	Lethargick-|slumber] ed.; Lethargick-slumber
33	dizzy] D1; dizze

49–50   Widow-|hood] ed.; Widow-hood
56–9   Quality. . . Thus:] Quality. Thus [*very Derectly*] to a Smug Pretend-
        ing Fellow of no Fortune: Thus [*as scarce seeing him*] to one that
        Writes Lampoons: Thus [*Fearfully*] to one one really Loves: Thus
        [*looking down*] to one's Woman, Acquaintance, from Box to Box:
        Thus
59   Woman͵] ed.; ~,
73   Men] D1; ~,
74   Scandals,] D1; ~͵
74   home͵] D1; ~,
107   *Mezentius*] D1; *Merentius*
139   the͵ matter,] D1; ~, ~͵
157   little] D1; little-
160–1   *Tom*; now *Tom*͵] D1; ~. ~ ~.
169   *Annum*] D1; *Ann.*
181   it] D1; it it
202   Instrument.] TJ1; ~;
205   Outhouses] ed.; Out-|houses
208   Underwoods] D1; Under-|woods
208–9   Water-|courses] ed.; Watercourses
210   Profits,] D1; ~͵
228   the] D1; the the
237   possible.] D1; ~͵
238   you;] D1; ~,
246   with] D1; wirh
253   Tautologist] D1; Tantologist

II. i

8   Male-|contents] ed.; Male-contents
17   Sir?] ed.; ~͵
24   *Jonathan*͵] D1; ~,
26   *percent*] ed.; *per-|cent*
36   Money-affairs] D1; Money—affairs
47–8   forth-|with] ed.; forthwith
53   be͵] ed.; ~,
53   to] ed.; too
75   How!] D1; ~͵
87   Conscious] D1 (conscious); Conscouis
107   Loves] D1 (loves); Love's
113   Humorous] D1; Humorons
181   recitativo] D1; recitatiro
198   Thou'rt] D1; Thour't
211   we've] D1; wh've
226   Company͵ with,] D1; ~, ~͵

II. ii

8   in‸ but . . . that)] TJ1; ~) ~ . . . ~‸
27   told] D1; to!d

II. iii

58   writing.] D1; ~‸
80   well?] D1; ~‸
102–3 on, the Musick Fits‸] D1; ~‸ ~ Musick-Fits,
185   not‸] D1; ~?
192   Vanquish'd] D1; Vanquish‸d
195   in to] D3; into
195   thus.] D1; ~‸
211   *Mantua.*] D1; ~:
283   Thin‸] D1; ~,
299–300 self-|examination] ed.; self-examination
304   me,] D1; ~;

III. i

7   She'll] D1 (she'll); She‸ll
37   *Trim‸*] D1; ~,
57   *Terim*] D1; *Treim*
65   stay‸] D1; ~.
76   *Generous*] D1; *Gene-|nerous*
77   *Widow's*] D1; *Widow‸s*
84   *Servant,*] D1; ~.
95   unconscionable] D1; unconsionable
105   Gra'mercy] ed.; Cra'mercy
105   *Trim,*] D1; ~.

III. ii

6–7   is, that‸] D1; ~‸ ~,
12   *Formal*] D1; *Formall*
49   Good‸] D1; ~,
75   believe‸] D1; ~,
102–3 Bashful-|look'd] ed.; Bashful-look'd
139   *Nutbrain*] D1; *Nut-|brain*
140   a'.] D1; ~‸

III. iii

1–2   Anti-|chamber] ed.; Antichamber
5   Why,] D1; ~‸
18   People,] D1; ~.
43   Me] ed.; me
90   Woman.] D1; ~‸

iv. i

3   him.) ed.; ~ₐ)
13   Wickedness] D1; Widkedness
16   Dishonour'd] D1; Dishonoun'd

iv. ii

108   I've] D1; Iₐve
123   compos'd] D1; compss'd
126   Advise.] D1; ~ₐ
127   Interr'd] D1 (interr'd); Interrₐd

iv. iii

0.1   *Fellows,*] D1; ~ₐ
6   Fight!] D1; ~.
12   back.] D1; ~:
29   a] D1; a a
31   Husband,] D1; ~ₐ
32   Footmanₐ] ed.; ~.
42   tellₐ you,] D1; ~, ~ₐ
45   Puffₐ Pyes. Have] ed.; ~. ~ₐ have
72   that,] D1; ~ₐ
86   Tragedy-Drum] D1; Tragedy—Drum
114   time.] D1; ~ₐ
128   in] D1; in in
138   Battle,] D1; ~.

v. i

17   Incarnate] D1; Incarnato
24   Iₐ] D1; ~ —
32   Good—] D1; ~ₐ
68   inestimable] D1; inestinable

v. iii

58   Pin-cushion] D1; Pin-|cushion
96   inₐ] D1; ~;
100   Whitherₐ] D1; ~,
102   Madam.] D1; ~ₐ
105   servants] D1; servant's
113   Sirrah?] TJ1; ~:
120   face.] D1; ~ₐ
124   Friend?] D1; ~:
132   fellow.] ed.; ~ₐ
136   *Sharlot,*] D1; ~ₐ
138   *Trusty.*] D1; ~ₐ

V. iv

16	of.] D1; ~:
23	Ground;] D1; ~ₐ
26	Occasion.] D1; ~ₐ
34	*Harriot*ₐ] D1; *Harriote,*
36	(what . . . have)] D1; ₐ~ . . . ~ₐ
38	weedsₐ] D1; ~;
60	How] D1; *How*
65	And] D1; and
73-4	Land-|steward] ed.; Land-steward
90	giv'st] D1; givest
95	Flowr'y] D1; Flowery
101	lov'st] D1; lovest
118	Animals!] D1; ~ₐ
125	*Harriot.*] D1; ~ₐ
126	*Sharlot.*] D1; ~ₐ
160	me,] D1; ~ₐ
162	What? can my Lord revive, Yet Dead to me?] D1; What can my Lord revive? Yet Dead to me,
171	Youre] ed.; You're
198	ev'ry] D1; every
216	now, Gentlemen,] D1; ~ₐ ~ₐ
230-2	Screen . . . Morality.] ed.; Screen . . . the| Laws . . . makest.	But . . . supererogatory	Morality. [different lineation.]
238	selfₐ] D1; ~.
261	Lord, the Entertainmentₐ] D1; ~ₐ ~ ~,
302	*Employ*] D1; Emply

Epilogue

8	*to-Night*] D1; *to. Night*
17	Picts] D1; *Picts*

THE LYING LOVER

Dramatis Personae

6	*Pinkethman*] D1; *Pinkeman*
7	*Charcole*] ed.; *Charcoal*

I

[title]	LOVER:] D1; ~,
49	why,] D2; ~ₐ
50	why,] D3; ~ₐ
55	Desireₐ—] D1; ~.—

105–6   Counter-|scarps] ed.; Counterscarps
134   Lapfulls] ed.; Lap–|fulls
143   Fortune˄—] D1; ~.—
149   Footman] D1; Foot-|man
236   *Gazette*] D1; Gazette
270   vanish'd] D1; van sh'd
279   Footman] D1; Foot-|man
313   Of] D1; of
325   handsome?] D4; ~˄
363   Orange˄] D1; ~,
384   Harvest˄—] D1; ~.—
385   *Ceres*] D1; Ceres
388–93   While . . . Love!] ed.; [set as prose]
388   While] ed.; while
389   Eccho'd] ed.; eccho'd
390   Than] ed.; than
391   All] ed.; all
399–412   As . . . Mirth.] ed.; [set as prose]
399   Fireworks] D1; Fire-|works
401   Whose] ed.; whose
403   And] ed.; and
404   You] ed.; you
405   Had] ed.; had
407   Which] ed.; which
409   He] ed.; he
409   *Thetis'*] D1; *Theti*'s
410   As] ed.; as
412   He] ed.; he
449   over-run] D1; over-|run

II. i

14   and] D1; aud
35   it.] D1; ~,
175   warrant] D1; warraut
196   Midnight] D1; Mid-|night
198   *Ceres*] D1; Ceres
309   *Penelope*] ed.; *Pen.*
311–12   Bosom-|friend] ed.; Bosom-friend
319–20   Creature,] D1; ~˄
324   Father˄—] D1; ~.—
344   *Penelope*] ed.; *Pen.*

II. ii

82   shed] D1; she'd

125	bleeding‸—] D1; ~.—
164	*Character*—] D1; ~‸
177	Read there] D1; [*Read there*
182	Extasies‸—] D1; ~.—

III. i

3	*Penelope*] ed.; *Pen.*
32	least—] D1; ~,
33	My] D1; my
66	are,] D1; ~.

III. ii

8	art‸—] D1; ~.—
16–17	*Book-|wits*] ed.; *Bookwits*
32	half-penny] D1; half-|penny
40	*Chairman.*] ed.; *Chair.*
48	smoothly‸—] D1; ~.—
148	She] D1; she
160	I'de] ed.; Id'e
169	Do] ed.; do
197	Fiddles‸—] D1; ~.—
197	Porter‸—] D1; ~.—

IV. i

23	remember‸—] D1; ~.—
53–4	Anti-|chamber] ed.; Anti-chamber

IV. ii

44	deserves.] D1; ~‸
81	it‸—] D1; ~.—

IV. iii

68, 76, 79	*Watchman.*] ed.; *Watch.*

IV. iv

42	what‸—] D1; ~.—

IV. v

1	*Turn-key*] ed.; Turnkey
13	High-road.] D1; ~‸
87	Tap-house] D1; Tap-|house

v. i

90	down‸—] D1; ~.—

v. iii

27	frank˄—] D1; ~.—
34	usage,] ed.; ~.
82	*thereabouts*] D1; *there-|abouts*
102–3	And . . . *Penelope.*] D3; [set as verse]
104	generous] D1; generons
128–9	She . . . side—] D1; [set as verse]
150	Infancy˄—] D1; ~.—
154–7	Oh . . . Pity.] ed.; [set as verse]
197	You've . . . Sound!] D1; [set as prose]
197	You've] D1; you've
282–3	And . . . besides,] ed.; [set as prose]
282	And] ed.; and
318	one,] D1; ~.
344	*Who*] D1 (Who); who

THE TENDER HUSBAND

Prologue

| 37 | *like*˄] D1; ~, |

Song

| 1 | *Eyes,*] D1; ~. |

i. i

45	might, if˄] ed.; ~˄ ~,
101	Justice] D1; Jnstice
111	Dear˄] D1; ~,
146	Habitation] D1; Habi-|bitation
179	10,000] ed.; 10000

i. ii

5	*September*] D1; *Sept.*
5	13th,] D1; ~.
5	*Annum*] D1; *Ann.*
14	Drugs] D1; Dtugs
20	*l.*] ed.; l.
20	*Annum*] D1; *Ann.*
21	Pin-Money] D3; Pin-Momey
24	*l.*] ed.; l.
26	*l.*] ed.; l.
61	˄*Don't* . . . *Sirrah,*˄] ed.; (~ . . . ~,)

85	‸*Clear*] D1; (~
89	know,] ed.; ~‸
89	so‸] ed.; ~,
135	Dear‸] D1; ~,
162	there,] D1; ~.
182	since‸] D1; ~,

II. ii

14	Good‸] D1; ~,
40	Good‸] D1; ~,
189	*Urganda*] D1; Urganda
264–5	Mid-|night] ed.; Midnight

III. i

41	Dear‸] D1; ~,
71	come.] D1; ~‸
78	Let us see it] D2; (*Let us see it*
111	Ladiship's] ed.; Ladiships's
133	Captain] D1; Capt.
138–9	out-|did] ed.; out-did
160	Windgall'd] ed.; Wind-|gall'd

III. ii

9	*Tipkin*] ed.; *Pitkin*
46	Harke'e] ed.; Harke's
69	well‸] D1; ~.

IV. i

5	downcast] ed.; down-|cast

IV. ii

52	not] D1; not not
99	make him] D1; make him him
136–7	Head-|strong] ed.; Head-strong

V. i

9–12	[inverted commas omitted in letter] ed.; [inverted commas used]
13	‸Adieu] D1; [~
57	*Titmouse*] D1; *Tit-|mouse*

V. ii

70	*Item*,] D1; ~.

73–4   forth-|coming] ed.; forth-coming
102   Sir‸] D1; ~,
185   two?] ed.; too.

Epilogue

21   *Command*] D1; *Commaud*

THE CONSCIOUS LOVERS

Prologue

20   *give‸ it,*] TJ; ~, ~‸

I. i

61   troublesome.] O2; ~‸
253   short-sighted] Du 1; short-|sighted

I. ii

260   But] O2; But But

II. i

35   good-natur'd] Du 1; good-|natur'd

II. iii

169   begone] O2; be-|gone

III

36–7   Hobble-|de-Hoy] ed.; Hobble-de-Hoy
93   see,] ed.; ~‸
93–4   in-|in-inadvertency] ed.; in-in-inadvertency
185–6   Well-|wishers] ed.; Well-wish-|ers
196–7   Waiting-|maids] ed.; Waiting-maids
316   *Geoffry*] O3; *Geoffrey*

IV. i

90   is.] O2; ~‸

IV. ii

156   over-fond] ed.; over-|fond
167   Resolution] O2; Resolu-|lution

V. iii

186   Suspicions,] ed.; ~;
208–9   I . . . him—] ed.; [set as separate line]
222   only‸] ed.; ~,
223–4   ever-|destined] ed.; ever-destined

PRESS VARIANTS

VARIANTS in first editions, specifically stop-press corrections, changes made between press-runs of a single edition, and variants occurring in the unexplained resetting of one page of *The Tender Husband*, are recorded. Discussions of the printing procedure by which changes other than stop-press corrections were made can be found in the introductions to the individual plays. Lists of copies I have examined precede the variants, which are recorded by forme and identified by signature and line-number. Lost type, such as letters pulled by the ink balls, is not noted unless it causes substantive variants.

THE FUNERAL

Sheet D, Outer Forme

First state. Copies at Harvard, Bodleian, Yale, Newberry, British Museum, University of Texas (two copies), Columbia, Cornell (two copies), University of California, Folger, Huntington, University of Chicago, Williams College.

Second state. University of Texas, Library of Congress, University of Pennsylvania, Princeton.

Sig. and line	First state	Second state
D2ᵛ.7	*Brumpton,* and	*Brumpton* ,
D2ᵛ.16	Young	Yonng

THE TENDER HUSBAND

Sheet D, Outer Forme

(Note. States are identified as A and B, since no order can be established on existing evidence.)

State A. Copies at Bodleian (two copies), Victoria and Albert Museum, Folger, University of Chicago, University of Texas, Harvard, Huntington, University of Pennsylvania, Yale, William Andrews Clark Memorial Library, Library of Congress, and Williams College.

State B. Copies at British Museum, University of Texas, Yale, University of Michigan, and Princeton.

Sig. and line	State A	State B
D3.1	Ladies⌄	Ladies,
D3.4	those⌄	those,
D3.8–9	*Pa-|ladin*	*Pala-|din*
D3.12	*Hu.*	*Au.*
D3.12	Niece,	Neice,
D3.15	Opportunities	opportunities
D3.25	*Grey-Goose,*	*Grey-Goose,,*
D3.30–1	love | with me	love with | me
D3.31	me⌄)	me.)
D3.35	Cleri	Cler.

Sheet H, Inner Forme

First state. University of Texas (two copies).

Second state. Bodleian (two copies), British Museum, Victoria and Albert Museum, Folger, University of Texas (two copies), Library of Congress, University of North Carolina, Harvard, Huntington, University of Pennsylvania, Yale (two copies), University of California, University of Michigan, Newberry, Princeton, William Andrews Clark Memorial Library, Williams College.

Sig. and line	First state	Second state
H1ᵛ. page number	58	50
H2. page number	59	51
H3ᵛ. page number	62	54

THE CONSCIOUS LOVERS

Because many variants arise from the use of standing type in this edition and these do not affect the text, changes in pagination, running-titles, press-figures, and ornaments are not recorded.

First state. Bodleian (two copies), Yale, Newberry, University of Illinois (two copies), Johns Hopkins, Temple University, Williams College, copy owned by Richmond P. Bond.

Second state. Bodleian, Folger (two copies), British Museum, Yale, University of Texas (two copies), Harvard, Library of Congress, Columbia (two copies), Princeton, University of Chicago, University of Pennsylvania, William Andrews Clark Memorial Library, University of California, Huntington (two copies), Victoria and Albert Museum, University of North Carolina, Lehigh University.

Sheet A, Inner Forme

Sig. and line	First state	Second state
A7ᵛ. catchword	*And*	*Your*

Sheet B, Inner Forme

B2.35	alone₌	alone,
B4.29–30	Con-|science	Cone|science

Sheet B, Outer Forme

B7.16	*Myrtle.*	*Myrtle?*

Sheet C, Inner Forme

C1ᵛ.7	you,	you.
C1ᵛ.32	but,	but₌
C2.2	seiz'd,	seiz'd₌
C2.32	and,	and₌

Sheet D, Inner Forme

D1ᵛ.16	Drawing-Room—	Drawing-Room.—

Sheet E, Inner Forme

E2.catchword	plain	plain-
E4.10	his own	his
E4.33	*me*	*hence*
E6.29	ather	rather

Sheet E, Outer Forme

E2ᵛ.1	plain	plainly
E3.26	if,	if₌

Sheet F, Outer Forme

F2ᵛ.24	Mannor	Manor
F2ᵛ.28	Mr	Mr.

HISTORICAL COLLATION

THE historical collation contains all substantive and semi-substantive changes, except those in stage directions, in editions published within Steele's lifetime and shortly after his death. The reading of the present text appears first, followed by any other readings which occur within these editions, and their sigla. If the accidentals are not uniform in all editions containing one reading, only the accidentals of the first one are recorded. A consecutive series of editions is indicated by hyphenating the sigla for the first and last, for example, D1–4 means all editions from the first duodecimo to the fourth.

THE FUNERAL

Dedication

0.1–38   To ... *Steele.*] [om.] TJ1–2, Du

Preface

2   the Duke of *Devonshire*] a very Great Man Q, TJ1–2
39   'twere] it were D4

Prologue

0.2   Spoken by Mr. *Wilks.*] [om.] TJ1–2
27   *nay*] *yea* TJ1–2

Dramatis Personae

1–16   [original cast listed] [om.] TJ1–2, Du

I. i

5   Laughers] Laughters Q, D1 second impression, D4
8   him] them D1–4, Du
53   Sorrowful] a sorrowful D1–4, Du
54   an] a TJ1–2
60   my Mourning Furniture] mourning-furniture TJ2
74   a what de' call] a what d'ye call D1, D4; what d'ye call D2–3, Du
96   Fellow's] Fellow TJ1–2
114–15   our Friend, tell Him Dr. *Passeport*] our Friend, tell him, Dr. *Passeport*, D1–4; tell him our Friend, Dr. *Passeport* TJ1–2
135   you're] you are D4
140   or] in Du
145   of] [om.] D2–3, Du

I. ii

59	Woman] Women TJ1–2
83	Lord's Foible] Lord *Frible* Q, D1–4, TJ1–2, Du
84	generosity] all generosity TJ1–2
91	to] in D4
92	Natural] your Natural D3, Du
99	give] gives Q
128	Interests] Interest TJ1–2
186–7	when . . . affected] when that there is indeed some Progress made in shall be wholly affected Q; when that there is indeed some Progress made in, shall be wholly affected D1–4, Du (effected D2–4, Du); when that wherein there is indeed some Progress made, shall be wholly effected TJ1–2
188	an Inn of Court] or Inn's of Court Q; an Inn's of Court TJ1–2
222	don't] you don't TJ2
223	out—you Read] out, read TJ1–2
240	thy sincerity] the sincerity Q
247	Virtue also—that] Virtue. Also that TJ1–2
256–7	'till she Trembles,] [om.] TJ1

II. i

21	Shillings] Shilling Du
39	an] a TJ1–2
46	I am] I'm D1–4, Du
58	loss] lose Q
95–6	to fold . . . Fair!] to Embrace that Beauteous— D1–4, Du
109	she's] she is D4
119	when] & when TJ1–2
122	*Brumpton*, and] *Brumpton* , Q (uncorrected state), D1–4, Du
202	Ow] Owe D3, Du
205	every] in every D3, TJ1–2, Du
207	willing] unwilling D2–3, Du

II. ii

5	*Lord Brumpton*] *L. H.* Q

II. iii

2	*as she*] *when she* D2–3, Du
8	Look'e you] Look ye D1–4, Du; Look'e now TJ1–2
19	a] [om.] D1–4, Du
23	know,]~; D3, TJ1–2, Du

25–6 Ay, but . . . self—] Ay, but Mr. *Campley*, will you gain Ground ev'n
      of that his Rival, your Dear self— Q; Ay, but Mr. *Campley*! will
      you gain Ground ev'n of that Rival, your Dear self? TJ1; Ay, but
      Mr. *Campley* will gain ground ev'n of that Rival, your dear self.
      TJ2
27   Oh!] Ha! TJ1–2
29   If I am] If I Q; If I be TJ1–2
35   at] [om.] D1, TJ1
91   'twill] it will D4
118   what's become] what becomes D4
123   *Harriot*] *Sharlot* Q, D1–4, TJ1–2, Du
141   nay] [om.] TJ1–2
159   would] would you D4
164   Power,] Power? D3, TJ1–2, Du
167   so] 'tis so TJ1–2
168   ingenuously] ingeniously D4; ingenuously now TJ1–2
179   And] And I Q, D1–4, TJ1–2, Du
191   an] a TJ1–2
192   was ever] ever was D3, Du
195   in to] into Q, D1–2
218   may] [om.] D1–4, Du
224   for] [om.] TJ1–2
242   have] [om.] Q
258   *Campley's*] Mr. *Campley's* TJ1–2
271   I'm] I am D2–3, Du
289   an] a TJ1–2
318   an] a TJ1–2
319   and Innocence] Innocence and Q
320   How] Now TJ1–2
321   Protection?—] Protection. TJ1–2
322   'tis] it is D3, Du

III. i

23   Promises] Premises TJ1–2
23   Lady] my Lady D1–4, Du
31   heard] hear Q
40   you] your Q
54   de] the D3, Du
56   I do] do I D1–4, Du
67   so] to Q, D1, D4
92   the] them Q, D1–4, TJ1–2, Du
93   is] [om.] TJ1
107   sometimes] sometime D2–3, Du

III. ii

70	Him] Her TJ1–2
70	an] a TJ1–2
91	Wife, pretends] Wife: she pretends TJ1–2
139	importune] importunate Du

III. iii

15	your] you Du
18	People, Ye] People. Ye Q; People, you D1–4, Du
22	know] I know TJ1–2
38	Words] Word TJ1–2
57	*Your*] *Tour* Q
88	en] in D1–4, Du

IV. i

15	all∧] ~; TJ1–2

IV. ii

1	Misfortunes] Misfortune Du
90	see you] see you, you D1–2, D4; See you; you D3, Du
121–2	Disfavour, and under the Rose. Be] Disfavour; and under the Rose— Be D1–4, Du; Disfavour. And under the Rose, be TJ1–2

IV. iii

5, 9, 13	*Swagger*.] *Sw.* Q; 2 *Sol.* D1–4, Du; *2d. So.* TJ1–2
72	Bumpkin] *Pumkin* Q, D1–4, TJ1; *Pumpkin* Du
74	Quarter'd] are Quarter'd Q
79–84	ha! *Ruffle* . . . Rot:] [om.] D1–4, Du
85	tight] right D3, Du
103	of] off TJ1–2
114	in] [om.] Q, TJ1–2
143	Army] [om.] D3, Du

V. i

23	Where's] There's Q
31	that] [om.] Q
33	wou'd not] wou'd Q; won't TJ1–2
37	Innocent—*Harriot*] Innocent *Harriot* TJ1–2
65	writ] writ it TJ1–2
75	an] a TJ1–2

v. ii

2	I] [om.] D4
11	to the House, half] [om.] TJ1–2

v. iii

1	It] I TJ1
30	't] it TJ1–2
63	dead] deaf Q, D1–4, TJ1–2, Du
63	forget] forgot D2–3, Du
105	servants] servant's Q

v. iv

7	that] [om.] TJ2
44	You are] You're D4
45	a] [om.] D3, Du
53	They] Thus Q
55	'tis] 'twas D3, Du
56	Endeavourers] Endeavours D4, Du
56	Mouth] Month Q
60	Ladyship] Lordship Q, TJ1–2
69	makes] make TJ1–2
73	now] [om.] TJ1–2
101	lov'st] lov'd Du
104	thy] my D1–4, Du
109	or fear] nor fear TJ1–2
111	Abode] Above Q
123	do] did Q, TJ1–2
129	your] the Q; that TJ1–2
139	that] hat Q
140	you'd] you had TJ1–2
153	Husband] my Husband D3, TJ1–2
163	To me] to make me Du
209	had] should Q, TJ1–2
211	am] am's Q
219	me] thee Q
224	their] her Du
244	others] other's TJ1–2
247	when] which Q
250	Sirs] Sir Q, D1–2, Du
268.4	Sung by *Jemmie Bowin.*] [om.] TJ1–2
275	*Bequeaths*] *Bequeath*, Q
280.2	Sung By Mr. *Pate.*] [om.] TJ1–2

282   *your Urns*] *Urns* D3, Du
283   *Drown'd*] *crown'd* D2–3, Du
296   of] to TJ1–2

Epilogue

14   *t'a*] *to a* Q, TJ1–2
31   *Bright*] *Right* Q

THE LYING LOVER

Dedication

0.1–44   [TO ... STEELE] [om.] Du

Preface

0.1   THE] [om.] Du
2   'em] *them* D2–4, Du
20   Friend] *Friends* Du
20   His knowing] *knowing His* Q

Dramatis Personae

1–11   [original cast listed] [om.] Du

I. i

14–15   Arm? ... is] Arm, ... is? D4
60   There's] There is D4
67   owe] own Du
74   Machines] Machine D3–4, Du
113   Parks] Park D4
147   asleep] sleep Q
203   there's] there is D3–4, Du
212   of] or Q, D1–4, Du
216   tho'] [om.] Q
225   find] find you D4
231   e'en] even D4
264   Warfare] Welfare Du
295   o'th'] o'the D4
309   thrust] trust D3, Du
340   and] or D3–4, Du
415   a] [om.] Du
457   Pleasure] a Pleasure D2–4, Du

II. i

193   of't.] of it? D4
243   He is] He's D4

282   Suiterer] Sui-|rer D2; Suiter D3; Suitor D4, Du
283   to one] to to one Du
284   'em] them D4
357   they're] they are D3–4, Du

II. ii

67   of] of the D1–4, Du
126   Sons'] ed.; Son's Q, Sons D1–4, Du
130   and] and to D3–4, Du
133   me] [om.] D3–4, Du
140   Looks] Look D1–4, Du
217   as frolick] frolick D3–4, Du

III. i

11   such] such a D2–4, Du
15   not] nor D2
45   Lies.—] Lye D4
58   Cheeks] Cheek D1–4, Du
73   Pout] Point D3–4, Du

III. ii

134   such a] a such Q
156   Courtesies] Curtsies D3–4, Du
173   humblest] Humble D2–4, Du

IV. i

11   Eyes] Eye D1

IV. ii

6   Suiterers] Suitors, D1–4, Du
31   you not] not you D2–4, Du
34   Messages] Message D3–4, Du
53   Passions] Passion D4

IV. iii

12   I'm] I'am D4
33   I am] I'm D4

IV. iv

12   He is] He's D4

IV. v

20   with] with a D2–4, Du

29	think] thing D2
71	Drink] Drinks D3–4

v. i

7	Oppressors] th'Oppressors D3–4, Du
18	wakes] awakes D3–4, Du
68	cannot] can D4

v.ii

27	*Lovemore*] *Lat.* Q, D1, Du

v. iii

5	they're] they are D4
52	*Lovemore.*] ~‸ D2–4, Du
66	not] not to D1–4, Du
161	the irrevocable] th'irrevocable D1–4, Du
184	Let] But let D2–4, Du
310	he is] he's D2–4, Du

THE TENDER HUSBAND

Dedication

0.1–31	[TO . . . *Steele.*] [om.] Du
5	You] [om.] D3

Prologue

13	*of*] *in* D2–3, Du
30	*for*] *or* D2

Dramatis Personae

1–11	[original cast listed] [om.] Du

1. i

72	she] he Q
85	*Captain Clerimont*] *Cler.* Q, D1–4, Du
92	*Clerimont Senior*] *Cler.* Q, D1–4, Du
129	*Captain Clerimont*] *Cl.* Q, D1–4, Du
162	certain] [om.] Du
164	Languer] languish D1–4, Du
181	confess] confest Q
183	be] [om.] Q
185	*Clerimont Senior*] *Cler.* Q, D1–4, Du
196	*Captain Clerimont*] *Cle. S.* Q

213	Pounds] Pound D1–4, Du
221	*Captain Clerimont*] *Cle. S.* Q
228	*Captain Clerimont*] *Cle. S.* Q
230	very] [om.] D1–4, Du
233	*Captain Clerimont*] *Cle. S.* Q
247	*Captain Clerimont*] *Cle. S.* Q

I. ii

49	it] [om.] D4
50	our] your D4
69	You are] Your Du
119	*your*] *you* Q
149	cannot] can't D1–4, Du
166	have been] has been D1–4, Du
198–9	I am] I'm D1–4, Du
221	least] lest D4

II. i

| 10 | so busy a fine] so busie and fine a D1–4, Du |

II. ii

23	with] with of Q
44	for] of Du
77	to you] [om.] D1–4, Q
96	a] [om.] D1
135	*Aunt.*] *Hu.* Q (State A)
250	you'll] you will D1–4, Du
291	have] [om.] D1–4, Du

II. iii

| 24 | Army-Friend] army-friends Du |

III. i

21	*Mrs.*] *Mr.* Q
68	Mute] Mutes D2–3, Du
85	*my Amorous*] *and am'rous* D1–3, Du; *an am'rous* D4
124	to] with D1–4, Du
166	Father is] Father's D4

III. ii

| 22 | not] [om.] Q |
| 109 | them] him Q; 'em D1–4, Du |

IV. ii

37	Colours] Colour D3, Du
44	you] [om.] D2
82	most] much Du

v. i

14	you] your Q
27	an] and D4
56	*Mrs.*] Mr. Q
62	*Mrs.*] Mr. Q
80	but] but by Q
104	six] sick Q
105	*Lucy*] *Jenny* Q, D1–4, Du
119	*Lucy*] *Jenny* Q, D1–4, Du
119.1	Fainlove] Jenny Q, D1–4, Du
146	the] [om.] D2
158	I've] I have D4

v. ii

1	dear] [om.] D1–4, Du
24	you] your Q
47	Pounds] Pound D1–4, Du
57	3998] 3990 Q
179	ye] you D2–3, Du
185	two] too Q, D1
190	do as soon] do so as soon D2–3, Du; as soon D4
198	*Captain Clerimont*] *Cler.* Q, D1–4, Du
199	I'll] I D4
204	*Clerimont Senior*] *Cler.* Q
209	*Clerimont Senior*] *Cler.* Q, D1–4, Du
218	*Captain Clerimont*] *Cler.* Q, D1–4, Du

THE CONSCIOUS LOVERS

Dedication

8	Majesty] Majesty's Du 1

Preface

56	told me] told O3

I. i

25	be at] beat TJ
102	there is] there's Du 2

106	to] [om.] D
113	I'm] I am O2–3
142	came] come O3
149	who] why Du 2
171	Top-Gamesters] Top-Gamester Du 2
187	there is] there's O2–3
191	Ay,] [om.] O2–3
209	It's] 'Tis Du 1–2
210	agreed] a greed TJ
279	a Part] Part O2–3
319	particularly] [om.] Du 2
321	Occasions] occasion TJ

I. ii

10	It's] 'Tis Du 1–2
28	beholden] beholding Du 1–2
36	greater] great O3
43	it's] 'tis Du 1–2
54	have] have have D
58	having] have Du 2
74	superfluous] superstitious Du 2
127	have] have had Du 1–2
128	Inclinations] Inclination Du 1–2
161	had] [om.] Du 2
188	his] this O3
231	loved] loved her Du 2
245	*Phillis*] *Lettice* O1–3, D, TJ, Du 1–2

II. i

45	his] the Du 2
89–90	immoral] immortal Du 1–2
92	Scene] Scence Du 2
94	Instructions] instruction TJ
98	all] all that Du 2

II. ii

2	all] [om.] Du 2
44	Oh! ho!] Oh! oh! D
44–5	thing right] right thing O3
72	have] [om.] Du 1–2
72	know] know know Du 2
105	you] your TJ

II. iii

19	it's] 'tis Du 1–2
22	something] nothing Du 2
146	these] those O2–3
201	I'm] I am Du 2

III

25	it's] 'tis Du 1–2
57	it's] 'tis Du 1–2
95	Good] God O1
117	you was] you were Du 2
122	has he] he has O3
142	admitting] admiring Du 2
145	How's] How is Du 2
155	it's] 'tis D, Du 1–2
200	I'll] I will Du 2
207	I am] I'm D
208	too wise,] [om.] TJ
211	It's] 'Tis Du 1–2
214	our] your Du 2
247	she] she she TJ
258	I am] I'm Du 1–2
297	I am] I'm Du 2
308–9	to beget] beget O2–3
319	I] a Du 2
327	it's] 'tis Du 1–2
341–413	*Tom . . . Myrtle* [speech prefixes] *Tar. . . . Bram.* O1–3, D, TJ, Du 1–2
374	plainly] plain O1(u), O2–3, TJ, Du 1–2
402	'em] them Du 2

IV. i

24	bad] bid Du 2
33	his] his own O1(u), TJ, Du 1–2
55	*hence*] *me* O1(u), D, TJ, Du 1–2
64	*inclines*] *incline* Du 2
69	her self] self Du 1
115	all] [om.] Du 2
120	'em] them Du 1–2
142	it is] 'tis Du 1–2
143	your loose] you loose TJ
201	me] me now Du 2
204	had] would Du 2

IV. ii

165   But] [om.] TJ

IV. iii

15   would] will Du 2
34   I a] a I O2; I Du 2
38   and] [om.] TJ

v. i

44   Sir] [om.] O1, Du 1
89   to] [om.] Du 2
101   as] a TJ
114   end] end end TJ
116   not] [om.] O1–3, D, TJ

v. ii

30   I] [om.] O3
35   can] will Du 2

v.iii

13   comes] come TJ
109   made] once made Du 1–2
133   I] [om.] Du 2
234   Affair] affaires TJ
246   his] [om.] Du 2

PRINTED IN GREAT BRITAIN
AT THE UNIVERSITY PRESS, OXFORD
BY VIVIAN RIDLER
PRINTER TO THE UNIVERSITY